RENTON'S
UNDERSTANDING THE STOCK EXCHANGE

THE ESSENTIAL REFERENCE
THIRD EDITION

RENTON'S

UNDERSTANDING THE STOCK EXCHANGE

THE ESSENTIAL REFERENCE

THIRD EDITION

N.E.Renton

First edition 1989
Second edition 1992
Third edition 1998

Published by:

Information Australia
A.C.N. 006 042 173
75-77 Flinders Lane
Melbourne VIC 3000
Telephone: (03) 9654 2800
Fax: (03) 9650 5261

Internet: www.infoaust.com

e-mail: nerenton@infoaust.com

By the same author:

*Guide for Meetings and Organisation, Guide for Meetings, Guide for Voluntary
Associations, Understanding Managed Investments, Understanding Investment Property,
Understanding the Australian Economic Debate, Taxation and the Small Investor,
Understanding Dividend Imputation, The Australian Wills and Record Keeping Book, The
Retirement Handbook, Elements of Style and Good Writing, Good Writing Guide, Family
Trusts, Negative Gearing, Company Directors: Masters or Servants?, Metaphors: An
Annotated Dictionary, Metaphorically Speaking (published in the United States), Public
Relations, Newsletters and Internet Usage for Organisations, Successful Clubs, (with
John Gurney), Understanding Finance: Balance Sheets (edited by N E Renton), How to
Prepare a Business Plan (edited by N E Renton), Dictionary of Stock Exchange Terms,
(edited by N E Renton).*

Renton. N.E. (Nicholas Edwin), 1931-
 Renton's understanding the stock exchange.

3rd ed.
ISBN 1 86350 242 4.

1. Stock exchanges - Australia. 2. Finance, Personal -
Australia. 3. Investments - Australia. I. Title. II.
Title : Understanding the stock exchange.

332.64294

Page Design/Desktop: Peter Conway
Printed and bound in Australia by Griffin Press

To my dear wife and children - plenty of
calls, but no sign of any dividends.

Any fool can make money, but it takes a wise person to save it.
— Scottish proverb

The inevitable never happens - it is the unexpected, always
—John Maynard Keynes

In every one of these reports you get a certain amount of sales-
manship ... it is not up to a chairman or a director to run his
shares down —Sir Arthur Warner

Learn to take losses quickly and cleanly—Bernard Baruch

The old adage of never putting all your eggs in the one basket is
still important—Daryl Dixon

If that is a healthy technical correction I hope I never see a real
slump—Austin Donnelly, just before the October 1987 stock market crash.

I read their balance sheets, not their editorials—Rupert Mur-
doch, in regard to his newspaper acquisitions.

Risk is not a dirty word—Walter Wriston

How come there's only one Competition Commission?—graffiti
seen in Canberra.

... for carrying on an undertaking of great advantage, but nobody
to know what it is—from a prospectus at the time of the South
Sea Bubble.

You know that you are old when the seat on which your broker
sat when executing your first stock exchange order is now treas-
ured as an interesting museum piece—the author, during a lec-
ture to the Australian Shareholders' Association.

STRANGE BUT TRUE

Compound interest, the tool of investors, also affects day-to-day
transactions.

An insurance company, hoping to attract as additional customers
people who had difficulty in paying premiums, recently published an advertisement asking: "Which would you rather pay: $250
a year or $25 a month?"

Those who chose the latter option probably did not realise that
this was equivalent to borrowing money at 51.16 per cent per annum!

Table of Contents

About the Author

Nick Renton was born in 1931 and qualified as a Fellow of the Faculty of Actuaries in 1957. He is also a Fellow of the Securities Institute of Australia and a Fellow of the Institute of Actuaries of Australia. He holds an Investment Adviser's Licence and qualifications as a commercial arbitrator.

After 15 years as Principal Officer of a life insurance company he became the first Executive Director of the Life Offices' Association of Australia from 1975 to 1979. He was Executive Director of the Life Insurance Federation of Australia from its formation in 1979 until 1986. In those capacities he acted as the official spokesman for the life insurance industry.

He is now an independent business consultant to leading stockbrokers, insurance companies, employer organisations, government agencies and others. He also serves on the boards of several financial institutions and is a frequent speaker at seminars and conferences.

He was the founder and first president of the Australian Shareholders' Association and has been Federal president of the Australian Society of Security Analysts and Victorian chairman of the Commercial Law Association of Australia.

His *Guide for Meetings and Organisations*, published by the Law Book Company, has been widely used as a reference work on all aspects of chairmanship and the running of voluntary associations since it first appeared in 1961. It deals with many practical aspects of meetings procedure not covered in Joske and is now in a two volume sixth edition.

He is also the author of books on investment property, managed investments, taxation, wills, good writing, family trusts, negative gearing, public relations, the Internet and the Australian economy, as well as of numerous papers to professional bodies and articles in newspapers and financial journals.

His popular dictionary of metaphors has been republished in New York.

In 1992 he was awarded the prestigious H.M.Jackson Memorial Prize for two of his works, *Understanding Dividend Imputation* and the *Retirement Handbook*.

In 1995 he received the Ken Millar Award for the second edition of this best-selling book and for his highly controversial *Company Directors: Masters or Servants?* with the citation reading: "For excellence in furthering the education and advancing the interest of investors."

He is married and has three children. He has long felt that every Australian family should aim not only to own its own home but also to participate in the growth of the nation by holding shares. He believes strongly that small savers should become better informed on investment matters generally as well as more aware of their rights as shareholders in listed companies.

N.E. Renton

Foreword

by
Alan Cameron AM, Chairman, Australian Securities
and Investments Commission

Foreword

I am very pleased to write the foreword to this third edition of Nick Renton's "Understanding the Stock Exchange".

The author is an independent expert who has devoted much of his spare time over the last 40 years to the twin objectives of advancing shareholder rights and educating investors to adopt sound investment principles.

It is timely that a new edition should be published now. Over the last few years, there has been a dramatic leap in direct, public share ownership in Australia. Two out of every five adult Australians now own shares in companies listed on Australian Stock Exchange Limited, courtesy of a number of well-patronised floats such as Telstra and AMP.

If one believes the tales around the marketplace, many of those shareholders are more than pleased with their debut in the often exhilarating and sometimes hair-raising world of the stockmarket. Too many have not yet experienced the downside, the sinking feeling as others appear to have sold and they are left with shares unsaleable at any price.

It is also timely having regard to the launch of the Australian Securities and Investments Commission (or "ASIC") on 1 July 1998 as the new regulator of consumer protection in the finance sector.

This gives us the chance to build on the work of the Australian Securities Commission for investors. For instance, in 1997 the ASC retrieved almost 100 million dollars for investors following the collapse of the Austwide group. It is therefore appropriate that consumers now have a "one-stop shop" regulator to protect their interests in the financial sector.

As the Australian market becomes more globalised and we enter the age of electronic commerce, more and more investment opportunities are being offered directly to the public, including via the Internet.

Investors need to be able to look after themselves: to understand what the terminology and the jargon mean, and how trading on the stock exchange works. That is why access to information of the kind contained in this book is essential.

I conducted investor meetings at six locations around the country in the last year. The response indicated a high level of interest in this subject, but also some scepticism of information from official sources. I therefore welcome the author's continued commitment to informing and educating the public.

Nick Renton has probably written books about more different topics than any other Australian author. In this book he has once again demonstrated his great skills in explaining a complex subject in clear English and with great attention to detail.

There are two final messages I would give personally to the readers of this text:

High Return = High Risk

If something looks too good to be true, then it probably is not true.

So many Australians have succumbed to the lure of returns which are much higher than a reasonable return, and have lost the lot.

If you do not know what a reasonable return is, then you need advice from a licensed adviser.

Secondly, never give anyone else's address for your CHESS notices. This is particularly important as the ASX moves fully to paperless shareholdings. Giving someone else's address for the receipt of notices is like handing that person a blank signed cheque; don't do it.

And finally, good luck !

Alan Cameron AM
Chairman, Australian Securities and Investments Commission

This certainly is a far more solid work than some of the light weight get rich quick books which appear from time to time only to fade away as fingers get burnt.

I thoroughly endorse Renton's philosophy of giving his readers the information they need to understand investments and then letting them make up their own minds as to the securities which they feel most comfortable in holding.

This book, while it was clearly a labour of love by the author, is highly professional as one would expect from a writer with his qualifications and experience.

Of course, this is not a book to be read from cover to cover in one go. Rather, it is a work of reference which can be consulted as the occasion arises.

No doubt many readers will also use it as a self teaching manual. It can certainly be used to learn any part of the craft of share investing which people are interested in, from types of shares to taxation and from theoretical concepts to the latest equity products.

Two earlier editions of Renton's work have been widely used as text books by bodies ranging from the Securities Institute of Australia to the City University of Hong Kong. Not a bad effort for a book that was originally aimed at ordinary mum and dad investors a market which it will no doubt continue to serve well for many years to come.

Ross Greenwood
Editor
Business Review Weekly

BRW Media

Level 2, 469 La Trobe Street, Melbourne Vic 3000

GPO Box 55A, Melbourne Vic 3001

Telephone: (03) 9603 3888

Facsimile: (03) 9670 4328

A division of John Fairfax Publications Pty Limited.
A.C.N. 003 357 720

Preface

You don't make the poor richer by
making the rich poorer
—Winston Churchill

The Telstra Factor

The recent float of Telstra, a company which is a household name in Australia, has brought a large number of new investors into the ranks of shareholders in companies listed on the stock exchange.

It also gave rise to a number of rather sad stories of unsophisticated "new chums" voicing some quite elementary questions. These persons wondered whether such shares could be bought in a shop or by mail order. Some even thought that payment could be made by posting off a plastic credit card.

Several brokers reported that even many comparatively wealthy applicants for the shares could not fill out the necessary forms correctly.

The need for a book which is objective and which can teach the basics of investment principles and practice to ordinary people, and to do so in an objective fashion, is thus greater than ever.

The New Edition

The text of this third edition has been completely revised and updated. A number of new sections and chapters have also been added in order to deal with recent developments or to expand on important topics.

However, to meet the convenience of the many students who use this work as a textbook the numbering of the paragraphs used in the previous edition has, as far as practicable, been kept unaltered.

Australia's Widening Shareownership

A person who has a stake in the Australian economy through being a shareholder is likely to be a better citizen and a voter who is better informed at election times.

A recent study by the Australian Stock Exchange showed that in May 1997 some 20.4 per cent of all Australian adults owned ordinary shares directly. This was double the 10.2 per cent figure of the corresponding 1991 survey mentioned in the previous edition of this book.

It is obvious that many astute people have realised that, generally speaking, it is better to buy shares in a bank than to make deposits in it, just as it is often better to invest in shares in a company which receives management fees from an associated unit trust than to become a unitholder in such a trust.

Some Dangers

It is, however, disturbing to find that some of the new investors on the stock exchange seem to be having difficulty in understanding important investment concepts such as dividend imputation, capital gains tax and negative gearing. Some of them even have trouble in grasping simple notions such as books closing dates.

New chums often naively believe that somehow a thousand dollars' worth of shares costing $30 each must automatically be poorer value than a thousand dollars' worth of shares costing $3 each.

In the light of all this the action of the Australian Stock Exchange in closing its own specialist bookshops in each capital city is most astonishing. This backward step will not aid the cause of investor education.

Price Volatility

Share prices are very volatile these days and equity markets are not for nervous Nellies. Even non-speculative shares can rise several percentage points in the course of a single trading day-by more than the total interest which can be earned on a one-year term deposit. Of course, a similarly sized fall in share prices can also take place.

Long-term investors can afford to ignore such short-term fluctuations. Furthermore—and this is particularly relevant to retired persons —while market values can fluctuate daily the stream of dividend income from a well-spread portfolio is much more stable. In all probability such income will merely rise gradually, year after year.

In fact, such dividend streams are less likely to show the type of extreme fluctuations experienced in the fixed interest market where interest rates are varied by official edict.

Superannuation

One reason for the rising prices currently being experienced on the stock exchange in this country and even more so on the markets in the United States of America is the rapid growth of superannuation assets.

The weight of money from this source is adding to the increasing demand for quality shares from non-superannuation savers investing directly or through managed funds. The total demand is currently greater than the supply of such shares.

In a period of relatively slow economic growth fewer companies than normal are raising fresh equity—and, in fact, some leading companies have even been buying back their own shares, while at the same time shares in some other companies have disappeared through takeovers made for a cash consideration. Many existing investors are reluctant sellers because of the capital gains tax legislation.

Of course, the various privatisation issues have worked in the opposite direction, increasing the quantity of listed shares available to investors.

Member Choice

Another aspect of superannuation is also worth mentioning—the forthcoming requirement that trustees will need to offer their members a choice of several different funds.

Competition and democracy are both wonderful principles—but the anecdotal evidence suggests that in regard to something as vital as retirement savings this new freedom will become a very real source of worry to many people. It will also provide an opportunity for intermediaries to enrich themselves at the expense of fund members by practices such as churning.

This poorly thought-through legislation actually poses concern in two conflicting ways.

Some members will be ultra conservative, choosing funds offering investments which are secure but which involve extremely low returns—thus cutting into the members' ultimate retirement benefits. Other members may go in the opposite direction. They will opt for funds promising seemingly very high returns, but in doing so they will be putting their capital at risk.

The need for education on investment aspects so that employees can make a sensible choice in this important area thus becomes greater than ever.

The Internet

The number of Australians using the Internet is growing rapidly, despite the fact that some conservative people are almost proud of still being computer illiterate. However, with younger age groups there is almost a feeling that if something is not on the Internet then it does not really exist.

While stockbrokers and listed companies in Australia have been relatively slow to embrace the new technology this is likely to change significantly over the next few years. Thus investors should really start to educate themselves now in regard to Internet usage, so as to be able to tap into the wealth of data useful to investors which is becoming readily accessible.

To some extent a vicious circle is involved here—the greater the use organisations across the board make of the Internet the greater the attraction of using this new source of information will become.

There is also not much point in a company complaining that its web pages are not being accessed by many shareholders or that it does not receive much e-mail from them if the relevant addresses have been kept relatively secret by not being included on its circulars or featured prominently in its annual reports.

Corporate e-mail

It is also rather pathetic that some listed companies which actually do have web sites do not then go on to include on them e-mail addresses which can be used by their shareholders.

Another sure way for a company to lose goodwill is for it to ignore legitimate questions from customers or shareholders, or to just send them robot-generated responses which demonstrate very clearly that no human being has even bothered to read their e-mail messages.

Tax Reform

The current debate on possible changes to the tax regime rarely mentions investors.

To illustrate, it seems likely that under a goods and services tax regime GST will have to be paid on brokerage. On the other hand, stamp duty on stock exchange transactions and financial institutions duty may disappear.

The more fundamental changes to the income tax rules which ought to be made on the grounds of equity will probably not be made.

The legislation will presumably continue to pretend that inflation does not exist and thus overtax interest earnings and not allow depreciation deductions based on replacement values.

The illogical anomaly which unfairly prevents the indexation of the cost price of assets in capital loss situations will presumably also remain in place.

A rather different anomaly also cries out for attention: why cannot the franking rebate be applied against the Medicare levy?

Ethics

The concept of ethics in relation to investment matters seems to be being debated more frequently than in former times.

It is, however, disappointing to find that a listed company which was queried recently in regard to its observance of the letter and spirit of the disclosure rules resorted to litigation against the regulator, as well as against the Australian Stock Exchange and even—in a blatant affront to the principle of free speech—against a number of reporters who wrote about the matter. Such attacks do little to raise lay confidence in the system.

It is also worrying to have a Federal Minister of the Crown assume a departmental portfolio in an area in which his family has a major investment stake—despite the clear potential for a conflict of interest which such a combination inevitably produces. Even more disappointing were the efforts of the Minister's colleagues in trying to defend the indefensible.

Less serious but still rather undignified was the action of one stockbroking organisation in circularising investors, urging them to apply for shares in a recent float and to lodge the forms through that organisation on the basis that subscribers would be entered in a special draw. Each of "five lucky applicants" was to receive a parcel of shares to the value of his or her allocated amount.

Banned Investment Advisers

One of the best-kept secrets in the investment world consists of the names of the investment advisers whose licences have been cancelled by the Australian Securities Commission in order to better protect the investing public.

The media usually ignore this subject and the Commission (now the Australian Securities and Investments Commission) relies on people searching its web site. This is fine in theory and convenient for people with access to the Internet and the necessary knowledge of where to look. However, it is not much use to people who are unaware that the ASC even exists, who have never heard of licensing and who may not even own a computer.

N E Renton
ner@melbpc.org.au

Chapter 1—Introduction

The first rule is not to lose. The second rule is not to forget the first rule.
—Warren Buffett

Preliminary Comments

101   Australia has a relatively high savings ratio, but for many years the investment "portfolios" of most people did not extend much beyond deposits in traditional low interest savings bank accounts or even zero interest cheque accounts.

102   There were many reasons for this, including a widespread ignorance of the alternatives, inertia, and an understandable fear of putting hard-won assets at risk. People seemed unconcerned with inflation. Naturally, the banks, being the main beneficiaries of this investment conservatism, had a vested interest in not disturbing the status quo.

103   Yet these days many people have significant funds requiring investment and this may be a cause of great worry to them. Typically, the source of such funds can include lifetime savings; proceeds from the sale of a home, a farm or a business; insurance or compensation payments; inherited assets; and so on.

104   Most people have had no formal training in investment matters and may be having trouble in coping even with household budgeting or the consumer finance aspects of daily living. It is little wonder then that they have difficulty in distinguishing between circumstances:

- when cash should be put away in something highly liquid in order to cater for a short-term need, and

- when more adventurous long-term investments such as shares can prudently be undertaken.

105   Australia now has an ageing population. As women tend to outlive men, there are also many widows in the community who are now in charge of large sums left to them by their late husbands. Often these persons lack the know-how which should ideally accompany such wealth.

106   In recent times there has been a tendency for occupational superannuation lump sum payments to become larger and for people to take retirement at earlier ages than formerly (sometimes not entirely voluntarily). Both are factors which further exacerbate the problem. With a trend towards trade union superannuation, many more employees will find themselves

with significantly larger investment problems in their retirement years than they ever encountered during their working lifetimes, when it might also have been easier for them to acquire the appropriate knowledge.

107 Simultaneously, several factors have emerged which all add to the difficulties of making sensible savings plans:

- taxation rules have become more complex

- social security legislation has also become more complex and is subject to frequent change

- deregulation has led to many new investment products being evolved

- markets have become more volatile

- the various privatisation issues have attracted large numbers of new and thus inexperienced investors.

Investor Attitudes

108 This book is designed to give a general understanding of the system as a whole, so that people can make intelligent and informed investment decisions and better appreciate the environment against which such decisions have to be made. The book does not, of course, seek to give recommendations as to specific investment situations and in any case it is obviously impossible for any general publication to take into account the individual circumstances of any particular reader. Nor does the book deal with the more esoteric investment vehicles, such as antiques, jewellery, postage stamps, paintings, currency plays or commodity futures. These are for specialist investors, not for the first time players.

109 Some people are so concerned with *minimising income tax* that they fail to focus on what should really be one of the prime investment objectives, namely, the *maximising of "after tax" income*. (After all, $1000 gross less $500 tax is better than $400 tax-free.) Similar remarks apply also in the case of people who concentrate unduly on maximising their social security benefits rather than on bettering their total position. Some persons are so keen to get a few hundred free dollars from the Government that they are willing to forego a few thousand earned dollars in potential investment returns.

110 Yet the very same people who worry about tax on the income side may overlook the tax rules governing their outgo. Thus they do not distinguish sufficiently between, on the one hand, interest incurred in earning investment income (which is, by and large, deductible, thus greatly reducing the apparent interest burden) and, on the other hand, non-allowable interest incurred in servicing housing loans or consumer debt.

111 Similarly, there is a tendency to ignore inflation, even during periods when the rate of inflation is relatively high. To illustrate, a 15 per cent per annum yield with the capital being eroded by 9 per cent loss of purchasing power each year is much less attractive than a 10 per cent per annum yield with the real value of the capital protected. Illogical tax treatment imposed by the authorities makes this problem even more serious.

112 There is also a tendency to chase so-called *tax-free* investments, such as insurance bonds held for 10 years or more and (following the introduction of imputation) shares in companies which are paying franked dividends. There is nothing wrong with such categories of investment, but it should be realised that they are not really exempt in a conceptual sense: what happens is that someone else rather than the ultimate investor picks up the tax bill (although not necessarily at the same rate in the dollar). The relevant legislation merely gives relief against *double* taxation.

The Role of Investment Advisers

113 A virtual "investment advice" industry has now sprung up in Australia. Some investment advisers and financial planners are remunerated by fees based on the time spent by them in acting for clients, on the lines used by solicitors, accountants and medical practitioners. But for the most part advisers are rewarded mainly or exclusively by brokerage or commission on the business generated. This is not necessarily improper and it enables the needs of small investors to be serviced. However, it also presents a potential "conflict of interest" situation which should be fully recognised by all investors who use and rely on intermediaries:

- Not everybody appreciates the important distinction between an enthusiastic sales pitch and truly independent advice.

- Another problem arises from the practice known as "churning"—the switching of investments in a portfolio in order to generate commission income for the adviser rather than to improve performance for the investor.

- A different problem again arises when an intermediary persuades a client to borrow money so that the client can make a bigger total investment than that possible by just using the client's own funds—one which, in the process, results in a bigger brokerage or commission payment to the intermediary.

114 Many advisers are specialists in particular areas (for example, real estate or pooled investments vehicles) and their inability to give a complete overview as to all the available investment alternatives should also be taken into account. Nor has it been unknown for some investment consultants themselves to become bankrupt.

115 Furthermore, most advisers would not have the time or the patience to explain the system as a whole, even if they understand it. Yet clients really need to appreciate the background against which their investment decisions are to be made. If they are unfamiliar with the language used then they cannot even communicate meaningfully with the advisers or assess their true capabilities.

116 All too often discussions between advisers and their clients focus on specific investment opportunities, rather than on the investor and the investor's real requirements. Yet there is no such thing as a universally ideal investment:

- A particular security may be very good buying for one person and very good selling for another person who is in entirely different circumstances.

- A particular security may also be very good buying for a person at one stage of that person's life and very good selling at a different stage.

117 Many inexperienced investors do not appreciate these aspects sufficiently and fail to brief their advisers adequately in regard to themselves. The advisers in turn no doubt find life easier if they do not unduly press their clients for such detailed personal information—despite "know your client" rules. (The other side of this coin is that some clients, on discovering that their advisers are giving such seemingly contradictory advice, may form a quite unjustified suspicion as to their bona fides.)

118 Of course, such briefings are feasible only if each client has first systematically defined the client's own circumstances, preferences and requirements.

119 A different problem arises in the stock exchange world. Many brokers, understandably conscious of their expense rates and the time needing to be spent in explaining even simple things to inexperienced investors, discourage new clients from initiating market transactions and prefer to head such persons into one or more pooled investment vehicles.

There are nowadays many hundreds of these available, with a vast variety of different investment strategies—managed funds, investment bonds, listed and unlisted unit trusts, listed investment companies and public superannuation funds.

Such an approach strategy has some legitimate advantages discussed later in this book, but it also has the "social" disadvantage that the investors concerned will not get a proper "feel" for the capitalistic system and will continue for all time to remain ignorant of investment principles and practice.

Unsolicited Offers

120 Telephone calls and letters out of the blue, particularly from overseas, which offer unsolicited investment opportunities should always be rejected out of hand. In many cases the securities offered will not even exist.

121 Unsolicited offers to buy shares or fixed interest securities already held, especially those which are unlisted or inactively traded, should also be treated with great caution.

Regulatory Change

122 In a deliberate move to give law reform in the corporate area a greater pro-business profile the Federal Government shifted responsibility for this from the Attorney-General's Depart-

ment to the Treasury. In March 1997 it set up the Corporate Law Economic Reform Program (CLERP) to replace the Simplification Task Force.

123 The Federal Treasurer subsequently announced the establishment of three new bodies of relevance to investors on the stock exchange. These commenced their operations on 1 July 1998. They are:

- the Australian Prudential Regulation Authority (APRA), a statutory body with headquarters in Sydney to facilitate co-operation with the Reserve Bank of Australia; this body will undertake the prudential supervision of deposit-taking institutions, of life and general insurance companies and of superannuation funds

- the Australian Securities and Investments Commission (ASIC), a statutory body with headquarters in Melbourne, which will replace the Australian Securities Commission (ASC); this will be the market regulator and consumer protection body

- the Financial Sector Advisory Council (FSAC); this non-statutory body will report directly to the Treasurer on regulatory and other changes required in order to make Australia the leading financial centre of the Asia Pacific region.

New Products

124 The Australian market has seen many new products developed in recent times.

125 They are usually not inspired by any real client needs. They result instead from marketing considerations on the part of imaginative entrepreneurs, whose principal desires are for:

- influence over a greater share of investors' dollars

- profits from the packaging process itself

- greater commission earnings for their intermediaries

- opportunities for cross-selling other products or services

- more difficult client comparisons of competitive products.

126 In the small Australian investment world such innovation is often a mixed blessing, because it also leads to increased overheads and to confusion among investors and even among financial advisers.

127 Some new products will succeed and some will not. The experimentation is healthy, but the community has to pay for the hidden costs. These are two-fold:

- monetary—for research and development, for advertising and promotion, and for profit

- non-monetary—in the form of a fragmented and therefore less efficient market place.

128 Furthermore, investors who buy products which they do not understand are very likely to get their fingers burnt.

Scams

129 Advertisements offering wonderful ways to make money on the stock exchange frequently appear both in print and these days on the Internet. In many ways they resemble those promising riches by backing horses or using lucky numbers in a lottery. A moment's thought will show that if someone really had a foolproof way of creating wealth he would exploit it himself in private rather than make it generally available.

130 Apart from the products from reputable organisations described above there are always the "get rich quick" schemes from fly-by-night operators.

131 The lesson should be that if an investment scheme looks too good to be true then it almost certainly is. It should be obvious that no promoter with any sense is really going to sell an asset worth two dollars for one dollar or somesuch.

132 Unfortunately the cause of financial education for the masses is not advanced when a major trading bank chooses to promote itself not on the price or quality of its banking services but rather on the opportunities for its customers to win tickets in a lottery.

Tax Minimisation

133 Many of the more imaginative new products in the investment world are purely or mainly tax driven. This means in practice that if they are successful in market terms then they will have only a short shelf life before the authorities catch up and the law is changed.

134 The general thinking by entrepreneurs in this area seems to be that if a particular economic activity can be packaged into a different legal form by a financial institution then that must automatically be progress.

135 The reality is that sensible investors set out to maximise their wealth and not to minimise their tax payments.

The Millennium Bug

136 Much has been written about the Year 2000 bug—the inability of many computer systems to distinguish between the year 1900 and the year 2000 because both are often recorded as just "00".

137 This can impact investors in relation to:

- their own records—for example, in regard to capital gains tax (see also Appendix 8)

- the profitability of the companies in which they invest, especially where these fail to cope with the problem

- the economy as a whole.

Conclusion

138 Two distinct investment styles are possible:

- Top down investors look at the overall economy and then pick market sectors which they believe will grow.

- In contrast, bottom-up investors start by looking at individual stocks.

139 Even in this computer age markets are made by people. Participants include optimists (called "bulls"), who buy in the expectation of a rise, as well as pessimists (called "bears"), who sell in the expectation of a fall. Rising prices across the board and the excitement of boom conditions constitute a "bull market"; the reverse situation is known as a "bear market".

140 The stock market crash on 19 and 20 October 1987 ("Black Monday" in New York and "Black Tuesday" in Australia) and the Asian crisis of October 1997 were useful reminders that booms do not last forever. However, the principles of sound investment apply equally whether share prices happen to be high, low or in between.

141 Sensible investors must know what they are doing. The material in this book is designed to assist people wishing to invest on their own account as well as those preferring to delegate all such detailed decision making to others. In either case, the book will hopefully give sufficient information to enable people to get started and to avoid the major pitfalls.

142 Nevertheless, all investment recommendations regardless of their source should always be treated as though they, in the manner of cigarettes, bore a compulsory message reading:

"WARNING: Investment is a wealth hazard".

Chapter 2—Background

*You don't get credit for being prepared—but
you do get results*
—Merle McCormack

Preliminary Comments

201　This chapter sets out some general information as background to the subject of investment.

202　Conceptually, the simplest form of investment is probably a savings account with a bank (or a similar account with a building society, credit union, etc.). Ignoring for the moment the question of taxation, $10,000 invested in such an account at, say, 12 per cent per annum would produce an income of $1200 each year.

203　If that income is not withdrawn, then the balance at the start of the second year would be $11,200. At the same 12 per cent per annum rate this would then produce an income of $1344 for the year. After 10 years of non-withdrawals the balance would be about $31,058 or $21,058 more than the original $10,000 investment (in other words, an increase of 210.58 per cent.)

204　Some unscrupulous promoters might want to describe this as representing 21.058 per cent per annum, implying simple interest (210.58 divided by 10)—but that, while accurate, would be quite misleading. The return is best described as 12 per cent per annum compound interest.

205　An entirely different form of investment is exemplified by the ordinary share, described in detail in Chapter 4. Its apparent return in the form of dividends might typically be only 4 per cent per annum rather than the 12 per cent return just mentioned. But the attraction to the investor would be that both the capital outlaid originally and the income stream resulting from that investment are expected to increase in value. If, after one year, that value had increased by, say, 20 per cent, then the total return from the investment would be 24 per cent, not 4 per cent.

206　While the expectation might be plus 20 per cent, the actual outcome might be plus 100 per cent or better; it could, of course, also be minus 50 per cent or worse.

Meaning of "Investment"

207　"Investment" can be defined as *an act of immediate sacrifice in the expectation of future reward.*

208 From a national point of view, investment means the construction of factories, machinery, roads, etc., together with the net increase in the level of stocks held by business enterprises.

209 But from a personal point of view, investment means the purchase of specific assets such as shares, bonds, real estate, etc. In some contexts deposits in banks and other savings institutions can also be regarded as a form of investment, although the word is used mainly to cover the other avenues just listed.

210 Whether a particular asset should be thought of as an "investment" or not may depend on the motives of the person acquiring it, as will be seen by considering the case of a house purchased for owner occupation or a work of art bought for aesthetic enjoyment.

211 The direct annual return on an investment is variously called:

- *interest* (in the case of loans)
- *dividends* (in the case of shares), and
- *rent* (in the case of property).

All three are similar in economic terms and represent a reward for the use of money and for the risks undertaken. In addition, investors can make a capital profit or a capital loss from the difference between the cost of an asset and the proceeds on its eventual sale or redemption. For some types of investment the prospect of making a capital gain are more relevant than the prospect of earning a periodical income stream. Such investments are often referred to as "growth" situations.

The Investment Return and Other Considerations

212 Only after an asset has been finally disposed of does it become possible to measure objectively whether it has been a good, bad or indifferent investment. This is done in part by calculating the compound rate of return per annum inherent in the transaction—a figure usually referred to as the *yield*—and comparing this with the returns which alternative investments would have produced.

213 "Yield" can be defined as *the net rate of interest at which the sum invested equals the present value of all income payments plus the present value of all capital payments*. This aspect is further discussed in paras 227 to 230 below.

214 Consider a work of art purchased for $1000 and sold for $2000. Was that a good investment? Well, it all depends.

215 Firstly, there is the question of timing. If the interval between the two transactions was 20 years, then the yield would have been about 3.53 per cent per annum; if only 12 months, then 100.00 per cent per annum. So the time at which money is put into or taken out of a particular investment is very relevant to its investment merits. Clearly, a dollar down the track is not as valuable as a dollar here and now. It is easy to be deluded by figures relating to long periods: $10,000 growing to $1,000,000 over 40 years might sound impressive, but the return inherent in such an investment would be only 12.2 per cent per annum. See also paras 1917 to 1919.

216 Secondly, it is necessary to allow for both taxation and infla-tion—topics dealt with in detail later in this book.

217 Thirdly, there is the question of whether the form of the investment meets the investor's convenience. For example, the work of art, regardless of yield, would have been quite unsuit-able to someone looking for weekly sums for household expenditure purposes.

218 Fourthly, the marketability of the investment needs to be considered. A work of art cannot be sold very easily (except possibly at an unrealistic price). It is thus comparatively illiq-uid. Its disposal may also involve relatively high transaction costs.

219 Finally, the degree of risk assumed by the investor needs to be taken into account. With a work of art—in contrast to, say, a deposit in a bank—there is no guarantee or even a great likelihood that the investor will ever get the original outlay back, let alone do better than that.

220 All the above illustrates that each investment needs to be assessed not in isolation but rather in relation to the circum-stances of the investor.

221 At the time of acquisition of an asset it is, of course, not possible to calculate *with the benefit of hindsight* the actual yield which will be achieved over the period during which the asset is held. In an extreme case, some specific investment might well result in a total loss, even if that possibility looked remote at the time of its acquisition. However, investments are

normally entered into on the basis of their prospective or expected yield, calculated on some set of expressed or implied assumptions. In many cases, several different alternative scenarios may be taken into consideration.

222 To further complicate matters, the general expression "yield" is often used in a different sense from that described above, particularly in the case of shares or property, where it may just represent the first year income divided by the market price.

Investment Objectives

223 The prime aim of all investors is to maximise the size of their total wealth.

224 In practice, an increase in wealth can be obtained in various different ways—for example:

- In the form of income or of capital growth or of a mixture of both.

- In a very secure way or in a less secure way but with the prospects of greater gain. (Put crudely, the choice is between "sleeping well" and "eating well".)

- In the short-term or in the long-term.

- Using readily marketable assets or less marketable assets with other offsetting attractions.

Capital gains (and losses) can be either *realised* (when the relevant asset is disposed of) or *unrealised* (when it is still held but its value has changed).

In the stock exchange context, the sources of wealth for an individual investor include:

- physical wealth creation—the value added to shareholder funds by companies through the use of labour and capital and the exploitation of management skills

- market wealth creation—the value added to share prices, often by changes in perception leading to increased price earnings ratios

- favourable zero sum game outcomes—for example, in regard to options and futures, where the gains of one player are at the expense of another player

- the exploitation of market anomalies by arbitrage
- the exploitation of tax concessions (often although not always resulting in benefits at the expense of the community).

Investment Risk

225 Most investments involve compromises between conflicting goals and investors need to bear that in mind. The old adage "the higher the return, the greater the risk" is still true today.

226 All investments involve some risk. To illustrate:

- Even holding cash exposes its owner to the chance of loss by theft or fire—quite apart from the quite separate risk of loss of purchasing power due to inflation (see Chapter 3).

- Investing in Government securities sounds safe enough—but only if there is no revolution.

- Investments in the corporate world involve the risk of loss due to management weaknesses; due to fraud; due to changes in economic conditions, in legislation, in taxation or in government policy; and so on. Droughts, industrial disputes, unexpected competitors, developments overseas and many other factors can ruin expectations or even cause insolvency. Company profitability and thus market values are directly affected by such factors.

Separate from all the above, market values while an investment is being held are also a function of the interest rate levels prevailing from time to time (see paras 263 to 268) and in some cases the exchange rate. The existence of such risks does not mean that such investments should not be made—only that investors should be aware of the dangers and take them into account when evaluating the expected returns.

Notes:

1. Some phenomena affect the market as a whole. This is known as "systemic risk". It cannot be avoided by persons who wish to be investors. Other phenom-

ena affect only specific companies or industries. Investors can to some extent safeguard themselves against such losses by using the principle of "spread"—see paras 256 to 262.

2.   Situations involving higher than normal risks should not be entertained unless they also offer higher than normal prospective returns.

3.   Furthermore, most investors should confine risky situations to a relatively small proportion of their total portfolios.

Capital and Income

227   Consider $100 invested at a 10 per cent per annum interest rate for 10 years:

1.   This could involve $10 income annually for each of the 10 years and the repayment of the $100 capital at the end of the 10th year.

2.   Alternatively, it could involve no annual payments during the 10 years, with the equivalent sums being reinvested at the 10 per cent rate, so that the final sum would then be $259.37 rather than just $100. ($100 plus one year's interest is $110; $110 plus one year's interest is $121; and so on.) (In some circumstances investments of this type would be described as "showing capital growth" and producing a "capital gain" of $159.37.)

3.   Alternatively again, it could involve annual payments of $16.27 during each of the 10 years rather than just $10, each payment representing partly interest and partly a return of capital, with no further payment then being made at the end of the 10th year.

- Example 1 could be a Commonwealth Bond.

- Example 2 could be a savings bank deposit, as in para. 203.

- Example 3 could be a loan involving regular periodical instalments comprising both principal and interest (a *credit foncier* loan), viewed from the perspective of the lender.

Many other types of investment can produce comparable patterns. For example, a 10 per cent return can also be obtained from, say, a 9 per cent 10-year debenture, face value $100, purchased at 93.86 or from a similar 12 per cent 10-year debenture purchased at 112.29. In such transactions the 10 percent return reflects the amortisation of the discount or premium and would be referred to as the *redemption yield*.

228 The above are just illustrations of various patterns and an infinite number of other combinations is possible. All are equally good in the sense that they are returning the same 10 per cent per annum, but whether or not any specific pattern happens to suit any particular investor will depend on that investor's circumstances. The important point is that only the redemption yield is relevant for investment decision making—not the *coupon* (the nominal rate being paid by the issuer) or the *flat yield* (the annual interest payments as a percentage of the price being paid by the investor). To illustrate, it would normally make sense to switch a 14 per cent loan security with a redemption yield of 10 per cent into an equivalent 11 per cent loan security with a redemption yield of 12 per cent.

229 Whether any given dollar is "capital" or "income" is relevant for some legal purposes (for example, the distributions from a trust fund) and involves a significantly different income tax treatment. But, apart from that, the label makes no difference to an investor and the two should not really be regarded as separate concepts at all.

230 There is one important proviso to all that. A well-known form of fraud on investors involves paying them back their own capital while *pretending* that it represents a true profit and thus a conventional investment return. For example, a swindler can promise a 30 per cent return on $100 on some project and actually meet that commitment even if no commercial profits have been generated at all, merely by distributing $30 after 12 months (thus impressing investors), while getting ready to disappear with the other $70. (For this reason, companies are precluded from paying dividends out of capital, although strangely enough no corresponding prohibition applies in the case of publicly-held unit trusts.)

Investment in Relation to the Investor

231 The market is made up of investors of all types, varying in size, sophistication, activity levels, temperament, tax status, and so

on. The requirements of a large superannuation fund on a relatively low rate of income tax may differ significantly from those of a small individual investor on a much higher rate of tax. Again, a young man in his twenties with some surplus income has a different set of needs from an elderly widow living on her past savings.

232 A potential investor should analyse his personal circumstances —assets and liabilities, income and outgo, the expected changes in these, and so on. Other possible questions are:

- Are his children dependants?

- Does he want to leave them assets in his will?

- Has he any other legal or moral commitments?

- How is he affected by taxation legislation?

- How are he and his spouse affected by social security legislation?

- Is he temperamentally a "high risk" person or the reverse?

- Is he impatient?

- Does he want to get actively involved in investment matters on a daily basis?

- Is he knowledgeable?

- Does he expect high inflation and therefore want, as a high priority, a hedge against it?

- Can he cope with the paperwork?

233 Furthermore, the investment of a one-off large sum needs to be handled differently from the regular investment of small amounts of ongoing savings.

234 People are often net savers at some stages of their lives (for example, before marriage and in the last few years leading up to retirement) and net dissavers at other times (for example, while having a young family and after retirement).

235 Some people need to get investment income in periodical instalments for living purposes while others would find the receipt of such income as a relatively unattractive feature, just increasing the problem of finding a satisfactory home for surplus cash.

236 Other persons again might desire not only to receive periodical instalments of interest, dividends and rent but also to uplift some of their original capital (that is, past savings) on a regular basis (although obviously this has its limitations).

237 As regards risk profile, some investors are natural gamblers, keen on the more speculative forms of investment; others would wish to stick to more solid paper. Many people are in between, willing to take a modest degree of risk with their entire portfolios or alternatively at least prepared to earmark a proportion (say, 10 per cent, or some other figure which they can afford to lose) to more exciting and potentially more rewarding but less secure categories.

238 Investors should also decide on the degree of involvement which they desire. Do they want to make an investment and then forget all about it? (This is, however, not a strategy which is really recommended.) Are they prepared at least to read the financial pages of a newspaper on a daily basis and talk to a stockbroker on average once every few weeks? Or do they want to make investment a serious hobby, studying financial publications and Internet pages as well as doing some research of their own? And, as a separate question, do they want to be active traders, long-term holders or something in between?

Another important point: Investors in companies who ignore relevant circulars to shareholders or who miss certain deadlines do so at their peril and can deprive themselves of large sums of money. The message "This document is important!" is not always just marketing baloney.

239 Each investor will need to make up his own mind in regard to the aspects discussed above and then evolve his own strategy accordingly, choosing a portfolio which fits in with his requirements as nearly as possible.

Portfolio Composition

240 Ideally, a "balanced" portfolio should be aimed at, although this may not be practicable if the total amount involved is small or in the case of some investment categories. It is highly undesirable to have all of one's eggs in the same basket—see paras 256 to 262 below. On the other hand, too much spread also has some disadvantages in the form of too "ordinary" a

performance, and in the form of higher transaction costs and additional administrative burdens.

241 The most general questions (types of investment and the proportion of funds in each category—in other words, *asset allocation*) should be decided first, along with the question of how many different individual investments should be acquired. The main categories for serious investors wishing to be in conventional investment assets are ordinary shares, property (real estate) and fixed interest securities. The latter can include long-term investments, as well as cash or "near cash" (see para. 276). The fixed interest component of a portfolio can be either positive or negative (as when borrowed funds are used—see Chapter 27). Other investment assets include:

- Gold (in various forms)—see Chapter 21.

- Derivatives, such as options—see Chapter 22— and futures—see Chapter 23.

- Collectibles (coins, stamps, antiques, etc.)—see paras 2402 to 2406.

- Life insurance.

- Superannuation (including rollover vehicles).

Examples of how individual portfolios could be composed follow:

	Portfolio I per cent	Portfolio II per cent	Portfolio III per cent
Ordinary Shares	40	33	75
Property	50	33	75
Fixed Interest Securities	10	34	-50
Total	100	100	100

See also paras 2717 to 2720.

Notes:

1. There are some classes of security which do not fit neatly into these categories. For example, listed property trusts could be put into the "ordinary shares" group, although treating them as "property" would seem more useful. Again, converting prefer-

ence shares—see para. 440—are probably best regarded as "fixed interest" until actually converted.

2. Liquidity aspects are also relevant: 100 per cent shares would be relatively liquid; 100 per cent direct property—because of the "all or nothing" aspect of real estate—would not be.

3. An alternative approach to the use of arbitrary percentages such as those shown above is to go for a fixed interest component which generates a return equal to the periodical cash required, net of other income. There are some problems with this—it ignores inflation; it disregards the possibility of changes to interest rate levels; it does not take into account the ability to cash in part of a growth portfolio; and so on.

242 Sub-category questions come next—for example:

- in the case of property: residential, industrial, offices or retail?

- also in the case of property: city, suburban, urban or rural?

- also in the case of property: in which State?

- in the case of shares: how much into industrials and how much into resources (mining and oil)?

- in the case of industrials: how much into each industry (banks, media, retail, transport, textiles, automotives, and so on)?

- in the case of resources: how much into producers and how much into pure explorers?

243 Specific questions (which particular property or which particular share) come last.

Types of Investment

244 As shown below, investments can be categorised in a number of different and overlapping ways. The word "security" is frequently used as a loose label for investments such as shares, debentures, notes, bonds and options; however, the word by itself does not imply:

- that the investment is necessarily "secure" in the sense of being "safe"

- that there is any guarantee or any charge over assets (as in the case of a "secured loan").

245 Firstly, one can distinguish between public sector investments (Commonwealth Bonds, semi-governmental debentures, etc.) and private sector investments (company securities, real estate, etc.)

246 Secondly, one can distinguish between "fixed interest" and "equity" type investments. The former involve a guaranteed, contractual rate of return and include most forms of loan securities (bonds, debentures, notes, deposits, mortgages) as well as most preference shares. The latter involve a variable, performance-based rate of return and include ordinary shares and real estate. There are also some "hybrid" securities, such as convertible notes (see paras 449 to 450). Options of the type traded on the stock exchange must also be regarded as equities.

Notes.

1. Sometimes the word "equity" is employed more narrowly as a synonym for just ordinary shares, but this is not really a desirable usage of the term.

2. The guaranteed nature of fixed interest paper does not eliminate the possibility of some default by the issuing entity or even total loss by the investor.

247 Thirdly, one can distinguish between redeemable securities (those having a predetermined repayment or maturity date) and irredeemable securities (those intended to last for ever). The latter are sometimes called *perpetuities* and include all ordinary shares and freehold property.

248 Fourthly, one can distinguish between securities listed on the stock exchange and all other investments.

249 Fifthly, one can distinguish between direct investments (those made by the investors themselves) and indirect investments (those involving an investment manager—for example: listed investment companies, listed and unlisted unit trusts, insurance bonds, friendly society bonds, public superannuation funds).

250 Sixthly, one can distinguish between investments in Australia and those overseas. In addition:

- Company securities can be sub-divided into those conferring ownership (ordinary and preference shares) and those creating a debtor/creditor relationship (deposits, notes and debentures).

- Loans can be categorised as being either "secured" (charged on some assets, as in the case of debentures and mortgages) or "unsecured" (see also para. 447).

Trustee Securities

251   Some investments thought to be particularly safe are given "trustee security" status by legislation which varies in each State. The concept means that trustees (including executors or administrators of deceased estates) can invest in them unless the relevant trust instrument specifically prevents this. Of course, this artificial status increases demand and lowers returns, and for this as well as for other reasons the trustees of most modern trusts are given wider investment powers.

Unfortunately some State Governments have granted trustee security status to some organisations in their State purely for parochial reasons. In the process they were exposing investors in those securities to bigger risks than these investors realised. The range of trustee securities has been widened in recent times, possibly in recognition of the fact that the intended safety of fixed interest paper in times of high inflation was rather illusory when its nominal value lost significant purchasing power each year. The concept itself has been abolished in some jurisdictions.

Types of Companies

252   Companies can be classified according to their principal activities.

253   Industrial companies are those engaged in commerce and industry. They can be classified into various sub-groups, such as some of those set out in Appendix 11, which—although somewhat arbitrary—are the ones used for compiling the various stock exchange indices mentioned in para. 979.

254   Resource companies include those involved with mining and oil, with sub-sectors such as gold. Producers and explorers can present rather different risk profiles. Unlike the position in industrial companies, even successful mines from the very nature of their operations involve wasting assets.

255 There are also "conglomerates" (diversified companies) which do not fit neatly into these categories.

Spread

256 If an investor has ten investments of approximately equal size and one of them goes bad then the investor has lost 10 per cent of his money—an unfortunate outcome, but not the disaster which would have occurred if *all* of his money had been put into that one investment. (The disturbing lack of spread inherent in many Australian portfolios held by individuals is obvious from the statistics at the end of Appendix 3.)

257 Similarly, in terms of income, if nine of the ten do well, returning, say, an average of 15 per cent per annum, then the non-receipt of income from the tenth would still produce a reasonable 13.5 per cent return on the entire portfolio. This applies equally whether one is considering, for example, shares—with some companies not paying a dividend—or income-producing real estate—with some individual property being empty and thus not generating rent.

258 For these reasons it is usually a sound strategy to have a "spread", in other words, a series of different investments rather than just a single one. Naturally, this works in both directions—just as portfolio performance overall will be better than that of the worst component, it will also be worse than that of the best component.

259 To be effective, spread must involve not only different individual investments, but also completely different categories. For example, shares in two retailers would not safeguard against a slump in retailing; similarly, two adjoining properties, even if leased to separate tenants, would not protect against an oversupply of space in that street or that neighbourhood. However, even a good spread would not necessarily overcome the adverse consequences of widely occurring economic or political phenomena, such as rising interest rates, tax changes, wars or recessions. Being in 100 different companies is not much help in an October 1987 style crash, when the whole market drops 50 per cent.

260 Spread is possible in various ways, for example:

- By class of investment (bank deposits, bonds, shares, property, etc).

- By institution within each class.

- By industry (food, steel, textiles, etc.).

- Geographically.

261 One can achieve a geographical spread of share investments within Australia either by buying into national companies or less satisfactorily by buying shares in locally-operating companies in several States. To the extent that the whole country really represents a single economy, neither strategy is perfect and some offshore investment is called for. This also provides spread in another useful way, namely, over more than one currency. However, the costs of investing overseas and the increased difficulties in monitoring such investments also need to be taken into account. On a separate aspect, various international agreements are in place in order to eliminate double taxation.

262 By a suitable mix of investments investors can also achieve any desired degree of liquidity.

Notes:

1. The disturbing lack of spread inherent in many Australian portfolios held by individuals is obvious from the statistics at the end of Appendix 3.

2. Once 10 or 15 stocks are held increasing the number further does little to reduce risk. To illustrate, with 20 stocks in equal weighting a failure reduces the total value of the portfolio to 95 per cent of its starting figure; with 40 stocks this becomes 97.5 per cent, which is not greatly different in a practical sense. However, owning more stocks may be useful in the context of priority issues or shareholder discounts. On the other hand, more stocks mean more paperwork and a harder task of monitoring individual company performance.

3. Investors already holding 10 or 15 stocks directly need not also use managed investments in order to protect themselves. However, they may find them

useful for other reasons—for example, to add an overseas exposure to an otherwise domestic portfolio.

4. Spread should always be measured in terms of current market value, not cost.

The Interest Rate Structure

263 Interest rates on loans are, in the absence of interference by governments, a function of supply and demand. Rates for individual transactions will vary according to assessments of the degree of security, in other words the likelihood that all interest will be paid on the due dates and that the capital will be repaid on the maturity date. Rates across the board will move from time to time in line with changes in monetary policy and as the relationship between the volume of funds available and the volume of funds sought changes. Of relevance also can be the degree of support from overseas lenders, which is influenced by overseas interest rate levels and by expectations as to future movements in the exchange rates for the Australian dollar.

264 Other things being equal, rates on securities of the type traded on the stock exchange can be listed in order of size as follows, starting with the lowest:

- Commonwealth Bonds.

- Semi-governmental debentures.

- Company debentures.

- Company unsecured notes.

Rates on other types of loan, for example, mortgages, and returns from all other categories of investment would be influenced by—and would in turn influence—this pattern. The Commonwealth Bond interest rate is often regarded as the yardstick for everything else, the Bond being regarded as a virtually "risk-free" form of investment.

265 Securities of large, well-known, old—established and highly profitable companies, especially those with total assets large in relation to their total liabilities, would command lower rates than similar securities of other companies lacking such attributes. Thus an unsecured note of a company would command a higher rate than an equivalent debenture of the same com-

pany, but the unsecured note of a leading company could well be regarded as worthy of a lower interest rate than the debenture of a second-ranking company.

266   Another factor of relevance is the term of the loan (usually, but not always, longer terms command higher rates; when they do not, an *inverse yield curve* is said to apply). A further important factor is the degree of marketability. For example, some semi-governmentals (generally securities issued by statutory corporations guaranteed by the State Government concerned) are very inactively traded and for that reason produce relatively high returns on secondary markets such as the stock exchange, although not necessarily on the primary market (that is, at the issue stage—a point which subscribers to such issues should always take into account). This has led to centralised borrowing in some States, creating paper which is much more liquid. For some types of company loan the interest rate would include margins for the administrative expenses involved and to compensate for the expected incidence of bad debts.

267   As mentioned above, interest rates on new loans (and, subject to the terms negotiated, on certain existing loans) tend to move up and down from time to time in line with changes in supply and demand and in line with the returns applying to existing securities of equivalent calibre. Inflationary expectations may also have some marginal influence —see para. 324.

268   Yields on equity situations can be either higher or lower than interest rates generally, using the term "yield" in the sense of the expected next year return divided by the outlay. An ordinary share is clearly less secure than a Commonwealth Bond, and should thus require a few percentage points higher return each year in order to compensate for the extra risk. But offsetting that are some tax aspects and the prospect of ever—increasing dividends in successive years and/or capital growth (these two aspects are connected). Thus good quality shares are often traded on quite modest dividend yields. This subject is discussed further in paras 926 to 935.

Deposits with Banks and Others

269   Depending on the investor's motives, interest-bearing deposits with banks and other financial institutions can be regarded as a form of investment. By virtue of supervision by the Reserve

Bank of Australia (RBA) all deposits with Australian banks offer a high degree of security. Deposits at call (that is, withdrawable without notice) offer convenience also, by virtue of a network of branches and automatic teller machines and because there is a right to make deposits and withdrawals in very small amounts. There may be a choice between different types of deposit, some involving a high degree of liquidity and low interest (or even no interest at all) and others a higher rate of interest in return for the client agreeing to lock his money away for a specified period and/or subject to some minimum size restrictions for transactions and/or balances.

Notes:

1.   A "deposit" with a bank is actually just an unsecured loan to that organisation. In legal terms it creates a debtor/creditor relationship. This is very different from, say, the purchase of units in a cash management trust, which results in investors actually owning a portion of a portfolio of fixed interest securities. It is, of course, also completely different from becoming a shareholder and thus part-owner in a bank.

2.   While the interest rate being paid on call deposits by different institutions can influence an investor's choice of institution in the first place, switches of funds already in place should not be made on the basis of the current interest rate alone without regard to the incidence of transaction charges, especially Financial Institutions Duty (FID)—see para. 3011.

3.   A bank account which does not pay interest can hardly be considered to be an "investment" at all, particularly if it involves periodical and/or transaction charges. Sometimes rebates which can eliminate these charges are available subject to the maintenance of certain minimum credit balances; such deals usually represent very poor value and a depositor would normally be much better off in making a deposit elsewhere at a commercial rate of return and putting up with the bank charges.

4.   The above reference to supervision by the Reserve Bank needs some qualifications. Australian bank

deposits are not formally guaranteed by the Government in the way that some such deposits are guaranteed in a number of overseas countries. Furthermore, the Bank's "Lender of Last Resort" (LLR) facility, which at one time ensured that no bank ever had a liquidity crisis, no longer exists.

270 The disadvantages come from the total absence of growth prospects and from the fact that after allowing for both income tax and inflation the true rate of return will usually be negative. For example, at some stage of a cycle a 12 per cent interest rate may be available and may even sound generous. It may well be marketed as a "high interest" package. However, if tax is imposed at 50 cents in the dollar, then the "after tax" rate of return will be only 6 per cent. If on top of that inflation is running at 10 per cent, then the actual rate of return to the lender will be minus 4 per cent. At that rate, depositors will obviously be getting poorer each year. (However, even a minus 4 per cent rate will still be better than the minus 10 per cent rate which would apply to money "hidden under the bed"!)

271 Fees vary, but then so do the transaction costs of other forms of investment. In both cases, they must be allowed for in assessing the returns. Non-banks are less safe than banks and for that reason often offer higher interest rates and/or other features such as zero charges. Some banks offer accounts which are free of fees and which may involve a waiver of government charges, subject to the maintenance of a certain minimum balance in a zero interest account; as indicated above, it will usually be better value to pay the normal fees and to earn proper interest on any credit balances.

272 With both banks and non-banks depositors face two different risks which, while relatively small, should be recognised. From their very nature all such institutions "borrow short and lend long". Thus, if all depositors were to want their money back on the same day, as happens when there is a "run on the bank", then clearly these demands could not possibly be met, because most of the assets are quite properly tied up in the form of long-term loans rather than being held in cash. Depositors thus run a liquidity risk even if the institution concerned is solvent. (Mortgage loans of the type under consideration can be sold to third parties, but they cannot

normally be called up unless the borrower has defaulted in some way.) Runs pose great dangers for depositors. The subject is discussed in greater detail in paras 3927 to 3941.

273 Separate from this liquidity risk is the risk that the total assets of the institution through excessive bad debts, mismanagement, fraud or other causes become worth less than the total liabilities. This position would be at its worst for depositors and other creditors without security, as these would rank behind the secured creditors.

Notes:

1. Some building societies issue withdrawable shares which are marketed as being equivalent to deposits. However, shareholders rank after all creditors and this can make a significant difference in the event of a failure.

2. Some building societies borrow extensively on a secured basis from banks or other third parties. Such a practice greatly reduces the security of depositors, as in the event of trouble all losses would fall on them rather than on those higher up in the security queue.

274 As explained in paras 256 to 262, individual customers can minimise their risk by spreading their deposits over several institutions, although this may lower the return where sliding scale interest rate formulae are in use. It is, of course, still possible that a failure by, say, one building society, will lead to a run on all others, a phenomenon referred to as *contagion*.

275 Many people maintain bank deposits not as part of a deliberate investment strategy but rather as a reserve "for a rainy day". Such people should at least consider the alternative of investing more heavily and drawing against a pre-arranged line of credit should some unexpected emergency arise. A simple example of such a facility is the unused limit on a credit card such as Bankcard or its competitors.

276 Certain assets can be regarded as being "near cash". These include deposits, short-term bills, units in a cash management trust and other income-producing assets which can be turned into actual cash very readily and generally without loss.

277 Bills can be subdivided into "bank-bills" (bills issued or endorsed—effectively guaranteed-by a trading bank) and

"non-bank bills". The former are safer but the latter command higher yields. Bills do not pay interest as such, but are issued at a discount on their redemption value. Normal terms go up to about 180 days and the minimum face value is usually $100,000.

278 Deposits can be at call, thus providing great flexibility, but without a guaranteed interest rate. Alternatively, they can be "fixed deposits" (also known as "term deposits"), usually at a higher interest rate, which is normally guaranteed for the term of the deposit (see also para. 444). Maturing deposits can generally be rolled over if desired (but only at the rates then current).

The Difference between Investment and Gambling

279 "Gambling" can be defined as *playing games of chance for money; taking great risks to secure great rewards.* There is thus some superficial similarity between investing (see para. 207) and gambling.

280 However, leaving the motives of some individuals aside, there is an enormous difference between gambling proper and using the stock exchange. True gambling involves a pool of money supplied by all participants, out of which a portion is used to meet, firstly, the administrative costs, secondly, the profit of the organisation conducting the activity and, thirdly, taxation. The balance is then distributed amongst some only of the participants on a basis determined purely or mainly by chance. The whole exercise, while no doubt giving pleasure to its participants, is basically unproductive. (While on the surface there may appear to be spin-offs in the form of employment creation and a widening of the government's revenue base, these are obtained at the expense of greater benefits from alternative uses of the resources involved.)

281 By way of contrast, in the case of investment the money is originally supplied to some commercially-run enterprise— say, to entrepreneurs in order to fund a factory, plant, equipment, raw materials, etc. The aim of the management would be to produce a profit by putting these assets to good use. At the end of an accounting period the physical assets would, by and large, still be intact and the primary reward for the inves-

tors would arise from the *increase* in wealth generated by the enterprise.

282   Investors can, of course, often achieve a secondary reward by disposing of their holdings to another person prepared to step into their shoes. If such a person is willing to pay more than the original consideration, then the investor concerned will have realised a one-off capital gain in addition to any peri-odical distribution of income which he might have received from the company.

283   It is true that some investors may be influenced into outlaying their money mainly or entirely by the prospects of such a capital gain—in which case they could technically be de-scribed as gambling or speculating. But these words are pejo-rative and disguise the fact that any such gain is only a by-product of a worthwhile and useful economic activity.

284   Furthermore, even speculators, by undertaking commercial risks, provide a very useful service to the community. Many unsuccessful ventures result in capital losses to their financiers and the prospect of high rewards from successful ventures is needed in order to induce people to provide money for enter-prises in which success is by no means certain. Without some gains to offset such losses many new ventures which benefit the nation would never get off the ground.

285   While the stock exchange is sometimes facetiously described as a casino, its main role (see Chapters 5 and 16) is really to provide a channel for the pooling of a large number of small investment amounts and to provide a means of liquidity for individual savers.

286   Speculators on the stock exchange perform a useful role by evening the market out-buying when others are selling and vice versa. By subscribing to new flotations, persons with speculative motives also assist companies to raise fresh capital and to expand.

Portfolio Reviews

287   Investors should not regard a decision to invest in a particular direction as the end of the matter. Portfolios need to be reviewed periodically, say three or four times a year even for relatively inactive investors. This does not, of course, mean that changes need be made at any particular review, only that

the relative merits of making or not making changes should be carefully considered. One cannot avoid decision making by ignoring the subject—continuing to hold a security amounts to a decision by default.

288 Particular regard should be had to any alterations in:

- The economy as a whole.

- The performance of each individual security.

- The circumstances of the investor.

289 This may lead to a rebalancing of the existing portfolio (for example, between ordinary shares and fixed interest paper) and/or to changes in specific holdings. However, having regard to the incidence of transaction costs, to the existence of certain tax rules relating to capital gains which are discussed later (see Chapter 29) and to the loss of the opportunity to participate in favourable developments affecting a company while one is out of the stock, a decision *not to sell* might well be appropriate even if a corresponding decision *to actually buy* would not be made.

Ideally, every investor would sell at the top of the market and then repurchase at the bottom. Obviously, in practice this is not achievable and an investor who gets his timing wrong in the attempt may finish up worse off than if he had stayed put.

290 In deciding whether or not to dispose of a particular stock regard should be had mainly to its future prospects, and never to its original cost price to the investor. The latter (apart from tax considerations) is utterly irrelevant to such decision making. Furthermore, investors should never allow themselves to get emotionally attached to their shares—judgements should always be made on objective considerations.

291 Nor should investors allow emotional factors to prejudice a decision to repurchase a share which they had once owned but disposed of, if it appears to be good buying in the light of current conditions and even if it has gone up in the meantime.

292 Another purpose of the review should be to reassess the strategy for the future investment of new money (or to allot priorities for the disposal of assets, if it is necessary to disinvest).

Pre-retirement Planning

293   Persons nearing retirement should engage in pre-retirement planning. Ideally, this should commence some five to 10 years before the intended retirement date and, in the case of married couples, should involve both partners. Investment aspects are an important ingredient of such planning, but should not be dealt with in isolation. Other relevant matters to be taken into account include:

- possible "second careers" and the extent of superannuation (in the context of likely income)

- the type and location of housing desired (in the context of asset rearrangements)

- budgeting

- non-financial aspects such as new hobbies, sports, travel and involvement in community affairs

- the desirability of having regular medical check-ups

- the importance of making and periodically revising wills.

These and other aspects are dealt with at great length in the present author's *The Retirement Handbook*.

294   Pre-retirement courses and self—help groups are useful in stimulating thinking and providing background information. However, every person is unique and has different requirements and priorities. For this reason independent counselling by trained personnel on a one-for-one basis is really needed.

Conclusion

295   Most of the large investors around today were small investors on the day they started. As in many other walks of life it is best to involve oneself gradually and to learn from practical experience as one goes.

296   People with only a few hundred or even a few thousand dollars available should not ordinarily contemplate turning themselves into share investors, *except in the context of taking a first step*. A number of factors all suggest that very small

players should stay out completely unless they expect to go on beyond their initial stakes:

- the impossibility of achieving spread
- the relatively high costs involved in making small transactions
- the unavoidable volatility in market prices
- the hardship likely to flow from mistakes or bad luck
- the possible embarrassment from a lack of liquidity.

In addition, there is always the danger that if the purchased shares go down and fingers get burnt then the new investor will be scared off for life, which would be a pity; while if the shares go up then he will get a completely misleading impression as how easy it all is.

297   On the other hand, it is better to learn the craft while one is young and while one's funds are relatively small rather than to have to make the first investment decision after receiving, say, a large superannuation lump sum payment at age 65. The penalty for making a wrong move then and thus prejudicing the savings of a lifetime are much greater.

298   Pooled investment vehicles are described in the companion volume by the present author, *Understanding Managed Investments*. They may be appropriate avenues for investors having more than a few thousand dollars but who regard themselves as still in a small league. Such vehicles suffer from some disadvantages and are not really ideal for people wishing to get more actively involved in the investment scene with all which that implies.

299   Finally, investors should carefully distinguish between three different situations:

- Savings earmarked for a specific purpose. These must be invested in a way which is consistent with the date on which the funds are likely to be required. Such sums should usually be invested in a "capital guaranteed" form, rather than in equities, notwithstanding the disadvantages discussed above.

- General reserves. These are less necessary if an assured positive cash flow is available and/or if there is access to credit facilities.

- long-term savings. These should generally be invested to best advantage without the investor's short-term liquidity requirements being amongst the goals.

In assessing value for money, investors should quantify the return required from any prospective investment by approaching it in stages—for example:

- The starting point is the current risk-free interest rate—say, the 10-year Commonwealth Bond rate.

- To this is added a margin to produce the return appropriate to, say, a high quality company debenture.

- To this is added a further margin to produce the return appropriate to, say, a lower quality fixed interest security.

- To this is added a further margin to produce the return appropriate to an equity situation.

Naturally, for ordinary shares "return" includes capital growth as well as dividends and imputation credits.

Chapter 3—Inflation

A billion here, a billion there, and soon you're talking about real money
—Everett Dirksen

Definition

301   "Inflation" can be defined as *the state of affairs when the value of money falls and the prices of goods and services increase, other things being equal.*

Perspectives

302   Fixed interest investments have for a long time been favoured as savings vehicles by conservative persons unwilling to gamble with their money. For understandable reasons such investments have been particularly popular with people at both ends of the age spectrum —youngsters starting out in the financial world in a very small way and retired persons dependent on investment income in order to maintain their standard of living.

303   Interest rates move up and down from time to time and so do rates of inflation. *At any stage of a cycle the current rates for both tend to look "normal" and it is hard to imagine anything significantly different.* Yet it is highly likely that a period of low interest rates will be followed in due course by a period of high interest rates and vice versa. Similar remarks apply to rates of inflation. Just how suitable is a fixed interest portfolio during a period of high inflation? To answer that question satisfactorily it is necessary to look at the nature of inflation in greater depth.

Inflation and Investors

304   Inflation is very relevant to investors. Its effect can best be illustrated by an analogy. If the Federal Government were to go to all owners of five-room houses and compulsorily acquire one of their rooms without compensation, then there would probably be a revolution.

305   Again, if the Government were one night to confiscate 20 per cent of all deposits in savings institutions—or to impose an equivalent special one-off tax-then the political outcry would be unbearable. But that is precisely what the Government does to savings during a period of inflation, except that it does it more surreptitiously, by keeping the number of dollars constant while reducing their unit value, rather than the other way around, and by doing this in small gradual stages rather than in one dramatic hit.

306 Investment in securities denominated in dollars is thus a sure recipe for disaster in times of high inflation and really poses a much larger hazard than most people realise. The risk is different in character from the risk inherent in equity situations, but the chance of loss—as the reduction in asset value is a virtual certainty —is in a sense much greater.

307 Nor, despite a popular belief to the contrary, can investors avoid erosion of their savings by making deposits on an "at call" basis rather than for longer terms. Either way, after 365 days a year's inflation will have been at work.

308 This situation affecting a unit of currency should be contrasted with the position of other units in common use. The length represented by one metre or the mass represented by one kilogram do not change each year.

The Measurement of Inflation

309 The rate of inflation is usually measured by changes in the Consumer Price Index (CPI), although other yardsticks such as the Gross Domestic Product (GDP) Implicit Price Deflator are sometimes quoted. The CPI is meant to reflect average movements in the cost of living. It is calculated by considering a carefully chosen representative basket of goods and services, with the components kept constant for relatively long periods in order to ensure that like is compared with like (this is sometimes difficult in an era of rapid technological change). Of course, different groups in the community have different spending patterns and thus an index based on the whole population may not really be appropriate to their own individual circumstances.

310 A hypothetical investor with a portfolio which yielded no income but the total value of which moved up exactly in line with the CPI would more or less preserve the purchasing power of his savings. However, such an investor would have had no reward for his sacrifice or his risks. Ideally, therefore, investors need to *outperform* the CPI *after allowing for tax*, and to do so by a reasonable margin each year, otherwise they are effectively going backwards.

311 Wage movements provide another yardstick by which inflation can be measured, particularly Average Weekly Earnings (AWE). In a sense this is more relevant to investors, as the

moral case for maintaining the purchasing power of capital is at least as strong as that for maintaining the purchasing power of labour. Over long periods wages have moved up to a greater extent than prices, partly because of industrial muscle and partly because productivity gains have been passed on to the workers rather than to the suppliers of capital and know—how which made such gains possible in the first place.

312 Demands by trade unions for wage increases to at least match price increases have some superficial logic but they ignore the law of supply and demand. If legal moves result in a level of minimum wages above that which the market will bear then the inevitable result is labour shedding and unemployment instead of growth.

313 Investment in ordinary shares is often recommended as a means of preserving purchasing power (as well as a means of benefiting from Australia's economic growth). While the rate of inflation fluctuates from year to year the long-term trend is always up.

Appendix 1 sets out some figures illustrating movements in inflation as measured by the CPI and comparing these with movements in share values. It will readily be apparent that unfortunately there is no great correlation and that it is quite possible in any particular period for share values to go down while prices go up.

Nevertheless, in the long run the value of shares across the board (and of other equity investments, such as property) tends to move in the right direction, while the value of fixed interest investments does not. The latter may offer advantages such as liquidity, convenience, security and high nominal returns—but such instruments clearly do not constitute a suitable hedge against inflation, especially for the long-term investor.

The Inevitability of Inflation

314 Inflation feeds on itself. For example, higher prices result in higher wages, which in turn cause higher prices. This then produces a loss of international competitiveness, leading to a worse exchange rate for the Australian dollar and to higher domestic interest rates, both of which result in higher prices yet again. And so it goes on.

315 Despite the rhetoric of politicians of all parties the inflation phenomenon is not readily fixable on a permanent basis. In fact, because inflation makes tax collecting easier in electoral terms—as rising dollar incomes mislead most voters into thinking that they are better off than they really are—and also because inflation makes it easier to service the national debt, governments are not in truth very keen to eliminate inflation.

316 The public sector is a significant net borrower from the private sector (in practice, mainly from small savers—both directly and indirectly through savings banks, life insurance companies and superannuation funds). Thus anything that reduces the burden of this debt—even if it means cheating millions of innocent people—is seemingly quite welcome.

317 In the Australian context there are also constitutional impediments which would prevent legislation dealing with prices and wages—although in practice such measures would do little more than slow down rather than eliminate the upward spiral. In any case, those calling for legislation fixing *maximum* prices see no inconsistency in the continued existence of industrial awards fixing *minimum* wages. While in public all employer groups oppose wage rises, businessmen really prefer paying these to losing production as a result of industrial disputes. In the long run it is much easier to pass extra costs on to consumers rather than to suffer losses by having expensive capital resources lying idle and through being unable to recover ongoing holding charges.

318 Governments also cause inflation by spending more money than they raise either through taxation or by borrowing from the public. Thus the money supply is increased without a corresponding increase in the volume of goods and services, resulting in higher unit prices.

319 From time to time various policies are suggested to governments as devices for fighting inflation, but most of these are two-edged swords. For example, high interest rates are said to discourage expansion and thus to lower the demand for resources—which would be deflationary. But high interest rates also translate into higher production costs and are thus inflationary.

Taxation Aspects

320 One effect of taxation in conjunction with inflation was demonstrated in para. 270. There are, however, other effects as well. The income tax legislation, with some exceptions, regards a dollar as a dollar and therefore taxes are imposed on the apparent rather than the real profits of all business enterprises—for example, without proper regard to the fact that the cost of goods to replenish stock levels after sales will be higher than the original cost or to the fact that the replacement prices of depreciating assets used in a business will be higher than their historical cost. Many companies therefore pay tax on more income than is just and in effect have their capital base eroded unfairly.

321 Again, the sliding scale of income tax rates in use for individuals means that effective tax rates increase each year as people move into higher tax brackets even if their incomes rise by no more than just to keep pace with inflation.

322 Some business taxes are particularly harmful in the inflation context—notably payroll tax, which increases the cost of labour and which is inevitably passed on in the form of higher prices. Similarly, petrol tax feeds into all transport costs and thus affects virtually all goods. This is particularly severe for Australia as a country with large distances separating small markets. Taxes imposed on businesses as distinct from those levied on individuals may be less damaging to governments in an electoral sense, but such taxes also tend to be more inflationary.

Investment Strategy

323 It follows that sophisticated savers who agree with the case made out above should adopt an investment strategy which recognises the inevitability of continuing inflation. This will not, of course, eliminate inflation for the nation as a whole, but it will at least transfer some of the burden from themselves to others less able to look after themselves. A *zero sum game* is involved here—the gains of one party (say, a debtor) are always exactly balanced by the losses of another party (say, a creditor). Similarly, gains to wage earners collectively are matched by losses to the rest of the community, including age pensioners and others who can ill afford such discrimination.

324   It is sometimes suggested that the level of interest rates current from time to time adequately allows for inflation and that therefore fixed interest investments can safely be made, notwithstanding the above analysis. To some extent the former statement is probably true. Interest rates can certainly be thought of conceptually as involving three separate components:

- a payment for the use of the money (the equivalent of rent)

- a payment for the assumption of risk

- a payment by way of compensation for inflation.

But the last-mentioned component is in practice quite inadequate, because the relative bargaining strengths of lenders and borrowers are not equal. Those with surplus cash need to find a home for it, while those with a use for money for some commercial activity have the choice of not going ahead if the borrowing terms are such that the chance of making a profit is regarded as too low. Thus lenders collectively (whether small savers or large institutions) are never in a position to say to borrowers "we believe that inflation will be x per cent per annum; therefore you must pay us $x+y$ per cent per annum".

325   Separate from that is the question of taxation already referred to in para. 270. The law treats nominal interest payments as "income" for tax purposes, even though the "inflation compensation" component should logically be treated as a non-taxable capital item. Lenders thus pay more tax than is equitable and correspondingly commercial borrowers get a bigger tax deduction than is really warranted. Naturally, this statutory distortion is taken into account by participants in the capital markets when arranging their affairs. However, as far as investors are concerned, even if the gross rate of interest received by them exceeds the rate of inflation then in practice the net rate (for tax-paying individuals) does not.

326   The word "real" is often used in economic discussions as meaning *inflation adjusted*. Thus if the rate of inflation is 10 per cent per annum and the price of something has gone up by 12 per cent per annum in dollar terms then it can be said to have gone up by only 2 per cent per annum in *real* terms. As

discussed below, one can also distinguish between *real assets* (equities) and *monetary assets* (loans).

327   A house is always a house. If in a space of 12 months its price increases from $100,000 to $110,000, then this does not actually mean that its owner is any better off. But, unlike the depositor in a savings institution, or the holder of a Commonwealth Bond, or the lender under a mortgage, the owner of the house has at least *preserved* his purchasing power (more or less). The same principle applies to other physical assets, such as shops, factories, office buildings and so on, as well as to plant and equipment and to stocks of both raw materials and finished goods. At one stage removed, this principle also applies to the shares of companies holding assets of this type (as distinct from assets such as loans, which are denominated in dollars). Some companies, such as banks and finance companies, hold mainly monetary assets.

328   Furthermore, real assets such as buildings (colloquially often referred to as "bricks and mortar") tend to keep their value because of the high labour cost involved in their construction (both directly and indirectly in relation to the labour component of their materials). If the cost of new buildings goes up in dollars because of increased labour costs then this factor enables the vendors of existing buildings to obtain more dollars for their buildings because the alternative of erecting a cheaper new building has been eliminated. The value of land, particularly land in desired locations, tends to rise at an even faster rate than inflation, because demand increases as population grows while supply is fixed.

329   Oversimplifying slightly, it can be said that a company makes a profit equal to the sale price of its goods and services less their cost price, interest and the expenses of running the operation. If the volumes stay the same but the unit prices in respect of both the "cost" and the "expense" elements rise by 10 per cent (if this is the rate of inflation), then the profit before interest will also rise by 10 per cent in dollar terms—while remaining steady in real terms. Thus, prima facie, ordinary shares in companies ought to be good inflation hedge investments.

330 In practice, this may not always work out. Higher prices, while no doubt also applying to the competitors of a particular business, may deter potential customers. Costs, particularly those for labour and in respect of government charges, may rise faster than the prices obtainable in the market place. Again, exporters have to take prices dictated by world markets, often dominated by countries with much lower inflation rates than Australia, while some local businesses are subject to competition from imports.

Leverage

331 On the other hand, companies which use borrowed funds can actually *benefit* from inflation (although at the risk of encountering certain other problems). This use of loan monies to supplement one's own capital is known as "gearing" or "leverage" and the advantage just referred to works something like this (again assuming for the purpose of illustration a 10 per cent inflation rate):

	Year 1 $	Year 2 $	Increase %
Profit before Interest	200	220	10
Interest	100	100	-
Profit after Interest	100	120	20

There is thus also scope for dividends to more than keep pace with inflation.

332 It also follows that a conservative company using borrowed funds the total of which is small in comparison with the total assets of the company may not really be acting in its shareholders' best long-term interests, although this is not a clear-cut issue. Other things being equal, investors expecting high inflation to continue would probably wish to concentrate on companies using a fair amount of borrowed funds and having mainly non-monetary assets.

333 Gearing as a tool in order to benefit from inflation can be employed by investors as well as by companies. Some warnings as to the hazards of using borrowed funds are given in Chapter 27, but in the context of inflation the attraction in respect to both asset values and income should be noted. For example, an investor might wish to put a net $100,000 into

income-producing real estate. The following two scenarios should be compared:

	Capital	Increase in Value over one Year	Income per annum	Together
	$	$	$	$
Scenario No. 1: Small Property, no Loan				
Property	100,000	10,000	10,000	20,000
Net Total	100,000	10,000	10,000	20,000
Scenario No. 2: Larger Property, subject to Loan				
Property	200,000	20,000	20,000	40,000
Less Loan	100,000	nil	16,000	16,000
Net Total	100,000	20,000	4,000	24,000

334 The analysis in this chapter suggests that inflation should always be considered when evolving an investment strategy and that certain categories of investment—equity situations, such as ordinary shares and property, both directly and indirectly through unit trusts and the like—have clear advantages over other categories—fixed interest securities. However, other investment principles are also relevant and inflation is, of course, only one factor—although an important one-in the overall context of the subject.

Bookkeeping

335 A separate factor of significance to investors should be mentioned at this stage, although it deals with a subject explained in Chapter 8. Inflation can cause distortions to company balance sheets, as for example when assets are kept in the books at cost rather than being written up periodically in order to reflect current values. This can result in the readers of such documents being misled as to the true underlying value of the shares concerned (and thus also as to a company's efficiency). Depreciation also tends to be understated if it is based on out-dated historical figures and this and other bookkeeping features can cause the true profit of a business enterprise to be seriously overstated. It is thus possible for companies to be

effectively paying dividends out of capital without this being obvious.

336   It is sometimes argued that accounting for inflation should not be introduced until the taxation system in Australia is amended to take inflation into account. This is actually a back-to-front argument: the cause of taxation reform in this important area would be greatly advanced if companies demonstrated in their published accounts that their present tax burden was excessive and that it affected different categories of taxpayer quite unevenly.

Trust Estates

337   Many old-style wills and trust deeds confer restricted investment powers on the executors or trustees and prohibit investment in other than fixed interest paper. The ravages of inflation in recent years will have demonstrated that such limitations, while no doubt inserted with the best of intentions, can greatly disadvantage the beneficiaries concerned.

The Future

338   The following sample figures will illustrate the points made in this chapter. They show the outcome of inflation at 10 per cent per annum over the next 50 years:

Item	Approximate Price $
Postage on a standard letter	40
4 Kg hamburger steak	1,350
One week's average wages	55,000
Motor vehicle (such as a Mazda 929)	3,800,000

Chapter 4—Company Securities

The engine which drives enterprise is not thrift,
but profit
—John Maynard Keynes

The Concept of a Company

401   The simplest form of business enterprise involves a sole trader—in other words, a single individual who puts up his own capital and labour into some commercial or industrial venture. This person takes all the risk and reaps all the rewards if the activity is successful. He can run the business in his own name or he can register (under State law) an appropriate business name. The use of such a name should be distinguished from the formation of a company, as discussed below.

402   A sole proprietorship can find that its financial and/or human resources prove to be too limited. One solution to this problem would be the formation of a firm or partnership—an enterprise where two or more individuals come together and share the financing, the work, the risks and the rewards—on some agreed basis.

403   Partners need not all make identical contributions or share profits equally. Frequently the skills of different individuals will be complementary, as when a technical expert teams up with someone having administrative skills or when an inventor links up with a person who is good at marketing. Similarly, partners can supply different amounts of capital—in an extreme case, there may be one "working" partner running the business on a day-by-day basis and one "sleeping" partner supplying all the money.

404   A partnership is not a legal entity and all partners are jointly and severally liable for the financial obligations of their partnership. This principle covers not only trade debts but also, for example, awards of damages or even losses caused by the fraud of an employee or one of the partners.

405   This aspect is a deterrent to potential investors, as these would naturally be unwilling to put their entire personal fortunes at risk for what might be a relatively small investment in some project. Recognition of this factor led to the invention of the joint stock company—an artificial body, treated by the law as a separate "person" capable of suing and being sued and able to own property. Furthermore, in the ordinary course of events companies—unlike natural persons—stay in existence in perpetuity.

406 Most companies have *limited liability* and this means that the members of the company—as distinct from the members of a partnership —are not liable for the obligations of the enterprise beyond some stated amount (see para. 413). This concept of limiting an investor's risk was quite a remarkable innovation, ranking in importance with the industrial revolution.

407 Early companies were set up by Royal Charter (letters patent from the King, usually also conferring some monopoly rights, as in the case of the East India Company of 1600, or the Hudson's Bay Company of 1670). Later on companies were incorporated one at a time by Special Acts of Parliament, as in the case of the Australian Mutual Provident Society (founded in 1849 as a friendly society but incorporated as a company by a Private Act of the Colony of New South Wales in 1857 —long before it was demutualised in 1998).

408 More general companies legislation was first developed in the second half of the nineteenth century. It is now relatively easy to form new companies using this standard machinery.

409 Modern business enterprises frequently require large sums of money and it is thus very convenient for entrepreneurs to be able to put together the relatively small individual contributions of a large number of unconnected investors.

410 A company can be thought of as a sort of club:

- with members (the shareholders, who technically *are* the "members" of the company);

- with an elected committee exercising delegated authority (the board of directors); and

- with formal rules (the *memorandum of association* and the *articles of association*).

As in the case of most clubs, the majority of the members do not involve themselves in the day-by-day running of the organisation. However, they retain ultimate control through their right to vote at general meetings. The shareholders collectively are the *owners* of the business. The directors have legal, moral and professional obligations to run the enterprise for the benefit of all shareholders—although they clearly also have ethical obligations to other stakeholders: employees, creditors, suppliers, customers, ultimate consumers and the community at large (for example, in relation to the environment or to paying a proper share of taxation).

411 The *memorandum of association*, generally speaking, deals with the relationship of the company to the outside world. It covers matters such as the name of the company, its objects, its authorised capital and a statement as to the limited liability of its members (if applicable).

412 The *articles of association* deal with the rights of members *inter se* (amongst themselves). The articles cover matters such as the various categories of shares, the voting rights attached to each share, the size of the board, proceedings at general meetings, dividend declarations, and so on.

Main Types of Company

Limited Companies

413 Commercial companies incorporated under the companies legislation with limited liability are known as "limited companies" and are required to have the word "Limited" (or the abbreviation "Ltd.") as the last word in their name. This was originally meant to serve as a warning to persons thinking of extending credit to the company, putting them on notice that the members did not have the same unlimited liability as applied in the case of the members of a partnership. However, these days this word seems to have the reverse effect and confidence tricksters frequently prefer to operate under some impressive sounding company name. (These days some organisations which are not companies, such as building societies and friendly societies, are also required to use the label "Limited".)

414 In the stock exchange context, limited liability works this way:

- Newly-created shares are offered at a certain issue price, payable either at once or on the basis of an initial amount and the balance by subsequent instalments (known as *calls*).

- The amount of each call and its due date can be set at the onset or alternatively it can be fixed by the directors from time to time. (In a few cases the shareholder has the right to nominate the date of the call.)

- If the company ever goes into liquidation owing money, then the liquidator is also entitled to call up the outstanding balance.

- However, once the total issue price has been subscribed the shares are described as *fully-paid* and no further amounts can be required from shareholders (in their capacity as such), no matter how large the indebtedness of the company.

- Any person who acquires existing shares from a quitting shareholder takes them subject to the same rights and obligations as applied previously. So the maximum liability of any shareholder is fixed as the amount of the unpaid calls, if any.

- Calls are levied on the shareholder who is on the register at the time, but if he does not meet them they can also be recovered from previous shareholders going back 12 months. For these reasons most companies do not allow shares which are subject to future calls to be registered in the names of minors.

- Shares still subject to calls are known as *contributing shares* or *partly-paid shares*.

<u>No Liability Companies</u>

415 Mining companies can be formed as limited companies in the usual way. However, there is another alternative—incorporation as a "no liability" company. Such companies have "No Liability" (or the abbreviation "NL") at the end of their names.

416 Shareholders in such companies have the privilege of not paying calls. They cannot be sued for unpaid calls, but shares on which calls are not made by the due date are then forfeited. Forfeited shares are auctioned a few weeks later (unless the arrears have been paid in the meantime) and any proceeds, after deducting the expenses of sale and the amount of the unpaid call (and, sometimes, of subsequent calls), are paid to the relevant shareholders pro rata. (If the shareholders cannot be traced, then the proceeds become unclaimed monies which are eventually paid to the government.) The reserve value at

such auctions is the amount of the call (plus subsequent calls, if any); shares not reaching this reserve remain at the disposal of the board and can be either offered to shareholders or placed with third parties at not less than this figure at some later time.

Proprietary Companies

417 The vehicles described above are all known as "public companies", meaning that members of the general public, by and large, can acquire shares. They are not "public" in the sense of being government-owned. In a different category are "proprietary companies" ("private companies")—companies which restrict the right to transfer shares freely, which limit the number of shareholders to 50 (apart from employees and ex-employees) and which prohibit both the offer of shares to the public and the soliciting of loan funds from the public. Such companies are distinguished by the words "Proprietary Limited" (or the abbreviation "Pty. Ltd.") at the end of their names.

418 Companies listed on the stock exchange, from their very nature, need to be public companies. However, their subsidiaries can be and often are proprietary companies. In practice most small family companies are proprietary companies. Many small businesses incorporate in order to get the protection of limited liability (as well as to get certain taxation advantages). Only a very small amount of paid-up capital, such as $2, is sufficient to achieve this purpose.

419 The terms "public company" and "private company" are also used in taxation legislation. The meaning there is similar to, but not identical with, the meaning under companies legislation.

Unlimited Companies

420 It is also possible to form companies with unlimited liability ("unlimited companies"). These have some advantages, notably the ability to reduce their capital without court approval. This feature in theory makes such a format very suitable for mutual funds (which need to offer a ready facility for redeeming investors' shares on request). However, the risks for shareholders which are posed by unlimited liability offset this advantage and most promoters of pooled investment vehicles

therefore prefer to create either unit trusts or investment companies.

(*Note:* Legislation to allow capital reductions without court approval has recently been enacted.)

<u>General Comments</u>

421 Limited companies with both fully-paid and contributing shares (or with more than one class of the latter) commonly provide that dividends will be paid in proportion to the paid-up value. In the event of liquidation the return of capital per share would take any uncalled amounts into account. If both fully-paid and contributing shares are listed, then the respective market values should theoretically reflect the amount and timing of the outstanding commitment (as well as any dividend differences).

In practice anomalies in price frequently arise, making one category or the other (usually the contributing shares) the better buy. Prepayment of calls is often permitted, but usually confers no advantage.

422 In contrast, no liability companies usually (but not invariably) provide that fully-paid and contributing shares rank equally, both for dividends and in liquidation.

423 While most partnerships involve unlimited liability, some of the smaller Australian States have machinery allowing the formation of limited partnerships. However, these must not involve more than 20 partners each.

Capital Structures

<u>Ordinary Shares</u>

424 Most limited companies have share capital and are technically known as "companies limited by shares". All companies listed on the stock exchange—apart from the "no liability" companies described above—are in this category. It is also possible to incorporate companies without shares as companies "limited by guarantee", a format used by mutual life insurance companies and by many non-profit bodies—although the latter can also incorporate under other legislation, such as the *Associations Incorporation Act.*

425 Subject to that exception, all companies *must* have "ordinary" shares. They *may* also have other *classes* of shares, such as

"deferred" shares and/or "preference" shares. A description of these is included in this chapter for the sake of completeness and also as an aid to an understanding of the whole system. There are furthermore a number of long-standing preference shares still listed and in any case the subject has historical interest. However, for the most part preference shares—having none of the advantages of either ordinary shares or fixed interest paper—are not in current circumstances suitable investments for small individual investors. This latter observation does not apply to convertible or converting preference shares (see para. 440).

426 The shareholders collectively *own* the company, meaning that they are:

- entitled to all the profits (after all expenses, interest on the liabilities and taxation);

- entitled, on liquidation, to all the assets remaining after all the liabilities have been met;

- able to exercise control.

However, the profits to which the shareholders are entitled are not necessarily distributed in cash each year.

427 The simplest capital structure involves only one class (or category) of shares, namely, ordinary shares as stated above. Each such share represents an aliquot part of the company. Thus, if there are one million shares, each represents a one-millionth part of the equity of the company. All shares in each class of shares have identical rights. Most ordinary shares carry voting power, although sometimes a class of non-voting ordinary shares also exists.

428 For historical reasons shares in Australia are legally required to have a "face value" or "par value" or "nominal value", such as 50 cents or one dollar. However, this concept hides more than it reveals. Shares are not necessarily issued for their nominal value and even if they are then the value of each share at any later time is likely to be either more or less than this figure (whether one is considering the market value of the shares on the stock exchange, or their value based on a valuation of the entire company either as a going concern or on break-up).

(*Note:* Legislation to abolish par values has recently been enacted. See paras 1247 to 1262.)

429 The terms *premium* and *discount* are used in this connection. Thus, a new 50 cent share may be offered to subscribers at a premium of 70 cents—in other words at a total issue price of 120 cents. While such language is frequently used in company circulars and in legal documents it confuses many readers and really serves no useful purpose as far as an investor or anyone else is concerned (see also paras 1245-1246).

Deferred Shares

430 Companies can create shares which are inferior to ordinary shares in some defined way—for example, non-voting ordinary shares or *deferred shares* (such as shares which do not participate in dividends for some years, automatically converting to ordinary shares at the end of this period). Deferred shares may be given a name such as *"Z" shares*. Some deferred shares may receive less favourable treatment than ordinary shares (as to amount and/or priority) in the event of the company's liquidation. Some companies acquire assets from their promoters in exchange for *vendor shares* which are subject to special conditions, such as limited dividends till certain profit targets are achieved and a prohibition on listing on the stock exchange before a certain date.

Preference Shares

431 Companies can also create shares which are superior to ordinary shares. These are usually just known as *preference shares*, although depending on the precise conditions other names such as *"A" ordinary shares* or *preferred ordinary shares* are sometimes used. Preference shares are normally entitled to a fixed rate of dividend, but this is payable ahead of any dividends available to ordinary shareholders. As dividends can legally be paid only out of the profits of the company, the so-called "fixed" rate is really a maximum rate. Any balance of the profits belongs to the ordinary shareholders.

432 In an economic sense preference shares and their dividends resemble loan funds and the interest thereon. But the legal status and the "place in the queue" of such shares is very different. Preference shareholders are part-owners of the busi-

ness (along with the ordinary shareholders, although with different rights). They are not creditors in the way that lenders are.

433 In the event of liquidation the preference shareholders once again rank ahead of the ordinary shareholders, this time in respect of the capital aspects. However, they rank behind all categories of creditors. Preference shareholders are normally entitled, in a winding-up, to the face value of their shares and to any arrears of dividend. They will get this, provided only that the assets remaining after satisfying all the liabilities are sufficient. Preference shareholders may therefore get *less* than their theoretical entitlement (or even nothing at all), but they can never get any *more*. As stated above, any balance remaining belongs to the ordinary shareholders, regardless of whether this is more or less than the money originally put in and irrespective of the cost to any particular investor.

434 In a successful enterprise the ordinary shareholders can thus find that their stake in the company (their "equity" in it) can be worth many times its original value. Conversely, if things go wrong, they risk losing their entire outlay—and because they are "at the tail end of the queue" their risk is the greatest.

435 Some companies have more than one category of preference share on issue—for example, "first preference" shares, ranking ahead of "second preference" shares, these in turn ranking ahead of "third preference" shares, and so on. These may all have different dividend rates and/or face values, the actual rates to some extent reflecting the different risks but also being a function of the interest rate levels prevailing at the time the securities were created.

436 Preference shares can in any combination be:

- cumulative or non-cumulative
- participating or non-participating
- redeemable or irredeemable
- convertible or non-convertible
- voting or non-voting.

Preference dividends can be made subject to franking, as in the case of ordinary shares. Alternatively, the terms of issue can provide that all dividends shall be unfranked; naturally, the dividend rate then needs to be correspondingly higher. (Neither the fact that dividends are franked in one case nor the fact that the rate is higher in the other mean that either version is necessarily better for a tax-paying investor.) See also para. 2890.

437 The term "cumulative" means that if any year's preference dividends are not paid out (for example, because of lack of profitability) then all arrears must be paid off before payment of ordinary dividends is permitted. Dividends on non-cumulative preference shares, by way of contrast, are looked at only one financial year at a time and shareholders have no protection against missed declarations.

438 Participating preference shares (sometimes also known as "preferred ordinary shares") entitle the holders to a stipulated minimum rate of dividend (subject, as always, to sufficient profitability) and to participation in higher dividends beyond that, on a formula related to the rate of ordinary dividend. The higher amount may, for example, be an extra one per cent, or the number of cents per share can be the same as for the ordinary shares. Most preference shares are non-participating.

439 Unless they are specifically labelled "redeemable" most preference shares are intended to be perpetual (that is, irredeemable) securities in the same way as ordinary shares are (apart from winding-up situations). However, some preference shares are created with a fixed maturity (or redemption) date, with the intention that (subject to certain statutory constraints) they will be redeemed at a pre-determined date and at a stipulated price (not necessarily their face value).

Variations to this theme can involve a range of dates during which redemption may take place (possibly at different prices depending on the date chosen) and/or vesting the right to call for redemption in the hands of either the company or the shareholder. Some redeemable preference shares are issued with a very low face value and a very high premium, as it is legally easier to make redemptions out of a share premium account than by reducing capital; in such cases the dividend rate as a percentage of the face value may sound ridiculously high.

440 Again, preference shares are non-convertible unless specifically labelled otherwise. Two main types of convertible preference share exist—and they are quite different:

- Most convertible preference shares are convertible to ordinary shares in some specified ratio on a specified date (or within one or more ranges of specified dates), either automatically (compulsorily) or more commonly at the option of the holder. Before conversion such preference shares are entitled to a fixed rate of dividend, often higher than that being paid to ordinary shares at the time of issue. Unlike most other preference shares, convertible preference shares usually participate in rights issues as though they had already been converted (see para. 708). The conversion ratio is normally adjusted in the event of a share split or a bonus issue; shares without this protection would pose serious risks of dilution to their holders. There should also be a right of conversion ahead of time in the event of a successful takeover offer.

- Some shares, under a name such as "converting preference shares", are compulsorily convertible to ordinary shares, often at a discount (for example, 10 per cent) to the market price prevailing on or near the conversion date. Such preference shares do not need entitlements to rights or bonus issues before conversion, as the market value formula ensures that a proper consideration is given. In effect, the preference shares have a redemption value of $111.11 per $100 face value (assuming the above-mentioned 10 per cent discount), but payable in kind (ordinary shares) rather than in cash. For analytical purposes it is much better to focus on this figure and the full market price, rather than on the face value and the discounted market price. Furthermore, any purchasers of the preference shares at a price above this $111.11 should take the certain capital loss at the conversion stage into consideration when assessing the yield.

The stock exchange trades converting preference shares in its equity list, but they are really fixed interest paper until actually converted. However, it is most important to realise that:

- in the case of true convertibles, a doubling, say, in the market price of the ordinary shares over time will result in a near-doubling of the market price of the convertible securities (as the conversion formula involves a specific number of ordinary shares).

- in the case of the converting preference shares described above, a doubling in the market price of the ordinary shares will not result in any change whatsoever in the market price of the preference shares (as in contrast the conversion formula involves a specific number of dollars).

441 Most preference shares carry no entitlement to votes at general meetings of the company, unless the dividends are more than six months in arrears. However, such shares can be voted at meetings of preference shareholders; such meetings would normally be necessary on all questions affecting their rights. Some companies' articles also make provision for the preference shareholders to elect their own director to the board, to monitor their particular interests (as well as those of all shareholders).

Loan Securities

442 Ranking ahead of all categories of shares are various types of unsecured liabilities. Ahead of these again are the different classes of secured liabilities. Because of this ranking loan securities are sometimes referred to as "senior securities".

443 As far as small investors are concerned, the only unsecured company liabilities of relevance are deposits and unsecured notes (including convertible unsecured notes) and the only secured liabilities of relevance are debentures. It should, however, be noted that in the event of liquidation unsecured liabilities arising from investment decisions rank equally with all other unsecured liabilities, such as those arising from trading,

from unsecured bank loans, from damages awards or whatever. Investment liabilities are sometimes referred to as "paper". Some high risk, poor quality company fixed interest securities are referred to as "junk bonds"; these are discussed in paras 1914 to 1916.

Deposits

444 Deposits on an unsecured basis can be made with banking and finance companies, either at call or for a fixed term of a few months or a few years (or for an indefinite term subject to some period of notice). Some industrial companies also accept money on deposit from their shareholders. Deposits are personal contracts between the lenders and the borrowers and are not usually transferable. They are thus not traded on the stock exchange.

Unsecured Notes and Debentures

445 The word "note" in "unsecured note" and the word "debenture" both mean "loan" and imply a transferable acknowledgement of an obligation. Debentures and unsecured notes can thus be listed, although there would not necessarily be any intention to take this step in the case of many of the securities offered to investors. This aspect would be set out in the initial prospectus.

The word "unsecured" means that no assets are charged by way of security, as in the case of debentures; the latter are really "secured notes". However, it should be realised that shares—while there is no requirement for them to be actually labelled as "unsecured"—are, in a technical sense, in fact significantly less secure than unsecured notes. In practice, notes and debentures usually involve a term of several years, although some irredeemable loan securities also exist.

446 Notes and debentures of the type under discussion are usually issued under a trust deed which imposes some restrictions on the borrowing company and which gives investors some degree of protection in the event of a default. An independent trustee is appointed, such as a statutory trustee company or a subsidiary of a life insurance company. If necessary, the trustee can take action on behalf of the note or debenture holders—for example, by arranging for a receiver and manager to be appointed. There would also be provision for meetings of holders

to be called. Naturally, a receiver in those circumstances has no obligation to act for shareholders or even to report to them.

447 Debentures are secured by a charge over certain assets of the borrowing company and of other companies in the group. Such a charge can be either "floating" (applying to assets at large, except to the extent of specific prior charges) or "fixed" (attached to specific assets). If the assets comprise freehold land and the security is a first mortgage for not more than 60 per cent of the value of the property then the debentures can be called "mortgage debentures".

448 Trust deeds would usually specify certain minimum ratios for income cover and assets cover which must be maintained. For example, it may be provided that during the currency of the loan the total secured liabilities must not exceed 40 per cent of the group's total assets (in other words, $250 cover would be available for each $100 of secured indebtedness; the higher this figure, the better for investors).

Similarly, it may be provided that during the currency of the loan the total liabilities must not exceed 60 per cent of the total assets or one and a half times shareholders' funds (in other words, about $167 cover would be available for each $100 of secured and unsecured indebtedness).

While such conditions benefit investors they naturally impose corresponding burdens on the issuing corporations. In current circumstances most industrial companies find it preferable to obtain their debt finance in ways other than by issuing debentures to investors. Instead of charging assets many companies prefer to use "negative pledges" to protect lenders.

Convertible Notes

449 Convertible unsecured notes (usually just called "convertible notes") are notes which give the holders the right at certain specified times to convert the loan into ordinary shares in some specific ratio such as 1 for 1 or 2.1 for 1 (the "conversion ratio"). If unconverted by the end of the latest conversion period they mature in the usual way on the specified maturity date shortly afterwards. Until they are converted they enjoy all the privileges of loan securities, including priority in the event of liquidation and (normally) the payment of interest at a much

higher rate than the dividends available on the shares which will be allotted on conversion.

However, other things being equal, convertible notes usually involve somewhat lower interest rates than the company would need to pay on equivalent unconvertible securities. As in the case of convertible preference shares (see para. 440), convertible notes need to embody protection for holders in the event of takeovers, share splits and rights and bonus issues.

(Notes convertible at the option of the company rather than at the option of the holder are sometimes issued, but such securities involve significant tax disadvantages for the issuing company. Until converted they rank ahead of shares in the usual way, but for analytical purposes they can be regarded as equity, unless the liquidation of the company before the conversion date is under contemplation.)

450   Convertible notes can be very attractive investments for some categories of investor. If things go well, they can always be converted and this privilege will ensure that their market price moves up in line with that of the company's ordinary shares. If things go badly, the notes can be redeemed for their face value and this tends to limit the loss an investor can incur.

The return is normally higher than the return on the corresponding ordinary shares and the market price on many issues is less than that which should theoretically apply—although each note must be examined individually in this regard and the relationship varies from time to time. Offsetting these features are the facts that note interest is fully taxable, without the imputation credits available for dividends—see paras 2833 to 2846—and that the volume of notes traded each day in most companies is relatively small, making buying and selling more difficult than in the case of shares.

Options

451   Some companies have another type of security on issue, known as an "option", and described in greater detail in Chapter 22. Each option gives the holder the right to acquire a share in the company at a specified price (called the "exercise price") on stipulated exercise dates (or sometimes at any time up to a maximum date). Options not exercised by the latest possible exercise date lapse and become worthless.

These securities can also be very attractive for investors, provided only that their cost is not excessive and that they have adequate protection against dilution (this does not always apply and needs to be checked out in each case). If things go well, they move up in value as the value of the underlying shares goes up, usually producing higher proportionate gains than those available from a direct investment in the shares (see paras 480 to 481). If things go badly, the options can be allowed to lapse, thus limiting dollar losses.

Scrip Certificates

452 Investors in company securities are often provided with documents of title by the companies concerned, setting out the size and other details of the holding. These documents, normally issued some weeks after allotment (in the case of new securities) or the receipt of a valid transfer form (in the case of existing securities), are known as "scrip certificates". (The word is not, as is sometimes thought, "script".)

(*Note:* An alternative system called "CHESS", which involves uncertificated holdings, is described in paras 1669 to 1681.)

453 In addition, the company would keep a record of the holding in a "register"—these days invariably in computer form. This gives rise to phrases such as "*registered* unsecured notes". Registers can be inspected and copied, but investors are free to have their securities registered in the names of nominees (although persons entitled to more than 5 per cent of a class of voting shares are defined as "substantial shareholders" and have to disclose details of their interest under Section 708 of the *Corporations Law*, as part of the legislation relating to takeovers). Mailing lists based on share or note register data are discussed in paras 3948 to 3957.

454 Scrip certificates (where they exist) need to be produced before a transfer of the relevant securities can be registered—although lost certificates can be replaced (admittedly at some cost and inconvenience and after some delay). Such certificates are also frequently deposited with persons lending money on the security of shares or other company paper. Furthermore, some stockbrokers insist on receiving the relevant scrip before accepting selling orders, especially from small or new clients (see also paras 1679 to 1689 for the

requirements of the "T+5" settlement system). For all these reasons certificates should be kept in a safe place.

455 However, scrip certificates are not "bearer certificates" and changes in the ownership of company securities cannot be effected merely by handing over scrip. However, the name on a certificate is *prima facie* evidence of title.

456 Many overseas jurisdictions allow companies to issue their securities in either "registered" or "bearer" form, but the latter would be illegal in Australia.

Illogical Transactions

457 Investors facing a loss because a fixed interest security has gone down in value sometimes seek to hold on to it in the knowledge that other than in exceptional circumstances it will be redeemable at its face value at maturity. In order to achieve the liquidity which they would have obtained by selling they then borrow, possibly on the security of the fixed interest investment itself. In practice the rate of interest on the loan is likely to exceed the return which would be given up on a sale. Such a strategy thus does not make sense unless the borrowing is at call and an early decline in interest rate levels is expected.

Dividends and Interest

458 Dividends are usually paid twice a year, although a few companies make distributions on either a yearly or a quarterly basis. On the normal pattern, a company would pay an "interim dividend" on its ordinary shares about eight months into financial year, based on its results for the first six months, and a "final dividend" about six months later when the results for the whole year are known. The interim dividend is traditionally between one-third and one-half of the expected total dividend for the year concerned.

459 Preference dividends and interest are normally paid twice a year in equal instalments, although again payments by some companies would be made either once or four times a year. The rate per annum is sometimes referred to as the "coupon". The term "accrued interest" (as at a particular date) is used in relation to loan securities to refer to the proportion of the interest which belongs to the period since the last interest

payment. The amount of accrued interest would normally be reflected in the market price of such securities.

Notes:

1. Investors wishing for monthly or quarterly interest payments from loan securities which pay interest on a half-yearly basis may be able to achieve their objective indirectly by acquiring stakes in several issues with different payment months. In the same way, share investors wanting dividends in particular months for cash flow reasons can have regard to the customary time of payment when picking companies.

2. Shareholders should, as far as possible, arrange to have their dividend and interest payments made directly into their accounts at a bank or other financial institution—preferably electronically and thus by way of cleared funds. This avoids the possibility of loss or delay in the mail and the inconvenience of banking cheques physically. It also puts the funds to work faster.

3. If the persons entitled to dividend or interest payments cannot be traced, then the sums concerned become unclaimed monies which are eventually paid to the government.

4. Shareholders sometimes complain about the length of time between the end of an accounting period and the declaration of a dividend and/or between that declaration and the actual payment of the dividend. However, this seems a very trivial issue-money in the hands of the company still earns interest and this benefits the shareholders collectively.

460 The formal announcement of a dividend by a company's board of directors is called a *declaration*. A company deciding not to make a distribution is said to have *passed* its dividend.

461 Dividend and interest announcements involve two dates—the "books closing date" (which determines who is entitled to the payment, namely, holders on the company's register at that time) and a "payable" date some weeks later, when the actual cheques (or statements and scrip certificates, in the case of dividend reinvestment plan participants) are posted.

For securities listed on the stock exchange a third date is also used. Seven working days before the books closing date the stocks go "ex dividend" or "ex interest", meaning that sellers rather than purchasers become entitled to the payment. Before that the stock is traded on a "cum dividend" or "cum interest" basis, meaning the reverse.

Theoretically, the market price at that time should drop to reflect the amount of the distribution. If it does not, and the "ex dividend" price is equal to the previous "cum dividend" price, then the shares are said to have "carried" their dividend. It will be observed that shareholders on the books on the last day of a particular half-year (or even for the whole of that half-year) would not necessarily get the payment nominally related to that period, as this distribution is invariably governed by the cut-off dates described above.

The word "Capital"

462   The word "capital" is used in various senses. Colloquially, it can be used by both individuals and corporations to mean just a supply of money, as in the phrase "I have built up some capital". It can also be used more technically, for example, to distinguish between "share capital" and "loan capital", or between "capital items" and "revenue items". The expression "working capital" is used in accounting to mean "current assets less current liabilities".

463   In relation to shares, a company has:

- "Authorised Capital" (also called "Nominal Capital"), meaning the maximum amount of shares which the company is permitted by its rules to issue; a higher limit than formerly can be authorised by the members in general meeting; certain fees payable to the government are based on this amount, a fact which acts as a useful discouragement to inflating it unduly.

- "Subscribed Capital" (also known as "Allotted Capital" or "Issued Capital"), meaning the shares actually issued, on the assumption that they are all fully-paid—in other words the Authorised Capital less the Unissued Capital.

- "Paid-up Capital" (also referred to as "Called-up Capital"), meaning the portion of the shares already issued which are actually paid-up—in other words the Subscribed Capital less the amounts yet to be called (and also less any calls in arrears).

In each case the face value of the shares concerned is used. Any amounts paid for the shares in excess of this face value must be credited to a special account which in many ways resembles paid-up capital and which is called the "Share Premium Account" (*Corporations Law*, Section 191).

Again, if a company redeems any preference shares out of profits it must credit a special "Capital Redemption Reserve" with the face value of the shares redeemed (*Corporations Law*, Section 192). The amount of "capital" is not a particularly useful figure. Neither is the amount of "reserves" (see paras 464 to 468). Investors should focus much more on the total *Shareholders' Funds*, in other words on the total assets less the total liabilities (see below and paras 809 and 907).

The word "Reserves"

464 The word "reserves" is also used in various senses. In popular parlance it means "surplus cash" and refers to an asset. In company accounts, on the other hand, it refers to a bookkeeping item on the other side of the balance sheet, namely, that part of the Shareholders' Funds which is not "capital".

465 Various labels—usually self-explanatory—are commonly applied to the several components of reserves, but the main distinction which should be made is between capital items, which are not available for dividend declarations, and revenue items, which are.

466 Revenue reserves include the balance in the Profit and Loss Account, also known by terms such as "Undistributed Profits", "Retained Profits", "Unappropriated Profits", "Accumulated Profits" and "Plough-back", and amounts which have been transferred from this at some stage (net of retransfers), such as a "General Reserve", an "Investment Reserve" or a "Contingency Reserve".

467 Capital reserves include the "Share Premium Account" (also known as the "Share Premium Reserve"), the "Assets Revalu-

ation Reserve", the "Realised Capital Profits Reserve", the "Exchange Fluctuation Account", the "Premium on Consolidation", the "Capital Redemption Reserve" and so on. Some of these capital reserves arise directly from moneys subscribed by investors, while others result from specific transactions—such as the acquisition or disposal of assets—or merely by way of book entry.

468 The exact titles are largely a matter of taste. The actual subdivisions of the reserves are relatively meaningless. Reserves belong to the whole body of shareholders and should be distinguished from the "Provisions" which are made in respect of specific *liabilities* such as future tax, individual doubtful debts or long service leave.

Holding Companies

469 Many companies listed on the stock exchange are "holding companies", meaning that they own shares in other companies-known as "subsidiary companies"—which actually run the business (the "operating companies"). The holding company may or may not also run part of the business. The holding company is the "parent company" of the group and the other companies are either wholly-owned subsidiaries (where 100 per cent of the shares is held, and the companies are virtually divisions of the parent) or partly-owned subsidiaries (where more than 50 per cent but less than 100 per cent of the shares is held and/or where the board of directors is controlled).

Other companies in which significant shareholdings are held (other than as a pure investment) and over which some influence is exerted are called "associated companies". A holding company and its subsidiaries are all said to be "related" to each other.

470 Investors in the holding company are really investors in the entire group. They are mainly concerned with the position of the enterprise as a whole. Such groups publish consolidated figures. These involve adding up all the assets and liabilities—or all the profits and losses—of each company in the group, but eliminating inter-company transactions. It is, of course, necessary to allow for the minority outside interests in any partly-owned subsidiaries.

471 However, the parent company figures may be relevant on some occasions—for example, when the sale of a subsidiary is being contemplated or when a parent company loan which is not guaranteed by the subsidiaries is being evaluated.

Priorities

472 As mentioned throughout this chapter, company securities can be ranked in order of the priority on a winding-up—in a typical situation, secured loans at the head of the queue, then unsecured loans, then preference shares, and finally ordinary shares at the end of the line. (There are also some statutory priorities, such as wages and taxation.)

Some companies have two categories of unsecured loan, one being "subordinated" to the other. On liquidation the owners of categories other than ordinary shares get their due, provided that the funds are sufficient after satisfying the owners of categories ahead of them. Within each category any shortfall would be borne proportionately. Ordinary shareholders are the residual group and get whatever is left over. Unlike the entitlements of other investors, the entitlement of ordinary shareholders is not related to the face value of their shares or anything similar.

473 Secured creditors—including debenture holders as described above, as well as mortgagees—rank ahead in the sense that they have certain assets pledged to them, assets which can be sold in the event of default. If these are sufficient, then the secured creditors get paid in full and the balance is added to the pool of funds available for the other categories. If the assets are insufficient, then the secured creditors rank with the unsecured creditors for the unsatisfied balance.

474 The year-by-year position is somewhat similar. A company's profit before tax and interest is available to meet this interest. The payment of interest is a legal obligation and companies with insufficient profitability which wish to avoid the consequences of default may choose to meet interest out of capital sources. The profit remaining after meeting the interest obligations becomes subject to income tax and the balance is available to meet the preference dividends (if any) and then the ordinary dividends. It is illegal (as well as immoral) to pay

dividends out of capital, but dividends can legitimately be paid out of the undistributed profits of earlier years.

It is also possible to eliminate debit balances in the Profit and Loss Account by reducing capital and/or the share premium account—this requires approval by the shareholders and by the court. Shareholders would normally vote in favour of such a move, as it would be a mere bookkeeping entry which in no way reduced their actual stake in the entity and as it would probably allow the sooner resumption of dividend payments. The court would mainly be concerned to ensure that creditors were not being prejudiced by the cash outflow from dividends following such a reconstruction.

Investor Aspects

475   Company securities can be acquired by investors in two quite distinct ways. Newly-created securities can be bought directly from the issuing company, usually without incurring any brokerage or stamp duty. This is known as the "primary market". Existing securities can be bought from their holders at the time, either privately or through the stock exchange—the "secondary market". With some minor exceptions, offers of new securities to the general public require a prospectus (see Chapter 43).

476   Investors in ordinary shares would expect to benefit both by receiving a stream of periodical income—the dividends—and by an increasing market value for their shares. The latter can come about for the variety of reasons described in greater detail in Chapter 10. A further expectation would be that the income would increase year by year.

477   Investors in the fixed interest securities discussed above would expect to benefit mainly from the steady income stream. Notes and debentures bought on the secondary market at other than the face value plus accrued interest (see para. 459) would also, if held to maturity, produce a capital gain or a capital loss at that stage—a factor which would be allowed for if the investment concerned is made on the basis of its redemption yield (see paras 227 and 1707 to 1712).

It is also possible to buy fixed interest securities with a different purpose in mind, so that a short-term capital gain rather than regular income is the primary objective. Such a strategy can be particularly appropriate when a downward move in interest rates is expected; in that case, paper with the longest achievable outstanding term would produce the best result.

478 It is often possible to get higher returns by buying existing fixed interest paper on the secondary market than by subscribing to equivalent new issues. On a separate aspect, investors wishing to make a short-term fixed interest investment may on occasions find that long-term securities give a better return than securities with an outstanding term more closely matching the investor's actual need—however, the purchase of long-term paper runs the risk of a capital loss if interest rates go up while the investment is still being held (as well as the chance of a capital gain in the reverse circumstances). Investors needing periodical cash but not minding an erosion of capital might find the purchase of high coupon securities at a premium attractive. The reverse can also apply.

479 Investors in convertible securities would expect to benefit both from the immediate income stream and from the prospects of acquiring a more valuable investment in due course (the ordinary shares to be allotted on conversion and possibly also entitlements to rights issues in the meantime).

480 Investment in contributing shares and options presents greater *leverage* than investing in the corresponding fully-paid shares:

- If, for example, the market price of a fully-paid share is 250 and an option exercisable at 200 exists, then the market price of the option would be, say, 70 (representing 250 less 200, plus a margin for the time value of the option and the advantage of leverage).

- If the price of the fully-paid share subsequently moves up, say, by 25, then the price of the option would in practice move up by a similar amount.

- In the case of the share this would represent a 10 per cent gain, but in the case of the option this would represent a much bigger 36 per cent gain.

- Of course, this aspect can work against the investor if the price goes down rather than up—but presumably investors would not buy into the company at all if they did not expect a price rise.

481 When examining their portfolios investors should allow for the future calls on contributing shares and for the cost of exercising any options held by them.

Buy-Backs

482 Companies were for a long time not allowed to purchase their own shares. In general terms this was a useful safeguard against market price manipulations, against insider trading problems, against fraud on creditors and against the unwarranted frustration of takeover bids. However, recent amendments to the legislation now enable companies to engage in buy-backs (self-acquisition schemes) to a limited extent and subject to some safeguards against abuses—see Chapter 40.

Elimination of Small Holdings

483 Investors sometimes finish up owning parcels of shares with a trivial total market value, even if they might once have been worth considerably more.

484 Companies can also use the above-mentioned buy-back provisions to mop up very small holdings of their own shares by offering to purchase them from existing shareholders at market value free of all charges and by subsequently cancelling them. Such a mechanism helps both the individual shareholders concerned and-by reducing share register expenses—the company.

485 Investors who prefer to retain their small holdings can continue to enjoy this right by advising the company concerned to that effect at the appropriate time. However, having regard to the paperwork involved in keeping proper records and to the high transaction costs in the form of minimum brokerage (see para. 532) on any subsequent disposal on the stock exchange, the retention of small parcels for sentimental reasons or in order not to face up to a loss which is already in place is usually not a sound strategy.

Deals with Subsidiaries

486 Subsidiaries and associates of listed companies are sometimes listed companies in their own right and/or engage in borrowing from the general public. The name of the subsidiary or associate may or may not resemble that of the parent company. It may or may not be using the parent's logo.

487 It should be noted that in the absence of specific guarantees or other contractual arrangements there is no legal obligation on a parent company to assist persons who may be investors in, or creditors of, one of its subsidiaries if such an entity gets into trouble. In fact, the primary obligation on company directors is to look after the interests of their own shareholders.

488 However, depending on the circumstances, a parent company may, of course, regard itself as having a *moral* duty to bail out persons who dealt with a subsidiary in the belief that the parent would always stand behind it.

Stapled Securities

489 Some companies create *stapled securities*. These are two legally different instruments which under their terms of issue are coupled together for certain purposes. In particular, they cannot be transferred separately either on-market or off-market.

490 Examples of such securities include:

- ordinary shares and units in an associated unit trust

- ordinary shares and unsecured notes

- ordinary shares and options.

491 A "parcel" consisting of one share and one unit or note or option is traded on the stock exchange as though it were a single security.

492 Stapled securities are sometimes created for tax reasons or to enable cash distributions to be made out of capital.

Instalment Receipts

493 Another instrument traded on the stock exchange is known as an *instalment receipt*. Typically, it arises when existing fully-paid shares in a company are offered to the public under a

prospectus with the vendor agreeing to accept payment for them in stages.

494   Thus in practice an instalment receipt closely resembles a contributing share as far as investors are concerned, except that:

- the outstanding amount is payable to the vendor of the shares in due course rather than to the issuing company

- the terms of the arrangement usually give the purchasers full voting rights and an entitlement to all the dividends instead of a smaller amount based on the proportion actually paid for

- the paperwork is probably different, involving a trustee company which controls the shares to which the instalments receipts relate until the final payment is made.

Derivatives

495   A *derivative* is a financial instrument that *derives* its value from the price of another more basic instrument—for example, an option (see Chapter 22) or a futures contract (see Chapter 23).

496   Schedule 5 of the *Company Law Review Act 1998*, when it comes into force, will abolish the concept of par values (see paras 1241 to 1256). Each company's share premium account and capital redemption reserve (if any) will be merged into that company's share capital account.

Chapter 5—The Stock Exchange

There is something about inside information which seems to paralyse a man's reasoning powers
—Bernard Baruch

Background

501 The term "market" can be used to describe any mechanism under which buyers and sellers in commodities deal with each other, especially a mechanism providing access in an organised manner and subject to recognised rules.

502 In the context of the subject matter of this book the word "market" is often used as a synonym for "stock exchange" or as a shorthand way of describing the interaction of buyers and sellers of securities ("market forces").

503 The "commodities" under discussion are mainly existing securities. For this reason the stock exchange is frequently referred to as a *secondary market,* in contradistinction to the facilities used for the issuing of newly-created securities, which are referred to as the *primary market.*

504 It should be noted that the trading of securities on a stock exchange in no way affects the physical assets of the company or other enterprise behind those securities. The market merely facilitates a change in the *identity* of the owners of those assets. (The ability to trade its shares in this ready manner does, of course, benefit the company indirectly, as it makes the raising of capital from the general public in the first instance easier— see Chapters 6 and 43.)

505 The origins of the modern stock exchanges operating on a large scale in cities such as London, New York (Wall Street) and Tokyo can be traced back to Italy in 1344, when the city-state of Florence converted some of its debts into 5 per cent stock, so that its creditors no longer had to wait for payment but could sell instead.

The Australian Stock Exchange

506 The Australian Stock Exchange Limited (ASX) was formed in 1987 out of the six separate State capital city stock exchanges, the origins of which go back to the 1850s and which now retain their existence as subsidiaries of the national exchange.

507 Members of an exchange are called "stockbrokers" or just "brokers" for short, a term indicating that for the most part they are dealing as *agents* (intermediaries) for their clients, charging a fee (called "brokerage") for their services (see paras

528 to 541). Except in relation to transactions clearly identified as such they do not deal as *principals,* actually buying and selling shares on their own account.

508 Originally all trading in shares (and bonds, etc.) in Australia involved a "call" system. Each broker had a "seat" on his exchange—literally a seat at a desk in a room resembling a school class room. Several times a day, at a fixed hour, a complete list of all companies dealt in was read out in alphabetical order. Brokers with buying and selling orders in a particular stock would identify themselves when it was reached in this call and would then complete the deals with each other.

509 Membership of the exchange became known as "having a seat on the exchange", a term which sometimes continues in use even today, long after seats were formally abolished.

510 In 1962 this approach was replaced by a "post" system of trading. This enabled continuous dealing on the trading floor of each stock exchange during its official hours (week-day mornings and afternoons).

511 The year 1987 saw the start of share trading on computer screens—the Stock Exchange Automated Trading System (SEATS) (see paras 1618 to 1624). This was gradually extended to all stocks and the physical trading floors finally disappeared in September 1990.

512 The "market" also includes the telephone network and the Internet. Not all deals arranged by brokers are made through SEATS.

513 Most overseas stock exchanges use broadly similar approaches. However, for a long time the London Stock Exchange used a system unique to itself, involving two distinct classes of members—brokers, who dealt only as agents with the general public, and jobbers, each a specialist in certain stocks. These latter were traded near particular posts on the floor of the London exchange. Jobbers dealt with brokers as principals. Jobbers did not charge brokerage, but instead made profits and covered costs by always trading at two different prices simultaneously—a lower one, at which they were willing to buy, and a higher one, at which they were willing to sell. The margin or difference between the two prices came to be

known as the "jobber's turn". The jobber was never told whether the broker wished to buy or sell.

514 The stock exchange in Australia, despite its virtual monopoly position, is not an arm of government in the way that, say, the Reserve Bank of Australia is. Nor, at the time of writing, is it owned by members of the general public on the lines applying in the case of the major trading banks, although that is about to change—see paras 550 to 554. Rather, the stock exchange is a sort of private club controlled by brokers. Of course, in theory other people could start a rival club—but in practice such a development would not easily be achieved.

515 The stock exchange lays down appropriate rules for its members. While these rules affect investors on the stock exchange and while they are no doubt in large part designed for their benefit the fact remains that the rules are primarily drawn up to meet the desires of the members of the "club"—the stockbrokers—rather than the wishes of their customers. For this reason, Section 774 of the *Corporations Law* allows the Federal Government to disallow proposed new amendments to the rules (presumably if these are felt to be against the public interest).

516 Transactions on the stock exchange are always "subject to the Articles, Rules and Regulations, customs and usages of the Exchange". The reference to the unwritten "customs and usages" should be particularly noted.

517 However, neither the stock exchange nor its members, nor any other authority (nor for that matter the issuing entities) determine the prices at which securities change hands. Such prices result from market forces—supply and demand, and the level at which (at the margin) buyers and sellers are willing to do a trade with each other. The principles—although not the detailed mechanics—are thus similar to those in a public auction system. Prices (and volumes) of all deals are publicly available—these days instantaneously on computer screens—and this, too, helps to ensure fair pricing. It should, however, be noted that the reported market value of a share is actually the price at which a relatively small proportion of the total shares on issue changed hands.

518 (In London, the buying and selling prices as well as the jobber's turn between these all fluctuated in line with market pressures. Different jobbers quoted different prices and this ensured competitive pricing.)

Stockbrokers

519 The system of dealing described below is extremely simple. It allows the ownership of very large volumes of securities to change hands at great speed and with a minimum of fuss and formality, despite very large sums of money being involved.

520 Because of the absence of proper documentation with signatures of the parties and of witnesses and the prior checking of title, etc., as is customary in some other markets (for example, in relation to the sale of land), it becomes doubly necessary for those brokers dealing with each other on the stock exchange to have complete trust in the integrity and solvency of their opposite numbers. There is thus some justification for a closed "club" with all that this entails, including the appropriate vetting of new entrants.

521 Brokers may no longer operate as sole traders and have to form partnerships or companies. Incorporation has been an option only since the substantial deregulation of the securities industry in 1984. Membership of the Australian Stock Exchange by stockbroking corporations is now permitted and this has allowed some Australian stockbroking businesses to be acquired in whole or in part by major trading banks, by merchant banks and in some cases by overseas stockbroking organisations. Some brokers have even become listed companies themselves.

522 In addition to acting as true "brokers" and earning brokerage on the lines described above, most stockbroking organisations directly or through associate or subsidiary companies engage in other profit-making activities such as:

- trading in securities as principals for their own account

- underwriting new issues of equity and loan securities

- soliciting subscriptions for unit trusts, insurance bonds, public superannuation funds, film investments and the like

- negotiating takeovers and other corporate deals
- writing independent expert reports for prospectuses and takeover documents issued by their corporate clients
- running "in house" cash management trusts
- running "in house" equity trusts
- lending money for margin trading
- lending money secured by mortgages on real estate
- dealing in options and futures.

Choosing a Broker

523 An investor seeking to deal on the stock exchange will first
need to select a broker. A list of brokers willing to accept new
clients can be obtained from the stock exchange, but it is
preferable if the choice of broker can be based on word of
mouth recommendations. It is also useful if the investor can
arrange for an introduction through some existing client of the
broker concerned.

524 The Australian Stock Exchange has about 85 active member
organisations (firms and companies) in the six State capitals.
The larger organisations maintain offices in more than one
city. Different brokers have different attributes. For example,
some may be more conservative than others. Some do mainly
institutional business while others welcome individual clients.
Some are better at the paperwork than others. Some have better
operators than others. The range and quality of research will
also vary. Most brokers send periodical newsletters to clients
interested in receiving them (but see also Chapter 14).

525 As a rough generalisation, a large broking organisation will
have the advantage of a larger capital base, access to a wider
range of associated activities (see para. 522) and the opportunity to engage in more flotations (see Chapters 6 and 43). On
the other hand, a small organisation may be able to offer a more
personal service and may be more expert in some particular
specialisation. Brokers headquartered in one of the smaller
States may be more familiar with companies based in their
home State.

526   There is nothing to stop a client using more than one broker. This can be useful in giving investors a better feel for the market and in allowing recommendations to be cross-checked. On the other hand, using several brokers may prove frustrating to some people who will be confused by getting conflicting advice. The smaller volume of business per broker may also mean that clients who spread their business too thinly are then regarded as unattractive clients by all their brokers and finish up with poorer service all round.

Notes:

1.   Some brokers delete the names of inactive clients from their mailing lists. In some cases this will prove to be counterproductive, as the clients will probably come under the influence of another broker and then be even less likely to give business to their original broker.

2.   In a formal sense, an investor is a client of a stock-broking organisation. However, in practice an active investor often develops a good working relationship with a particular person in that organisation and may deal with that person for years. That would certainly help the quality of the advice being given in the context of the "know your client" rule. If that person leaves that stockbroking organisation in order to join one of its competitors then his clients have the choice of staying with their existing stockbroking organisation or becoming clients of the other one or doing both. However, it would seem rather unethical for a person changing positions to make a blanket mailing to all names on his previous client list, asking the clients concerned without any prior discussion to formally close their existing accounts.

527   It is, of course, unwise for an investor to split an order in a particular stock between two or more brokers. Quite apart from the higher level of charges which this may incur, it would result in the investor competing with himself and thus pushing market prices up or down against himself.

Brokerage Rates

528   Until 1984 minimum brokerage rates were fixed by the stock exchange and rates were therefore uniform amongst all bro-

kers. A period of "negotiated" rates then commenced. In practice, most brokers are charging their smaller clients on a basis similar to that applying in the period before deregulation, with major and minor variations as indicated in paras 530 to 537. Larger and/or particularly active clients can achieve considerably lower fees from some brokers, depending on factors such as the size of the individual orders, the total business over a period, the volume of research data required, and so on.

529 The main elements of the old scale for ordinary shares, convertible notes, options and rights in listed companies were as follows:

- On the first $5,000 of consideration: 2.5 per cent
- On the next $10,000 of consideration: 2.0 per cent
- On the next $35,000 of consideration: 1.5 per cent
- On the balance over $50,000 of consideration: 1.0 per cent

In addition, a flat "order fee" of $5.00 applied.

530 Shares in unlisted companies (see paras 2001 to 2004) were subject to brokerage at double the above rates (apart from the $5.00 order fee).

531 The above scale applied on each order given at the one time to buy or sell on behalf of the one beneficial interest securities in any company of the same class and paid-up value, provided that the entire order was completed within one month from the date of the first transaction.

532 Many (but by no means all) brokers have dispensed with the rather unpopular order fee and have introduced minimum fees instead (predominantly in the $60 to $100 range, with some as low as $40 and others as high as $125). Some brokers charge lower minima on selling orders than on buying orders—a gesture not related to the work involved, but rather to the fact that the client has less control over the size of a selling transaction, particularly where holdings may have been held for a long time or where the shares have gone down in value since purchase—perhaps even because of the broker's own

poor advice in the past! Some brokers charge higher minima on orders involving mining shares—again a distinction without much logic behind it.

533   Some brokers have varied the basic scale, for example, by charging 2 per cent instead of 2.5 per cent in the bottom bracket or moving down the thresholds at which the lower rates commenced. Some brokers charge lower rates to clients who are senior citizens or for orders placed electronically. However, Australian rates, by and large, remain high by international standards.

534   During boom times certain brokers charge higher brokerage rates to new clients than to established ones. While this may have some logic as a "rationing" device for scarce human resources, it seems rather shortsighted.

535   Some brokers have continued to use another controversial feature of the old scale—in the case of rights issues (see Chapter 7), brokerage on buying transactions is charged not on the amount of the deal but on that amount together with the minimum amount payable to the issuing company by the "applications closing date" at the end of the rights period (even if the rights are allowed to lapse because of changes in market conditions or the securities are onsold as "rights" rather than as "new shares"). (The expression "minimum amount payable to the issuing company" refers to the fact that sometimes the investor has a choice between fully-paid and contributing shares.)

536   Fixed interest securities—apart from convertible notes— are subject to lower rates of brokerage than in the case of shares. Brokerage is normally based on the face value rather than on the consideration.

537   No brokerage is charged on prospectus applications for new securities which are lodged through a stockbroker, as the issuing company usually pays him a fee for this service.

538   Another phenomenon of deregulation was the emergence of a discount house, a broker charging a flat fee regardless of the size of the order—see paras 1650 to 1652.

539   Differences in brokerage rates should not be viewed in isolation. Operating efficiency, although not so visible and not easily measurable, is probably much more important. There is

little point in saving one percentage point in brokerage if the price of the trade is two or three percentage points worse than might have been achievable.

The quality of the advice is also relevant—a one per cent difference in brokerage is neither here nor there if a share doubles in value. Long-term investors will find that the total brokerage (and stamp duty) paid by them as a proportion of the market value of their portfolios may be quite small, having regard both to capital growth and to the absence of such charges on:

- shares taken up in rights issues
- shares taken up in dividend reinvestment plans
- shares taken up in share purchase and similar plans
- shares taken up in flotations

540 Brokers are contractually entitled to earn brokerage from both buyers and sellers even if both legs of a transaction affect their own clients. This is different from the common law position under which agents get remunerated only once. Such transactions are known as "crossings". They must take place at a true market price and conform to certain rules to ensure this.

541 Despite popular belief to the contrary, a broker has little incentive to recommend a particular stock to a client as a good buy merely because he holds an unexecuted selling order in it from another client—his remuneration is the same whether the buying client's money is invested in that stock or in some other.

Listing

542 About 1200 companies are listed on the Australian Stock Exchange. Before a company can achieve the privilege of listing it has to formally make application for this to the exchange and to meet certain conditions. These relate to the minimum size of issued capital and to the maintenance of a sufficient spread of shareholders (in an attempt to ensure that an active market will really exist in the stock concerned); to the provision of certain information to the exchange (and thus to the general public) as soon as it becomes available and within certain time limits (in order to ensure an informed

market—see also Chapter 33) and to the payment of appropriate listing fees each year and on the listing of new securities.

543   Other matters of concern to the stock exchange include:

- The contents of the articles of association.
- The contents of prospectuses.
- In the case of unit trusts, the contents of trust deeds.
- In the case of loan securities, the contents of trust deeds.
- The issue of scrip (where applicable) and the conduct of the share registry.
- The contents of annual reports.
- Books closing dates.
- New issues.

In earlier times prospectuses were examined by the exchange authorities before their release, but pre-vetting no longer takes place. Large overseas companies which are listed on stock exchanges in their home countries can be listed on the Australian Stock Exchange without fully complying with most of the rules binding local companies. About 70 such companies are listed in Australia.

544   Rules promulgated by stock exchanges have some advantages over legislation enacted by governments. In particular:

- they can be altered much more rapidly in the event of changing conditions
- they can be drafted less formally
- they can be interpreted by stock exchange committees rather than by the courts
- regard can be had to the spirit as well as to the letter.

545   Both the stock exchange rules and the companies and securities legislation are in part designed to discourage dishonesty. Of course, they can never be completely successful in this objective. However, neither the rules nor the legislation can ensure corporate profitability or even sound management for all listed companies.

ASX Codes

546   Every separately-traded security has its own distinctive acronym, known as the "ASX Code". This is the Australian equivalent of the well-known Wall Street "ticker symbol".

547   In the case of fully-paid ordinary shares the code consists of three letters based as far as practicable on the company's name. For other securities, such as partly-paid ordinary shares, preference shares, convertible notes, options, etc., one or two further letters are added.

548   These handy codes, apart from being used internally in the ASX computer system, are often used in the stockbroking industry as convenient abbreviations.

549   However, rather surprisingly, the stock exchange is doing nothing to encourage their wider use either by listed companies in their own printed material (annual reports, prospectuses, circulars, dividend advices, etc.) or by the media in news reports. Nor is the exchange seeking to promote their use by clients of member organisations.

The ASX Demutualisation

550   The Australian Stock Exchange is in the process of abandoning its mutual structure and turning itself into a listed company. That process is expected to be completed in 1998. As in the case of other demutualisations, reserves built up by past generations are being turned into windfall gains to the current owners.

551   The ASX will be listed on the ASX. The concept of a stock exchange being listed on its own board is indeed unique. It raises certain obvious conflicts of interest, although supervision will come from the Australian Securities and Investments Commission. Perhaps it might have been better if the ASX had opted for listing on some overseas exchange instead.

552   While the "members' club" aspect of the traditional structure was not ideal from the perspective of investors, a corporate entity dedicated to making commercial profits also raises some concern for its customers. For example, will adequate resources be devoted to watching out for market manipulation? Admittedly, the exchange has a long-term interest in

preserving the integrity of its market—but monitoring per se costs money and does not directly yield any income.

553 Similarly, will public education have any priority? In the long run better informed investors would generate additional savings— capital funds which could be invested on the stock exchange. Such investors would also institute increased trading activity, which would feed into additional revenue from brokers and listed companies. However, cost-cutting accountants or executives with share options (and with an eye on the ASX dividend rate or the market price of its shares) may not always see it that way.

554 Hopefully, the clients of brokers will not notice any difference in regard to their normal trading activities.

Chapter 6—Flotations and Placements

None of us really understands what's going on with all these numbers
—David Stockman

Background

601 As a small business grows and expands it frequently needs more capital than can be provided by its founders and/or than is generated by the business itself. This applies particularly in times of inflation, when additional funds will be required merely to "stand still" in physical terms.

602 Additional money can be obtained in a variety of ways, including:

- Loan funds raised from banks or other professional lending institutions.

- Loan funds raised from the general public.

- Share capital raised from institutional investors.

- Share capital raised from the general public.

603 The availability of such loans on reasonable terms would depend on aspects such as the size and quality of the assets available as security, the subsequent ratio of total debt to total shareholders' funds and the expected ability to service such debt each year.

604 Issuing additional ordinary shares would naturally dilute the equity and voting power of the original entrepreneurs and may thus not be welcome on that score alone. Admitting outsiders would also restrict the freedom of the board and the management to run the enterprise as they see fit. However, that is the price they would have to pay if they wish to "go public".

605 Of course, it is possible for the entrepreneurs to get the best of both worlds to some extent by ensuring that they maintain their own shareholdings at more than 50 per cent of the voting capital, thus at least retaining control. However, this may also reduce the attractiveness of investing for outsiders.

606 Capital raisings of the type described in this chapter are, generally speaking, in the national interest. They promote economic growth, open up employment opportunities, increase the tax base, and so on.

Flotation on the Stock Exchange

607 Raising money from the general public is facilitated if an issue of new shares is accompanied by flotation—in other words, by a listing on the stock exchange. In the United States the

descriptive term *Initial Public Offering* (IPO) is used for this process. Owning listed shares greatly increases the ability of investors to quit their individual holdings on reasonable terms and with reasonable speed, and this feature can be an important consideration when prudent investors are deciding whether or not to invest in a particular project in the first instance. Owning unlisted shares means being less liquid and running the risk that any available exit price is not a fair one; furthermore, many people would not be interested in being locked into minority holdings in private companies.

608   Flotation is not confined to existing businesses. A brand new enterprise would also be eligible for listing, although clearly the risks for investors would be greater than in the case of an old-established enterprise with an attractive track record.

Prospectuses

609   Raising money from the general public in the way described above and in the next chapter requires the issue of a *prospectus*. This is an important document, with many important messages for prospective investors—especially if they read between the lines. Prospectuses and certain warnings for potential applicants are discussed in Chapter 43.

      (*Note:* The plural of "prospectus" is "prospectuses", not "prospecti".)

610   If the company is to be listed on the stock exchange then the proposal to list would naturally be highlighted in the prospectus. If in such cases listing is subsequently not granted for any reason then all subscribers to the issue would receive their money back (usually without interest).

611   If oversubscriptions are to be allowed, then the prospectus has to set out the upper limit for these and to give all relevant figures on a "worst case" scenario.

612   The "opening date" of an issue is purely nominal. In practice applications can be lodged as soon as the prospectus containing the application form is available. Popular issues often close one minute after the official opening time and applications received after this would then be rejected.

613   Readers of a prospectus will need to focus on different aspects of the information according to the type of security being

offered (equity, fixed interest, managed fund, or whatever) and according to their own investment objectives. In addition, they will need to draw on complementary relevant data in the public domain but not necessarily in the prospectus itself (see also Chapter 43).

Underwriting

614 Companies seeking to raise funds for expansion purposes may wish to enter into spending commitments before actually getting the new money in. They therefore find it useful to obtain a guarantee from a third party, called an *underwriter*, to the effect that the money being sought from the public will actually be forthcoming. If members of the public (individuals and institutions) fail to provide the underwritten amount by the closing date of the issue then the underwriter or nominees of the underwriter have to subscribe the shortfall. For providing this service the underwriter will receive a fee, details of which will also be set out in the prospectus. The size of the fee, per dollar of money being raised, is relevant in at least two different ways:

- as a factor reducing the asset backing being acquired by incoming investors

- as an indication of the degree of risk perceived by the underwriter.

615 Underwriters are frequently stockbrokers or merchant banks. They will normally lay off much of their risk by engaging a panel of "sub-underwriters", mainly institutions such as investment companies, life insurance companies and superannuation funds, which have the necessary capital and/or cash flow and the potential to hold any stock which they may be required to take up.

616 Underwriting is not restricted to new flotations—many companies making rights issues (see paras 701 to 746) also find it attractive to use this mechanism.

Brokers to the Issue

617 Whether an issue was underwritten or not, a proposal to seek listing on the stock exchange once required the appointment of a specific member of the exchange who was willing to act as its "sponsoring broker". However, this requirement no

longer applies, although one or more "brokers to the issue" may be appointed in order to assist in publicising the issue and in soliciting subscriptions through as wide a client base as practicable.

Issue Price

618 The price at which shares in new companies are offered to investors is very relevant to their attractiveness or otherwise as an investment. There is no such thing as a "good share" in isolation—it can only be good or bad in relation to its cost. Potential investors will therefore wish to make their own assessments of the likely market price on listing. Unless this exceeds the issue price by a reasonable margin for the risk involved they may be better off avoiding the company altogether or alternatively waiting and buying the shares on the market after they are listed.

619 The main factors affecting the market price of shares which are already listed are set out in Chapter 10. The same factors also have relevance when flotations are being evaluated. In the case of new issues of ordinary shares the various key indicators for the stock (in respect of its issue price) should be compared and contrasted with the corresponding indicators for any comparable stocks which are already listed (in respect of their current market prices) and possibly also with industry averages. In particular, attention should be paid to:

- the earnings yield or its reciprocal, the price earnings ratio, (the most important single indicator)
- the dividend yield (but having regard to the franking ratios)
- the dividend payout ratio or its reciprocal, the dividend cover
- the ratio of price to net tangible asset backing per share
- the gearing ratio (the ratio of debt to equity)
- the risk factors generally

but taking care to always compare like with like. For example, last year's result for an existing company is not directly comparable with a forecast of next year's result for a company being floated (a period which might be some two years later). Some particular yardsticks may be more important to some categories of investor than others—for example, retired persons in need of a good cash flow may prefer a high payout ratio for the dividends, while other investors may be quite relaxed about having some of the profit retained within the company.

(*Note:* There are also non-mathematical factors affecting the demand for shares. For example, many institutions like to have portfolios which replicate the ASX All Ordinaries Index—see paras 647 to 654. While this is not a very sensible investment strategy the fact that is widely used is undoubtedly a factor affecting the demand for shares in newly listed companies.)

620 The promoters of the float will, no doubt, also have done such sums. Their interest is, of course, the reverse of that of the investors—they will want to issue the shares at as high a price as possible. However, if they pitch the price too high, then the issue will fail (or at the very least a high proportion will be left with the underwriters, thus overhanging the market). If they pitch the price too low, then they will merely be handing windfall profits to the successful subscribers.

621 The market will perceive some floats as being overpriced. As further discussed in Chapter 43, these issues will often be characterised by huge advertisements, by long periods during which the issue is open, by mailings to people on "sucker lists", by the use of glossy paper, by the inclusion of irrelevant features such as the photograph of a State Premier, and so on.

622 The market will also perceive other floats as being underpriced. These will be characterised by being "taken firm" by the underwriters, by being offered only on a restricted basis to favoured clients of the brokers associated with the issue (as distinct from being a genuine "public issue") and by the shortness of the period during which the issue is open. Prospectuses—or at least prospectuses with a blank application form left in them—will be hard to get.

623 Of course, the market is not always right. Sometimes very popular issues, heavily oversubscribed, with allotments severely cut down, prove flops on the open market after listing. The reverse can also apply. In addition, market conditions across the board can change in the few weeks between the close of an issue and the commencement of trading, just as

they can—to the worry of underwriters—in the weeks between the setting of the issue price and the closing date for applications.

Stags

624 Applicants to new floats will fall into two main classes—long-term holders and "stags". The latter are investors who subscribe to such issues with the express purpose of selling out shortly after listing commences. They run a risk each time they do this, but they hope to make a profit overall. They serve a useful market function in helping to get new issues off the ground. By and large, promoters of new issues—particularly those underwritten by the major stockbroking organisations which depend on client goodwill—err on the side of underpricing rather than overpricing such floats.

Listing Existing Shares

625 The above description focused on newly-created shares. However, the shares offered in a float can also be:

- existing shares which are made available for that purpose by some of the current shareholders, or

- a mixture of such existing shares and shares newly-created by the company.

626 Quite often the founders of a business wish to sell some of their existing holdings to new investors as a means of:

- raising cash for themselves, and/or

- diversifying their own investments, and/or

- obtaining a public market for the shares.

627 Furthermore, an existing enterprise which already has a sufficient spread of shareholders can seek listing without any offer of shares to the public by the either the company or its current shareholders. This is known as a *compliance listing*.

Placements to the General Public

628 Placements of newly-created shares to the public at large or to the clients of a particular stockbroker are sometimes made by companies which are already listed. Apart from raising money, such issues can increase the spread of shareholders, leading to

a more active market and perhaps safeguarding the company's listing status.

629 Such issues, which cannot without the consent of a shareholders' meeting exceed 10 per cent of the company's capital in any year, are usually made at a small discount to the prevailing market price.

630 The new shares may not immediately rank equally with the existing shares—for example, in regard to dividend entitlements. Naturally, any such differences need to be taken into account when evaluating the generosity of the issue price.

Placements to Institutions

631 Placements of newly-created shares can also be made to one or more institutional investors, such as life offices or superannuation funds (provided the total number of new shares is within the above-mentioned 10 per cent limit).

632 Such issues are usually made at around the market price or at a modest discount to that price, although sometimes—when the institutions are particularly keen to get stock—the issues may actually be made at a slight premium.

633 Placements can be unfair to existing shareholders if they are made at a too low a price (see para 1211) or if they are made for the wrong motive—for example, in order to frustrate an expected takeover bid (see paras 1149 to 1150).

634 The reasons given by companies for making placements to strangers rather than making pro rata issues to the existing owners (see Chapter 7) include the following:

- that the cash is received much faster

- that the administrative costs are much lower

- that the ability to dispense with a prospectus in some cases means that the issue can be made even if certain up-to-date audited figures are not available.

635 Of course, sometimes shareholders will be grateful not to have a rights issue pushing down the price of their shares—especially if the state of the economy makes new cash for investment scarce and/or where there have already been large capital raisings in the recent past (either generally or in the company concerned).

636 Occasionally, the alleged prime motive of a placement will be not so much to raise cash as to cement some business relationship. Such arguments are of doubtful validity, as a deal which makes commercial sense does not need such a prop, and one which does not is unlikely to become viable by virtue of being accompanied by a share issue.

Vendor Shares

637 Shares and options issued to the promoters of a company for the transfer of either tangible or intangible assets may be classified as "vendor securities" where the arms' length value of these assets is not readily establishable. The vendor shares and options are then held in escrow and are not listed on the stock exchange or otherwise tradeable for at least 12 months.

Conflicts of Interest

638 Attention is drawn to the fact that a stockbroker acting as underwriter and/or broker to an issue has a conflict of interest problem if his clients look to him for advice in relation to such a new issue. Other conflicts can arise if a broker becomes a director of a listed company, particularly one which he has helped to list. There is nothing necessarily sinister in such conflicts, which are normally disclosed in accordance with legal and moral requirements, but they add to the difficulties faced by investors.

Investor Strategy

639 Investors interested in participating in a float available to them will need to give some thought as to the number of shares for which they should apply. If the issue is oversubscribed, then applications will be cut down.

640 The proposed basis for this rationing may be spelt out or hinted at in the prospectus; ideally, this important piece of information should always be provided and the allotment basis should not involve an "at the directors' discretion" vagueness. Floats which are particularly popular might go to a ballot, with those selected receiving, say, 1000 shares each and the rest missing out completely.

641 A common approach is to allot small applications in full and to reduce large applications pro rata. Thus in order to finish up with, say, 1000 shares an investor might have to apply for 2500.

If he has guessed wrong then he will finish up with either too few or too many shares. Getting the number actually applied for in an issue which turns out to be undersubscribed—and which then trades at a significant discount on the issue price for a long time—can prove expensive.

642   Application monies in respect of shares not allotted will be returned—usually without interest—after about one month, a further aspect which needs to be taken into consideration, both in regard to its effect on the investor's liquidity and to the loss of income.

Sweeteners

643   Sometimes promoters try to make a borderline issue look more attractive by adding a *sweetener*. For example, a share issue might be accompanied by "free" options, on, say, a one for two basis.

644   Of course, this does not add value in an absolute sense—if the company is worth a particular amount if there are two million shares then it is still worth the same total amount even if there are instead two million shares and one million options. At a micro level, two share worth, say, 20 cents each become instead two shares worth perhaps 17 cents each and one option worth 6 cents.

645   However, the "share plus option" alternative does have some attraction to investors by creating greater flexibility. Individual investors have the ability to sell the shares and keep the options if they so wish, or vice versa. In practice this privilege is likely to translate itself into extra value on the market.

646   "Share plus option" arrangements can also feature in rights issues—see para. 740.

Index Funds

647   Institutional portfolios administered by full-time professional fund managers who devote all their energies to the task—and who have access to all published information and to security analysis—should in theory produce investment returns which are well above the average of those obtained by all investors or those obtainable by picking stocks at random.

648   In practice this does not always happen, leading to a move in recent times towards the formation of some "index funds".

The managers of such funds use computers to build up a portfolio which replicates the ASX All Ordinaries Index or some other stock exchange index (see paras 979 to 985).

649   The intention is to avoid conscious decision making and its associated expenses and mistakes and to replace them with an automatic stock selection process. The proponents of this theory claim that it is better to *ensure* an average performance than to risk having a below average performance.

650   However, such a theory would work only if the fund incurred:

- no administration expenses
- no brokerage when buying or selling
- no stamp duty when buying or selling
- no income tax on realised gains.

In the real world an index fund is inevitably going to *under-perform* the index to which it relates.

651   Furthermore, investing in the index naturally does not eliminate price volatility.

652   Nor is it clear why investors would want to pay for the privilege of specifically *aiming* at achieving only an ordinary performance.

653   Nevertheless, as indicated in para. 619, the existence of index funds is a factor affecting share prices. There will be extra buying pressure for shares in the All Ordinaries Index and less buying pressure for shares not in this Index.

654   Shares in newly floated companies are not admitted to the Index until some weeks after they are first listed, to allow trading to settle down. However, in the case of companies which because of their size and liquidity are clearly going to be included in the Index, the extra demand from the managers of index funds will be there right from the first day of trading.

Chapter 7—Share Issues

*What's breaking into a bank compared
with founding a bank?*
—Bertolt Brecht

Rights Issues: Background

701 Listed companies which require additional capital for expansion purposes or in order to reduce debt can obtain it by creating additional ordinary shares. One way to do this is to make a placement to institutions at around the current market price (see paras 631 to 636). Another way is to make what is called a "rights issue" to their existing shareholders on a proportionate basis, at a rather lower price. It may aid the understanding of some important theoretical concepts if a few hypothetical numerical illustrations are first given. These ignore capital gains tax, which is separately discussed in paras 2906 to 2908.

702 In accordance with market practice all figures relating to shares in this chapter are expressed in cents per share (thus $2 is shown as 200).

703 If a company is "worth" $24,000,000 and has 4,000,000 ordinary shares of the one class on issue, then each share can be said to be have a value of 600. (It is immaterial, at this stage of the argument, whether the "value" being considered is the market price or the net tangible asset backing per share on either a break-up or a "continuing entity" basis.)

704 If the company, feeling that it needs more money, raises, say, a further $3,000,000 by issuing fresh shares, then it will be worth $27,000,000 (ignoring expenses). This is true *regardless of the number of new shares being created in the exercise.*

705 The $3,000,000 could, for example, have been raised

- (1) by issuing 2,000,000 new shares at 150 each, or

- (2) by issuing 1,000,000 new shares at 300 each.

Apart from tax considerations—which are discussed as a separate question in Chapter 29—is either one of these versions better for shareholders than the other?

706 Under the first version the company will on completion have 6 million shares worth a total of $27,000,000 on issue—producing a "post issue" value of 450 per share. Under the second version the company will have 5 million shares worth a total of $27,000,000 on issue—producing a "post issue" value of 540 per share.

707   If the new shares were to be allotted to outsiders, such as friends of the directors, then under either version the recipients would make large windfall gains. The existing shareholders, although collectively still owning the same *number* of shares as previously, would have suffered corresponding losses. Each share would be worth less than before the issue—the capital would have been "watered".

708   To prevent this happening listed companies normally offer new shares in the first instance to the existing shareholders on a proportionate basis (pro rata to their existing holdings at a clearly defined time—the "books closing date"). Holders of convertible securities are normally treated as though they already held the equivalent number of ordinary shares. For the treatment of optionholders, see para. 2206.

As an inducement to investors to put up the necessary cash such issues are usually made at a discount to the market price of the shares at the time of the announcement. As shown below, this results in the rights themselves having some value. The existing shares, once they become stripped of this separately-tradeable entitlement, fall in value by a corresponding amount. To preserve their investment, prudent shareholders must therefore take some action—either selling their rights before the deadline or taking them up.

Choices for Shareholders

709   Shareholders can then take up their entitlements by subscribing for the new shares at their stipulated issue price (see paras 720 to 734). This is Scenario A of para. 716 below. Alternatively, they can dispose of the rights by selling them on the stock exchange (or privately). This is Scenario B. Either way, shareholders will have exactly "preserved their equity"—in other words, made neither a gain nor a loss from the issue (assuming always that the market prices stay in line with the theoretical position—see paras 714 to 719; in practice, of course, market prices will often be different). Both versions (1) and (2) of para. 705 above are equally fair.

710   However, the cash position of shareholders under both these scenarios (A and B) will have changed—they will have either made an additional investment or sold off part of their existing investment, according to the alternative chosen. They may

appear to have made a capital gain under the second alternative, but in reality they will have sold off "part of the farm" by selling their rights, even though the *number* of shares actually held by them will not have changed. Shareholders may also *appear* to have got a bargain by being able to buy new shares at a relatively low price, but actually the value of the existing shares normally falls correspondingly and they are actually only lineball.

711 Alternatively again, shareholders can sell some rights and take up the balance (Scenario C). By an appropriate choice of numbers shareholders can also stay "cash neutral" (at least in theory).

712 There are many other variations to this theme. For instance, instead of selling rights, shareholders can sell off existing shares—either before or after the issue, with a similar outcome (Scenarios D and E respectively). They can also sell off new shares in due course.

"Cum Rights" and "Ex Rights"

713 The existing shares are traded on the stock exchange on a "cum rights" basis till seven trading days before the company's books close for the purpose of fixing entitlements to the issue. This means that buyers of the shares cum rights acquire the entitlement to the new shares (whether they actually get onto the company's register in time or not—although the seven-day period just mentioned and T+5 assist in that regard). After that time, shares are traded on an "ex rights" basis, meaning that the sellers retain the privilege of taking up the rights themselves (or of selling them separately). Naturally, the price on the market will reflect the appropriate status of the shares.

The Theoretical Value of Rights

714 The following figures—applicable to version (1) above— will illustrate the points just made and also show how the theoretical value of rights is calculated:

Issue: one for two @ 150 Price cum rights: 600

2 existing shares @ 600	=	1200
1 new share @ 150	=	150
3 shares post issue	=	1350

Therefore the theoretical price of each share ex rights is 1350 divided by 3, that is, 450 (as in para. 706 above). This 450 less the application money of 150 is 300, which is therefore the theoretical price of each right.

715   The arithmetic can readily be checked. The price of one share ex rights plus the price of half a right (reflecting the one for two ratio) must equal the price of one share cum rights. 450 plus half of 300 equals 450 plus 150 equals 600, as it should. (It also follows that if new shares are issued to non-shareholders at a discount on the market price then this produces a gain to the new investors and an equivalent loss to the existing holders.)

716   Consider a holder of 4500 shares (one for two = 2250 rights):

Scenario A: Taking up the entitlement:

4500 shares worth 600 each	=	$27,000
plus 2250 shares @ 150 application money	=	$3,375
6750 shares worth 450 each	=	$30,375

Scenario B: Selling the entitlement:

4500 shares worth 600 each	=	$27,000
less 2250 rights @ 300 sale price	=	$6,750
4500 shares worth 450 each	=	$20,250

Scenario C: Taking up some of the entitlement and selling the balance:

4500 shares worth 600 each	=	$27,000
plus 1500 shares @ 150 application money	=	$2,250
6000 shares = $29,250		
less 750 rights @ 300 sale price	=	$2,250
6000 shares worth 450 each	=	$27,000

Scenario D: Taking up the entitlement after selling some shares cum rights:

4500 shares worth 600 each	=	$27,000
less 500 shares @ 600 cum rights	=	$3,000
4000 shares	=	$24,000
plus 2000 shares @ 150 application money	=	$3,000
6000 shares worth 450 each	=	$27,000

Scenario E: Taking up the entitlement either before or after selling someshares ex rights:

4500 shares worth 600 each		=	$27,000
plus 2250 shares @ 150 application money		=	$3,375

6750 shares = $30,375
less 750 shares@ 450 ex rights   = $3,375

6000 shares worth 450 each   = $27,000

717   It will be noticed that Scenarios C, D and E all result in the same "cash neutral" position and that the number of shares held at the end of the exercise (6000) is the number of shares held at the beginning (4500) multiplied by the ratio of the cum rights price (600) to the theoretical ex rights price (450). This principle is of general application.

718   The above calculations assumed that the dividend entitlements of the old shares and the new shares were the same—in the jargon of the industry, that the shares ranked "pari passu". Frequently, the new shares created in the rights issue will participate in dividends only from some future date (see para. 723) and there may thus be a dividend difference between the new shares and the old shares in favour of the latter. Allowance for this needs to be made in the calculations. If, for example, each old share in para. 714 is to get 9 cents more in dividends than each new share, then the equivalent ex dividend price of 591 should be used instead of the cum dividend price of 600, producing a theoretical ex rights ex dividend price of 294 instead of 300. (It would not be correct to use the cum dividend price and then subtract the dividend at the end.)

719   More often than not, the actual market values will be below the theoretical levels, because the incidence of the issue itself will result in additional selling pressure which is not matched by any additional buying pressure.

The Mechanics of a Rights Issue

720   The procedure for a new cash issue is as follows. The first step in the process is a company announcement to the stock exchange (in accordance with the listing requirements), giving the general terms of the proposed issue—the purpose of the issue, its size, the ratio being offered to existing shareholders,

the price per share, the name of underwriter (if any), the various dates, and so on. The expected future dividend policy for the company as a whole, as well as the specific participation rights of the new shares, will also be given. The company will also indicate how fractions are to be treated (ignored, rounded up or rounded down)—see also paras 1642 to 1644.

721 This announcement may or may not be communicated to shareholders by circular, it may or may not feature on a web site, and it may or may not receive publicity in the press. It will, however, reach all brokers.

722 The market price can move in either direction following the announcement of the issue. The price may also be influenced by other announcements made at the same time, such as in relation to profits, dividends or expansion plans. In times of low liquidity or in the case of companies making frequent or large issues the price may fall because some shareholders may not find it easy to raise the necessary cash and may therefore choose to sell out instead. Potential purchasers may also hold off for the time being—see para. 729.

723 For fully-paid shares there are a number of critical dates:

- The day on which the issue and its terms are announced.

- The first day of trading for the rights, and for the existing shares on an "ex rights" basis. Other things being equal, the market value of the latter will fall to the theoretical equivalent of the closing cum rights price (see para. 714).

- The "books closing date" for the issue. As explained in para. 461, this is seven trading days later.

- The date on which the entitlement and acceptance forms to the issue and the prospectuses are sent out to existing shareholders. The "low point" on the market is often reached a few days later, as many of the less sophisticated investors rush to sell their rights.

- The last day of trading for the rights.

- The "issue closing date"—the latest date for the lodging of valid applications (including cheques) for the new shares (see para. 730). This is often but not always the same as the last day of trading for the rights.

- The date from which the new shares rank for dividends.

- The date on which certificates for the new shares are dispatched to non-CHESS holders.

724 If the new issue involves contributing shares then the announcement would also set out the portion of the application money which is required by the issue closing date and the amounts and due dates of the further calls (or an indication of the expected call program). Some issues offer a choice between fully-paid and contributing shares. The dividend entitlements of the contributing shares would also be provided.

725 The company will send out, about two or three weeks after the books closing date, formal advice to each shareholder, showing the number of shares held on that date and the number of rights to which the shareholder is entitled and the total cost of the new shares, etc., together with appropriate explanatory material in the form of a prospectus. Such notifications are ignored by investors only at their peril. In particular, deadlines should not be missed by shareholders anxious to act in their own best interests.

726 Shareholders not wishing to take up the new shares themselves normally have an important privilege—the ability to "renounce" their entitlements in favour of someone else, including a purchaser willing to pay a consideration for such a transfer.

727 It will be noticed that rights can be traded as soon as the stock exchange quotes them. Sellers do not need to await the books closing date or the receipt of official advice from the company.

728 Many shareholders unfamiliar with the market or not keeping an eye on the financial press may be unaware of an impending rights issue and of their ability to trade rights or shares ex rights. They may therefore decide to sell only when they get the company's circular and the "Entitlement and Acceptance Form" setting out their exact entitlement.

729 As a general rule the best strategy for selling is to avoid this time and to sell either well before or well after this mailing. On the other hand, the best strategy for buying is to await this customary low point in the middle of rights trading. In rising or falling markets, it may, of course, be advisable to depart from this standard approach.

730 Shareholders wishing to take up some or all of their entitlement should complete the acceptance form and return it to the company with the appropriate payment by the due date (either directly or through their broker). In due course the company will send out a scrip certificate for the additional holding (except where holdings in uncertificated form are being used by the shareholder). There is, of course, no advantage in sending the money to the company much before the deadline—although missing the deadline can be even more disadvantageous. Acting shortly before the closing date gives subscribers an interest saving and preserves flexibility in the event of a market downturn.

731 Shareholders wishing to sell some or all of their rights on the market should place an order with their broker in the usual way (see paras 1601 to 1608).

732 In some cases brokers receive a handling fee for new issue applications lodged through them.

733 The new shares will be quoted on the stock exchange as from the trading day following the cessation of rights trading. Until the scrip is issued by the company concerned they will be quoted on a "deferred delivery" basis, meaning that, while the ownership of the shares can change in the usual way, settlement does not take place until the scrip is available and can be delivered by the seller (or its electronic equivalent).

734 If there is no difference between the old shares and the new shares either in regard to the paid-up amount or the dividend entitlement, then they will "equate" as soon as the scrip is available—in other words, they will no longer be quoted separately. In other cases the separate basis of quotation will continue until the difference ceases to apply.

Deals not Involving Brokers

735 The procedure for private sales of rights is broadly similar to that described above, except that an off—market "Standard

Renunciation and Acceptance Form" (gold) needs to be used. See also paras 1632 to 1634.

Prospectuses

736   Before the *Corporations Law* became operative proportionate rights issues were not regarded as being made to the general public and therefore did not require prospectuses. However, since 1 January 1991 prospectuses have been required even for such issues, in an endeavour to better protect investors. (Such prospectuses need to be "lodged" with the authorities, as distinct from requiring registration.)

Furthermore, the liability of company directors for any misleading information in such documents has been greatly increased. As a result, considerable costs are now being incurred by many companies in gathering together all possibly relevant data and in producing quite thick prospectuses. In practice much of this material probably remains unread by its recipients. Apart from the "wasted expense-aspects, some undesirable side—effects of the new legislation are beginning to emerge:

- Small companies cannot afford to make rights issues at all, as the cost per dollar being raised is far too high. This is not healthy for the economy.

- Large companies can afford to make such issues, but tend to do so less frequently and for very large amounts when they do, in order to amortise the costs of prospectus preparation more efficiently. However, this pattern does not help their shareholders, and cash raised before it is really needed leads to lower earnings per share.

- Companies are induced to make institutional placements (of at least $500,000), as these are exempt from the prospectus requirements. Again, this is to the detriment of the existing shareholders.

- Companies are induced to make rights issues at the time of releasing their annual reports. This allows up-to-date financial information to be provided in a prospectus at minimum extra cost, but it also means that rights issues can become "bunched" into the main reporting season, with the attendant risk that the market could become oversaturated.

However, the government intends through its *Corporate Law Economic Reform Program* to make legislative changes to overcome some of these problems.

Maximum Size for New Issues

737   The aggregate face value of the new shares (not the issue price) must not take the issued capital above the authorised capital figure (see para. 463).

Non-renounceable Rights Issues

738   The above paragraphs described the normal situation for listed companies, which involves the making of renounceable rights issues. However, some rights issues—particularly those made at a price near their market value—are made on a non-renounceable basis. The procedure is similar, except that there is no rights trading and that the quotes on the stock exchange are called "cum entitlement" and "ex entitlement" instead of "cum rights" and "ex rights". Shareholders not wishing to take up their rights can simply lapse them. If market conditions permit, they can, of course, sell shares instead of selling rights.

Rights to other Securities

739   Rights issues do not always involve ordinary shares. On occasions rights may be in respect of other equity securities, such as options or convertible notes.

740   Occasionally a new issue will comprise both shares and options, offered together in some defined proportion, on the basis that shareholders must subscribe for both or neither. In such cases the rights traded will be the rights to a particular "parcel" of both securities. Only after the issue closes will the shares and the options be traded separately.

Spin-off Companies

741   Sometimes a company floats off a subsidiary company by offering shares and/or options in it to its own shareholders on a pro rata basis, as a preliminary to having that subsidiary's shares listed separately on the stock exchange. This is called

a "spin-off". The parent company can retain a majority or minority interest in the spin-off company.

One reason for such a divestment might be to accommodate shareholder desires for a direct investment in a separate industry from that represented by the parent. Another reason might be to try and increase the total market capitalisation of a group, by separating out a profitable subsidiary entity from a debt-burdened parent. The procedure is similar to that described above, with either renounceable or non-renounceable rights. Naturally, a detailed prospectus needs to be distributed. The capital gains tax implications are discussed in paras 2955 to 2957.

Notes:

1. Companies can also distribute shares in spin-off companies to their shareholders without raising cash. This would normally be done through machinery in the *Corporations Law* known as a *scheme of arrangement.*

2. An alternative to this, *targeted shares* or *letter stock,* is described in Chapter 41.

742 Some spin-offs involve issues to the general public, in which case shareholders may be given some priority. However, ASX Listing Rule 3J(2) requires that a listed company should not transfer major assets to a separate company without first giving its own shareholders the opportunity to preserve their equity.

On a separate aspect, shareholders sometimes resent having to pay for shares in a spin-off company, on the basis that they already own the equity in it. This is partly correct, and as indicated above a distribution without cost to the shareholders is certainly possible.

However, companies engaging in spin-offs frequently desire to raise further funds and just use this route as an alternative to issuing more shares of their own. By paying for shares in the spin-off company the shareholders will have outlaid more cash, but they will also own a correspondingly bigger asset. The cash paid over by the shareholders collectively finishes up with the company owned by them and they still retain the equity in it. The claim that shareholders are paying a second time for the same asset is thus a myth.

Lapsing Entitlements

743 It is, of course, never compulsory for shareholders to take up and pay for rights, in the way that it can be compulsory for shareholders to pay calls on contributing shares in limited companies owned by them. Investors always have three main choices:

- to take up the rights

- to sell them

- to let them lapse.

Investors would, of course, be silly to let unwanted rights lapse if they can turn them into cash by taking simple action. They would also be silly to take up the new shares if the market value of the existing shares is less than the cost of the new shares (allowing for any dividend difference), although the absence of brokerage and stamp duty can make a slight premium on the market price acceptable to some investors wishing to increase their holdings. Allowing rights to lapse does not, of course, affect the *number* of existing shares held—although their value might have changed.

744 The discrepancy referred to above can happen because of changes in market conditions since the time at which the terms of the issue were set and announced. Another factor can be the rather stupid provision in the companies legislation which prevents limited companies from making cash issues at a price below the par value without special court approval. (This provision is likely to be repealed in due course.)

Protection for Shareholders who do not take Action

745 The terms of a rights issue may or may not protect certain shareholders: those who do not act by the closing date for the issue, either by taking up their entitlements or by selling their rights—regardless of whether this inaction is due to ignorance, forgetfulness, incapacity, failure to receive the material or any other cause.

746 Enlightened companies allot the shares not applied for to a trustee who takes up the shares and sells them, distributing the net proceeds (after deducting costs and the application money) pro rata to the shareholders concerned. Less enlightened companies vest the entitlements to such shares in the underwriters

or put them at the disposal of the board. Depending on the precise terms, this can cause large losses to the shareholders who do nothing (see also paras 1234 to 1235).

(*Note:* If a purchaser of rights on the market allows them to lapse then there will be no entry in the company's share register relating to that purchaser and any proceeds from the trustee would as a matter of mechanics be sent to the vendor. However, the money belongs to the purchaser and would need to be passed on, through the two brokers concerned.)

Assessment of Rights Issues

747   As indicated in paras 1044 to 1050, whether a particular rights issue is good, bad or indifferent for shareholders does not really depend on the issue price or the so-called "bonus element" inherent in it (see para. 765). Rather, it is a function of the use to which the company will put the additional money and the expected rate of return on it. The post issue ratio of shareholders' funds to loan funds also has some relevance.

748   An issue price well below the market price (known as a "deep discount") may seem attractive to unsophisticated investors because it *appears* to offer a bargain. (The common journalistic approach of using terms such as "a generous discount" is to be deprecated— see also para. 1047.) As demonstrated in para. 715, this is quite illusory: any "gain" made in acquiring new shares cheaply is exactly balanced by a "loss" on the existing holding. Some specific tax disadvantages are analysed in para. 2908. However, markets do not always act rationally and—notwithstanding the above—the ex rights price may well rise to the previous cum rights price or even higher. In that event, shareholders may indeed have benefited.

Bonus Issues: Background

749   A "bonus issue" (sometimes also called a "free scrip issue") is an issue of fully-paid ordinary shares to existing shareholders, pro rata to their existing holdings, but (unlike the rights issues discussed above) without any payment being required.

750   Technically, a bonus issue is a dividend not paid in cash. The company puts through a book entry, crediting the share capital account with the face value of the new shares and debiting some other account, such as the share premium account or an

assets revaluation or realisation reserve, with the same amount. This overcomes the prohibition on issuing shares for less than their face value. The taxation implications of such transactions are discussed separately in paras 2844 to 2857 and 2905.

751 Although widely perceived both by some company directors and by unsophisticated investors as a benefit, bonus shares are really nothing of the kind (although they do not cause much harm either). Clearly, a company putting through a few book entries and printing additional pieces of paper does not improve the total size or quality of its assets or the profitability of the enterprise to the slightest degree. A shareholder who owned, say, one per cent of the company before a bonus issue will still own only one per cent after it is all concluded. Thus typical press comments to the effect that "the shareholders in ABC Limited have been *rewarded* with a one for three bonus" are rather a nonsense. (To use another analogy, if a person owning two houses on one title arranges for a subdivision then he will get two title certificates, but the total value of his property will not have doubled.)

(*Note:* In this zero sum game the only benefits which bonus issues can really confer on some shareholders must be at the expense of other shareholders—as, for example, when the holders of one cent paid shares in an executive share plan rank equally (share for share) with the holders of fully-paid ordinary shares, whose stake in the total dividend pool then gets watered in the process.)

The Mechanics of Bonus Issues

752 In many ways, a bonus issue can be regarded as a rights issue made at a zero issue price. However, there is nothing corresponding to rights trading and there are significant differences under the capital gains tax legislation—see Chapter 29. There is no need for investors to fill out any forms or to take any other action (apart from adjusting their own records), as everything will happen automatically as far as the shareholders are concerned.

753 There are five critical dates relating to the official announcement of an impending bonus issue:

- The day on which the issue and its terms are announced.

- The first day of trading for the bonus shares on a deferred delivery basis (see para. 733) and for the existing shares on an "ex bonus" basis. Other things being equal, the market value will fall in line with the ratio of the issue.

- The "books closing date" for the issue. As before, this is seven trading days later.

- The date from which the bonus shares rank for dividends.

- The date on which certificates for the bonus shares are dispatched to non-CHESS holders.

754 Thus, if a bonus issue is made on a one for one basis and the bonus shares rank pari passu, then the theoretical ex bonus price is half the closing cum bonus price. The transaction is really equivalent to a two for one share split. Similarly, a one for two bonus issue involves an ex bonus price of two-thirds the previous price and is the mathematical and economic equivalent of a three for two share split. Such a move might be described in company publicity and in media reports—and even in some brokers' circulars—as a "capital benefit". However, it was really nothing of the sort.

755 In practice, the ex bonus price may turn out to be higher than warranted by the theory. If the bonus ratio is high, as in the illustrations just given, then the resultant lower price per share may attract some additional small investors who might have been deterred from entering the stock because of its previous high-sounding unit price. Actually, this would not have been logical, but psychological factors also come into market behaviour. However, large investors, focusing more on the number of dollars which they wish to invest, would be less affected—and these collectively really have much more influence on prices.

756 If, on the other hand, the bonus ratio is low, say, one for 10, then the ex bonus price may creep back to the previously prevailing cum bonus price because some people have got used to that sort of price level for the stock and forget the dilution

which has taken place. (This is called "carrying" the bonus and corresponds to the phenomenon of carrying the dividend, which occurs when the ex dividend price moves back to the cum dividend level. A similar phenomenon can also occur in the case of rights issues.)

757 Share prices often move up at the time of bonus issue announcements—or even ahead of them, if they are anticipated. This may partly be because of the perception—illogical though it is—that bonuses confer a benefit. (The perception thus results in a self-fulfilling prophecy—at least in the short-term; ultimately, share prices will reflect fundamental factors such as earnings per share.) It may also be because of associated announcements, such as of current profitability and of the likely future dividend distributions. Bonuses are usually declared only when profits are rising.

Other Aspects of Bonus Issues

758 The perception that bonuses are desirable has an understandable origin. Companies that do well often make bonus issues. But the bonuses are the *result* and not the *cause* of the company doing well.

759 Companies tend to make bonus issues for a variety of reasons, including:

- To keep the unit share price down and thus increase market interest in the stock.

- To hopefully boost total market capitalisation and thus facilitate takeovers by the company while simultaneously making bids for the company itself more expensive.

- To keep the dividend rate (expressed, as it ought not to be, as a percentage of the face value) low, in the naive hope that the making of large or increased distributions by the company will be less conspicuous to trade unions, politicians, consumer advocates, regulatory authorities and customers.

- As a symbolic gesture, to signal to the market that the company is doing well.

760 Bonus issues with the half-yearly dividend in cents per share then being kept constant are often made as an alternative to increasing the dividend *rate* per share. Companies are required to indicate their future dividend intentions as part of the bonus announcement. Any rise in the market value which seems to result from the bonus may well also have occurred on a simple announcement of future higher total dividend payments.

761 A bonus declaration frequently follows a revaluation of assets made so that the company's book values will more closely correspond to the true value of the assets. Such revaluations are highly desirable in their own right, as an aid to having a fully informed market. They may, of course, also lead to a reassessment of the stock by investors. However, the declaration of a bonus is a completely separate step.

762 Sometimes a bonus issue and a cash issue at a premium will be made simultaneously. Such a procedure is completely illogical.

763 Shareholders are, of course, free to sell their bonus shares on receipt and to treat the proceeds as a capital profit if they so wish. But in reality such a move amounts to selling a part of their holding and the liquidation of a portion of their original investment.

764 Bonus issues involve some minor disadvantages, such as the cost to the company of the associated paperwork and the fact that some shareholders who like round numbers may be left with a holding not conforming to this criterion. They may also endure a slight reduction in equity if fractions are disregarded. The company may also encounter difficulties in future years if the lower post issue market value ever drops to below par, making cash issues difficult. Depending on how they are handled, bonus issues can also cause inequities between the holders of different classes of security.

The "Bonus Element" of Rights Issues

765 The example in para. 716 showed how a shareholder with 4500 shares cum rights could finish up with 6000 shares ex rights, *without* laying out any more money. In other words, that particular rights issue could be regarded as similar in ultimate effect to a one for three bonus issue. For this reason some

commentators talk—quite unhelpfully, as it happens—of rights issues containing a "bonus element".

Minimum Brokerage

766 Disposing of small parcels of rights on the stock exchange would in some cases involve more brokerage than the transaction is worth. Because of this some companies have made special arrangements with their underwriter to handle such sales without imposing the usual minimum brokerage. Such arrangements also have regard to the high turnover which occurs during the limited rights trading period. It should also be noted that depending on the circumstances brokerage can kill deals which would otherwise make sense—for example, buying into rights priced at one cent with a view to selling them at two cents, as distinct from taking up new shares costing several dollars.

Round Numbers

767 Many investors who start off with round number of shares such as 500 or 1000 finish up with a distinctly non-round number after a rights or bonus issue. There is no great virtue in buying or selling shares just in order to finish up with a nice round number again, as that action in itself would incur relatively heavy transaction costs (which probably include minimum brokerage) for no particular investment advantage. If the company concerned makes frequent issues then such action could be required each time.

Priority Issues

768 On occasions companies make issues to their shareholders, or both to their shareholders and to the general public, not as rights issues but on the basis of a general priority to shareholders registered on a specified date. This method is favoured by some boards for convertible or unconvertible notes or preference shares. The directors then use their discretionary power and allot shares to applicants as they see fit.

769 Such an approach is highly unsatisfactory. If the terms of the issue are attractive—for example, because the interest rate being offered is relatively high and/or because the conversion terms are generous—then the issue will probably be oversubscribed and allotment will amount to windfall gains for those

lucky enough to achieve it, at the expense of everyone else, including unsuccessful applicants and existing shareholders whose interests are being eroded.

770   If the basis of allocation is arbitrary then the main beneficiaries might turn out to be friends of the directors. If on the other hand a passably reasonable basis is used, such as either pro rata to the stock applied for or pro rata to the number of existing shares held, but with the rationing method announced only after the issue has closed, then that still amounts to an unfairness, as investors are denied the opportunity of rearranging their affairs so as to take advantage of the precise terms.

771   Unsuccessful applications, with the money returned after some weeks without interest, can be quite costly. The position is made worse if the company hints before the event that all applicants will receive a minimum parcel and then welshes on that half—promise.

Reconstructions

772   Company reconstructions can take many forms, the most common being:

- Share splits—for example, dividing each $1 share into two 50 cent shares.

- Consolidations—the reverse of this, for example, converting ten 20 cent shares into one $2 share.

- Capital reductions involving the writing off of capital regarded as permanently lost. As the losses concerned have already taken place, such a paper exercise really has no further effect on investors, although it can make the payment of dividends out of future profits easier.

- Reductions involving the share premium account (see para. 474), again to make the payment of dividends out of future profits easier.

- Capital reductions involving a partial repayment of capital in cash or through a distribution in specie.

- Schemes of arrangement involving share and/or loan securities in one company being exchanged for securities in another company (a de facto takeover).

- Schemes of arrangement involving share and/or loan securities in one company being exchanged for different securities in the same company.

In some cases shareholders affected by such moves need to lodge Section 160ZZP elections with the Australian Taxation Office to protect their capital gains tax position—see paras 2974 to 2976.

773 Capital reductions and schemes of arrangement require 75 per cent majority approvals at general meetings and subsequently the ratification of the move by the court.

774 The reason often advanced for splitting shares—that a lower market value will bring in more investors—is probably specious. To a person with $10,000 to invest it makes little difference whether this involves 1000 shares at 1000 or 2000 shares at 500.

775 Similarly, the reason sometimes put forward for consolidating shares—to stop the number of shares on issue becoming "too unwieldy"—is also quite unimpressive. It cannot make the slightest difference to a share registrar whether he has to deal with 1000 shareholders holding between them, say, 1500 million 20 cent shares or with the same 1000 shareholders holding 300 million $1 shares. However, the impression that some shareholders have that a reduction in the number of shares held by them as a result of a consolidation somehow constitutes "theft" by the directors is also totally erroneous.

Optional Share Purchase Plans

776 A few companies have taken the concept of dividend reinvestment plans (see Chapter 32) one step further and allow their shareholders to take up *additional* shares (up to some limit) at a market-related price but free of brokerage and stamp duty. Sometimes these arrangements supplement conventional dividend reinvestment plans and sometimes they take their place— probably in a deliberate endeavour to slant them in favour of small holders rather than institutions. Some plans allow top-

ping up to some round number of shares—a relic of earlier times when odd lots involved buyers and sellers in additional charges (see para. 1637). To the extent that these plans involve a fixed issue price and a closing date some weeks after the price is set they also effectively confer a useful fringe benefit on the shareholders involved —a free call option, which can be exercised if the shares go up but allowed to lapse if they go down.

777 The existence of such a plan, as well as directly helping investors who want to top up their holdings in a modest way without incurring minimum brokerage and other charges, also acts as a factor increasing the popularity of the company in the market place, thus probably leading to a slightly higher share price.

Miscellaneous

778 The adjustments required to earnings per share figures to allow for rights and bonus issues are discussed in Appendix 7.

779 Companies with dividend reinvestment and/or dividend election plans should, but do not always, make sure that the desires of members of these plans in regard to the enrolment or otherwise in those plans of the newly-created shares are ascertained and acted on, where these shares arise from the exercise of rights or options.

780 Sometimes a rights issue can significantly reduce the attractiveness of investing in a company. For example, the market price of a share with a net tangible asset backing of 100 per share might be only 50, or a 50 per cent discount on that asset value. If the company later on makes a one for one rights issue at, say, 40, then the market price ex rights will be 45 (on the theoretical basis), while the net tangible asset backing per share will fall to 70. The discount on that asset value after that is then only 36 per cent.

Legislative Changes

781 As indicated in paras 1247 to 1262, the concept of par values is likely to be abolished in the near future. With this the distinction between the share capital and the share premium accounts of a company will also disappear. These two separate accounts will just be amalgamated into a single share capital

account. Bonus issues on the lines of those made in the past, as described above, will thus no longer be possible in the future.

782 The replacement of bonus issues by share splits will no doubt help newer and less well informed shareholders to understand better what is really going on with their investments.

Buy-backs

783 As indicated above, a company needing more cash from its shareholders can make a rights issue. In the reverse situation— if a company has too much cash—it can make a partial return of capital to its shareholders (see para. 772).

784 An alternative device is also available. The company can buy back some of its issued shares, on either a proportional or a non-proportional basis. This aspect is explained in Chapter 40.

Capital Gains Tax

785 As explained in para. 2906, shares which have pre-85 status for capital gains tax purposes lead to:

- shares which have post-85 status, where these arise from a rights issue
- shares which have pre-85 status, where these arise from a bonus issue.

Arbitrage Opportunities

786 Arbitrage at large is discussed in paras 986 to 989. Sometimes the price of the old shares ex rights and the price of the rights (after allowing for the application money and any dividend difference) get out of line. Theoretically, this could allow profits from selling one and buying the other, but in practice transaction costs and capital gains tax considerations usually make such moves unattractive.

Chapter 8—Annual Reports

The stock market is but a mirror which provides an image of the underlying or fundamental economic situation. Cause and effect run from the economy to the stock market, never the reverse. In 1929 the economy was headed for trouble. Eventually that trouble was violently reflected in Wall Street.
—John Kenneth Galbraith

Background

801   For many years all companies have been required by law to produce an annual report which is sent to all shareholders shortly before each Annual General Meeting and filed with the Australian Securities Commission. In the case of listed companies copies of these reports must also be filed with the stock exchange. The exchange has always required considerably more data from companies than this legal minimum, in order to ensure that the market is properly informed.

The information in annual reports can be very important to the market in general and to security analysts in particular. It becomes the starting point for appraising the investment merits of each company's securities—see further in Chapters 9 and 10-thus allowing investors to make meaningful decisions to buy, to sell or to hold.

802   Annual reports contain accounting, statistical and certain other relevant information and statements prepared:

- in compliance with the *Corporations Law*
- in accordance with the appropriate professional accounting standards
- (in the case of companies listed on the stock exchange) in compliance with the listing rules.

In particular, all annual reports must contain a *balance sheet* and a *profit and loss account* with the latest available figures and—for comparison purposes—the corresponding figures for the preceding year. The provisions currently in force ensure a measure of uniformity in presentation. Listed companies also need to include a funds statement—a summary of the source and application of funds for the year (again with comparative figures).

803   These are accompanied by a *directors' statement* certifying that the accounts give a "true and fair view" and by a report from an external auditor. This chapter briefly describes these documents, but without going into the numerous technical aspects involved in their preparation.

804   Another formal component is the statutory *directors' report,* which contains the replies to certain questions set out in the legislation. Most listed companies also provide non-statutory reviews of the company and its operations and prospects,

usually in the form of reports by the chairman and/or the chief executive. These often provide valuable clues—likely changes to dividend rates, future capital raisings, personnel changes, new products, and so on. Of course, bad news may also be buried in small print in one of the notes to the accounts. Readers really need to study the whole document.

805 Many companies also use their reports as marketing and public relations tools and for this reason such documents are often produced on glossy paper, with photographs, charts, etc. Analytically—minded readers will, no doubt, prefer to focus on the facts rather than allow themselves to be diverted too much by the pretty pictures. They will also get more out of "cents per share" data than out of the much grander—sounding "millions of dollars" totals for the whole group.

Many listed companies have large numbers of relatively small shareholders. It is an unfortunate fact that most such shareholders are apathetic and do not normally bother to read or study the annual reports sent to them (but see para. 833).

The Balance Sheet

806 The balance sheet is a statement of the financial position of the enterprise. It shows the worth of the company as at one particular day, often the preceding 30 June or some such date, depending on the "financial year" (reporting period) adopted by the company. It sets out, in summarised form and under appropriate headings, the various categories of assets held and their book values, together with similar information relating to the liabilities. The difference between the total value of the assets and the total value of the liabilities indicates the net worth of the company, effectively the amount which is owned by the shareholders collectively and which is known as the "shareholders' funds" (or "shareholders' equity").

807 The main categories of assets are:

- Current Assets (cash, or assets likely to be consumed or converted into cash within 12 months) .

- Non—current Assets, including investments, inventories, property, plant and equipment, and intangibles.

808 The main categories of liabilities are:

- Current Liabilities (liabilities likely to be discharged within 12 months).

- Non—current Liabilities.

809 Shareholders' Funds include:

- Paid-up Share Capital.

- Reserves—for example, share premium account, asset revaluation reserve, general reserve (see paras 463 to 468).

- Retained Profits or Accumulated Losses (the balance in the Profit and Loss Account).

810 The quality of the assets should be noted, as should the relative size of the external liabilities to the shareholders' funds. For most analytical purposes intangible assets such as goodwill and patent rights are best treated as a deduction from the Shareholders' Funds, so that these then equal Net Tangible Assets. NTA per share can be compared with the market value. (See also paras 972 to 978.)

811 Whenever assets are acquired or liabilities are incurred they are entered in the company's books at cost. Subsequently the book values may need to be adjusted up or down in order to bring the figures more into line with the then current conditions. Sometimes this is done with rose-tinted spectacles—as when the purchase of a new asset by the company itself at an inflated figure then becomes the justification for the writing up of similar assets already held. If the existence of ultimate capital gains tax liabilities is ignored then such creative accounting is likely to be even more deceptive.

Of course, bookkeeping going in the opposite direction can be just as bad. Leaving assets in the books at cost when they have actually increased in value—at least in dollar terms—was once considered conservative, but it can actually be grossly misleading and can cause shareholders to quit their holdings too cheaply. The writing up or writing down adjustments should normally be made through the profit and loss account.

812 There is, of course, no unique "true value" for any asset except at the moment of its sale. Shareholders may not always appreciate that the valuation of assets is an art rather than a science. To illustrate:

- The value of a company in a forced fire sale is one thing.

- Its value on a leisurely voluntary winding-up is another.

- Its value as a going concern is different again.

- Its value to keen bidders in a takeover duel, especially when these are looking for an alternative to the expense of setting up a fresh organisation, may be considerably higher than this latter figure.

All these values will, except by coincidence, be different from historical cost, as well as from such a cost indexed for inflation. In particular, the assets held on any particular balance date and shown in the balance sheet at what is referred to as their "book value" may have a very different value to the enterprise while it is a going concern from the value which they might realise in other circumstances. To illustrate this aspect further, the stock on hand can be valued, inter alia, at cost, or at its market selling value, or at its replacement value. This naturally also affects the company's disclosed profit. For example, if an item of stock costing $1000 is sold for $1500 then clearly the profit is $500 (ignoring expenses). But if that item is unsold at the balance date then various scenarios are possible, including:

Valuation Basis	Book Value	Profit
Cost	$1000	Nil
Replacement Value	$1100	$100
Market Selling Value	$1300	$300

The true value of stock can vary substantially according to the precise circumstances and its ascertainment and audit can cause great difficulties in practice. Fashion goods, for example, can carry significant mark-ups at the start of a season, but if left over then they can be practically worthless at its end. In a different area, spare parts can be extremely profitable if sold to a customer who needs them, but they can also sit on shelves for long periods, taking up valuable space and incurring overheads such as insurance.

(*Note*: If, in the above example, the item is sold in the following year for, say, $1600, then the profit for that year will be $600,

$500 or $300, depending on which of the above three valuation bases was used at the balance date. While the figures in each trading year are different for each of the three bases, the total profit for the two years combined is naturally the same for all three—namely, $600, being the $1600 realised less the $1000 original cost.)

814 Certain assets, such as plant and machinery, have a limited economic life, after which they are worthless or nearly so (scrap value). In such cases, it is appropriate to write down or "depreciate" the original cost in gradual stages each year over the expected lifetime of the asset and in due course to write off completely any excess of the residual book value over its realisation price at the time of its disposal. Such charges constitute part of the costs of running a business. More than one method for depreciating assets is available.

815 Working in the opposite direction is inflation. For example, land purchased some years ago for, say, $1 million may now be worth several times that figure. To leave the book value unaltered in such circumstances would be rather misleading.

816 Apart from showing present liabilities companies would normally wish to allow for expected future obligations, such as in respect of long service leave for their employees or for tax payable in later years. This leads to certain "provisions" being made in the balance sheet. Contingent liabilities also need to be mentioned—this is usually done by way of a note to the accounts.

817 All these things involve judgement on the part of the directors in the first instance and later on on the part of the auditor. The precise valuation approach adopted has to be spelt out in notes to the accounts.

The Profit and Loss Account

818 Unlike the balance sheet, which relates to a single day (the "balance date"), the profit and loss account covers the whole reporting period (normally one year) ending on that date. The net profit divided by the number of shares on issue gives an important figure which is usually also highlighted elsewhere in the report—the earnings per share. The safety of the investment can be judged in part by comparing interest payments with the earnings before interest and tax (often called "EBIT").

819   The "retained profits" shown in the profit and loss account as at the balance date are part of the shareholders' funds and are the historical build-up of all credit and debit entries relating to revenue transactions since the formation of the company (both cash items and book entries):

- Credits would include gross trading profits and investment income.

- Debits would include running expenses (wages, rent, interest on borrowed funds, depreciation, and so on), as well as taxation and dividends to the company's own shareholders.

820   The profit and loss account sets out, in summarised form and under appropriate headings, such transactions over the reporting period.

Consolidated Accounts

821   Companies with subsidiaries present two sets of accounts, one set for the holding company and another set for the group as a whole, the *consolidated balance sheet* and the *consolidated profit and loss account.* These two are obtained by combining the separate information for the parent company and for each subsidiary company, after eliminating inter—company transactions. (The latter, particularly in the case of wholly-owned subsidiaries, are often influenced by tax considerations and do not necessarily represent commercial realities.) The following jargon terms are often used in these contexts:

- *economic entity*, the group as a whole

- *parent entity*, the holding company

- *controlled entities*, the subsidiary companies.

822   Investors in ordinary shares of listed companies should normally focus on the consolidated accounts only, as these relate to the enterprise actually backing these shares. Holding company figures by themselves would have relevance in special circumstances only, such as when the disposal of all subsidiaries is imminent or when those loans to the parent company that are not supported by guarantees from the other companies in the group are being considered.

823   It should be noted that profits from other companies are treated in three different ways, according to the circumstances:

- Where less than 20 per cent of another company is owned, then the shareholding is treated as an investment and credit is taken only for the dividends actually received or receivable.

- If between 20 and 50 per cent is owned then "equity accounting" can be used, meaning that credit can be taken for a proportionate share of the profits, whether this is distributed or not.

- If more than 50 per cent is owned, then the company becomes a subsidiary and this latter principle again applies: credit is taken for all the profits, less the proportion belonging to the outside minority shareholders (if any).

Audit Reports

824   The figures and explanations in the reports sent to the shareholders are the responsibility of the board of directors. However, an independent auditor has to report on them to the shareholders. Normally he will be able to certify that they are in order.

825   However, on occasions an auditor will issue a "qualified" report, that is, he will draw some irregularity to the attention of the shareholders. Most qualifications encountered in the case of reputable companies are minor and relate to somewhat technical disputes as to the appropriate accounting treatment of some transaction. However, some qualified reports can raise more serious issues.

826   Shareholders should, of course, be equally wary of both overstatements and understatements of assets. Both can arise either unintentionally (for example, because of poor bookkeeping, stock control or internal audit practices) or intentionally (for example, because some insiders desire, fraudulently, to take advantage of share prices which are either too high or too low).

827   Sometimes assets are deliberately undervalued in order to hide a company's inefficiency, as this means that the return on the funds will appear to be higher than it really is. On a completely different aspect, profits are frequently overstated—even in the

case of major companies—because inadequate allowance is made for inflation.

The Needs of Small Shareholders

828 Many companies have large numbers of relatively small shareholders. It is a well-known fact that most such shareholders are apathetic and do not normally read the annual reports sent to them—as some share registrars have found out to their cost when trying to save money by putting dividend cheques in the same envelopes as reports. (The registrars then have to replace large numbers of lost cheques, thrown out with the reports in unopened envelopes!)

829 However, even such shareholders benefit from the contents of the reports indirectly, as these are a prime source of data for stockbrokers and others advising investors. Naturally, such experts would regard the reports as only one ingredient in their total knowledge base and would interpret the information in those reports in the context of external factors, such as the performance of competitors, the state of the economy and any recent government initiatives. For investment choice purposes it is also necessary to compare different companies with each other.

830 Mention should be made of one purpose of company reports which is rarely discussed—the encouragement of new direct investors. It would be unfortunate if the only shareholders in Australia were to be large institutions managing pooled investment funds. People who own shares themselves tend to know more about how the whole economic system works and this makes them better citizens and more informed voters. Furthermore, a wide shareholder base assists companies to raise fresh capital from time to time. Such support also helps to maintain an active market in the company's securities. Naturally, well-prepared annual reports would be only one factor in encouraging people to buy shares—but a factor nevertheless.

831 Companies offering goods and services to the general public find it of particular advantage to have a large number of individual shareholders, as these become potential customers and ambassadors for their products.

Employee Reports

832   Some companies provide their employees with a second, simplified version of their official annual report—a version which does not have to comply with the more formal disclosure requirements of either the *Corporations Law* or the stock exchange listing rules, but which is designed to explain facts in a way which helps good employee relations.

833   Many individual shareholders might also prefer to get such an "easy to read" document. Companies which produce a staff version of their annual report often publicise its existence and make it available to shareholders on request.

Glossy Presentations

834   The lavishness in the production of some companies' annual reports is a subject for occasional criticisms. Glossiness in reports is a two-edged sword. On the one hand, a high quality article creates an image of solidity and prosperity. On the other hand, such reports give the impression of waste and a misuse of shareholders' funds. In a large company, of course, the cost per copy may not be particularly big. Especially when considering the minimum expenses needing to be incurred in any case in producing data for management purposes and in complying with the statutory requirements and also to the fact that part of the money would, if the report did not exist, be spent on other marketing hand—outs. In fact, much of the cost may be incurred in hidden ways—in the use of the company's own managerial resources and in fees for outside professional advice—rather than for the actual printing and distribution.

835   There are no doubt many shareholders who would, if given the choice, opt for a higher dividend and a cheaper annual report containing only the basic information in duplicated form. Such shareholders may well think that the expenses incurred in producing a fine-looking document are larger than they really are, with the result that the company loses rather than gains investor goodwill.

836   In this context, a recent change in the legislation is welcome. Shareholders can now elect to be taken off the mailing list for annual reports. This serves to eliminate much wasteful expenditure—not only in regard to reports which would be discarded for lack of interest but also in respect of multiple copies of

reports which would otherwise need to be sent to the one address.

Some Desirable Reforms

837　Investors tend to be forward looking, more interested in the future than in the past. Facts and figures relating to the last 12 months are relevant in the course of evaluating the directors' stewardship, but even more so as the starting point for forecasting the future.

838　It might thus be helpful and also conducive to better understanding, if balance sheets and profit and loss accounts were always accompanied by some of the key indicators derivable from them, such as those discussed in Chapter 9—earnings per share, dividend cover, net profit per dollar of sales and net tangible asset backing per ordinary share, as well as the return on shareholders' funds, the earnings before interest and tax as a proportion of the total assets, the cover for interest, and the gearing and working capital ratios.

　　Many companies give such data already, although the rationale behind the number of shares used for some of this arithmetic is not always clear (see also Appendix 9). Other worthwhile figures would be the interest rates payable on major loans and the total outlay on all forms of taxation.

839　In the case of those companies which have convertible securities and/or options on issue, a second set of such indicators, showing the effect of the dilution in respect of these, should also be given. Such figures would actually be much more meaningful than the corresponding undiluted figures.

840　In the case of companies operating in more than one industry, subdivisions of profit, net assets and turnover by industry would also be helpful. Similar remarks apply in regard to companies operating in more than one country or currency, where a corresponding dissection on these lines should be shown in respect of all significant subdivisions. The word "industry" may be hard to define in a legal sense, but in practice company managements and their auditors would know what an appropriate disaggregation for any particular enterprise should be for such reporting purposes.

841　Details of minority shareholdings in other listed companies are at present frequently given only in the aggregate. However, full details should be given of all material holdings of shares in such companies—showing the name of each company, the number of shares held and the proportion of the capital which this represents, the price paid, the market value as at the balance date, the annual amount of dividends receivable and the equity share of the earnings and net assets, together with the reason for making such an investment and a statement as to any intentions in regard to its retention or disposal.

842 Such information would be useful market knowledge at the best of times. It becomes even more important for shareholders in cases where the prime motivation for acquiring such holdings bears on the rights of shareholders, as when strategic parcels of shares in other companies are acquired as part of a takeover defence.

843 Except in the case of genuine investment companies, the reasons for making and retaining such holdings really ought to be given in more meaningful terms than just stating that they represent "a good long-term investment". In particular, in the case of companies owning shares in each other there must always be a feeling that the prime results of such cross—holdings are to deny shareholders voting power commensurate with their holdings, to eliminate takeover premiums and to encourage inefficiencies by making it harder to remove ineffective managements. Explanations by the directors of their investment motives and of the justification for any "above market" prices which may have been paid would therefore be particularly in order.

844 The company's future dividend policy should always be set out, especially following any changes in either tax rules or market conditions. Shareholders also appreciate advance warning of possible capital raisings or confirmation that none is planned for the foreseeable future.

845 The extent of litigation by companies is growing and it would be relevant to shareholders that both the direct and indirect costs in this area of activity should be made available for scrutiny and discussion. Similarly, because of the importance of these subjects, a summary of the company's industrial relations philosophy and of its attitude to technological change could also be set out.

846   Forecasts as to future performance are always difficult. However, directors are in a better position than outsiders to make such estimates and should thus endeavour to keep their shareholders fully informed of likely developments and available budget figures. It is recognised, of course, that directors can find themselves in a "no win" situation in that they may be criticised by someone or other regardless of whether their predictions later on turn out to have been too high or too low.

847   Some old-established listed companies include in their reports figures showing the current value of $1000 invested in the company's shares, say, 10 years ago, allowing for the notional reinvestment of dividends and the proceeds from the sales of rights. Others compare the movements in the market price of their shares with those of the All Ordinaries Index (see para. 982). While such figures need to be interpreted with some caution, their inclusion is to be encouraged as providing a spur to managerial effort.

Secrecy in Accounting Information

848   Companies sometimes resist calls for greater disclosure on the grounds that this would assist competitors. Frequently such claims have little substance, as the competitors probably know more of what is going on than the owners of the business, the shareholders. But in any case the privilege of listing and thereby inviting the general public to become stakeholders brings with it an obligation, namely, the need to have regard to the rights of those who risk their money and to keep them fully informed.

If any company feels that secrecy is particularly important for it then it has to weigh the disadvantage of openness against the advantage of having public shareholders. (Directors also tend to overuse the "aiding our competitors" argument during question periods at annual meetings. It can provide a convenient excuse to avoid responding to legitimate but unpalatable questions. Silence is an effective way of hiding inefficiencies.)

849   As mentioned above, there are words in the statutory certificates given by the directors to the effect that the accounts present a "true and fair view". Yet in some cases takeover documents issued a few months later make claims that the balance sheet data did not tell the whole story and that the

company is really worth much more than the annual report indicated. Such comments deserve to be treated with cynicism.

850   It is strange that many companies indulge in all sorts of artificial devices in attempts to boost the market value of their shares, but fail to use the most obvious method, namely, to disclose both up-to-date "going concern" and break-up values of their assets instead of just including them at a historical cost price. Companies which give meaningful information as to the true value underlying their shares have an excellent and perfectly proper protection against takeovers designed to exploit undervalued situations. It is, of course, true that if such disclosure reveals earnings on funds below what they ought to be then it highlights a weakness—but one which is probably already fairly obvious both to the market and to the takeover merchants.

Material for Reference

851   Another purpose of the annual report should be the putting together of some useful reference material relating to the company in a readily accessible and permanent form. It is somewhat surprising that many companies which produce expensive and otherwise elaborate reports do not even assist investors by including in them such obvious details as:

- their own telephone and facsimile numbers
- those of their share registrars in each capital city
- those of their auditor
- appropriate e-mail addresses
- the address of their World Wide Web site.

In the case of companies which have changed their name, the previous name should be prominently displayed for at least 10 years.

852   Other information which could routinely be shown as a matter of record by more than the handful of companies which now provide it is set out below:

- A summary of the major announcements made during the preceding 12 months.
- The amounts (both per share and in the aggregate) and all relevant dates for dividends, calls,

share issues and other capital changes since the start of the financial year covered by the report.

- The franking status of each of the above-mentioned dividends.

- The balance of the company's franking account.

- Details of the terms and conditions relating to all outstanding convertible securities and options.

- Full details of the dividend entitlement, calls program and voting power of any contributing shares.

- A reconcilliation between the number of shares on issue as at the balance date and the corresponding number 12 months earlier.

- The dates on which each director comes up for re-election.

- A 10-year table of key financial data and ratios, and of figures such as the number of shareholders, the number of employees and the range of market prices for the company's shares.

853 Such data would greatly assist investors trying to trace information which while publicly available is otherwise scattered over numerous separate pieces of paper. Where applicable, details of the company's dividend reinvestment plan (see Chapter 32) and statistics as to its utilisation would also be of interest.

Corporate Objectives

854 Reports should include in their opening pages a brief summary of the company's main activities. All reports should then set out the company's corporate objectives, both short-term and long-term. These objectives should be stated in meaningful language such as the aimed—for earnings as a proportion of shareholders' funds, of total assets and of turnover, and any intended expansion into other markets.

855 Vague phrases such as "to be a good employer, "to provide a service to our customers, "to improve our products, "to earn a satisfactory return, "to increase our market share" or "to meet our obligations to the community" are not particularly helpful.

Objectives such as "to maximise shareholder returns" or "to increase the value of our shareholders' investment" show the right spirit but say only the obvious.

Post Meeting Reports

856 Companies in Australia rarely issue a "post meeting" report after each annual general meeting, although such reports are quite common in some other countries. Many local companies already circulate their chairman's prepared address, which is frequently a sort of supplement to what is in the annual report itself and a means of bringing it up to date.

857 Ideally the post meeting report should cover much more than just the chairman's formal address, although that should be one item. Each question asked by any shareholder should be included, together with the answer given. If desired, elaborations on these impromptu replies could also be put on the public record in this way.

858 The annual general meeting is an important forum enabling shareholders to exercise their democratic rights. While few shareholders actually attend such meetings—partly because of the physical difficulties of doing so—all are entitled to learn what really went on. Good post meeting reports in themselves would also act as a factor encouraging more meaningful participation at meetings in future years.

Chapter 9—Theoretical Aspects

Never invest in anything that eats or needs repairing
—Stephen Lewis

Background

901 Chapter 10 sets out and discusses various factors affecting the market price of shares. Some of these relate to the economy at large and others to non-numerical information originating from the company concerned. However, several of the factors involve ratios and other figures derivable from the company's own published accounts (balance sheet, profit and loss account, directors' report, auditor's report, etc.). Study of such data is an important ingredient of security analysis.

902 For convenience these concepts and some other theoretical and mathematical aspects are now grouped together and dealt with below. This will assist investors who wish to carry out their own analyses. It will also be of interest to other investors seeking to understand better the basis of the reasoning used by professional advisers. This chapter concludes with some comments on stock exchange indices.

903 Some other chapters also deal with related matters. For instance, the theoretical values of rights and bonus issues are analysed in paras 714 to 719 and 754.

904 Many of the ratios and other figures (and their trend over time) provide a useful starting point for estimating the future. Investors—unlike historians—are rarely interested in the past for its own sake. Useful comparisons can be made of performance in the one company over time, as well as between different companies in the same industry or between different industries.

905 Comparisons can also be made between different categories of investment—for example, between the returns available from fixed interest investments (see the definitions of "yield" in paras 213 and 222 and of "redemption yield" in para. 227) and the various types of yield on shares (see paras 920 and 930). However, allowance must be made for the different character involved—clearly a steady 13 per cent per annum is of different quality from an income return starting at 4 per cent in the first year but expected to increase in future and to be accompanied by capital growth.

906 In the case of holding companies (see para. 470) regard should be had to the consolidated figures only, and not to the parent company figures which are also provided for legal reasons—

except in special circumstances (see para. 471). The published figures for the separate companies in a group, including the holding company, may be misleading, as certain transactions may have been arranged in particular ways for tax minimisation reasons.

907 Some calculations affect the enterprise as a whole and others are made on a "per share" basis. Other variations in approach are also possible. For example, in the former case one can look at:

1. Total assets; or

2. Net assets (total assets less total outside liabilities), also referred to as "shareholders' funds" or "shareholders' equity"; or

3. Ordinary shareholders' funds (total shareholders' funds as in 2, less preference capital).

In calculating a ratio it is, of course, essential to use consistent concepts for both the numerator and the denominator.

908 For some purposes calculations are best made on an "after tax" basis—as, for example, when investors wish to see the effect on their pockets of making two alternative investments. For other purposes calculations on a "before tax" basis may be preferable, as when it is desired to measure the efficiency of a particular company's management; or to distinguish between actual performance and profit variations beyond the control of the company caused by changes in the tax regime. As always, it is most important to compare like with like.

Net Tangible Assets

909 The "net tangible asset backing per ordinary share" figure, often abbreviated "NTA" or shortened to just "asset backing", is one possible measure of the worth of a share, although its usefulness is subject to some reservations.

910 In an ongoing company measures related to income tend to be more relevant, as the asset backing of a share is not normally available to shareholders unless the company is placed in voluntary liquidation or makes a capital return or unless a takeover offer reflecting this backing is made and accepted. In any case, the assets are usually much more valuable on a "going concern" basis.

On the other hand, in the case of a company in financial difficulties and facing bankruptcy, the book values used for the assets may turn out to have been too high and not realisable under the fire sale conditions then likely to prevail. Book values can also be too low rather than too high, particularly if assets have not been revalued recently in order to allow for inflation.

911 The company's total net tangible assets for this purpose are its shareholders' funds after deducting (where they exist):

- minority shareholders' interests (as these are separate from the interests of ordinary shareholders)

- preference share capital (as the calculation is concerned with the assets remaining after satisfying the prior claims of any shareholders who rank ahead of the ordinary shareholders)

- intangible assets.

The term "intangible assets" includes items such as goodwill (see paras 972 to 978), patent rights, trade marks and licences. Many analysts would also deduct a future tax benefit as an intangible asset, but—especially in the case of a company which includes such an item in its balance sheet because its availability is regarded as near certain—a more meaningful figure is probably arrived at by not disregarding it.

It should be noted, however, that the value of the benefit can go up or down with changes in the tax rate. The book value of listed investments should be adjusted for the market value disclosed in a note to the accounts—although large parcels can be worth considerably more or considerably less than this.

912 If there is only one class of ordinary shares then the "per share" figure is obtained by dividing the company's adjusted total net assets by the total number of ordinary shares on issue.

913 If there are fully-paid as well as contributing shares then the total assets must first be further adjusted by the total amount yet to be paid by way of calls on the contributing shares (whether by way of capital or premium). The division by the total number of ordinary shares then gives the net tangible asset backing for the fully-paid shares. The corresponding

figure for the contributing shares is derived from this by subtracting the amount of the future calls per share.

914 The ratio of the market value to the NTA can be compared with similar ratios for other companies. Prima facie, if the market value is at a discount to a correctly-measured NTA then the share can in theory be regarded as being available at a bargain price—but it does not, of course, follow that that particular share will in practice turn out to be a good investment. The reverse also applies.

Earnings

915 Companies report their profits (earnings) on both a "before income tax" and an "after income tax" basis. For analytical purposes *extraordinary* (in other words, non-recurring) profits need to be disregarded. However, *abnormal* profits should be taken into account—that term is used to describe items which are large and unusual but part of the usual costs of doing business—for example, costs relating to branch closures or the provision of bad debts. The company's reconciliation of its tax charge with the prima facie tax payable on its disclosed earnings provides a useful cross-check as to the validity of the declared figures.

916 The ratio of profits before tax to shareholders' funds is a measure of the company's efficiency. For example, a company which consistently underperforms the Commonwealth Bond rate on this yardstick would clearly make its shareholders better off by liquidating and allowing them to make such a (risk-free) investment instead. In practice this concept needs modification, because regard also has to be had to growth expectations, but it provides a useful starting point for identifying weaknesses.

917 Another measure of efficiency, which isolates the operating performance from the effect of gearing, is obtained by dividing the earnings before interest and tax (often called "EBIT") by the total assets.

918 In the case of companies with preference capital the net earnings rate on ordinary shareholders' funds is a very relevant figure. It is obtained by dividing the net profit less the preference dividends by the total shareholders' funds less the preference capital.

919 "Earnings per ordinary share" (usually referred to as "eps") are obtained by dividing a company's net profit (notionally adjusted where contributing shares exist) less the preference dividends (if any) by the total number of ordinary shares on issue. Such a figure is best expressed in cents per share. (An earnings rate expressed as a percentage of nominal capital is meaningless.) Suitable adjustments will also be required if the company has made any issues or repaid any capital during the year (see Appendix 7), and also if convertible securities or options exist (see paras 959 to 961).

920 The "earnings yield" is obtained by dividing the *eps* figure (in cents per share) by the current market price of the share (also expressed in cents). This is a measure of the performance of the company to an investor and can be compared with interest rate levels generally. It is a much more useful yardstick than the "dividend yield" discussed in paras 930 to 931, which—because it is a function of the payout ratio—ignores the fact that ordinary shareholders benefit from a company's earnings irrespective of whether these are actually distributed or not. Yields are normally expressed as percentages (thus *eps* 10.8 and market price 150 give an earnings yield of 7.2 per cent).

921 Other things being equal, the higher the earnings yield the better the value inherent in a transaction for a purchaser. However, things are never equal and some apparent bargains may be quite illusory. Distortions can arise from the mechanical nature of the arithmetic. Investors are much more interested in the future than in the past—and market prices reflect such expectations. Dividing the *last* published earnings figure by a *current* market value can produce a nonsense result, especially if losses or significantly reduced profits for subsequent years are now expected. Just before a new annual report is due the available full year data will normally refer to a period which ended about 15 months earlier and which commenced 12 months before that, in other words 27 months ago, perhaps under very different conditions.

922 A more common way of looking at the above-mentioned concept is to divide the market price per share by the earnings per share figure, instead of the other way round. The result, this time expressed as a number and not as a percentage, is

called the "price earnings ratio" or "PER" (sometimes shortened to just "PE"). (Using the same figures as before, namely *eps* 10.8 and market price 150, the PER comes out at 13.9; it should be noted that 7.2 multiplied by 13.9 equals 100.) In effect the PER represents the number of years' purchase available. Other things being equal, the lower the PER the better the value is for a buyer and the worse for a seller.

923   The market price of a share can also be regarded as the present value of its future earnings stream in perpetuity, whether these earnings are constant or not. To illustrate, consider three alternative scenarios, each involving an initial market price of 1000, a "return" to investors of 15 per cent per annum, a steady growth rate and the same PER each year:

(a)   Constant earnings of 150 per year (15 per cent of 1000)—a PER of 6.67.

(b)   Earnings in the first year of 100 instead of 150, but increasing at 5 per cent per annum—a PER of 10. The market price grows similarly at 5 per cent per annum, so that at the end of the first year it is 1050. The investor still gets 150, as in (a), but this time in the form of 100 earnings and 50 capital growth.

(c)   Earnings in the first year of 50 instead of 150, but increasing at 10 per cent per annum—a PER of 20. The market price grows similarly at 10 per cent per annum, so that at the end of the first year it is 1100. The investor still gets 150, as in (a) and (b), but this time in the form of 50 earnings and 100 capital growth.

Thus price earnings ratios of 6.67, 10 or 20 (and other figures) can all represent the identical 15 per cent return on different growth assumptions.

924   Average price earnings ratios (weighted by market capitalisation) are also published for the market as a whole. These can be used to assess its overall level in an endeavour to see whether shares in general are overpriced or the reverse. In times of boom the average price earnings ratio might be around 20, against about 10 in times when a more conservative view is taken. This yardstick can also be used to compare the Australian market with its overseas counterparts, but it is necessary to bear in mind that the bookkeeping conventions

for striking profit results are not uniform throughout the world. Japanese companies, for example, do not publish consolidated accounts.

925 Although price earnings ratios are regarded as modern and are frequently quoted in newspaper listings and in brokers' circulars and the like, this alternative approach is for many purposes not as useful as the less popular earnings yield. The latter can be more readily compared directly:

- with other yields, such as those obtainable on fixed interest paper

- with interest rates generally, including especially the cost to the investor of using borrowed money

- with the dividend yield on the shares being considered and on other shares.

Dividends

926 Some of the earnings available for a company's ordinary shares in respect of any year are usually distributed in the form of dividends. The rest are "ploughed back", in other words retained in the business.

927 Dividing the total earnings (net of any preference dividends) by the total ordinary dividend payout for the year (interim plus final distributions) gives the "dividend cover"—a yardstick which gives a rough indication as to how secure the continuation of the rate of dividend might be.

928 Dividing the dividend payout by the earnings gives the "payout ratio", the reciprocal of the dividend cover. In the past typical payout ratios have been in the 40 to 60 per cent range. However, both the popularity of dividend reinvestment plans (which give the companies readily-raised additional share capital) and recent tax changes (the imposition of capital gains tax and the introduction of imputation) have started to alter the traditional pattern and higher payout ratios are likely to become more common in the future.

929 Dividend rates are best expressed in cents per share (often referred to as "dps"), although some companies persist in quoting them as a percentage of the face value—which is confusing and unhelpful.

930   The "dividend yield" is obtained by dividing this *dps* figure (in cents per share) by the market price of the share (also expressed in cents). However, dividing a historical dividend figure by a current market price can be misleading—the remarks relating to earnings in para. 921 apply also to dividends. As explained in para. 905, the apparent annual return from ordinary shares as measured by the dividend yield is not at all comparable with the return from fixed interest investments, as the true return from shares includes the capital growth element.

931   An average dividend yield figure for the market as a whole (again weighted by market capitalisation) is also published. This can be used in the way described in para. 924. In times of boom dividend yields might fall to as low as about 2 per cent, but levels of 4 to 6 per cent would be regarded as more typical over long periods.

932   In making international comparisons it should be remembered that payout ratio patterns also differ from country to country—many prosperous United States companies, for instance, as a matter of policy never pay a dividend at all, preferring to retain all profits for expansion purposes. American investors appear to be much more sophisticated than Australian investors and accept this quite readily, although presumably investors in need of a cash flow make other arrangements.

933   The important tax concept of "franked" and "unfranked" dividends is discussed in paras 2833 to 2846. Dividend declarations need to indicate the "franking ratio", in other words the proportion of the distribution which is franked and therefore associated with an imputation credit. The important theoretical considerations which flow from the imputation system and the concept of "grossing up" are discussed in detail in Chapter 35.

934   Price earnings ratios and dividend yields for individual companies and specific industries also provide useful yardsticks for investors studying the prospectuses of companies which are seeking listing for the first time and for shareholders wishing to judge the generosity or otherwise of takeover bids.

935   The dividend cover referred to above can also be obtained by dividing the earnings yield by the dividend yield.

Ratios for Fixed Interest Securities

936 In the case of an ordinary share the net tangible asset backing is a measure of its worth, because collectively all the ordinary shares represent the residual value of the company after all prior charges have been satisfied. It is also possible to calculate a net tangible asset backing figure for loan securities and preference shares, but for these the meaning is quite different—it is a measure of the extent by which the assets can fall before the redemption or maturity value starts being eroded.

937 For secured loans the asset backing (best expressed in dollars per $100 maturity value) is obtained by dividing the total tangible assets by the total of the secured loans. A typical industrial company trust deed limitation restricting secured obligations to 40 per cent of total tangible assets thus implies an asset backing figure in excess of $250 per $100.

938 For unsecured loans the asset backing (again best expressed in dollars per $100 maturity value) is obtained by dividing the total tangible assets by the total of *both* the secured and the unsecured loans. *It is, of course, not correct to use the technique employed for ordinary shares and divide the assets net of prior charges by the total of the unsecured loans by themselves.* A typical industrial company trust deed limitation restricting total liabilities to 60 per cent of total tangible assets or 1.5 times shareholders' funds thus implies an asset backing figure in excess of about $167 per $100.

939 The asset backing for preference shares can be calculated in a similar fashion. If all preference shares rank equally, then the asset backing per share is the total shareholders' funds divided by the number of preference shares on issue. As shares are involved this time the backing is normally expressed in cents per share.

940 Another useful measure is the "interest cover" figure, which shows how far the company's profits can fall before the annual interest burden cannot be met. As interest is a tax deduction the company's gross earnings must be used for this purpose and naturally the earnings before the deduction of the interest are the relevant ones.

941 For secured loans the interest cover is the ratio (for example, 3.21 times) obtained by dividing EBIT (earnings before inter-

est and tax) by the annual interest commitment on these secured loans. (A less conservative—and therefore less desirable—approach is to place greater emphasis on cash flow and therefore to use earnings before interest, tax and depreciation.)

942　For unsecured loans the interest cover is the ratio obtained by dividing EBIT by the annual interest commitment on *both* secured and unsecured loans.

943　For preference shares the dividend cover is calculated by dividing the profit after tax by the annual preference dividend commitment.

944　The method described above compares the gross earnings before deducting interest with that interest. However, interest is not the only or necessarily even the most important fixed charge. Conceptually, a comparison of earnings before deducting interest, rent, wages, etc., with the total of that interest, rent, wages, etc., might be more appropriate.

Gearing

945　The shareholders' funds divided by the total assets, with the result usually expressed as a percentage, is called the "proprietary ratio". It is a measure of the how safe the company is—the greater the proportion of the total value of the company represented by the shareholders' equity the less the likelihood of creditors ever being able to institute receivership or liquidation proceedings.

946　However, as explained in paras 331 to 333, in times of prosperity the use of other peoples' money (provided the interest rate is lower than the return achieved on the funds employed) can considerably increase the yield on shareholders' funds and from that point of view the lower the proprietary ratio the better. There is obviously no "ideal" ratio—investors must do a trade off between risk and reward. The process of using outside funds to supplement the proprietors' money in this way is called *gearing* or *leverage*.

947　There are several other ways of looking at the same scenario, including the following:

- the *gearing ratio* (also known as the *debt to equity ratio*), obtained by dividing the total outside liabilities by the shareholders' funds

- the ratio which is obtained by dividing the total outside liabilities by the total tangible assets

- the ratio which is obtained by dividing the interest-bearing debt by the sum of that debt and the shareholders' funds.

Working Capital

948 The excess of a company's current assets over its current liabilities, called its "working capital", is one measure of a company's financial soundness. (As explained in paras 807 to 808, the word "current" in the context of balance sheets means cash or items which in the ordinary course of business would be consumed or turned into cash within 12 months.)

949 The current assets divided by the current liabilities gives the "working capital ratio", also called the "current ratio".

950 A variation of this theme is the "quick ratio", also known as the "quick assets ratio" or the "liquid assets ratio", obtained by dividing the sum of cash, debtors and those securities which are readily convertible into cash by the current liabilities. The quick ratio differs from the working capital ratio in that it disregards stock. If the quick ratio is too high, then this indicates idle funds which could be better employed; if it is too low, then this gives a warning sign as to a potentially dangerous situation.

Turnover

951 The "turnover" or "revenue from operations" (often referred to as "operating revenue" or just "revenue" or described more loosely as "sales") is the total amount receivable by a company in the ordinary course of its business for goods and services supplied by it during a financial year, excluding any inter—group transactions. (Deducting all expenses including the net increase in the provisions from this figure gives the profit.) The attention paid to sales figures is often overdone, as exemplified by the aphorism "turnover is vanity, profits are sanity".

952 The ratio of EBIT to total assets was mentioned in para. 917. For analytical purposes this can usefully be dissected into two components or factors, namely, EBIT as a percentage of turnover (the "profit margin") and turnover as a proportion of

total assets. (The two components multiplied together give the original ratio.) Both factors measure different aspects of efficiency; the second factor can also give an indication of the likely future capital requirements if physical expansion and/or inflation is expected.

953   Turnover figures for conglomerate companies need to be broken down into components for different divisions or industries. This is known as "segment reporting".

954   Another measure of efficiency is obtainable from the ratio of stock on hand to turnover. This indicates how long on average the company took to make a sale.

955   A yardstick of a different type is given by the turnover per employee and/or per dollar of wages.

956   Ratios such as those mentioned in the two previous paragraphs do not mean much in isolation, but an examination of the trend over time and comparisons between a company and its competitors can give a useful insight.

Employee Ratios

957   In the same vein one can calculate ratios of profits, assets and shareholders' funds per employee and/or per dollar of wages.

958   The ratio of fixed assets per employee is another interesting yardstick. It shows the degree of capital intensiveness and thus indicates the company's potential exposure to wage escalation and labour shortages.

Adjustments for Convertible Securities and Options

959   The NTA and interest cover figures for fixed interest securities which are convertible into ordinary shares before these securities are actually converted can be calculated in the same way as for unconvertible securities. But allowance for the existence of such securities must also be made whenever ratios such as the NTA or the earnings rate are calculated in respect of the existing ordinary shares. This is so regardless of whether the conversion is imminent or some years away.

960   For this purpose it is best to establish the figures on the two alternative assumptions of "full conversion" and "nil conversion". It is necessary to add back to the net profit the annual interest commitment, net of tax, in the case of calculations using earnings figures for the first assumption. Whichever

approach gives the *lower* values is then adopted. After all, noteholders are likely to convert rather than to redeem when it is to their advantage to do so. As a *zero sum game* is involved here, this means that they will convert when that is to the disadvantage of the remaining equity stakeholders.

961 Similar principles apply in the case of options. However, here the arithmetic must allow for the new funds, or for the after—tax earnings on those new funds, as the case may be, as well as for the increased number of shares on issue.

Other Ratios

962 The ratios and statistics discussed above are, of course, not the only ones which can be extracted. Other figures used by security analysts and commentators include the following:

- Market capitalisation—the market price per share multiplied by the number of shares on issue. Other things being equal, large companies can borrow at lower interest rates than small companies and they can compete better internationally. Their shares are also more marketable. They are thus more acceptable to institutions and to overseas investors.

- Cash flow—the company's net profit plus all the non-cash items taken into account in striking that profit, especially the amount charged for depreciation. A "price/cash flow" ratio corresponding to the PER can also be derived.

- The ratio of fixed assets to shareholders' funds. A ratio greater than one would give comfort in times of high inflation, but would also indicate that temporary creditors are financing part of the company's permanent assets structure.

- The ratio of short-term loans (net of cash on deposit) to total loans. This shows the degree of vulnerability to credit squeezes and can indicate the likelihood of imminent equity raisings.

- Growth rates for sales, earnings, earnings per share, NTA per share, etc. These may need adjustment for capital raisings, etc. (see Chapter 7),

but, subject to that, can be compared with the
rate of inflation to see whether the company is
genuinely improving its performance.

General Comments

963 The above comments represent a deliberately oversimplified
exposition of a complicated subject. In practice various adjustments beyond those already mentioned may be required.

964 In particular, the use of "end of year" figures is not appropriate
where a company has issued shares or made other capital
changes during the course of the year. Suitable adjustments for
bonus issues, share splits or consolidations, cash issues, capital
returns or shares issued as consideration for assets need to be
made. This process is illustrated in Appendix 7.

965 For some purposes regard can be had to the weighted average
number of shares on issue or to the weighted number of dollars
of shareholders' funds.

966 Companies with significant investments in associated companies (shareholdings of more than 20 per cent of the investee
company's capital, especially with some influence over its
board) also need special consideration. For some purposes
"equity accounting" figures are more meaningful than the
conventional accounts. The former allow for the actual proportional share of earnings rather than just dividends and
similarly for the actual proportional share of assets rather than
the cost or the book value on some other basis of the investment
in the associate. Equity accounting figures are normally included in the annual reports of companies where they are
relevant.

967 Generally speaking, Australian companies are not allowed to
own shares in themselves. The United States practice of a
company owning what is there called "treasury stock" is illegal
in this country. However, a company can finish up in that
position as the result of taking over another company which
already owns a parcel of such shares. The legislation gives
companies 12 months to rectify the position by disposing of
the shares and/or by cancelling them. In the meantime, "net"
figures should be used for all analytical purposes—the total
assets and the shareholders' funds should be reduced by the
book value of the shares concerned and the total number of

shares on issue should be reduced by the number of shares in the parcel.

968 It must be remembered that security analysis is an art as well as a science. Furthermore, accounting standards are often arbitrary. There is usually no single "correct answer" to a question involving value judgement. Different analysts may well choose to use different approaches, to make different adjustments, and to interpret data differently. Some of the views set out in this chapter are possibly controversial. However, this diversity of ideas helps to make an interesting market.

Misleading Figures

969 Companies often seek to highlight statistics which, while technically accurate, give incorrect impressions. For example, earnings per share can be up—while the earnings rate on shareholders' funds can be down. Again, a company's total earnings can be up after a takeover, but earnings per share for the original shareholders can be down.

970 A company can claim that its current year sales are "up on the budget". This is clearly meaningless, as the budget could have been set at any figure at all.

971 Again, a statement that sales are running at 98 per cent of some target may sound not too bad. However, for a company with a 2 per cent profit margin, if the company does not manage to reduce its expenses, then such an outcome would completely wipe out the profit. In such circumstances a statement that sales are 96 per cent on target could be even more misleading—as this would be sufficient to turn a given profit into a similarly-sized loss.

Goodwill

972 A compulsory Accounting Standard (ASRB 1013), entitled "Accounting for Goodwill", applies to companies for financial years ending on or after 19 June 1988. Companies purchasing assets which fall within the general scope of this standard are expected to write goodwill off out of their profits after tax over a 20-year maximum period.

973 As a result, companies in their balance sheets are forced to set out some meaningless figures and their published profit or loss

figures can be positively misleading. Investors need to make their own adjustments in order to overcome this statutory piece of nonsense. Shareholders who take a company's reports at face value may well be induced to let their shares go too cheaply.

974 As mentioned in para. 812, valuing assets is often an art rather than a science. The value of a company in a fire sale is likely to be much less than its value on a leisurely voluntary winding-up. Its value as a going concern will be different again.

975 However, writing one particular asset off over an arbitrary 20 years and regardless of the circumstances, especially when its commercial value and income-producing ability may easily then be considerably greater than before, must produce results which are neither fish nor flesh nor good red herring. It would be far better for balance sheet purposes to have regard to net tangible assets only and to write intangibles off "below the line" immediately on purchase.

976 The published profit would then represent the true accretion of wealth during the year, and at least results would be consistent from company to company and comparable from year to year.

977 Writing off intangible assets is very different from depreciating most tangible assets over their working lifetime. While the precise period for such an asset to lose its value completely and the pace at which this happens may both require a value judgement, at least any estimates made in practice tend to be of the right order of magnitude in the aggregate. Writing off goodwill over 20 years is not approximately right—it is 100 per cent wrong.

978 One possible side effect arising from this strange accounting standard should also be mentioned. It tends to discourage economic growth as companies become reluctant to make expansion moves because of its existence and enforcement.

Stock Exchange Indices

979 Nearly 100 different Australian Stock Exchange Share Price Indices are now being produced. Some cover shares in specific industries-metals, oil and gas, insurance, retail, media, and so on. Others cover combinations of these—All Resources, All

Industrials, All Ordinaries. Further indices cover the 50 Leaders, the 20 Leaders, and so on.

980 In each case the index number represents the market capitalisation of all the shares concerned, expressed as a number relative to a base number (500.0 as at 31 December 1979). Thus if an index is 1500.0 on a particular day and the shares concerned in total go up 1 per cent in value (after adjustment for any capital raised or repaid) then the index will be up 15 points at 1515.0. Indices thus give a quick picture of the weighted average price movements in the market as a whole (in the case of the All Ordinaries) or in a particular sector of the market (in the case of the remaining indices). The *percentage movement* up or down—rather than the precise number of points—gives the message. While such indices have some conceptual limitations they can be used as yardsticks by which the performance of a particular portfolio can be measured objectively. Movements in indices can also be used to make comparisons between Australian and international markets.

981 The best-known overseas index is probably the *Dow Jones Industrial Average* (DJIA), which is often used as a proxy for the United States equity market—although it is actually not as broadly based as the All Ordinaries in this country. The Dow covers only 30 stocks and its construction (based on an unweighted average of the individual share prices rather than the market capitalisation of the companies concerned) leaves a lot to be desired. The effect of this approach is that:

- the stocks with higher prices move the index more (up or down) than the stocks with lower prices

- if one of the thirty stocks is split (a relatively common event for US stocks which go up in price) then subsequently that particular stock moves the index less than it would have in the absence of that share split.

Appendix 1 features figures which compare the performance of the All Ordinaries and the Dow Jones indices in recent times. The fact that in the last 11 years (which include the October 1987 crash) the Dow has increased 4.17 times (in US currency terms) while the All Ordinaries has increased a mere

1.78 times (in Australian currency terms) goes a long way to explaining why so many commentators feel that the local market is not overheated by world standards.

982 The All Ordinaries Index is also used for the SPI Futures Contract described in paras 2329 to 2340.

983 In compiling these indices brokerage and stamp duty are ignored. No adjustments are made for either the sudden price drops as particular shares go ex dividend or the gradual build-up of prices between successive dividend distributions. The number of companies actually included in the All Ordinaries Index is only about 300 of the total 1200 listed companies, but it is fairly representative of the whole market because the companies included are chosen from time to time on the basis of their size (market capitalisation) and liquidity.

984 Corresponding to each of the above-mentioned straight indices is an "Accumulation Index". This measures share price movements in a similar fashion as before, but on the assumption that all dividends are reinvested back into the underlying security. For this purpose the incidence of income tax and the effect of the imputation system are both ignored. This index can be used to judge the performance of funds which do not make income distributions, but the comparison will, of course, not be valid except in the case of tax-free funds. It will, however, be much fairer than using a non-accumulation index.

985 The base of the Accumulation Indices was 1000.0 as at 31 December 1979. The actual base and the actual numbers from time to time again do not matter, as in the case of all index numbers only the *relationship* between the numbers at different times has any significance.

Arbitrage

986 The word "arbitrage" is used in relation to many commodity markets, including those dealing in shares, bonds, currencies, metals, and so on. It refers to the purchase of an asset in one market and the simultaneous sale of an equivalent asset at a higher price, usually in a different market. Ideally, this produces a risk-free profit for the arbitrageur ("pure arbitrage"). The term "arbitrage" is also used more loosely in situations which only approximate to this ideal, as, for example, when the two legs of the transaction are not quite simultaneous or

when the two lots of assets are not quite identical—circumstances in which the arbitrageur is then exposed to some minor risk. Arbitrage activity is useful in that it helps to smooth out anomalies between different markets.

987   To illustrate, investors or speculators could arbitrage between:

- Shares of a company traded on the Australian Stock Exchange and the same shares traded on the New Zealand Stock Exchange.

- Shares in the offeree company in a takeover which involves a share exchange and shares in the offeror company.

- Options and the underlying shares.

- Futures contracts and the corresponding physical assets.

988   While any investor at all who notices a market anomaly is free to engage in arbitrage activity, transaction costs in many instances are so high that only brokers who do not incur these outgoings are able to arbitrage effectively.

989   Brokers can also use short selling in order to arbitrage between Australian and overseas markets (see paras 1685 to 1698).

Options

990   An option has a market value which is determined by supply and demand, in the same way as for other securities. But it is also possible to calculate a number of alternative theoretical values for an option which have regard to the value of the underlying security and to the special features of the option which are particularly attractive to investors.

991   On such an approach, the theoretical value would reflect:

- the current market price of the underlying the security

- the exercise price (as a negative item)

- the "time value" of the option, this being an allowance for:

  - the fact that some of the money is not needed by a purchaser until the exercise price has to be paid

  - the "leverage" aspects discussed in para. 480

- the possibility of earning relatively high interest rather than relatively low dividends in the meantime(allowing for tax)
- the fact that the option does not have to be exercised at all and that potential losses thus have a relatively low and known upper value.

If the exercise basis is other than one for one, then the calculations need to reflect this. See also Chapter 22 for further explanations.

Convertible Notes

992   Similarly, a convertible note also has a market value which is determined by supply and demand. Again, it is possible to calculate a number of alternative theoretical values for a note which have regard to the value of the underlying security and to the special features of the note which are attractive to some investors.

993   On such an approach, the theoretical value would reflect:

- the current market price of the underlying the security

- the interest to be earned on the notes, less the dividends which would be received on the shares, allowing for tax including (in the case of companies paying franked dividends) the franking rebate

- an allowance for the fact that the notes can be redeemed at the instance of the investor rather than converted, and that this gives some protection against falling share values.

If the conversion ratio is other than one for one, then once again the calculations need to reflect this.

Chapter 10-Factors Affecting the Market Price of Shares

All you need is to look over the earnings forecasts publicly made a year ago to see how much care you need to give to those being made now for next year
—Gerald Koeb

Background

1001 For ease of exposition this chapter lists under about 25 different subheadings some of the identifiable factors which in combination can influence the market price of a share. Of course, many of these factors are interrelated—higher earnings by a company may lead to higher dividend distributions and/or to a higher net tangible asset backing per share; these in turn may lead to an improved perception of the company by investors; and so on.

1002 Some factors, such as those just mentioned, are peculiar to a specific company. Others, such as those discussed in paras 1004 to 1013, because they impact on companies in general and/or on investors at large, are likely to affect the market as a whole. Ratios based on a particular company's accounts should generally not be looked at in isolation—for example, they may need to be compared with the corresponding ratios for other companies or with the average ratios for all companies in the same industry or with ratios for the company concerned in prior years.

1003 The list does not purport to be exhaustive. It should also be remembered that the market is frequently not logical and that market sentiment can change without an obvious rationale. In reality there is only one single factor governing the price of a share, namely, the degree of supply and demand for it at the time.

Economic Factors

1004 The many economic, political and "natural phenomenon" factors of relevance to the prospects of companies and the market for their shares, in no particular order, include the following:

- interest rates
- inflation
- taxes
- tariffs
- subsidies
- she availability of credit
- unemployment

- budget deficits or surpluses
- budget speculation
- election speculation
- war and peace rumours
- commodity prices
- exchange rates
- exchange controls
- droughts, floods, cyclones and earthquakes
- industrial disputes
- wage rates
- technological advances
- monetary controls
- the balance of payments.

Developments both in Australia and overseas have their influence. Nowadays the world is really a single big market both for business enterprises and for stock exchange transactions. Value judgements and perceptions about factors such as the above get built into the market price of all shares—so that a set of positive factors for a particular company does not automatically mean that its shares are a bargain buy, or vice versa.

Interest Rate Levels

1005 High domestic interest rate levels, for example, affect companies directly, because such rates increase the cost of servicing the borrowed funds used in the business—cost increases which cannot always be passed on to customers. High interest rates also affect companies indirectly, because high rates slow down the economy—other businesses will postpone or abandon expansion plans for ventures no longer regarded as economic; housing starts will slow down, as less people will be able to afford home purchase mortgages; consumer spending will also go down, as people need to devote a larger proportion of household disposable incomes to servicing any credit already extended to them; bad debts will increase; and so on.

All these factors in turn will have multiplier effects—for example, if domestic consumers buy less, then manufacturers will have less call on them and transport groups will have less goods to carry; if less new houses are constructed then there will be less need for refrigerators, carpets, taps, and so on; if all this leads to fewer jobs and to less overtime then there will be less retail spending; and so it goes on.

1006 Increases in interest rates in Australia which are not matched overseas will affect the exchange rate by attracting funds into the country for both portfolio and direct investments and by thus pushing up the value of the Australian dollar. This is good for importers, but bad for farmers, miners and other exporters and for those local manufacturers who are subject to import competition.

1007 High interest rates also affect investors directly. If yields obtainable on new fixed interest paper rise then investors will switch out of the lower-yielding existing paper until its price falls sufficiently to bring its yield into line. Similarly, the prices of ordinary shares will fall, as investors switch out of low-yielding shares into high-yielding fixed interest securities.

Prices of investments will also fall as the demand from investors who are using borrowed funds falls in the light of the reduced opportunities to make a profit from gearing of this type once the cost of borrowing money has become more onerous. Offsetting this in a small way will be a tendency at the margin for the supply of investment funds to increase if persons are induced by the attractive rates being offered to save rather than to consume.

1008 Low interest rates work in reverse. It will be seen, therefore, that interest rate movements are one of the more significant economic factors affecting share prices. However, the above brief discussion glossed over other aspects—such as the differences between short-term and long-term interest rates (which do not always move to the same extent or even in the same direction) and the fact that markets are always forward-looking—more concerned with expectations of future interest rate trends than with the precise levels prevailing at the time.

Inflation

1009 Inflation has already been analysed in Chapter 3. It affects company profitability adversely because it increases the cost of labour and materials. The need to increase prices for goods and services may slow down sales. An inability to increase prices because of market conditions may cause losses. Working in the opposite direction is the fact that inflation allows profits to be made from the use of borrowed funds.

1010 Labour-intensive companies are more likely to be hurt by high inflation than capital—intensive companies (that is, those with a high level of assets per employee).

1011 Inflation also affects investors. In particular, when choosing between different categories of investment, investors should have regard to the respective expected real "after tax" returns from each. To the extent that investors do this, any changes in inflationary expectations will thus feed into share prices.

Taxation

1012 Taxation is discussed in great detail in Chapter 28. Changes in the rules under which companies are taxed or in their rates of tax will affect not only their net profitability but also, understandably enough, the way in which companies behave.

1013 Changes in the rules under which different categories of investor are taxed or in their respective rates of tax will affect their choice of investments. Thus announcements or even rumours of changes will impact on share prices.

Hypothetical Share Prices

1014 Generally speaking, investors want to buy shares at prices below their "true value", because that way the chance of a fall is less and the opportunity for making a capital gain is enhanced. Gains can come about both if the share price rises towards to its "true value" and as the "true value" itself rises. In the meantime a share acquired at below its "true value" would show a higher annual return than if it had been acquired at its "true value".

1015 As between the shares of different companies, clearly the ones available at the highest proportionate discount to the corresponding "true values" would constitute the greatest bargains, the best "value for money". Subject to other important criteria, such as the desirability for spread and possibly for ready marketability in a hurry, any "shopping list" for shares should obviously give priority to such relatively cheap stocks.

1016 In the same way, investors want to sell shares at prices which happen to be above their "true value", because that way the chance of incurring a fall is reduced, and because the proceeds from the sale can be reinvested in something else with better prospects. If a great number of shares are selling at prices well above their "true values", then this indicates an overheated market. It represents a good time to get out and to stay liquid.

1017 In practice selling decisions are harder to make than buying decisions, because capital gains tax needs to be taken into account (see Chapter 29). Furthermore, in the case of proposed switches the sale price *net of two lots of transaction costs* needs to be used—and that might considerably alter the picture.

1018 The exercise then is to find the hypothetical "true value" which was postulated for the purpose of the above analysis. Of course, there is no such thing as a single "true value" if one means by that phrase a value determined objectively in the abstract, as distinct from a "market value" as established in an arm's length transaction between "a knowledgeable willing buyer and a knowledgeable willing but not anxious seller". It is, however, possible to make value judgements as to the "true value" of a share. The fact that different analysts reach different conclusions from the same set of facts is, of course, one factor enabling the market to function.

1019 The most useful approach to estimating the "true value" of a share is to apply an appropriate price earnings ratio to an appropriate earnings per share figure (or to divide the latter by an appropriate earnings yield, a result which arithmetically is the same). This method is further discussed in paras 1022 to 1031.

1020 Another, but less useful, approach to estimating the "true value" of a share is to divide the (adjusted) dividends per share figure by an appropriate dividend yield. This method is further discussed in paras 1032 to 1038. The reason that it is less useful than the approach based on earnings referred to above is that ordinary shareholders have an equity (or stake) in all earnings, whether these are being distributed or not. Furthermore, the payout ratio depends on an arbitrary decision by the directors of the company.

1021 A third approach to estimating the "true value" of a share, but one less useful again (see para. 910), is take the net tangible asset backing per share figure. This method is further discussed in paras 1039 to 1043.

Earnings

1022 Some theoretical aspects of earnings were discussed in paras 915 to 925.

1023 A suitable price earnings ratio for some companies can be obtained by looking at the ratios applying to the shares of their competitors and to the shares of other comparable companies. The warnings set out in para. 921 should, however, be borne in mind. Adjustments based on other aspects can then be made if felt appropriate—for example, to allow for a particularly high or low gearing ratio, or to take cognizance of announced expansion plans.

1024 To obtain a hypothetical market value for a share this price earnings ratio is then multiplied by the prospective earnings per share figure for the current year (or for some other year in the near future, possibly with some allowance for the delay).

1025 The prospective earnings per share figure for the current year for the purpose of this arithmetic can be one contained in company announcements. However, it is preferable for the analyst himself to make his own estimates, having regard to the trend of actual figures from the recent past, adjusted as thought appropriate for known or suspected changes in the pattern of the company's activities, for trends in the industries in which the company operates, and for any changes in the tax regime and in the economy generally. It may be necessary to make separate forecasts in relation to:

- the size of the market in a company's goods or services
- the company's share of that market
- the profit margin achievable on such a share.

The specific result for the first half or any other portion of the current year, if known, should, of course, also be taken into account.

1026 The performance of competitors may give some indication of how well a company is likely to be doing, although such information has to be interpreted with caution. For example, if one company in a particular industry is doing well, is that because conditions are good all round or because that company is managing to capture market share from its rivals and its success is thus being achieved at their expense?

1027 The bookkeeping treatment adopted by a company will also affect its published results. For example, is the profit on the sale of a major asset a one-off capital gain which should properly be reported "below the line" as an extraordinary item, or is it part of the recurring profit generation of the company, a transaction in the ordinary course of business which should be reported "above the line" as an item of normal operating profit?

1028 Again, how should work in progress be valued? If a contract lasts three years, should credit for all the profit be taken in the last year, when the work is complete? Or in the first year, when the sale was achieved? Or should some credit be taken in each of the three years?

1029 How realistic are the various provisions in the balance sheet? For example, is the provision for doubtful debts either too large or too small? Setting up a provision or writing down an asset reduces the profit of the year concerned. (See also para. 813 and paras 972 to 978.)

1030 Analysts may also wish to make appropriate adjustments when companies acquire or dispose of major assets or subsidiary companies or when the status of companies in which they hold interests changes from "associate" (50 per cent or less owned and thus not consolidated) to subsidiary (more than 50 per cent owned and thus consolidated) or vice versa. Sometimes only a single share needs to change hands in order to alter the status of a company in this way and such a transaction can be deliberately engineered in order to allow consolidation or deconsolidation to take place.

1031 Where a company has been paying a zero or low rate of tax for a specific non-recurring reason, such as the utilisation of past tax losses, the earnings figures for forecasting purposes should be adjusted to reflect the normal rate of tax expected to be applicable in due course.

Dividends

1032 Some theoretical aspects of dividends were discussed in paras 926 to 935.

1033 A suitable dividend yield for some companies can be obtained by looking at the yields applying to the shares of their competitors and to the shares of other comparable companies. The warnings set out in para. 921 should, however, again be borne in mind. Furthermore, regard should be had to the franking status of the dividends (see paras 2833 to 2846). The dividend yields from companies paying fully franked dividends are not really comparable with the dividend yields from companies paying unfranked dividends, an aspect expanded on in Chapter 35.

1034 To obtain a hypothetical market value for a share this yield is then divided into the prospective dividend per share figure for the current year (or for some other year in the near future, possibly with some allowance for the delay).

1035 The prospective dividend per share figure for the current year for the purpose of this arithmetic would be based on the rate for the previous year, subject to any later information provided by the company. Companies making new issues are expected to indicate the likely new dividend rate in future.

1036 Most companies pay two dividends each year—an interim dividend based on the results of the first six months, and a final dividend which takes into account both the outcome of the full year and the interim dividend already paid. If the rate of interim dividend has varied from the corresponding rate a year earlier than a similar change to the final dividend can also—subject to any other indication from the company—be expected. (For example: Last Year: 4 cents interim, 8 cents final, 12 cents total. This Year: 5 cents interim; thus the likely final dividend will be 9 or 10 cents.) Sometimes companies label a dividend, or portion of a dividend, as "special"—the implication being that it is a one-off declaration.

1037 Another approach is to estimate the likely earnings per share figure and to apply the company's traditional payout ratio to that.

1038 Investors sometimes need to choose between shares in two companies with different earnings and dividend yield relationships—for example, other things being equal, is a dividend yield of 10 per cent (from a company with an earnings yield of 15 per cent) really more attractive than a dividend yield of 5 per cent (from a company with an earnings yield of 20 per cent)? Clearly, the latter share provides considerably less immediate income per dollar invested but it has more scope for higher dividends in the future and for a higher growth rate (because of the additional retained profits) in the meantime. The latter company is also of much greater appeal to takeover bidders, as these would naturally on completion of an offer obtain access to the entire stream of earnings.

Net Tangible Assets

1039 The valuation of company assets in general was discussed in paras 806 to 817 and in paras 972 to 978. Some theoretical aspects of the net tangible asset backing per share figure were discussed in paras 909 to 914.

1040 To obtain a hypothetical market value for a share its NTA figure can be used as it stands. Alternatively, this figure can be multiplied by the ratio of market value to NTA for other comparable companies or for the company itself at some other point of time regarded as more typical.

1041 The shares of companies in some industries traditionally trade at prices well above the NTA backing—in other words, the market price reflects a large "goodwill" component. This is not necessarily bad if the earnings performance of the company concerned justifies its share price, but such a relationship must be regarded as a warning signal.

1042 Correspondingly, the shares of companies in some industries traditionally trade at prices well below the NTA backing. Any new money raised by such companies tends to suffer a similar erosion.

1043 The NTA figure is not particularly relevant to the share price of most companies because it cannot be made available to the shareholders. However, it does become important in the following circumstances:

- If liquidation is likely.

- If a substantial return of capital is envisaged.

- If a takeover offer is expected or has actually been made (see Chapter 11). The value of tax losses (an intangible asset—see para. 911) can be relevant in takeover situations (but see also para. 2896).

Rights and Bonus Issues

1044 Two other significant factors affecting the market price of a share are its past pattern of making cash and bonus issues and the actual announcements of such issues. (See, however, para. 781.)

1045 Many investors appear to like a steady stream of rights issues made at a seeming discount to the market price of the existing shares at the time. Actually, this is a piece of nonsense, because the true total value of a company immediately after a new cash issue cannot really be different from its total value immediately before the issue plus the net new funds raised.

1046 It is a fallacy to regard a share ex rights as equal in value to a share cum rights—see para. 715. In this context the effect of a new share issue is neutral, neither good nor bad in itself. However, if the funds are used wisely and to good advantage, then the new issue will have been a good thing for the shareholders in the long run. One of the attractions of investing in ordinary shares is the opportunity for shareholders from time to time to put more money into enterprises which prosper and grow and which thus produce good returns.

1047 There is also a mistaken belief in circulation to the effect that ordinary share issues made at par are somehow better than share issues made at a premium to their face value, and also that share issues made at a deep discount are somehow preferable to share issues made at a slight discount on their market value—see para. 748. The use of the technical word "discount" in this context does not, of course, imply a bargain.

1048 There are at least two reasons for the feeling that new share issues are good in themselves. The first stems from the fact that companies doing well are more likely to expand and thus to need to raise more capital. Companies doing well are also likely to have increasing dividend distributions and earnings rates and therefore (other things being equal) increasing market values. These aspects are thus indeed correlated. But "doing well" is the cause of the new issue, not the other way round. However, companies doing poorly may also need to raise further share capital.

1049 The second reason is that rights trading provides an opportunity for shareholders to raise cash by selling their rights. Some investors foolishly think that just because they still have the same *number* of shares after that sale then they have generated some profit. However, as the shares ex rights are less valuable than the shares cum rights they have in reality sold off some of their capital, in the same manner as if they had sold off some of their holdings in a way unconnected with the new issue.

1050 Actually, cash issues are a two-edged sword. They tend to send share prices up because investors like them and because the dividend yield on the new dollars being invested may be relatively attractive. But they can also depress prices because not all shareholders will wish to put up more money and a considerable volume of selling pressure can thus develop around the time of a new issue or even when its imminence is merely being suspected.

1051 As explained in paras 751 and 754, bonus issues are effectively nothing more than share splits and again their real effect is neutral, neither good nor bad (apart from involving the company and its shareholders in needless administrative expenditure). However, shareholders seem to like bonus issues, again no doubt because of the confusion between cause (the company doing well) and effect (the bonus issue and the expectation of higher dividend distributions in the future).

Quality of the Management

1052 The quality of a company's direction and general management can probably best be judged by its results. However, the market's perception of the board and the management team will have some effect on the price of its shares.

1053 For example, a company which is run by a single individual as both its chairman and its chief executive poses certain dangers, particularly if he was also its founder. The combined office reduces the checks and balances. There are also questions such as:

- What happens if he dies suddenly?

- Has his strong personality allowed a professional team of successors to develop?

- Is his personal shareholding so large that its dispersal could depress the market?

- Is a controlling interest held by his family and might they, for sentimental or other non-commercial reasons, hand over control to a son lacking the skills of his late father?

- What if, instead of dying, the chief executive just gradually becomes senile without realising this and handing over the reins?

1054 Again, the separately listed Australian subsidiary companies of overseas parents may be at a disadvantage compared with purely domestic enterprises. Decisions may be forced on local managements in ignorance of some relevant local factors. Alternatively, decisions may be taken which benefit the group worldwide and which make commercial sense on that basis, but which are taken at the expense of the Australian operation and the minority shareholders in this country.

Offsetting this is the possibility that the overseas parent will one day seek to acquire these minority holdings on attractive terms—although there is a risk in the reverse direction: the parent's large stake may one day be disposed off instead, in a sale which then depresses the market for the stock.

1055 As regards the quality of management generally, some specific danger signs are:

- Splits in the board of directors.

- Frequent or unexplained changes of chief executive.

- Directors sitting on too many other boards.

- A declining market share for the company's main products.

- Falling profit margins (see para. 952).

- A declining earnings rate on the funds employed (see para. 916).

- A failure to revalue assets, thus disguising the company's true performance.

- Inadequate research and development expenditure.

- Excessively generous management contracts.

- Onerous trust deeds.

- Imprudent overexpansion.

- Prolonged or frequent industrial disputes.

- Irrational hostility to mooted takeover bids.

- Poor handling of questions at annual general meetings.

- Leaks to the media designed to affect the market price of the company's shares.

- Prosecutions for breaches of the law.

- Excessive related party transactions.

- The watering of the capital by placements below the market value or the asset backing.

- A failure to keep up with technological change.

- A failure to set up a high quality site on the World Wide Web.

- A failure to deal adequately with the millennium bug.

If the directors own reasonable parcels of shares in the company then there is a greater chance that their interests will parallel those of other shareholders than if they do not. Correspondingly, small parcels demonstrate a lack of faith in the company. However, the absence of large holdings by well-qualified but not necessarily wealthy individual directors should not automatically be held against them.

At the other extreme, a very substantial holding by a super-rich director would not necessarily signify all that much, as even the total loss of his entire investment in the company would probably make little difference to his standard of living. Each director's shareholding is set out in the annual report, subdivided into shares held beneficially (really owned by him) and shares held non-beneficially (registered in his name as a trustee or nominee for someone else).

1056 Investors should be particularly wary of companies making vague official announcements or issuing reports by directors which are full of excuses for poor results, blaming everybody but themselves—for example:

- government action or inaction
- adverse weather conditions
- computer problems
- trade union intransigence
- customers not being loyal
- criticisms by consumer groups
- a failure to get or retain licences
- activity by environmentalists

or even "the advent of unexpected competition"!

Diversification

1057 The extent of diversification instituted by a company's management will also affect its share price. However, as with so many issues of this type, there is no single "right answer" as to the degree of diversification which is best for any particular enterprise.

1058 There are clearly advantages in a company engaging in a spread of different activities, just as there are advantages in investors holding a spread of different stocks. If something goes wrong in any one line of business then this is not the same disaster as if something goes wrong in a company's sole line of business—and the "going wrong" may be due to circumstances beyond the control of the company, such as natural disasters, tax changes or adverse legislation.

1059 Declining market share may be due technological advances, fashion changes, variations in the exchange rate, different attitudes to health or environmental issues, increasing competition from imports, and so on, or from a number of such factors in combination. Expansion into growth situations in other areas can thus be an appropriate solution to difficulties of this sort.

1060 Diversification by product line can help to smooth out seasonal fluctuations—for example, it makes sense for an ice cream manufacturer to enter the hot pies business, and vice versa. Diversification geographically can overcome localised problems and some demographic changes. However, diversification offshore introduces an exposure to exchange rate fluctuations, to political risks and to mistakes stemming from unfamiliarity with local conditions. Earnings and assets when expressed in Australian dollars can move up or down even if unchanged in the local currency.

1061 Separate from that are the advantages flowing from sheer size. This can provide economies of scale, lower distribution costs, lower interest rates on borrowed money, and so on.

1062 The negatives to diversification arise because it is all too easy to devote excessive management effort to a company's less profitable non-core activities or to expand in the mistaken belief that distant fields look greener. The difficulties in a different industry may be greater than those in one's own, but less apparent from the outside. Expanding into other areas if the necessary management resources are not on hand may turn out to be a recipe for disaster. However, appropriately qualified staff can usually be recruited from outside if required.

Types of Industry

1063 The market tends to assess some types of industry less harshly than others. In particular, defensive industries (food, beer, newspapers, etc.) are accorded higher price earnings ratios than cyclical industries (automotive, building and construction, commodities, etc.). Sometimes premiums are accorded to:

- monopolies, because of their ability, within limits, to dictate prices (but they can also become complacent and inefficient)

- very large companies, because their shares are more liquid and because they can borrow more cheaply (but they also have greater difficulty in changing directions)

- very small companies, because their shares have the potential to increase in value by much greater multiples than large companies (but they also have a greater chance of failing).

Trends in the Relevant Industries

1064 Many entrepreneurial companies are involved in more than one industry. Whether the industries in which a company operates are growing or declining will obviously affect the market's perception of the company. For example, many forms of manufacturing are adversely affected by high labour costs and by import competition—quite apart from the special features of, say, the tobacco industry.

1065 Potential weaknesses include:

- Lack of growth potential.

- Past overproduction.

- Excess capacity.

- Inadequate returns on the equipment used.

- Excessive competition.

- Overdependence on tariffs and subsidies.

- Competitors from overseas setting up in Australia regardless of the short-term cost.

1066 On the other hand, some industries will benefit from Australia's ageing population—drugs, medical equipment, spectacles, hearing aids, retirement villages, and so on.

Technical Factors

1067 Sometimes the price of some individual stock is temporarily depressed because a large parcel is known or suspected to be overhanging the market—for example:

- the underwriting residuum following a cash issue

- shares held by the deceased estate of the company's founder

- shares being quit by a major shareholder in order to comply with some statutory requirement

- shares likely to be quit by overseas investors because of problems in their own countries.

1068 Anomalies often arise between two closely related but separately traded securities. Examples include:

- rights and the corresponding shares ex rights

- fully-paid and contributing shares

- "Old" and "new" shares (involving a different dividend entitlement)

- ordinary and deferred shares

- ordinary and converting preference shares

- ordinary shares and convertible notes

- ordinary shares and options

- shares subject to immediate delivery and the corresponding shares on a "deferred delivery" basis

- shares in an offeror corporation and the shares in the offeree corporation for which they can be exchanged (see paras 1107 and 1183).

Such anomalies can be expected to disappear in time when the two separate issues merge. In the meantime arbitrage opportunities may be possible (see paras 986 to 988). Convertible securities with a conversion ratio (see para. 449) other than unity seem to confuse the market.

1069 Anomalies can also arise between:

- ordinary and participating preference shares in the same company

- ordinary shares in two different companies of similar quality, the shares of one of which may be trading at higher earnings and dividend yields than the shares of the other.

Here, of course, the differences may last indefinitely, but at least the scope for price increases may be greater in the one issue rather than in the other. Of course, when two companies are involved the risk is that the market is right and that the anomaly is only an apparent one.

1070 The price of a share should in theory also reflect the amount of accrued dividend, moving up in gradual stages from an "ex dividend" value to a "cum dividend" value and then dropping back by the amount of dividend as soon as the basis of quotation is "ex dividend" again (see paras 459 to 461).

Newness

1071 The market is irrational in its assessment of brand new companies or new ventures by old-established companies. Sometimes the market accords a speculative premium to such shares for the "blue sky" element. The price can go to a level beyond that which seems justifiable on analytical grounds, particularly if investors buy the shares not in order to hold them, but rather with the intention of selling them to an even bigger optimist (or sucker) later on.

1072 At other points of the cycle the market may discount such shares excessively, being highly suspicious of mere newness and preferring to wait until actual results are available—at which time, of course, with much of the risk taken out of the stock, the share price may be many times higher.

Gearing Ratio

1073 As explained in paras 945 to 947, a gearing ratio which is either too high or too low will harm a company and thus adversely affect its share price. The fact that a company has a low gearing ratio and thus good capacity for additional borrowings may make it an attractive takeover target for companies in the reverse situation.

Scarcity Value

1074 Particularly in times of boom the shares of certain popular companies with a small number of shares on issue (or the shares of which are tightly held) are accorded a premium for scarcity. Phrases such as "scrip shortage" are used to describe such a phenomenon. This is probably another of the great myths of the stock exchange. There may be some investors who collect companies in the same way as a philatelist collects postage stamps, but it does not make sense for a serious investor to pay more for the shares of a particular company than they are worth relative to other shares more freely available.

Institutional Preferences

1075 Institutional investors prefer stocks with large turnovers, enabling them to buy and sell meaningful quantities quickly. They also prefer companies with exchange traded options (see paras 2207 to 2214), as these give them the opportunity to make additional profits from the writing of such options. See also paras 647 to 654 for demand distortions caused by the existence of index funds.

Notes:

1. Some institutions use mechanically applied formulae for buying and selling shares—for example, when certain ratios are exceeded on the way up or when yardsticks are breached on the way down.

2. Some institutions have regard to forecasts made by others, not so much for the absolute figures but rather for the trend which a change in such forecasts can reveal.

3. Some institutions use the *top down* equity management style, which begins with an assessment of the overall economic environment and then makes a general asset allocation decision regarding various sectors of the financial markets and various industries. Such institutions select a portfolio of individual securities within the favored sectors. Other institutions do the reverse and use the *bottom up* equity management style, which places less emphasis on the significance of economic and market cycles and focuses instead on the analysis of individual stocks.

Recovery Stocks

1076 Some companies which are making losses or relatively small profits may be regarded by the market as being on the brink of recovery. In that case the shares of such companies may be being purchased with that potential in mind at prices well above those warranted by other considerations.

1077 Companies starting to produce good results after a long period of disappointing figures would, of course, still be regarded with caution until the permanence of the recovery becomes evident.

Rigging the Market

1078 Creating a false or misleading market for any share or artificially rigging its price is a serious criminal offence. In particular, Section 998(3) of the *Corporations Law* reads as follows:

"A person shall not, by means of purchases or sales of any securities that do not involve a change in the beneficial ownership of those securities or by any fictitious transactions or devices, maintain, increase, reduce, or cause fluctuations in, the market price of any eligible securities".

1079 Notwithstanding such provisions, the temptation to drive prices up or down to one's advantage can be very great. The dividing line between genuine market activity and rigging is a thin one and, despite the efforts of the stock exchanges and the authorities, the difficulty of proving rorts beyond reasonable doubt in a court of law is enormous. Professional riggers would obviously cover their tracks quite well. The establishment of separate markets in futures and options in recent years has increased both the opportunity for manipulation and its potential rewards.

1080 Ordinary investors thus have to accept the possibility of share rigging to their detriment as one of the unavoidable risks of equity investment.

Glamour Stocks

1081 From time to time certain industries become fashionable and the shares of certain companies become "glamour stocks" trading at premium prices. However, the market is fickle and fashions change. Recent favourites since dethroned have included high technology stocks and gold stocks.

1082 Another group of companies now no longer popular but once selling at considerable premiums to their asset backings comprised the so-called "cashbox" companies—companies with assets mainly in cash, run by entrepreneurs regarded as skilled in making profitable corporate plays.

Takeover Stocks

1083 Every stock on the list is a potential takeover target (see Chapter 11). Notwithstanding this, some companies are more likely to be taken over than others, for example where the net tangible assets per share figure significantly exceeds the market value.

1084 The presence of holders of large parcels on a company's share register is a two-edged sword. On the one hand, such shareholdings can make the success of a hostile bid at a generous price more difficult, but on the other hand:

- such stakes can become the springboard for a potential bidder who manages to acquire them

- the large shareholders may become bidders themselves

- their bargaining power may result in a higher bid being received.

Insider Trading

1085 Insider trading is another criminal offence which is not easily proved in a prosecution despite being defined in some detail in Section 1002 of the *Corporations Law*. Directors, employees and other persons connected with a company are often by virtue of their office in possession of price—sensitive information which is not publicly available. If they use it in order to buy or sell securities or if they pass the information on to friends or relatives for this purpose then this is likely to be at the expense of the other party to the transaction on the stock exchange (or of the company itself).

The authorities may be able to detect insider trading constituted by the actual placing of buying or selling orders. However, it is also possible for a person who *otherwise* might have bought or sold shares to refrain from doing so because of information learnt as an insider. It would obviously be impossible for the authorities to prosecute such *lack of action*. Of course, inside knowledge of facts in advance and trading on the basis of such information do not in themselves automatically guarantee profits—sometimes markets fall when good news is actually announced or vice versa.

1086 Unusual buying or selling activity ahead of a company announcement is quite common and is in itself not firm evidence of illegal insider trading. It may be based on bona fide analyses by outsiders using published data. It may even be based on guesses and hunches by uninformed speculators. It may also be based on knowledge by people who are in no position of special obligation to the company, such as competitors or even observant delivery personnel. But then again it may also be related to special briefings which company spokesmen have, probably unwisely but in good faith, given to selected stock-brokers or institutions.

1087 Again, such trading is not necessarily always profitable, as when a hunch does not pay off or when a hunch is right but the market reaction to some actual result is not as anticipated.

1088 Chartists plot price and volume movements of shares listed on the stock exchange. They work on the theory that the emergence of certain trading patterns gives useful buying or selling signals to investors and that whether or not these patterns have been caused by insider trading is immaterial to the opportunity to profit from the signals.

Official Documents

1089 Previously unavailable information contained in official documents issued by a company can influence its share price. For example, unexpected good news can result in a price rise—but if there has been over-anticipation in the market then good news announcements can also send prices down.

1090 Some of this material may be stock exchange related—for example: prospectuses, takeover documents, "substantial shareholding" notices, applications for listing on overseas exchanges, and so on. Other material can take the form of papers filed in the course of legal proceedings, submissions to public inquiries, licence applications of various types, publicly-available documents filed with regulatory bodies, and so on.

1091 Again, other material may be less formal than this—speeches by company officials, media releases, television interviews, and so on.

Legislative Changes and Government Intervention

1092 The fact that changes in the taxation laws of the Commonwealth and the States can affect companies for better or worse has already been mentioned. However, many other legislative changes can affect particular industries, as can rulings by courts and regulatory bodies.

1093 Changes in companies and securities legislation and in quasi-legislation such as stock exchange listing requirements and accounting standards can also affect the market.

Changes in the Investor Profile

1094 Share prices over time will also be affected by changes in the
investor profile. For example, the ageing Australian population
may lead to a higher proportion of investors:

- who prefer secure stocks rather than speculative
ones

- who prefer high income to high growth securities

- who prefer fixed interest paper to ordinary shares

and so on. The spectacular expansion of both superannuation
and the pooled investment funds industry at the expense of the
individual investor will also have its effect. Separately from
this "change of party" element, the spectacular overall growth
of superannuation must increase the total demand for investments of all types.

Changes on the Supply Side

1095 The volume of listed ordinary shares on issue in dollar terms
varies from time to time. Such changes can exert upward or
downward pressure on share prices overall. Supply is:

- Increased by cash issues by companies already
listed.

- Increased by new flotations.

- Increased by shares issued under dividend reinvestment and other plans.

- Increased by calls on contributing shares.

- Increased by payments to exercise options.

- Decreased by capital reductions.

- Decreased by buy-backs.

- Decreased by liquidations.

- Decreased by takeovers made for a cash consideration.

Overseas Aspects

1096 Prices on the Australian Stock Exchange are, of course, affected by political, economic and other developments overseas
as well as by happenings in Australia. Major events such as
the Asian economic and banking crisis of 1997 and the forth-

coming introduction of the euro as a single common currency for 11 nations on the other side of the world all have their effect. To some extent Australian share prices are also influenced by movements on overseas stock exchanges, although neither day-to-day fluctuations nor long-term trends in any particular centre are necessarily mirrored all that closely. The effect is partly psychological.

1097 However, foreigners can invest in Australia and local residents can invest offshore. Australian companies can list overseas and vice versa. In that sense the world constitutes a single market, with the Australian Stock Exchange accounting for only about two per cent of the total global trading. Thus a decision by overseas investors to buy or sell local securities can have a relatively very large effect on prices in this country, even if the activity involves only a minor rearrangement of overseas portfolios.

1098 Because of the relative illiquidity of the Australian market the major foreign investors tend to be interested in only the most active of the listed stocks. However, to some degree buying pressure on any one sector of the market, by lowering yields, spills over into all other sectors. The reverse also applies.

General Comments

1099 Markets are made by people. Perceptions can be as important as reality. Investors are more interested in the unknown future than in the known past. They will try to estimate not only how companies will perform but also how other investors will react to this ever-changing scenario. There can thus never be a single "correct" market price for any particular share.

Chapter 11—Takeovers

Money makes a man laugh
—John Selden

Background

1101 A "takeover" occurs when a company—the "offeror" or "bidder"—seeks to acquire a significant parcel of shares in another company—the "offeree" or "target". The bidding company is usually, but not always, larger than the target company.

1102 Frequently ownership of 100 per cent of the shares in the offeree company is sought—a "full takeover". If the offer is successful then the offeree company will become a wholly-owned subsidiary of the offeror company. In effect a merger or amalgamation of the two enterprises will have taken place. If the offer does not succeed in 100 per cent acceptance but the bidder goes ahead anyway then a partly-owned subsidiary may result. Stock exchange listing can continue, subject to a sufficient spread of shareholdings.

1103 On occasions less than 100 per cent of the company is sought, in which case the transaction is described as a "partial takeover". All shareholders will be invited to part with a specific proportion of their holdings.

1104 In either event the takeover offer can be regarded as nothing more than a special case of shares being bought by a willing buyer and sold by willing sellers at a mutually acceptable price.

1105 However, the authorities have seen fit to draw a distinction between an investor buying a few hundred shares and a company seeking to acquire a controlling or other significant interest in another corporation. The dividing line in Australia has arbitrarily been drawn at the level of 20 per cent of the offeree company's voting capital (in the United Kingdom it is 30 per cent). 20 per cent is also the threshold for equity accounting (see para. 823). Shares in excess of this level can be acquired in certain circumstances without the need for a takeover bid—for example, a further 3 per cent of the capital can be legally acquired every six months. Moreover, securities which are not voting shares, such as options and warrants, are not affected by the 20 per cent rule.

1106 The current legislative provisions are set out in Chapter 6 of the *Corporations Law*. These are often referred to as the "takeovers code". This legislation provides a very detailed and somewhat complex set of rules which have to be observed in takeover situations. The main purpose of these rules is to ensure that all shareholders in the offeree company are treated equally and fairly, that they are given sufficient relevant information to enable them to make an intelligent decision as to whether or not to accept any offer and adequate time in which to make a decision or get independent advice.

Some changes to the details of these rules are being contemplated under the Corporate Law Economic Reform Program (CLERP), but these will not affect the basic thrust of the legislation being described here.

1107 The consideration offered in takeover schemes can consist of:

- shares in the bidding company
- cash
- a mixture of both shares and cash.

Some takeovers involve other forms of consideration, such as:

- convertible notes
- fixed interest securities
- options
- some combination of the above

or on rare occasions shares in other companies. Sometimes shareholders are given a choice between several alternative forms. Naturally, shareholders who accept a consideration other than pure cash can make additional gains or losses, depending on the subsequent market movements of the securities concerned.

1108 Investors should always take the possibility that a takeover offer may at some time be received into account when making decisions as to whether to buy, sell or hold shares.

1109 This chapter first of all discusses the subject in general terms and then against that background concludes with advice to shareholders as to their best course of action when a bid is received or mooted. The important capital gains tax aspects of takeovers are discussed separately in Chapter 29.

Mechanics: Part A and Part C Offers

1110 Takeovers can involve either formal offers, often referred to as "Part A Offers", or simple announcements to the effect that the bidder is willing to acquire shares at a specified price on the stock exchange for a period of one month. The latter are known as "Part C Offers". Some takeovers involve both processes concurrently. Under Part A offers the accepting investors usually pay no brokerage or stamp duty.

1111 The offeror company has to send the shareholders of the offeree company full details of the offer and certain other data required by the legislation (the Part A or Part C Statements). The offeree company then has to make available certain further information and its comments on the bid (the Part B or Part D Statements respectively).

1112 Some mergers can also take place using other provisions of the companies legislation, namely, those originally designed to facilitate corporate reconstructions and compromises with creditors. These involve a "scheme of arrangement", requiring a 75 per cent vote of approval at a shareholders' meeting and court endorsement. While the legal route for such amalgamations is different, the economic effect is much the same.

1113 Bidders typically seek to acquire:

- 90 per cent of all shares not already held by the bidder, if any, this being the level at which compulsory acquisition (see paras 1167 to 1170) can take place; or

- 75 per cent of all shares on issue, this being the level at which the passage of special resolutions can be assured; or

- 51 per cent of all shares on issue (actually, 50 per cent plus one share would suffice), this being the level at which the passage of ordinary resolutions can be assured; or

- about 40 to 50 per cent of all shares on issue, this being a level sufficient for effective control, but without the target company actually becoming a subsidiary.

Main Objectives

1114 In general, companies launch takeover bids because they expect that increased profitability and other benefits will flow from such a move. Common objectives include the following:

Benefits in Terms of Assets

1115 In a typical case, a successful takeover bid will be made at a price about 50 per cent higher than the market value prevailing before the offer was announced (or before rumours of an impending bid started to circulate). In the event of poor past performance such a bid value can easily represent a substantial discount on the true asset backing of the shares, thus providing the successful bidder with the opportunity to capitalise on this discrepancy and on the fact that the gains have not been previously unlocked in a voluntary liquidation.

1116 In this way the bid can be an effective means of splitting the profits to be made between the buyer and the sellers, as in the following example:

Market price pre-bid	200
Bid price	300
Net tangible assets per share being acquired	400

1117 Assets which have not been properly exploited in the past can be put to better ongoing use in the future, possibly after replacing an inefficient management team. Often the assets were undervalued in the company's books, thus disguising the inadequacy of the returns which they have been yielding.

1118 Alternatively, the assets of the company being acquired can be broken up, realising a capital profit in the process. Some of the assets may also be more usefully employed in the bidding company's own business, particularly assets such as land and buildings. Cash, or assets readily converted to cash, can also be used to improve the bidding company's own liquidity, possibly even repaying some of the funds borrowed in order to finance the bid.

Benefits in Terms of Earnings

1119 Most mergers, including those achieved through takeovers, provide the opportunity for cost savings through rationalisation and thus greater profitability. Significant efficiencies can often be achieved by combining the administration of the two enterprises at both head office and branch levels, by sharing office and factory premises, and by integrating distribution networks, computer facilities, treasury operations and the like. Other things being equal, larger companies can also borrow funds on better terms than smaller companies. Lower unit costs mean that the whole—in terms of earnings—is greater than the sum of the parts.

1120 As in the case above, the takeover provides a means of sharing the benefits of rationalisation between the two parties—the selling shareholders often get their benefits in the form of one-time capital gains, while the bidding company and its shareholders hopefully get their benefits in the form of enhanced profits each year in the future.

Benefits from differing Market Perceptions

1121 Some companies, because of their successful past record and their anticipated future growth, are particularly well regarded by investors. On the stock exchange this reflects itself in a higher than average price earnings ratio (see para. 922). Such companies can then make highly effective takeover offers for companies less well regarded by the market-offers which thus are simultaneously attractive to the recipient shareholders and inexpensive for the bidder.

1122 In the process the bidding company's earnings per share figure is boosted, thus also benefiting its own existing shareholders, as the following example involving a one for one share swap shows:

	Market Price per Share	Earnings per Share	Price Earnings Ratio
Offeror Company	300	30	10
Offeree Company	200 (pre-bid)	40	5

The offeree company shareholders achieve a one-off 50 per cent capital gain, while the offeror company shareholders get a lift in their earnings per share figure each year, despite more shares being on issue. If the market does not downgrade its assessment of the offeror company's shares then the higher earnings per share resulting from the acquisition will—even in the absence of any benefits from rationalisation—in due course cause its shares to rise more than otherwise would have been the case.

1123 Such a process can be repeated many times, but as the bidding company grows in size it will gradually find it more and more difficult to make acquisitions of the right calibre which are large enough to produce further significant increases in its earnings per share figure.

Benefits from not incurring Establishment Costs

1124 Expansion into new geographical areas or diversification into totally different activities or product lines can involve a company in heavy setting-up costs and long delays. To start from scratch would frequently mean a loss—making period of some years, during which key employees are recruited and other staff is trained; during which plant and premises are built and stock is acquired; during which distribution systems are organised and a customer base is built up; and so on.

1125 Many of these problems can be avoided if an existing business is taken over instead. A takeover offer in such circumstances probably involves some outlay for a goodwill element, but this could be money well spent, especially if valuable intangible assets such as well-known brand names are acquired as part of the deal. A bid can thus be a very attractive and practical alternative to starting up a new activity in the conventional way.

Subsidiary Objectives

1126 Takeovers frequently take place for more than one reason. Typically, other purposes achieved by the acquisition of a suitable company would include one or more of the following:

Horizontal Integration

1127 Competitors can be absorbed, although only to the extent permitted by law. Companies can get a better market penetration and thus a bigger market share, enabling economies of scale, lower unit costs and greater profits. Depending on the elasticity of demand, there may be scope for price increases.

Vertical Integration

1128 The source of raw materials and/or outlets for finished products can be tied up. Captive markets can produce greater stability.

Diversification

1129 Diversification can be achieved. As explained in paras 1057 to 1062, companies may wish to involve themselves in activities quite unrelated to their traditional operations, in order to counter seasonal or other trade cyclical problems, or just to reduce expense rates by spreading fixed overheads over a larger volume of business.

Pure Investment

1130 An investment in income-producing assets can be made. A company may as the result of changed circumstances find itself with surplus funds, but may not wish to make a capital return to its own shareholders (despite this being a desirable course of action). For such a purpose the industry in which the company to be acquired operates would within limits be quite immaterial, provided only that the yield on the funds involved were regarded as attractive.

Listing on the Stock Exchange

1131 A backdoor listing on the stock exchange can be achieved. An unlisted private company seeking to expand and/or to raise money from the public can acquire a company which is already listed on the stock exchange in order first of all to restructure it and then to refloat it. The business conducted by the offeror can be sold to the offeree for cash and/or for newly-created shares. In this way the bidding company can get listing at a lower cost and with less delay than if it applied for it in the normal way, while the shareholders in the company being acquired get a premium over the value otherwise available to them, by way of reward for being parties to the deal.

Retaining existing Listing on the Stock Exchange

1132 A takeover involving a share exchange can be made as a means of widening a listed offeror company's share register. To retain listing on the stock exchange a company needs to maintain a certain minimum number of shareholders. A company in danger of running foul of this provision can improve its position by offering its own shares in exchange for those in a suitable offeree company.

Plant and Equipment

1133   Plant and equipment can be acquired at an effective price well below its current cost or replacement value.

Dispute Resolution

1134   Difficulties arising from the joint ownership of enterprises can sometimes be resolved by one partner acquiring the other.

Cash

1135   Assets which can be either sold or used as security for loans can be acquired. Such an approach thus serves as an alternative to conventional fundraising techniques.

Forestalling a Takeover of the Bidding Company

1136   The possibility of a takeover bid for the present bidding company itself can be reduced. The number of potential bidders falls as the outlay needed to absorb a target company rises.

Miscellaneous

1137   Miscellaneous useful items can be acquired, such as key staff, production facilities, cash flow, retail outlets, a share portfolio, patent rights, marketing franchises, mining leases, interests in associated companies, business names, freehold and leasehold property, statutory quotas, tax losses (see, however, para. 2891) and the like. Becoming part of a larger operation can also be psychologically satisfying to the directors and management of the bidding company.

Opposition to Bids

1138   On occasions takeover battles become highly emotive affairs. Some boards of directors on receiving an unsolicited offer institute great resistance to it, even when the terms of the offer would seem to be highly attractive to the shareholders concerned. Possibly the opposition to bids by such directors is unduly influenced by their reluctance to lose their prestigious board seats or the other perks of office.

Directors may also regard—probably quite correctly—such offers as an implied criticism of their past stewardship. It is, of course, understandable that some directors with only a nominal holding of shares in a company might have a different viewpoint from that of a typical profit-oriented and unsentimental portfolio investor (see also para. 1055). However, the use of shareholders' funds in expensive advertising and public relations campaigns and/or in court cases against bids which shareholders might find attractive is a matter of some concern.

1139 Xenophobia also causes quite illogical opposition to some bids. Even some Australian States are notoriously hostile to so-called "predators" from other States, even though a change of ownership might, in fact, lead to greater local growth, employment, expansion and profitability. Bids by overseas interests are also frowned on. Actually, successful offers from such quarters can benefit Australia because they free local investment capital for other productive purposes.

Economic Benefits to the Nation

1140 Many takeovers assist the economy by leading to a better use of assets. Under-utilised resources do not help the nation. On the other hand, distant fields often look greener than they really are, and companies making takeover bids into industries which they do not understand and into activities which they cannot adequately control may find that profitability goes down rather than up.

1141 The effects of takeovers on employment are more complex. Vertical integration makes jobs more secure, but rationalisation may eliminate some positions, either immediately or in the long run. Many companies make it a condition of a takeover offer that no employee of the company being acquired will be declared redundant. Staff numbers are then reduced gradually by attrition or voluntary early retirement schemes.

The ability to lower costs by eliminating some duplication of jobs may be one of the attractions of a merger. However, as a result of a successful takeover other jobs may be created elsewhere in the community, either inside or outside the group of companies concerned.

For example, the more efficient economic unit arising out of an amalgamation may be able to attract more business than the two separate entities could have. In the absence of a merger a complete company failure could have occurred, costing many times the number of jobs. Again, an enlarged Australian enterprise might be able to compete more efficiently against overseas competitors. The greater profits when they materialise may also lead to further capital investment or—if distributed in the form of higher dividends—to increased consumption by shareholders, all creating additional jobs. Higher profitability also benefits the nation directly, through increased tax collections.

1142 It should be noted that not all takeovers work out as intended. Some acquisitions turn out to be disasters for the successful bidders, particularly when unexpected management problems manifest themselves or when the consideration paid turns out to have been excessive. Heavy interest costs associated with raising finance to fund an acquisition can also be a source of trouble, especially if the physical realisation of assets to repay such loans proves to be more difficult or slower than envisaged or if market conditions change.

Some attempts have been made to measure statistically the benefits or otherwise arising from consummated takeover offers. However, surveys comparing the post-takeover profits of merged groups with the totals of the corresponding pre-takeover separate figures of earlier years lack credibility because of the absence of a satisfactory control group.

1143 Frequently small businesses are started by some brilliant entrepreneur with vision and great ability, who works hard and spends long hours on the job because he owns the company. While small, such enterprises can have a spectacular growth rate, which makes them appear to be worthwhile takeover targets. However, after a successful bid such an entrepreneur may leave because he cannot fit in with the bureaucratic rules of a big company or, if he stays, then his new status as a salaried employee can effectively kill his initiative. A business which is taken over may also suffer from employee morale problems down the line. These are not helped by the wider span of control then operating.

1144 Despite some beliefs to the contrary, takeovers have no effect on inflation, as only a change in the ownership of assets is involved. There is no increase in the volume of money in circulation and no change in the level of goods. Any cash received by offerees is exactly matched by cash given up by the offerors or by lenders to them. Similarly, money from overseas bidders or from overseas lenders to local bidders in takeover situations has no economic effect one way or the other. Australia incurs a current account deficit each year and needs an equal net inflow on the capital account in order to square the ledger. Any such inflow attributable to a specific takeover would just be in place of some other capital inflow which would have occurred in any case.

1145 The possibility of a takeover bid and the existence of professional company raiders act as spurs to company managements to lift their efficiency—this is very healthy. However, it is also true that management resources can be diverted from their main task in order to fight off real or perceived takeover threats.

Defences against Unwanted Bids

1146 A few companies actively seek to be acquired—for example, undercapitalised companies with growth potential which are experiencing difficulty in raising additional risk funds or companies under the control of a founding family which is keen to diversify or to raise cash. But most companies are not in this category.

1147 Some companies on receiving an unsolicited takeover bid welcome it if its terms appear generous and acceptance is likely to confer benefits on their shareholders. However, in many cases such bids are regarded as unwelcome by the directors of the offeree company. Typically they will engage in verbal abuse, branding the bidder as a "raider", a "predator" or even a "vulture". They will make much of the fact that the offer was "unsolicited", as though that in some mysterious way had a bearing on a decision as to whether shareholders should accept it or not. Sometimes directors even use back-to-front arguments, such as that the company will be delisted if too many shareholders accept the offer; the likelihood of such a development is more a reason for acceptance than for rejection.

1148 More seriously, the directors will engage in one or more of the over 20 different defensive measures set out below. They are also likely to describe the bid as "totally inadequate", although this is quite a good negotiating ploy even if the bid is really regarded as satisfactory. Such an initial rejection may result in a higher offer either from the original bidder or from some counter-bidder.

1149 Common defensive moves—some of which may well be made in anticipation that a hostile bid may come one-day-include the following:

- A strong recommendation to shareholders to reject the offer and to disregard any communications from the bidder.

- An increase in the dividend rate, whether or not justified by the circumstances.

- A revaluation of assets.

- A bonus issue.

- The disposal of surplus assets.

- A capital reconstruction (such as a split of shares into shares of a lower denomination).

- A change in bookkeeping procedures.

- A merger with some other company.

- A partial repayment of capital.

- An issue of shares (possibly on the basis of a low paid-up value) to employees and/or to a staff superannuation fund.

- The creation of an employee share option plan.

- A placement of shares or convertible securities with some other party or parties thought to be friendly.

- A share swap with another company in a similar position.

- A takeover bid of its own.

- A rights issue designed mainly to make the company bigger.

- An approach to the authorities in terms of legislation relating to trade practices or licensing.

- The soliciting of political intervention.

1150 The intention of some of these moves would be to increase the company's total market capitalisation in order to make a successful bid more expensive and thus less likely. Of course, some moves on the above lines can be appropriate for reasons quite unrelated to any takeover activity. Others, such as the creation of cross-holdings, would rarely have any economic justification.

1151 Another favourite device involves the acquisition or disposal of a major asset, significantly changing the company's range of activities and/or its balance sheet ratios and thus reducing the attraction which the company holds for potential bidders. Unfortunately, such measures can also reduce the ongoing value of the company for the existing shareholders.

1152 Frequently companies under attack reveal favourable facts previously kept hidden and/or make unsubstantiated promises of much better performance in the future. Shareholders should, of course, regard such "deathbed conversions" with considerable suspicion and scepticism. They should also deny support to boards who waste shareholders' funds by resorting to legal action instead of letting markets decide.

1153 Alternatively, certain disclosures may be made in an attempt to frighten off the bidder—for example, the revelation of onerous service contracts or redundancy commitments ("golden parachutes"), or of substantial deficiencies in the offeree company's staff superannuation fund. There may also be suggestions that some important franchises will be lost, that key executives will resign, that the unions will cause trouble, and so on. There may in addition be hints from the target company's board as to the imminence of rival bids—at the very least, such tactics buy time for the company.

1154 Another form of defence involves the offeree company or its associates buying up shares in the offeror company. A large stake may be thought to increase the offeree's bargaining position in a takeover battle. In an extreme case the outcome may even be that the original bidder becomes the victim of a rival bid for its own shares launched by the offeree.

1155 Sometimes a company under attack will seek the support of a "white knight", a person or company willing to acquire (on the market or by placement) a significant stake in the offeree—a stake which, it is hoped, will be sufficiently large to deter or block the unwelcome bidder. In practice, such support has proved to be a mixed blessing. While it may succeed in frustrating the original bid, at a later stage the white knight may become a bidder himself. Alternatively, such a holding may become the springboard for some other bidder to whom it passes in due course.

1156 The success record of the above-mentioned blocking techniques as a whole has also been mixed. Institutions are now much more performance-oriented and thus tend to accept bids where this is commercially justified, although small individual shareholders, the company's own employees and some members of an enterprise's founding family may choose to hold on to their shares for sentimental or job-related reasons.

1157 A pleasing feature of recent years has been the trend for the trustees of staff superannuation funds, which often hold significant parcels of shares in the employing company, to seek independent advice as to its merits when a takeover offer for that company is made. The directors of companies receiving bids can thus no longer assume the automatic support of such funds regardless of the circumstances.

1158 Companies which are performing well, or which are large, or which have a single controlling shareholder, are relatively safe from attack—but even these attributes do not guarantee invulnerability. On the other hand, companies with under-utilised assets—or, worse still, with assets the true value of which greatly exceeds the value disclosed to investors—and companies which fail to communicate adequately with their own shareholders and the market at large are at particular risk.

Partial Bids

1159 Partial bids, that is, bids for less than 100 per cent of the shares, can be a means of obtaining de facto control of a company at a much smaller outlay than is involved in a full acquisition. Sometimes the fact that the remaining shares will continue to be held by a wide spread of shareholders and thus remain listed would also in itself be regarded as a useful advantage. The successful offeror under a partial bid can later move to a full acquisition, possibly even at a lower price than would otherwise have applied, because of the absence of a "control premium" in the market place. Alternatively, the offeror company may be able to dispose of its stake at a capital profit if some other bidder makes a full takeover at a later stage.

1160 Partial bids can leave investors as minority shareholders in a company run by a completely different board from that in office when they first purchased their shares and possibly one with a very different corporate philosophy. Frequently the takeover consideration offered may also be felt to be inadequate when regard is had to the likely market value of the remaining shares after control has changed —yet shareholders who refuse a partial bid because of such a factor may finish up being even worse off because a sufficient number of their fellow shareholders have accepted the proposition.

1161 The making of a partial bid, of course, also benefits shareholders if it sparks off a takeover battle and thus leads to a full bid (possibly at a higher price) from another party.

1162 Because of the above-mentioned problems a number of leading companies have in recent years adopted provisions in their articles of association which prevent partial takeovers unless these are first approved by shareholders in general meeting. On the surface, this seems fair enough, as such provisions are clearly intended to prevent control of a company passing too cheaply.

1163 The adoption of such articles is now specifically sanctioned by Sections 669 to 672 of the *Corporations Law*, but only for three years at a time, possibly demonstrating their experimental nature. However, such provisions are conceptually objectionable. Shareholders who do not like partial bids in general or a specific partial bid in particular can always reject such a bid for themselves. They should not, however, be allowed to interfere with the rights of other shareholders who might feel quite differently.

1164 It seems quite immoral for a majority to be able to dictate to a minority in respect of how the latter should choose to dispose of their own property—whether on the market or to a bidder under a takeover scheme. Such a principle is not found elsewhere in most articles. For example, a majority of shareholders might regard the market price of a company's shares as too low—but they could not stop a minority disposing of their shares at such a price.

1165 It is true that restrictive articles of the type under discussion do not affect partial bids thought attractive enough to a majority at the time—but then again such an article is not needed in such circumstances. But the disadvantage for shareholders of having such a rule on the books is that a bid which might otherwise be forthcoming might not ever be made, as the delays, controversy, expense and uncertainty might deter potential bidders. If a bid is not even put on the table for consideration then the opportunity for an auction by competing bidders is also lost.

1166 Various other clauses are sometimes inserted into a company's articles of association in an endeavour to deter unwanted takeover bids. Some of these provisions bear interesting sounding slang names, such as "shark repellents" or "poison pills". Shareholders who support the adoption of any such restrictive articles are not acting logically or in their own best interests. They are unwittingly helping to keep the market price of their shares down. This happens in two separate ways—the elimination of buying pressure from potential bidders and the removal of buying pressure from investors acquiring shares in the expectation of some bid.

Compulsory Acquisitions

1167 Despite some beliefs to the contrary, shareholders receiving a bid which they do not welcome are under no obligation to accept it. They have two other choices—to continue holding their shares, or to sell them on the market. The only exception to this is the "compulsory acquisition" provision of the legislation. This is designed to allow a bidder who acquires at least 90 per cent of an offeree company, from at least 75 per cent of the shareholders by number, to mop up the shares belonging to non-acceptors, including deceased estates and shareholders who have just disappeared. For technical legal reasons executors or administrators of deceased estates cannot enter into contracts affecting shares until probate or letters of administration have been granted.

Shareholders who have not advised changes of address frequently do not receive mail sent in accordance with out-of-date particulars shown in the register of shareholdings. (This 75 per cent rule is being modified, so that in future a holder of at least 90 per cent will more easily be able to achieve 100 per cent.)

1168 The theory behind the compulsory acquisition rule is sound. If the vast majority of shareholders have in effect voted to accept a bid then it can be presumed that the small minority whose shares are still outstanding would also benefit from acceptance. This minority, apart from the shareholders in the categories already mentioned, would also include:

- Shareholders who are too apathetic to respond to the offer documents or to make appropriate inquiries of their investment advisers as to their best course of action.

- Shareholders who intend to accept the offer but who are careless in regard to their financial affairs and who thus fail to act by the required deadline.

- Shareholders who make a conscious investment decision that they wish to continue holding the shares under offer.

1169 Shareholders in the first two categories are probably pleased when their shares are compulsorily acquired, as they are then entitled to exactly the same terms as those investors who accepted voluntarily. Shareholders in the third category may resent this legal provision on the basis that it interferes with their normal rights, but on balance the law works well. In any case, such dissenting shareholders have a right of appeal to a court—although naturally such litigation would not be cheap.

1170 There are substantial advantages to a bidder in obtaining 100 per cent ownership, rather than, say, just 80 or 85 per cent. Full ownership and control facilitate tax minimisation. They also allow more flexible dividend distribution policies and internal rearrangements within the group, without a need to be concerned about possible injustices to the holders of outside minority interests.

Total ownership would also enable capital reconstructions to be instituted more readily. These could range from liquidation on the one hand (the elimination of one corporate entity would result in some savings in overhead expenses) to significant expansion on the other hand (a course of action which might cause considerable resentment if minority shareholders were either called on for further substantial capital subscriptions or put in the position of having their equity eroded).

Legislative Weaknesses

1171 The present takeovers legislation is designed to protect shareholders, but only those in offeree companies. Shareholders in a company which *makes* a bid can be adversely affected if the consideration being offered is too high, possibly leading to a reduction in earnings and/or asset backing per share and thus to a fall in market value. However, the legislation ignores this possibility and they get no say in the matter.

1172 It would be better if the shareholders in an offeror company were given the opportunity to consider the terms of a takeover to be made by it and to vote in general meeting on the desirability or otherwise of such a transaction, especially where the assets being acquired are large in relation to the company's existing assets. Quite apart from the possibility that the consideration, whether in paper or cash, might be excessive, a further problem can arise in the case of takeovers involving a consideration in shares or convertible securities. Such bids have the undesirable effect of diluting the equity of existing ordinary shareholders.

1173 For these reasons takeovers made by a company should be treated differently from other purchases of assets, the authority for which is normally quite properly delegated to the board of directors. Shareholder consent is, of course, already required by law for some other matters felt to be significant, such as changes to the company's name, authorised capital or articles of association, capital reductions, a voluntary winding-up, and so on.

Stock exchange listing requirements also insist on such consent for a number of transactions, including the disposal of the company's main undertaking and certain purchases from, or sales to, a director or his associates. Pertinent precedents for requiring the making of takeovers to be first approved by shareholders in general meeting thus exist.

1174 The takeovers legislation, which at present covers only shares, is being extended to also cover options and convertible securities (in the case of companies) and units (in the case of listed and otherwise publicly-held unit trusts). Such an extension will benefit both investors and bidding companies. The former will get extra safeguards and the latter will get the ability to use the compulsory acquisition mechanism described in paras 1167 to 1170, thus enabling them to mop up small residual holdings.

Alternatives to Takeovers

1175 A bidding company can frequently make a profit out of a takeover simply because the bid enables it to acquire underutilised assets relatively cheaply. It would clearly provide greater benefits to the shareholders in what would otherwise be the offeree company if they could get access to all the advantages of a takeover without having to split the gains with another party. This can happen if the directors of the company concerned take appropriate action on their own initiative.

1176 One approach would be for the directors to reorganise the company themselves, disposing of surplus assets and either putting the proceeds to better use within the group or preferably passing them on to shareholders in the form of a partial return of capital.

1177 Another approach, which is particularly appropriate if circumstances have changed since the company commenced in business, would be to put the entire company into voluntary liquidation. If this is done properly, then its assets can be disposed of in an orderly manner for the full benefit of the shareholders who own the company and as part of an arrangement which involves reasonable compensation for the employees being made redundant. By way of contrast, an unplanned takeover would result in both the shareholders and the employees becoming relatively worse off, with an enterprising outsider in the process getting the benefit of past thrift by other people.

Action by Shareholders on receiving a Bid

1178 As indicated above, shareholders on receiving a takeover bid always have three distinct choices. They can:

- accept the offer; or

- sell their shares on the market (or privately); or

- do nothing and thereby continue to hold their shares.

If enough shareholders do nothing (either deliberately or through inertia) then naturally the bid concerned will fail. This can be a mixed blessing. If the company is being poorly managed then its market price may subsequently fall; however, it is also possible that the bid will have frightened the board and caused it to institute its own changes for the better.

Furthermore, the chance of another bid later on, from either the same or another party, remains—although, of course, if the company performs poorly in the meantime then next time the consideration might be lower. If the bid succeeds then the shareholders who declined it will enjoy some advantages and suffer some disadvantages. The advantages include:

- the probability that the company's profitability will improve under the new management team

- the chance that the remaining public shareholders may receive a generous "mop-up" bid later on (a higher price per share may be feasible if the number of shares in the hands of minority holders is relatively small)

- the possibility that a third party will one day make a higher offer for both the majority and the minority holdings

- the possibility that the company may be wound up voluntarily, thus releasing its hidden value.

The disadvantages include:

- the possibility that the minority may be oppressed by the majority

- the likelihood that profits will be ploughed back and no dividends will be paid

- the probability that the market value will fall once the takeover premium no longer applies

- the probability that the stock will become illiquid because future turnover will be small

- the possibility that the company will be delisted (although this would not happen without some prior period of notice).

Of course, these aspects all become academic if compulsory acquisition takes place.

1179 Strategies such as changing the management or putting the company into voluntary liquidation might conceptually seem to be more attractive alternatives, but these would not normally be available to most shareholders in any practical sense.

1180 If the share price has risen in response to the bid then selling on the market can lock in profits which might easily disappear if the bid does not proceed. Quitting in this way involves brokerage and stamp duty costs, but produces cash faster than accepting a formal bid. However, it is usually better for investors to wait in case a higher bid emerges, either from the initial bidder or from some other party. If a shareholder does decide in favour of accepting the bid, then the best time to do this may well be shortly before its final closing date, although depending on the precise terms of the offer earlier acceptance might result in earlier payment. (The closing date of an offer is frequently extended during the course of a bid—often on more than one occasion.)

1181 Decisions should be made on rational grounds, and never on sentiment. The views of the boards of both the offeror and the offeree companies should be listened to, but treated with great caution. Often specious and emotional arguments are used by both sides. As explained above, sitting directors may well have rather different interests from those of other shareholders. Reports by independent experts and sometimes by specific directors of the target company may accompany the documents and these may assist shareholders. However, at the end of the day each investor must make up his own mind as to what is the best course of action for him.

1182 If shareholders are given a choice between two or more different forms of consideration then they will have to weigh up the relative attractions of each.

1183 Furthermore, if the consideration involves shares of the bidding company then shareholders of the target company will have to consider whether they wish to become investors in the bidding company. Even if they do not really want to become long-term holders, another alternative needs to be considered, namely, accepting the new shares in the first instance, with a view to disposing of them on the market in due course. This may or may not turn out to be better than selling the existing shares.

1184 The takeover documents and other announcements should be studied carefully, attention being paid to the matters discussed above and aspects such as the following:

- The size and adequacy of the consideration.

- Dividend entitlements.

- Conflicts of interest of parties making recommendations.

- The likely market value of the target company's shares if the bid fails.

- If the consideration is in shares, the likely market value of the bidding company's shares if the bid succeeds.

- The attitude of major shareholders unconnected with the bidder.

- The closing date.

It should, however, be borne in mind that in practice offer terms are often varied. In fact, statements by bidders to the effect that they do not propose to increase the consideration and/or to extend the closing date should never be taken literally.

1185 Like should always be compared with like. It is, for instance, nonsense to compare the past dividends from ordinary shares with the returns available from putting a cash consideration into fixed interest investments.

1186 In assessing the "true value" of shares investors should use the price earnings ratio, the net tangible asset backing and the other approaches set out in Chapter 10.

1187 The market price during the course of a takeover bid can be either higher than the offer price, if the market expects further bids, or lower than the offer price, if the market is concerned that the bid may fail, and also to reflect the interest element until any cash is received. However, bids once made cannot legally be withdrawn other than in exceptional circumstances. On the other hand, bids can fail if all the offer conditions are not either fulfilled or waived.

1188 Once an offer is formally declared "unconditional" shareholders can be assured of receiving the cash and/or scrip within the time frame set out in the offer document. They can then take this certainty into account when deciding on how to react to the bid.

(*Note*: Some offers are unconditional from their very commencement.)

1189 Similarly, once a bidder achieves the "compulsory acquisition" level (see para. 1167) and announces the intention to mop up the outstanding shares there is nothing to be gained in practice by hanging out. At that stage it is in a shareholder's best interests to accept the offer as quickly as possible, as thereby any cash received from the bidder (or obtainable by selling the scrip received on the market) will earn more interest. Furthermore, voluntary acceptance may preserve for the offeree a choice between alternative considerations, whereas a compulsory acquisition would, of course, not involve this element.

1190 Alternatively, the shareholder can sell the existing shares on the market. This course of action may be attractive if the cash can be used to advantage elsewhere at the time. It can also be attractive in pure money terms, but only if the arithmetic is right, in other words if:

(a) the achievable market price, net of the considerable brokerage and stamp duty costs, after allowing for capital gains tax (if applicable)

plus

(b) interest on the net market price for the period between the expected settlement from the stock exchange transaction and the expected settlement under the takeover, less income tax on this interest

exceeds

(c) the actual cash takeover consideration, after allowing for capital gains tax (if applicable).

1191 The taxation aspects of bids are discussed in detail in paras 2918 to 2923. It is pointed out there that shareholders who acquired their shares before 20 September 1985 and who desire to avoid the disadvantages flowing from the capital gains tax legislation face an insoluble dilemma:

"They can, of course, always reject the bid, especially if its terms do not adequately compensate them for the tax aspects. However, this strategy will not avoid the problems if compulsory acquisition takes place in due course and in any case it poses the risk that the investor will become 'locked in' as a minority holder in a company which is then controlled by the bidder and the shares of which may become delisted".

1192 Investors should watch the basis of quotation of shares during takeover bids, as in the case of some bids "offer accepted" shares in the target company may be being quoted separately from the normal shares. On a different aspect, the new shares issued by the bidding company as takeover consideration may be being quoted on a "deferred delivery" basis and/or may involve a dividend difference.

Credibility Aspects

1193 In some takeover duels the quality of the arguments on both sides leaves a lot to be desired. The list of points made will typically include some which are highly relevant, some which are trivial, some which are misleading and some which while technically correct are irrelevant. In their enthusiasm some boards fail to realise that the inclusion of half-truths is likely to destroy the credibility of their whole message.

Management Buyouts

1194 Sometimes a takeover bid is made not by an outsider but rather by a syndicate involving the management team of the company concerned. Such a proposal is known as a "management buyout" (MBO) or sometimes as a "leveraged buyout" (LBO). Typically it involves the use of large amounts of borrowed funds, to be charged on the assets of the enterprise itself, possibly supplemented by equity funds from an organisation specialising in packaging such deals.

However, a panel of owners running their own business has a strong motivation to make the venture succeed. In the case of professional managers who were previously repressed by an incompetent board of directors the chance to be free to make commercial decisions can also be a factor lifting profitability significantly.

1195 From the point of view of ordinary investors such takeovers should be treated on their merits in the same way as other bids. However, quite apart from any "insider trading" implications, the actions of managers who should be producing optimum results for their existing shareholders in effect seeking to produce such results for themselves, must be a cause for concern.

Telephone Campaigns

1196 One or both parties to a contested takeover battle may engage a specialist organisation to telephone some or all of the shareholders in the target company:

- to remind them of the fact of the offer, and of its terms and closing date

- to stress the recommendation to accept or reject the offer, as the case may be

- to give, if desired, a contact point for further information

- to ascertain the shareholder's intentions, in order to provide strategic information for the party commissioning the exercise.

1197 Such approaches may be helpful in jogging the memory of busy people and in providing a means of replacing lost documents. However, the staff engaged to make such telephone calls normally follow a carefully-prepared script and are themselves quite unequipped to discuss the substantive merits of the offer or to answer other than the simplest factual questions.

Warehousing

1198 The 20 per cent threshold for takeovers was mentioned in para. 1105. The 5 per cent limit for the public disclosure of substantial shareholdings was mentioned in para. 453. Companies contemplating bids sometimes seek to get around these limits and to increase their strategic advantage by inducing other parties friendly to them to acquire additional parcels in the proposed target company and to hold these as principals.

1199 Such a device is known as "warehousing". It can also help potential bidders who wish to offer a share exchange, by allowing them effective control of a larger proportion of the target ahead of the bid than their own limited cash resources might conveniently allow.

Chapter 12—Shareholders' Rights

Sir, I have two cogent reasons for not printing any list of subscribers: one, that I have lost all the names; the other, that I have spent all the money
—Samuel Johnson

Introductory

1201 Shareholders in listed companies outnumber employees in those companies by about two to one, but rather surprisingly to date only the rights of employees have been the subject of much discussion in the community. It is worth noting that employees can in theory opt out of their relationship with a company-by striking or even by resigning en masse—but shareholders as a class cannot really abrogate their contracts in these ways.

1202 The main objective of investment in such companies is to maximise the wealth of their shareholders. In order to achieve this aim shareholders, whether large or small investors, in effect delegate control over some of their money to other people whenever they acquire shares on the stock exchange. While collectively remaining the owners of the enterprise, they hand over the day to day responsibility for the running of the business to the boards of directors and management teams of the companies in which they own shares.

However, shareholders are entitled to expect that this delegation of authority will be regarded as a sacred trust in pursuit of the above-named objective and that those in charge of each company will at all times carry out their duties both diligently and ethically.

1203 The principal legislation of relevance to investors in this context is the *Corporations Law*. There is also a special supervisory authority, the Australian Securities Commission (ASC), which recently became the Australian Securities and Investments Commission (ASIC), with a role as both market regulator and consumer protection body.

Legal Rights

1204 Shareholders enjoy the privilege of limited liability under companies legislation. They also have certain other specific legal rights and—subject to statute law—various rights under each company's rules (the articles of association).

1205 In particular, shareholders normally have:

- an entitlement to a proportionate share of the company's profit each year

- an entitlement to a proportionate share of the net assets of the company on a winding-up

- the right to attend meetings and to speak and vote at them (and to appoint proxies)

- the right to receive certain information relating to the company

- the right to dispose of their shares.

1206 The last-mentioned right includes the right to accept or reject offers under takeover schemes, a subject covered in great detail by specific legislation (see Chapter 11).

(*Note:* Shareholders are entitled to vote their shares at general meetings even if they have some vested interest in the subject matter—although there are some exceptions to this general principle—for example, in relation to the sale or purchase of assets to or from the company. This is quite different from the position at board meetings, where directors with a conflict of interest must absent themselves.)

1207 In the case of listed companies, certain further rights are spelt out in the stock exchange listing requirements. Some of these are relevant to potential shareholders as well as to current investors.

1208 Shareholders are, of course, entitled to sell their shares privately as well as through the stock exchange.

Moral Rights

1209 In addition to the legal and quasi-legal rights of shareholders mentioned above, it is possible to stipulate certain moral rights, although these involve some degree of value judgement. A basic tenet is that nothing should ever be done which significantly reduces any shareholder's equity (or relative stake) in a company without that shareholder's consent.

1210 For example, any action by the directors which would have the effect of reducing the value of the shares held by one group of shareholders (and in the process no doubt correspondingly increasing the value of the shares held by another group in this *zero sum game*) would be quite unfair.

1211 This principle can best be illustrated by discussing some typical cases:

- Issues of new shares made other than on a pro rata basis to existing shareholders and particularly placements offered to outsiders at a price which is less than either the market value or the net tangible asset backing of equivalent existing shares have the effect of diluting the equity of the current investors in the company. Such issues are therefore quite immoral. The practice is known as "watering the capital".

- Bonus issues made to holders of partly-paid shares at a lower ratio than that applying in the case of fully-paid shares similarly erode the equity of such holders and thus cause injustice.

- Pro rata issues confined to the holders of ordinary shares when options and/or securities convertible into ordinary shares are outstanding can also cause inequities unless the terms of such paper are suitably adjusted.

1212 Bonus issues are really share splits in a slightly different legal form. For example, if the holder of a contributing share which requires the payment of a further 50 cents in order to turn it into a fully paid share were involved in a two for one share split then he would, immediately after the split, hold two contributing shares with a further 25 cents outstanding liability on each (a total of 50 cents, the same as before). A one for one bonus issue is virtually the same as a two for one split, holders of fully paid shares finishing up with twice as many pieces of paper, each of them half as valuable as just before the capital was altered.

The holder of the contributing share in this example thus needs to receive one fully paid bonus share (the same ratio as in the case of holders of fully paid shares) to supplement his existing contributing share with 50 cents outstanding, in order to put him in the same aggregate position as in the case of the share split.

1213 Similar logic applies in relation to optionholders, who (in economic terms) are virtually shareholders who "owe" the amount of the exercise price and who because of this temporarily have no voting rights or dividend entitlement. It is, of course, true that in legal terms optionholders are not yet shareholders and that they have by way of offset the benefit of leverage and the privilege of forfeiting their options instead of taking the new shares up if this should prove to be more attractive at the last available exercise date. However, morally such optionholders should always be regarded as a special class of deferred shareholders for new issue purposes until that time. (The options created by some companies by virtue of their particular issue conditions specifically exclude entitlements to new issues. In such cases it could, of course, be argued that to allow participation would be unfair in the reverse direction, namely, to the ordinary shareholders.)

1214 The wider principle can also be illustrated by some other examples:

- A company finding that some or all of its traditional activities are no longer viable should make a partial capital return to its shareholders or invite them to place the company in voluntary liquidation rather than put their stakes at risk by diversifying into completely unrelated activities in different industries. The necessary management experience for the latter may be lacking, thus exposing shareholders to risks of a type which they may not have been expecting when acquiring their shares in the first instance. In such cases it is always better for each shareholder to be given the opportunity to make his own individual decision as to how to reinvest the surplus cash.

- Artificial devices by boards of directors intended to defend their companies against actual or expected takeover offers clearly interfere with the rights of shareholders to receive such offers and to decide for themselves whether to accept them or not. Some such measures are doubly wrong—for example, placements to so-called "friendly" parties at prices below the market.

A different breach of the moral rights of shareholders can occur in relation to personnel appointments as, for example, when a person is appointed to an executive or board position not on merit but rather because of a relationship by blood or marriage to some of those in control of the company.

Changes to the Rules

1215 As mentioned in para. 410, a company can be thought of as a sort of club—with members (the shareholders), with an elected committee (the board of directors) and with formal rules (the memorandum of association and the articles of association).

1216 Persons joining the "club" (investors buying shares in a company) do so on the basis of the rules in force at the time. If they do not like the prevailing conditions then they do not have to come in. However, a future general meeting of the company— subject to certain formalities—can change the rules, which are then binding on all shareholders. In some circumstances the altered rules may reduce the demand for the shares and thus adversely affect their market price.

Rule changes require shareholder approval with at least three-quarters of the votes cast in favour of the change. However, subject to that, a simple majority can outvote and thereby impose its wishes on a minority. This is fine (democracy at work) if the interests of each shareholder happen to be identical. But usually they are not—employees, customers, suppliers and even competitors may be large shareholders. These are all groups with vested interests of their own, interests which may well be different from those of pure investors.

Proxies

1217 Directors and executives enjoying the perks of office require special mention. The number of shares which they actually own may be very large or it may be quite small, but either way their influence can be considerable. Their advice to shareholders may be influenced by non-investment considerations—a fact which shareholders should take into account before blindly acting on it and—as normally suggested in company circulars—sending their proxies to the chairman. Of course, in normal situations non-controversial proposals get passed with such enormous majorities on the basis of votes cast by institutions and associates of the board that even hostile proxies lodged by small shareholders as some sort of protest will have little practical effect.

(*Note:* Trustees have a duty to exercise their voting power in the best interests of the beneficiaries of their trusts. This includes trustees of staff superannuation funds, who may on some occasions find it necessary to cast votes against the wishes of the employing company.)

Annual General Meetings

1218 Shareholders have a formal opportunity to put their views on the running of the company to its board and to their fellow shareholders at the Annual General Meeting which the law requires every company to hold each year (see also Chapter 13).

Such meetings have to transact certain standard business, but they also provide the opportunity for shareholders to ask questions and to make comments. All too often this opportunity is wasted, with shareholders—because of shyness or lack of knowledge of procedure—either remaining completely silent or at best raising some poorly-prepared point, a trivial matter or even a complete irrelevancy. In the light of such investor apathy it is understandable that most company directors would regard their stewardship as having received the tacit endorsement of the owners of the business!

1219 But company meetings do give shareholders the chance to have their say and—provided that they have done their homework and that they refrain from making only superficial comments—to influence the board. Furthermore, valid criticisms made at general meetings might well attract press attention and thus have a desirable effect on other companies as well.

1220 Company annual reports (see Chapter 8) are getting better all the time, but there will always be some aspects of a company's affairs where elaboration might be useful. For example, most companies were very slow to indicate a new dividend policy following the announcement that imputation was being introduced.

1221 Investors can also seek to improve their environment in less formal ways—for instance, by writing on appropriate occasions to specific companies, to the Australian Stock Exchange, to State or Federal Attorneys-General, to the Australian Securities and Investments Commission to Government, Opposition and third party politicians, to the Australian Shareholders' Association or to the media.

Unitholders

1222 To some extent unitholders in listed and unlisted unit trusts have similar rights to shareholders in companies, with the added advantage (at least in theory) of having the services of an independent trustee to stand between them and the fund manager. An important question arises in the case of trusts investing in shares: How are such shares going to be voted at the relevant shareholders' meetings and who in practice is to make the decisions in this regard? With a trend to a much greater concentration of shareholdings in institutional hands this subject is not unimportant for the community.

Delisting

1223 One further right of investors on the stock exchange should be mentioned—the right to permanent access to a free market by virtue of their shares continuing to be listed securities. At present shareholders are vulnerable, because this right exists only at the pleasure of the stock exchange. Suspension or delisting can occur for a variety of reasons, including requests to this effect from the company concerned or its failure to pay listing fees, or at the initiative of the stock exchange authorities or the Australian Securities and Investments Commission in order to "punish" the company for some breach.

In such instances those who suffer most are the innocent shareholders who often receive a double blow—not only has their investment turned sour but also they are denied the ability to cut their losses by quitting it on equitable terms. Of course, a company which has been delisted but which is still in existence can apply for relisting at a future point of time, possibly after it has been reconstructed. The same ASX formalities as for a brand new listing would naturally apply in such circumstances. (See also paras 2009 to 2016.)

Law Reform

1224 Companies legislation is designed in part to protect small shareholders. Yet some provisions are for all practical purposes useless in this regard.

Directors' Obligations

1225 For example, Section 232 of the *Corporations Law* requires that a director or other officer of a corporation "shall at all times act honestly in the exercise of his or her powers and the discharge of the duties of his or her office". Prosecutions for breaches of this provision are very rare—no doubt because of the difficulty of proving an offence beyond reasonable doubt (the normal standard for criminal charges). Again, Section 592 makes it an offence for directors to incur debts without reasonable grounds for expecting that they can be met when due.

1226 Possibly such matters should be tried before special juries composed of people who are active shareholders (in companies at large; not, of course, in the company involved in the charge). Such a tribunal would at least understand the issues and apply a proper value judgement to the facts of the case. Even an unsuccessful prosecution under this section would send a most valuable message to many people. Of course, dishonesty must be distinguished from actions taken in good faith but which with the benefit of hindsight turn out to have been poor commercial judgements.

1227 The above suggestion, while improving the quality of justice, would admittedly involve the community in some additional expenditure. Naturally, there would be some administrative effort required in order to establish rolls of suitably qualified people able to act as special jurors. Such persons should also be remunerated at a more realistic rate than applies in the case of common juries.

Oppression

1228 Again, Section 260 of the *Corporations Law* provides for certain remedies if the court is of the opinion that the "affairs of a company are being conducted in a manner that is oppressive or unfairly prejudicial to, or unfairly discriminatory against, a member or members". This sounds fine as a general proposition, but no sensible holder of 100 shares or so is going to risk incurring the costs involved in fighting a test case against a wealthy corporation, no matter how justified his case might be in theory.

1229 The authorities should provide some special official who could at public expense institute such civil actions on behalf of all shareholders on suitable occasions—after all, shareholders directly and indirectly make considerable contributions to State and Federal coffers! While legislation under the Corporate Law Economic Review Program is expected to expand the rights of shareholders to take action on behalf of companies this will still expose them to expense and the risk of costs orders against them—so these reforms will be of little practical benefit to individual small investors.

Voting

1230 The voting system used for electing directors is another area requiring legislative attention. To ensure that minorities can be equitably represented, proportional representation (as used for the Australian Senate) should become compulsory for company elections. This would also automatically ensure that groups of small shareholders with common interests as well as large investors who build up significant stakes in companies could obtain, as an entitlement, board seats based on the size of their respective holdings, should they so wish. (Some such persons might not desire involvement as board members, either because of potential conflicts of interest or because the insider trading legislation would unduly reduce their freedom to buy and sell shares in the company concerned.)

1231 In order to make this system work properly it would, of course, be essential to have quotas of reasonable size. This could be achieved by prescribing a minimum number of members for each board and by limiting the terms in office to one year at a time.

1232 On a separate but related matter, the sliding scale voting basis still used by some older companies when a poll is taken should be outlawed. The "one share, one vote" system is patently more equitable. While sliding scales are intended to benefit small shareholders by reducing the relative voting power of large holders, such provisions are often counterproductive in practice and harmful to the interests of small investors, as, for example, where they make takeovers more difficult.

Share Issues

1233 Another desirable area of law reform relates to new cash issues of ordinary shares or securities convertible into ordinary shares (see Chapter 6). It should generally be compulsory for such new issues to be offered in the first place to all existing equity holders on a pro rata basis, except in the case of some clearly—defined special circumstances, such as shares issued under dividend reinvestment plans or as consideration in takeover schemes. Any lesser requirement would give too great an opportunity for the watering of capital—the dilution of the interests held by existing investors—and the frustration of legitimate takeover bids, notwithstanding the advantages of speed and relatively low administrative cost claimed for share placements.

1234 Furthermore, it should become compulsory for all companies making rights issues (see Chapter 7) to protect the interests of those of their shareholders who for one reason or another do not deal with their entitlements by the closing date. A trustee should always be appointed to take up the new shares and then to sell them and distribute the net proceeds pro rata to the beneficial owners concerned. Many reputable companies already adopt this principle on a voluntary basis and the rest should be made to fall into line.

The use of a trustee handling sales in bulk would also avoid the need for shareholders, when disposing of their rights, to incur the relatively heavy minimum brokerage charges which normally apply to small sales (see para. 532). Furthermore, it would assist shareholders who through illness or absence from Australia have difficulty in dealing with such matters.

1235 It is true that this approach could impose some additional costs on the whole body of shareholders (both for clerical services and in the form of a higher underwriting fee if the issue is underwritten and the underwriter is deprived of the opportunity to make a windfall gain out of non-acceptances). The existence of the facility itself might also encourage shareholders not to deal with their own rights, especially if they think that this might result in a better price than from a disposal during the rights trading period. Because of these aspects a discount of, say, 10 per cent from the net proceeds which would otherwise be available might thus be appropriate.

Rights of the Press

1236 One aspect of meetings procedure badly needs reform. There should be a statutory right for the media to attend and report on all general meetings of listed companies. The privilege of access to a public market involves some corresponding obligations. Shareholders unable to attend a meeting personally because of time or distance limitations should at the very least be able to learn what transpired at it from the media.

The presence of the media can in practice also improve the quality of the conduct of the meeting, as no chairman wishes to be held up to ridicule for oppressive behaviour or evasive answers to legitimate questions. Luckily, attempts by boards to exclude journalists are comparatively rare—although such moves tend to occur in the very situations when reports by an independent press are needed the most. The statutory right to attend should be absolute rather than subject to approval by the meeting (democratic though that might sound), as otherwise the actions of a board-controlled majority could deprive outside minority shareholders of the opportunity to become informed.

Defamation

1237 The law of defamation also warrants attention. Sometimes corporate dishonesty needs to be exposed and this process is not helped by the quasi-censorship which is the de facto by-product of the present rules governing libel. The power of the purse is usually far too heavily weighted against any potential whistle blower. (See also paras 2519 to 2521.)

Proxies

1238 Proxies are normally sent to the registered office of the company concerned. It would be better if they were sent to some person independent of the company—for example, the auditor or a statutory official appointed as returning officer.

Minimum Shareholdings

1239 Some companies have adopted rules which prevent the registration as shareholders of persons owning less than a specified minimum number of shares. A legitimate reason for such a rule is that it keeps expenses down—a company incurs certain basic costs per shareholder which are unrelated to the actual size of the holding.

1240 However, the real motivation of companies using such provisions is usually political—they desire to keep out persons who are not genuine investors but who desire to own a single share or some such because of the rights this ownership gives to attend and speak at annual general meetings (see para. 1323).

The End of Par Values

1241 Australian company law will soon be brought into line with economic reality and overseas practice. The concept that shares must have a face value is to be abolished. All shares will become just "shares of no par value" (NPV). This feature will become compulsory for both existing and new companies.

1242 The revised nomenclature will undoubtedly aid better understanding of what an ordinary share really is and always has been—a defined part of the equity of a company, as distinct from an entitlement to a specific number of dollars.

1243 In practice this significant change in the law will also mean the end of bonus issues (see paras 749 to 764)—a greatly misunderstood concept, although one which has been remarkably popular with many small investors for a long time.

1244 Conservative investors may lament this particular reform, but it will probably encourage greater national savings by helping people to understand better exactly what an ordinary share really is.

1245 Most other assets held by individuals—for example, houses —do not involve the concept of par values. This does not seem to perturb anyone. Nobody thinks of a car as somehow costing, say, $9000 plus a $5000 premium. Even units in listed unit trusts have always lacked a face value, but this has never worried unitholders.

1246 The earliest securities to be traded on a commercial basis, in the fourteenth century, were effectively loan securities— pieces of paper acknowledging a debt of a certain amount. The concept of having a face value for such an item thus had a natural origin.

1247 When the first companies were set up it was thus understandable that the equity interests in these should also be given a face value. The initial investors had paid a defined sum for their shares and they received a certificate mentioning that particular figure. It was seen as representing the "par value" of the shares.

1248 But the reality was that the investor in such a situation was not actually making a loan to the company which received the cash. What the investor was doing was acquiring a part of the "equity" in the company. The investor was buying the right to participate in a defined portion (or *share*—hence the name) of the profits of the enterprise (and of its net assets in the event of its liquidation). The investor became a part owner of the business and not one of its creditors.

1249 The original sums invested, while perhaps of some mild academic or historical interest, had no bearing on the value of the company either as a going concern or on a winding-up. They had even less bearing on the value of its shares on the stock exchange. This latter value was governed entirely by supply and demand.

1250 In recent years companies have frequently made their initial share issues to the public at a premium, so that the face value then did not even give future investors a clue as to the actual flotation price.

1251 The new rules will have no material impact on partly-paid shares, as any outstanding liability (in cents per share) will remain the same.

1252 The law which is about to change also presented some industrial companies with a problem. They could not readily issue shares at a discount on their face value, although this could be done by going to court—a process which involved needless expenses and delays, and which sometimes led to unfavourable publicity.

1253 A company in financial difficulties and desperately needing further working capital could easily find that the market price of its 50 cents (face value) shares was only, say, 40 cents on the stock exchange. A placement at around this figure or a proportional rights issue at, say, 30 cents might bring in the necessary cash, but an issue at or above 50 cents as required by law would have been impossible.

1254 Presumably the original reason for this illogical restriction was investor protection. However, a ban on share issues at a discount is useless in this regard if that discount is measured against a meaningless face value. If the market value or asset backing of a share is 300 then an issue to the favoured few at, say, 100 would be quite immoral—even if that price were well above a 50 cent face value and thus no breach of the law was being committed.

1255 Companies will soon be free to issue shares at any price they choose without requiring approval from a court or from any other external authority. The terms of any such capital raisings will thus be able to reflect the wishes of their shareholders and the realities of the market place.

1256 Dividend reinvestment plans will be able to adopt simpler rules, as they will no longer have to prohibit allotments at less than the par value of their shares—a feature which sometimes caused losses for investors when a company continued a plan despite its shares having fallen to a discount.

Shareholder Discounts

1257 Some companies involved with retail products give their shareholders a discount on the goods and services marketed by them. Such plans are very popular with small shareholders—although less so with institutions, who regard them as a form of cross-subsidisation.

1258 The extra demand for the shares arising from the existence of such a plan and the disincentive for holders to quit the stock are no doubt factors boosting its share price.

1259 However, if the company concerned is operating on thin gross profit margins and sales of its products which would have taken place in any event just occur at lower prices, then the effect on overall profitability may be negative. On the other hand, *additional sales* taking place at the margin can often be very lucrative and the value of additional goodwill is not easily measured.

1260 Of course, investors as always need to do their sums. There is little point in incurring a large capital loss on shares which go down, merely in order to make a small gain from the discount on an occasional small purchase.

1261 On the other hand, some customers may be able to benefit from the discount on a large volume of purchases in comparison with the minimum investment necessary in order to qualify for the benefit. This could have the result of effectively trebling or quadrupling the after tax return on their shares.

1262 Not all shareholder discount schemes are worth considering. Some offer benefits on only a limited range of products and these may not be of much interest to many shareholders. Some plans are unlikely to create much goodwill because they are little more than cynical marketing exercises dressed up to give the superficial appearance of conferring benefits on the owners of the business.

Chapter 13—Annual General Meetings

Business will get better, but we won't know
it when it does
—Henry Ford

Background

1301 Section 245 of the *Corporations Law* requires every company to hold an Annual General Meeting each year and Section 316 requires the directors to lay its accounts and certain reports before the meeting.

1302 Such a meeting (often referred to as the "AGM") serves much the same purpose as the annual meetings of less formal organisations such as a local tennis club or the like—namely:

- to provide an opportunity for the committee (in other words, the board of directors) to give an account of its stewardship

- for the consideration of the accounts

- for the election of office-bearers (directors) by the membership as a whole.

Section 225 requires motions for the appointment of directors to be voted on individually.

1303 Small shareholders can make much better use of the annual meetings of the listed companies in which they hold a stake than they often do. They should not regard going to them as just a waste of time and effort. Furthermore, the cynical view of some investors that the holding of such meetings is a waste of money completely overlooks the role of such gatherings in providing a safety valve which helps to protect the interests of shareholders.

1304 In practice most annual meetings are attended by only a small proportion of those entitled to be there. This is in part explainable by the fact that such meetings are normally held during office hours, thus making it difficult for people in the workforce to get to them—although one or two companies have seen fit to hold their meetings at night in order to overcome this problem.

1305 Furthermore, in the case of national companies, many shareholders live in a city other than the one in which the meeting is being held—although, again, a few companies have endeavoured to assist in this regard by arranging either live television hook-ups or by holding informal "information" meetings in each State in the weeks following the legal meeting. Some companies rotate the cities in which annual meetings are held in successive years.

1306 Most of the shareholders who do attend a meeting do not seem to participate in it in any meaningful way. Possibly they are intimidated by the atmosphere, although the chairmen of many companies go out of their way to make shareholders feel at home. Some small investors may think that their contribution to a discussion might not be welcomed, but the fact remains that a good idea is a good idea whether it comes from the individual holder of 50 shares or the institutional holder of 50 million shares.

1307 Perhaps the reason for silence is that many people are very conscious that they are not skilled in company law, in accounting principles, in the economy, in meetings procedure or in public speaking and that they really know too little of the company's affairs to want to ask an intelligent question in public. Some shareholders may not even have bothered to read the company's annual report and do not wish to be shown up by raising something which has already been fully explained in that document. It is a fact that meaningful attendance does require investors to do some homework in advance—but they will also become more skilled investors in the process.

1308 The education system should probably teach students not only investment principles but also about shareholder democracy and how investors can participate in company meetings, in the same way as the principles of voting in parliamentary elections are now presented.

1309 Many investors do not even realise that shareholders have a right in law to originate their own resolutions at general meetings of companies in which they hold ordinary shares. To that extent they have a privilege (technically called the "initiative") not yet accorded to Australian citizens in regard to originating their own legislative proposals.

1310 It is, of course, true that this right is more academic than practical. It is rarely exercised by small investors, as the need to find 100 or so shareholders to sign the appropriate requisition and the need to reimburse the company for its expenses in circulating the resolutions act as a deterrent.

1311 Another difference between voting patterns in the companies arena and those in the political world is more puzzling. People in the wider community nearly always decide constitutional referendum questions in the negative while at the same time similar people in their capacity as members of a company are usually willing to entrust their proxies to the directors at shareholders' meetings (thus virtually ensuring a "yes" vote).

Defamation

1312 While debate in Parliament carries absolute privilege, the discussions at shareholders' meetings do at least enjoy qualified privilege. This defence to defamatory statements extends to any occasion where the person making the statement has a legal, social or moral duty to make such a statement and the persons to whom it is made have a corresponding interest or duty in receiving it.

Business of the Meeting

1313 The notice for a typical annual general meeting includes items to the following effect:

- To receive the accounts.
- To declare a dividend.
- To elect directors.
- To transact any other business.

Many chairmen on opening a meeting and indicating that a quorum is present will introduce the directors and the company secretary seated at the top table. The notice convening the meeting and the minutes of the previous AGM are usually taken as read. The chairman may announce the number of proxies held, partly as a genuinely interesting piece of information and partly as a not very gentle hint to dissident shareholders that they would be wasting their time in challenging the board's control of the business of the meeting by calling for a poll on any matter.

(Most resolutions are decided by a show of hands, each shareholder present having one vote. However, there is a right for the chairman or some stipulated number of shareholders—say, three—to call for a poll. On a poll both shareholders and proxyholders can vote, and the number of votes is related to the number of shares held.)

"To Receive the Accounts": Questions to the Board

1314 The item of business usually taking the most time and attention is the proposal to receive and consider the accounts and the reports of the directors and the auditor. This is the occasion for the chairman's prepared address to the shareholders (and, effectively, to the world). It also provides the opportunity for shareholders to quiz the board as to the affairs of the company and—although this may not be encouraged by some chairmen—to speak to the motion without asking a specific question.

1315 If shareholders choose to stay mute at that stage then the incumbent board is clearly entitled to regard that as an unqualified endorsement of all its policies and practices. Yet one often hears of shareholders, *after a meeting,* uttering complaints about some aspects of a company's activities.

1316 It should be noted that this agenda item is not worded explicitly as "Questions to the Directors". Because of this some investors may in ignorance fail to use their chance to raise issues before it is too late to do so legitimately. However, some enlightened companies issue a form which specifically invites shareholder questions. This form is then included with the material accompanying the notice of meeting. The form allows shareholders who are unable to get to the meeting or who do not want to engage in public speaking to pose their questions in writing. The company can then respond at the meeting, perhaps saving time by grouping similar questions together.

1317 Just as in Parliament Ministers can avoid replying to difficult questions from Opposition backbenchers so can company directors deflect awkward questions from shareholders. In both cases there is no obligation to answer a question at all or to do so in a meaningful fashion. Naturally, companies and directors risk adverse publicity if such tactics are adopted.

1318 However, shareholders should persist. If, for example, after five minutes of waffle the chairman concludes by asking the shareholder, "Does that information answer your question?" then the shareholder should respond by smiling sweetly and saying, "Actually, Mr Chairman, the question which I asked was ...". If the chairman demonstrates unfamiliarity with issues which he could be expected to know, the questioners can use phrases such as, "As chairman, and in the light of your long experience with this company, could you please elaborate on ...".

Notes:

1. Technically, the asking of questions is part of a speech on the motion before the chair. Under the normal rules of debate only one such speech by any member—apart from the mover of a motion—is permitted. However, many chairmen are indulgent in this regard and allow or even encourage questions to be asked and answered one at a time, which usually produces a much more satisfactory result for the meeting.

2. For what it may be worth, the legislation is to be amended to provide explicitly that the chairman of an AGM must allow a reasonable opportunity for the members as a whole at the meeting to ask questions about or make comments on the management of the company.

1319 The chairmen of some less reputable companies engage in all sorts of dirty tricks, for example, trying to intimidate or embarrass a questioner by drawing attention to the small number of shares held by him or by insisting that all questions be asked one after the other, with the replies later on being given en bloc. This latter tactic is clearly quite unsatisfactory, as the opportunity for appropriate follow-up questions is then undemocratically denied to the members and the board can pick and choose which questions will be dealt with. For similar reasons moves to *require* all questions to be submitted in writing ahead of the meeting should also be resisted.

1320 Another device is to offer to answer the question privately after the meeting. Quite apart from the insider trading implications of such a practice the answer to a question asked in public should also be on the public record. Actually, the asking of questions can serve a number of different purposes beyond the obvious one of seeking information. For example, questions can be so framed as to make the directors think about some issue. The quality of the answers can also be used to assess the calibre of those responding. A chairman who does not know something but gets some other director or an executive officer to reply gives out a different message from a chairman who does not even realise that he does not know something.

1321 Worse still is the practice of some companies to exclude the media from their meetings. As indicated in para. 1236, it should be made compulsory for companies enjoying the privilege of listing to allow their affairs to be reported freely.

1322 For their part, shareholders have a duty not to ask trivial or irrelevant questions, or to raise matters which are not the concern of the company. However, questions need not be confined to the accounts—they could, for example, relate to government policy affecting the group, or to conditions in the industry concerned.

Shareholders will also be more effective if they are not long—winded and if they remain polite and respectful to the chair. Shareholders wishing to ask questions which may require some research would, of course, be well advised to submit these in writing some time before the meeting, with a request that the considered answers be made available at the meeting. Such a move would also make it rather difficult for the chairman to avoid answering the questions on the ground that it is unreasonable to expect him to provide the necessary information on the spot.

1323 The proceedings at some meetings have been disturbed by people who are not genuine investors in the company concerned, but who have acquired a small holding of shares for the express purpose of mounting a demonstration in respect to environmental or political issues, such as uranium mining, pollution, resource security, Aboriginal land rights, or involvement in certain countries not renowned for civil rights. Such antics and time wasting are quite unfair to bona fide shareholders who get only one chance a year to quiz their directors on their stewardship.

"To Declare a Dividend"

1324 The articles of association (rules) of modern companies quite sensibly normally delegate the power to declare dividends to the board. However, some older companies vest this power in the shareholders in general meeting—although only in a circumscribed way. Shareholders can reduce the rate recommended by the directors, but they cannot increase it. It is not hard to predict the effect of such a provision.

"To Elect Directors"

1325 Some directors (usually one-third of the board) retire each year "in rotation". Those with the longest terms of service since their last election or re-election get this distinction. Directors appointed to fill casual vacancies (or as additional directors) during the year also have to submit themselves for re-election, as do directors over the age of 72 years (who can be appointed for only one year at a time). Directors are voted on individually and a simple majority is sufficient (within the limit for the size of the board stipulated in the articles). This method makes it virtually impossible for candidates opposed by the existing directors to ever get elected.

1326 A much fairer election system than that just discussed would be to use the proportional representation method described in paras 1230 to 1231. For example, in the case of a board consisting of nine members, shareholders who between them held 10 per cent of the voting power could then ensure the election of their nominee.

(*Note:* It would be desirable that candidates for a board, including existing directors standing for re-election, should give a brief oral exposition of their philosophy before the vote is taken.)

"To Transact any Other Business"

1327 Most annual general meetings have a final agenda item on the following lines:

"To transact any other business which may be brought forward in conformity with the articles of association".

This is one of the great myths of the stock exchange scene— there is usually no such business, although the item is sometimes used to pass votes of thanks or congratulations.

Other Items

1328 Depending on the circumstances, the agenda of an annual general meeting (or, for that matter, of an extraordinary general meeting) may also include items on the following lines:

- To appoint an auditor.

- To make a bonus issue.

- To introduce or vary a dividend reinvestment plan.

- To authorise a share split or consolidation.

- To authorise a change of name.

- To authorise an increase in the authorised capital.

- To authorise asset acquisitions from or asset disposals to associated parties.

- To amend the articles of association.

- To authorise buy-backs.

- To raise the level of directors' fees.

- To introduce or vary a staff share purchase plan.

- To authorise the allotment of options to key executives.

This list is, of course, illustrative rather than exhaustive.

1329 The item relating to the appointment of an auditor is required only if a vacancy exists or arose during the year, or if a change of auditor is under contemplation. In terms of the law auditors can continue in office indefinitely, but a change of auditors every three or four years would be very healthy.

Information and Influence Aspects

1330 There are four main benefits flowing to shareholders who attend annual meetings:

- *Self-education.*

  Shareholders will become better informed, not only in regard to the company's operations and prospects, but also in regard to its philosophy. The manner in which questions are handled can give those attending a valuable "feel" for the company and an opportunity to assess the quality of its board and management.

- *An exercise in democracy.*

  Shareholders have an opportunity to vote on the election of directors and on other matters before the meeting. Shareholders should not blindly vote in favour of everything put up by a board—sometimes their best interests are served by voting "no".

- *An opportunity to shape a company's policies.*

  It is true that one vote on a show of hands (or 100 votes on a poll) may not go very far, but collectively shareholders are able to exercise control. Furthermore, even a small number of speeches against a proposition or a handful of negative votes can serve as a useful warning to a board of directors that there are limits as to what is acceptable to the shareholders.

- *An opportunity to influence companies at large.*

  Criticism of some proposal at the meeting of one company and the publicity which this attracts can also serve as a useful means of discouraging similar adverse moves on the part of other companies.

Of course, many shareholders also enjoy the opportunity of talking to fellow investors and board members over refreshments at the conclusion of the formal proceedings.

1331 Shareholders wishing to address the meeting should give some consideration to where they should sit. Often a central position near the front is best, as this allows the shareholder to catch the chairman's eye when desired and to address the audience most effectively. Other aspects to be taken into account should be the acoustics of the room, the availability of microphones and the location of the media table.

1332 A series of questions to a board will be more effective if these are posed one at a time by different shareholders working as a team rather than if they are raised by a single shareholder in a long list. Such a technique also makes it harder for the board to gloss over any difficult questions. The later questions in the series should, of course, take the answers given to the earlier questions into account—they should follow up weaknesses or deal with additional angles and not just be repetitive. For maximum impact each member of the team should be seated in a different part of the room and not give the impression of being a member of an anti-board clique.

1333 A shareholder who wishes to raise a particularly important point does not have to confine himself to asking questions and speaking on the resolutions placed before the meeting by the board. He can also use the rules of meetings procedure in order to move an appropriate amendment. It is generally best not to do this on the spur of the moment in the middle of an excited debate.

It is preferable that the wording of any proposed amendment should be drafted very carefully in advance of the meeting, so that it conveys a clear and unambiguous message both to its intended audience and to the world at large—even if, as is likely, the numbers to have it actually adopted are not reached. For example, when the usual resolution to receive the accounts is being considered, an amendment along the following lines could be proposed:

"That the following words be inserted before the full stop at the end of the resolution:

', but that, having regard to the fact that the company's earning rate on its shareholders' funds was only 3 per cent last year, the board be requested to institute as a matter of urgency a suitable program of asset disposals in order to lift the earning rate to at least the level being attained by the company's major competitors'"

1334 After such an amendment has been moved a sheet of paper setting out its text and the name, postal and e-mail addresses and telephone and facsimile numbers of the shareholder who proposed it, can be ceremoniously handed up to the chairman, further emphasising the shareholder's genuine concern in regard to the matter.

Additional copies of this should be distributed to all media representatives present and immediately sent to relevant media organisations not represented—a step which may lead to a more accurate reporting of the issues raised. The shareholder should preferably also make arrangements in advance for some other shareholder to second the amendment.

1335 A recent stock exchange survey (see Appendix 3) has shown that nearly three million Australians own shares in listed companies in their own right, although admittedly only three-quarters of them hold shares in more than one company. This "shares in only a single company" phenomenon is surprising having regard to the lack of spread which it provides, but it is no doubt explained in part by the growing popularity of employee share schemes. Some recent well—publicised mega-loats of privatised corporations have also played their part.

These figures of overall ownership represent a much lower percentage of the population than in the case of the United States, although they exclude the millions who hold shares indirectly through equity trusts, life insurance policies or superannuation funds. The numbers of individual owners are to some extent influenced by families registering shares in more than one name in order to get bigger entitlements in new issues subject to rationing and in share plans with dollar limits per shareholder. (However, such duplicate registrations may also involve disadvantages—for example, more bookkeeping effort, higher marginal tax rates, additional minimum brokerage charges and so on.)

1336 A person who holds only 100 or 200 shares in a company may regard himself as just an investor simply looking for income and/or capital growth. But, unlike a depositor in, say, a bank or building society or credit union, a shareholder is really a joint venturer with others in a business enterprise. As explained in Chapter 2, he is a co-owner of the assets, and quite literally a "member" of his company, with the ability at law to influence its affairs through the voting power conferred by this rather special relationship.

Post Meeting Reports

1337 Very few listed companies in Australia currently produce a "Post Meeting Report". Such reports would keep shareholders properly informed as to what happened at the Annual General Meeting, apart from the prepared chairman's address. A good post meeting report would include the comments from the floor, as well as questions and answers. It could usefully also set out considered elaborations on the impromptu answers given at the time.

1338 Such reports would also help to educate investors and increase shareholder goodwill to their companies. The concept would furthermore lift the standard of conduct at meetings.

Candidates for the Board

1339 Persons wishing to put themselves forward as serious candidates for election to the board of directors of a listed company against the wishes of the incumbents would be well advised to do some homework first.

1340 Obviously, they need to comply with all technical requirements in the company's articles of association, such as those relating to share qualifications, signatures on nomination forms and deadlines.

1341 At another level, such candidates need to have a well thought-out policy, which they can present both orally and in writing, not only at the meeting itself but also beforehand. Talking to the media without such a policy is likely to be counterproductive.

1342 Then they need to have a strategy for communicating with shareholders and for soliciting the shareholders' proxies. They also have to have the financial resources to enable them to do this effectively.

1343 Finally, they need to have regard to the election process itself. For technical reasons it may well be advantageous to stand as a member of a team consisting of as many candidates as there are vacancies, rather than just as a single person.

Announcements

1344 The use of the chairman's address to make major announcements of new share issues, expansion moves and the like sounds very democratic. Actually, in the case of information likely to affect the market price of the shares, it can be very unfair to those members actually in attendance, as persons outside the meeting room but with access to the concurrent official announcement to the stock exchange would be able to act on it much more promptly.

Chapter 14—Advice from Brokers and Others

*Advice is the only commodity on the market where
the supply always exceeds the demand*
—Anon

Background

1401 Some important aspects of getting investment advice from stockbrokers and other experts have already been presented in earlier parts of this book or are dealt with later, including:

- The role of investment advisers (paras 113 to 119).

- Investment in relation to the investor (paras 231 to 243).

- Choosing a broker (paras 523 to 527).

- The placement of orders on the stock exchange (paras 1601 to 1608).

- Pre-retirement planning (paras 293 to 294).

1402 Chapter 7 of the *Corporations Law* requires persons who give investment advice to be licensed either as "dealers" or as "investment advisers". This allows the authorities to vet applicants for licences in respect of their character, education, experience in the investment industry and solvency. There are also provisions enabling licences to be revoked or suspended in appropriate circumstances.

1403 A few general points should be made:

- Advice always needs to have regard to both the investor and the investment.

- An investor should in his own interest give his adviser sufficient information about himself for this purpose.

- No adviser can possibly be an expert on all types of investment.

- Advice involves making value judgements and normally comes without any guarantees.

- Advice given at any particular time may not hold good at a later time.

- Vague questions will lead to vague answers.

- Advice is just that—decisions still need to be made by the investor himself.

1404 Before seeking outside advice an investor should be clear in his own mind in regard to certain matters, in particular:

- His investment objectives and priorities.

- His future income requirements.

- His existing assets and liabilities.

- His risk profile.

- His desire to be involved or otherwise in the on-going management of his portfolio.

- His taxation status.

- His social security status.

Obviously, he should also be able to tell an adviser precisely how much money he wishes to invest now; what further sums he expects to have available for investment purposes in the foreseeable future; and for what duration he is able to commit his money. An investor who is unfamiliar with the stock exchange scene should in his own interest point that out to the adviser so the adviser can pitch his advice at the right level and not assume a greater understanding than really exists.

1405 Much investment advice currently being given is not really *independent* advice. In fact, it would be quite unrealistic to expect advisers who are remunerated by commission from the recipients of investment funds (as distinct from being remunerated by, say, an hourly "fee for service" charged to the client) to be entirely disinterested. There is nothing wrong with such an arrangement as long as the investor understands the situation and allows for it when assessing the advice and deciding whether or not to act on it.

It does not follow that "free" advice is necessarily worse in quality than expensive advice. On a different but related aspect, "tied" intermediaries posing as "independent" can also constitute a danger for unsuspecting investors.

1406 In many cases, of course, an adviser's likely bias will be obvious and even welcome—as when an investor deliberately seeks out a stockbroker, a real estate agent, a bank or a life insurance agent. There is, furthermore, nothing to stop an investor getting advice from two or more sources and testing out the suggestions from one adviser on the others. Naturally, such a course of action should not be taken too far, as otherwise the investor will only find himself utterly confused by the legitimately-held but conflicting opinions. Furthermore, the seeking out of information too often without ever acting on it may wear out his welcome with advisers remunerated on turnover.

1407 Regular contact with more than one adviser can have other advantages, particularly having regard to the frequent personnel changes in the industry. Furthermore, from time to time advisers die or retire, or go out of business, either as a result of mergers or more sadly when a licence is withdrawn.

1408 There is a distinct tendency for advisers to put small and/or new investors into pooled investment vehicles, such as unit trusts, investment bonds, or personal superannuation products. There is nothing wrong with such an approach if it suits the investor's requirements or as a deliberate first step while both investment experience and financial resources are being built up. In fact, the use of such vehicles may well be the only practicable way for some people to benefit from the tax concessions available in the superannuation area.

However, persons who would prefer to make direct investments, such as in shares, property, bank bills or whatever, should not allow themselves to be diverted from such an objective by advisers who find indirect investments more rewarding purely from *the advisers'* point of view.

1409 As explained in paras 287 to 292, investment portfolios need to be reviewed periodically. This can introduce another set of conflicts of interest on the part of those called on to give advice. If they recommend changes, are they really acting in the client's best interests or are they simply touting for business which earns them a financial reward? A proper system of charging for time on the lines of most professions and then rebating any commission in full would, of course, avoid such problems.

Advice from Stockbrokers

1410 The role of stockbrokers is explained in Chapters 5 and 16. The giving of advice to investors who request it is a normal function of the stock exchange system, at least as far as full service broking organisations as distinct from the discounters are concerned. Brokers usually give such advice on a one-to-one basis prior to accepting any orders. While acting on a broker's suggestions can never be a guarantee of success, it should be recognised that all brokers have a strong vested interest in giving good advice, as this will result in long-term client relationships and in valuable word of mouth recommendations to other investors. Apart from that, today's small client may become tomorrow's large client.

1411 In addition to giving such individual advice many brokers send out periodical circulars to clients on their mailing list, reviewing the market generally and/or recommending particular stocks. Some put such information onto a web site on the Internet. All such advice can be useful in stimulating an investor's thinking, but it should not be acted on without further discussion. From their very nature such suggestions deal only with generalities and thus they may not be suitable for the specific needs of any particular reader. For example, even if a share mentioned is a desirable investment for the client concerned in an absolute sense, it may not be appropriate in the context of his existing portfolio and the importance of maintaining spread (see paras 256 to 262). Furthermore, circumstances may have changed between the preparation of the material and its being read. There will also usually be alternative propositions worth considering.

1412 Brokers tend to have a relatively small number of favourite stocks with which they are particularly familiar—including the leading shares on the stock exchange list, various "house" stocks (companies for which the broker acts as underwriter), and a few other securities considered especially good value but regarded as overlooked by their competitors. This is fair enough, as with 1200 or so companies listed on the stock exchange it would be unreasonable for a broker even with extensive research facilities to be an expert on all of them. However, this is not much help to a client interested in getting advice about a particular stock which is not among those being actively monitored by the broker concerned.

1413 Brokers often issue buying recommendations. Selling recommendations are less frequent, possibly because to tell a large number of clients that they should all sell a particular share at once would be difficult in practical terms and might be counterproductive if the price then falls too much as a result. The question of which clients to contact ahead of others could also be a cause of considerable embarrassment. Such advice can also antagonise the listed company concerned—and it, too, might be an existing or potential client of the broker.

1414 If the broker had previously been actively recommending the share concerned as an especially "good buy" then reversed advice which is volunteered might also be regarded as involving a greater loss of face than just keeping quiet about the changed viewpoint and waiting to be asked. Some brokers might also be reluctant to advise clients to quit a previously recommended share in case the client thinks that the broker is merely trying to drum up business or in case the turning of an unrealised capital loss into a realised one upsets the client and prejudices his goodwill towards the broker. (Of course, much greater goodwill could be lost if the client is not told to sell and the share later on falls even further.)

At a practical level, brokers for understandable reasons periodically revise the list of stocks which they research on a continuous basis; a past favourite may be dropped in the light of changed circumstances, but the absence of full data would add to the broker's reluctance to discuss the company.

1415 Some brokers, on being asked about a particular company, inquire whether the client is thinking of buying or selling. A sensible client will refuse to answer such a question, which is irrelevant to the matter under discussion. The broker's views of a company should be the same either way—and, in any case, the investor could become either a buyer or a seller, depending on the information which is forthcoming.

1416 Another favourite and equally absurd response to a client checking up on what to do with an existing holding is for the broker to ask, "What did you pay for them?" or, more poetically, "What do they owe you?" Apart from capital gains tax aspects (see Chapter 29) the price paid for a particular share is completely irrelevant to a decision as to whether to sell it or not, which should always have regard to the future, and not to the past. It is *doubly* irrelevant to a broker's assessment of a share.

1417 Brokers who do not really know what a share price is going to do sometimes suggest to a client that he should sell half of his holding. If the share then goes down the broker is able to claim,

"Wasn't it good that I got you to quit some?" In the reverse situation he can say, "Wasn't it good that I got you to keep some?" But such advice is not intellectually honest—if a share is regarded as overpriced then the entire holding should be quit and vice versa. In any case, if half is sold now, does half of the remainder get sold each time the client asks about the stock and where does this halving stop?

Furthermore, a client selling off bits of his holdings and then reinvesting the proceeds in other shares will finish up with too many small parcels which are difficult to watch and expensive to administer and eventually to sell. The sole exception to this should be where the portfolio has become unbalanced by some freak appreciation in one specific stock.

1418 Conflict of interest situations can affect members of the stock exchange on occasions—as when a broker is a company director, or when a broking organisation is an underwriter to an issue or is acting for vendors of a large parcel of shares to whom a duty to get the best price is owed. The particular inability of an underwriter to give impartial advice during the period an issue is actually open is obvious and hardly needs stressing.

1419 Another aspect which investors should watch is described in paras 1068 to 1069 and paras 1659 to 1660—namely, that anomalies can arise in the prices of certain securities. Brokers frequently fail to alert their clients in regard to such buying opportunities.

1420 Some other facets of this subject are presented in Chapter 15.

Talkback Programs

1421 In recent years a number of talkback programs have sprung up on radio, with a format under which callers ask questions on investment matters of an "expert" in the studio. Such programs are often listened to by people nearing retirement or already retired, or by persons keen to help elderly relatives with their finances.

1422 Such sessions can be useful in stimulating interest in the topics discussed, but their regular presenters breach a fundamental tenet which should apply to all investment advice—namely, "know your client".

1423 In particular, radio programs of this type pose a number of
dangers:

- Even if the advice happens to be suitable for the
  original caller it may not be appropriate for other
  people hearing it, because their individual circumstances will be different.

- A caller cannot, within the limited time available
  to him, adequately describe his own circumstances, so that the answer may not be very satisfactory even for him.

- Each answer, again for time reasons, has to be
  given in a grossly oversimplified form and without elaboration.

- The questions can range over such a vast variety
  of different investment topics that no presenter
  regardless of how well qualified he might be
  could be expected to be an expert on all of them.

- Important qualifications to general advice will of
  necessity be omitted.

- The consideration of alternative propositions
  will also be omitted.

- The technical terms used will probably not be defined properly.

- The format of the program and the speed with
  which the various different subjects are disposed
  of do not allow works of reference or other
  authorities to be consulted.

- Listeners can all too easily mishear the names
  mentioned.

- Listeners can also misinterpret the specifics of
  the advice.

- Because of the off-the-cuff nature of the answers
  the scope for error on the part of the presenter is
  considerable, both in regard to investment aspects and in regard to taxation.

- There is no practical method of ensuring that any corrections, even if made on air later, will actually come to the notice of all persons who heard the original broadcast.

- The impression is usually given that there is a single "right answer", whereas normally there will be many possible alternatives, each with its own set of advantages and disadvantages which need to be weighed.

1424 Appropriate warnings are rarely given or emphasised sufficiently—for example, to the effect that past investment performance is no reliable indicator of future results.

1425 Similarly, the fact that tax provisions, social security rules and other legislation are liable to change may need much greater stress.

1426 There is often a conscious or subconscious bias towards the investments with which the presenter is most familiar and also in favour of pooled investment vehicles and other products which pay commission.

1427 There can also be a bias in favour of switching investments rather than in favour of retaining existing holdings, partly because this may generate commission income, but also because such suggestions make for more stimulating listening. Repeated advice to callers to the effect that they should not make any changes to their existing portfolios would sound rather dull, although this might well be the best course of action in a particular case.

1428 Certain other attempts to make the programs more interesting are also a cause for concern—for example, recommendations to listeners to take up new shares in a float which has been announced in only very general terms, without mention of the key data, such as the proposed issue price, the price earnings ratio at that price, the hoped-for dividend yield or the net tangible asset backing per share.

1429 Within these limits the programs are good for arousing interest and increasing knowledge. But they can also create a feeling of confusion and give the impression that investment is a subject which is unduly difficult. Furthermore, it should be recognised that half-truths and vague generalisations can sometimes be more misleading and dangerous than outright lies.

1430 To sum up, investors will probably be better off if they do not look to such sessions as a means of getting their own specific investment problems solved. Even less should they ever regard the answers given to someone else's questions as a satisfactory basis for decision-making by themselves.

Advice from Friends

1431 Many people seek investment advice on an informal basis from friends and acquaintances who they think are both knowledgeable and trustworthy. The comments in paras 1403 to 1404 in regard to professional advisers apply equally in such situations, but a few additional points should be made.

1432 The friend concerned may not really know all the investor's circumstances and on either lack of time or invasion of privacy grounds may be reluctant to ask the searching questions necessary for the task. The friend may not be as fully informed about the range of investment opportunities as either the investor or the friend himself thinks. The friend may also be reluctant to give advice, realising that if the transaction turns out well then he will get no particular thanks for his effort, while if it turns out badly then the friendship could be prejudiced. Apart from all that, the friend would have no machinery in place which would enable him to get in touch with the investor if and when circumstances or his views change and the investment should be varied.

Advice from the Investor's own Bank

1433 The possible bias of certain advisers is mentioned in para. 1406. One aspect worth stressing is the special relationship of Australia's trading banks to their customers. There is a long tradition of bank managers being looked at as impartial and expert sources of advice on anything to do with money.

1434 However, there are two problems with this. One is the obvious factor that the bank's interests and the customer's interests do not really coincide even in the traditional banking relationship—for example, a bank fee represents a profit for the bank but a cost for the customer.

1435 The other is that these days the banks market a range of investment and savings products of their own and cannot possibly be objective in evaluating either these or competing products. In any case, the banks' own performance in some recent years throws doubt on their ability to guide others in investment matters.

Taxation Aspects

1436 While some advice seems to be primarily tax-driven, the reverse can also apply. For example, an investor might be told to sell certain shares, or to transfer them into a different name, without any consideration being given to the capital gains tax implications of such a move.

Rules of Thumb

1437 Various commentators have postulated certain basic principles for selecting stocks, such as:

- Buy shares with low price earnings ratios.
- Buy shares with high dividend yields.
- Buy companies with low gearing and good interest cover.
- Buy large companies, because they survive hard times better.
- Concentrate on solid businesses with good long-term growth prospects.
- Avoid new ventures.
- Buy companies with rising earnings per share.
- Avoid shares on everybody's "buy" lists.

1438 Such mechanical rules of thumb are too simplistic to be of much value—they tend to be dangerous half-truths. Furthermore, any such list tends to have some internal contradictions.

1439 As explained in para. 921, the arithmetical ratios have their own limitations.

1440 One other problem is that a share is only as good as its price. To illustrate, a company with "rising earnings each year" may indeed be a very good company in an absolute sense, but if the market price of its shares has already risen to more than is warranted by its current figures and its further prospects, then these shares can represent a very poor buy indeed.

1441 Some investors in fact adopt a "contrarian" approach and buy shares presenting the opposite criteria to those favoured by the herd, in the belief that these represent better value for money. While this theory has some logic, it also is too simplistic to warrant a blind following.

Miscellaneous

1442 Investors are frequently given the unhelpful advice to "be selective". Actually, even this plausible approach is not necessarily sound, as the experience of certain hypothetical "dart funds" has shown—funds which regularly outperform many portfolios which are based on research. (A "dart fund" is a fund constructed by picking stocks determined by darts thrown at a board covered by a financial page which lists all shares in alphabetical order.)

1443 Sometimes advice seems to be designed more to cheer the investor up than to help his pocket. For example, an investor with shares which have gone down in value may be told, "If you are a long-standing holder, then hang on." In other words: "These shares will go up for you but down for everyone else".

Chapter 15—Some Investment Myths

*Successful men follow the same advice
they prescribe for others*
—Anon

Background

1501 This chapter complements the preceding one. It analyses a number of common sayings and miscellaneous widely-held beliefs relating to investment matters. Investors who subscribe to the various myths or half-truths in current circulation are likely to lose money.

1502 Some words of warning relating to advertisements are also included. A brief discussion of compound interest follows in Chapter 19. The fallacy that fixed interest securities are always safe is analysed in Chapter 17. Some further myths are dealt with in other parts of this book.

Myths Relating to Ordinary Shares

1503 "This share is good buying at any price."

Such advice is obvious nonsense—any asset for which too much is paid must turn out to be a poor investment. Indeed, a better cliche would be:
"A share is only as good as its price."

1504 "You can lock these shares up and forget all about them".

Wrong again—all investments should be reviewed periodically. Even good shares can become overpriced, either absolutely or relatively; companies which were once prosperous can fail; markets can become overheated; the needs of individual investors can change. Furthermore, to overlook one's holdings when developments such as rights issues or takeovers occur is asking for trouble.

1505 "It is never wrong to take a profit."

If this were really true then every time a share moved up in price ever so slightly it would have to be disposed of, regardless of its future prospects. In practice, following this dictum even in a less literal fashion would cause investors to dispose of their best stocks and to hang on to their worst duds—the exact reverse of what they should be doing, namely, cutting their losses if they find that they have made mistakes.

Furthermore, there is little point in an investor quitting a particular stock if the proceeds are then used to buy an equivalent but different stock by way of replacement—the only beneficiaries of such a strategy would be the recipients of brokerage, stamp duty and capital gains tax. It should also be recognised that sometimes the apparent profits are due to inflation and do not really represent an increase in wealth.

(*Note:* Another version of this myth is:

"Nobody ever went broke taking a profit.")

1506 "You have not made a profit until you have actually sold the shares."

This is really the same myth as in the preceding paragraph. If an investor really wants the satisfaction of feeling that he has made a profit then he can always *pretend* that he has sold the shares and then repurchased them—at least that way he will have avoided the charges which would be involved in actually making a switch.

1507 "It is only a paper loss."

These words of consolation imply that an investor has not made a real loss when his shares go down unless he happens to sell them. The sentiment is sometimes expressed as "You have not made a loss until you have actually sold the shares." The proposition is just as incorrect on the downside as it is on the upside, as discussed above. The current value of an equity asset is determined by market forces and only rarely is this value identical with the original cost price of the asset. A loss is a loss whether it is realised or unrealised, as would become obvious to any person taking an inventory of his assets and measuring his net worth.

1508 "You should average down."

This is the same absurd proposition in yet another guise. The basic argument of its proponents can be illustrated by the following numerical example:

- An investor buys 100 shares at 400.

- They fall to 320, so that he has lost 80 cents per share.

- He should then buy another 100 shares, this time at 320.

- His average cost price will then be 360.

- Therefore his loss has been halved to 40 cents per share.

The conclusion is perfectly correct, but utterly misleading. He now has half the loss per share, but on twice the number of shares! 100 times 80 cents is $80, as is 200 times 40 cents, so his dollar loss has not fallen one cent. Whether the investor should buy more shares or not ought to be based on his assessment of the *future* movements of the stock, not on its historical cost price to him.

1509 "You can come to no harm, because you are holding these shares for nothing."

Such words are generally used to describe a scenario such as the following, involving a rise in share prices after purchase:

The purchase of 3000 shares at, say, 100 = $3000

The sale of 2000 of these at, say, 150 = $3000

This leaves the investor with 100 shares at a net cost of nil (but with a current market value of $1500). However, he can still come to "harm" if things go wrong from now on, in the sense that he could become up to $1500 poorer than he is now, which would be a pity.

1510 "A takeover offer expressed in shares costs only the cost of printing."

In other words, a cake can be divided into five quarters.

1511 Some myths regarding rights and bonus issues are discussed in Chapters 7 and 10. Of course, some cliches have more logic behind them than those just discussed. For example, the advice "to leave some profit for the next person" refers to the impracticability of picking the peak of the market when trying to sell:

"Nobody rings a bell at the top or the bottom of the market."

Investment Advertisements

1512 Investment advertisements should always be read critically. For example, if the word "guaranteed" is used, who is doing the guaranteeing and what exactly is being guaranteed? A guarantee is only as good as its guarantor. If a $10,000 company "guarantees" the repayment of $100 million then that guarantee is not worth having. On a slightly different aspect, it is also nonsensical for the contractual obligations of some entity to be "guaranteed" by the entity itself—the word implies a promise by a third party.

1513 Some advertisements soliciting fixed interest funds have curious angles to them. To illustrate, one recent advertisement contained the following gems:

- "You fix the term." Of course.

- "Get interest seven days a week." As everywhere else.

- "Earn interest on your interest." Hardly special.

- "Fixed term means that the interest rate is fixed for the entire term." It means much more than that: the investor's capital is also tied up for the entire term. It also means that if interest rates move up then existing depositors will miss out.

1514 A real estate advertisement seeking to sell an investment property said proudly: "You choose the tenant!" This being translated means: "The present owner tried for many months to lease this lemon and did not even get close. If you are silly enough to buy it, good luck to you."

The Par Value Trap

1515 Sometimes the argument runs something like this:

"A $1 share selling for $6 is too dear."

The face value of an ordinary share is a purely nominal figure of no significance whatsoever. In one company a $1 share selling for $6 could be very good value; in another, a $1 share selling for 60 cents could be grossly overpriced.

1516 The factors affecting the market price of shares are discussed in Chapter 10. The proposed abolition of par values is discussed in Chapter 12.

The Role of Profit

1517 A myth believed by some non-investors is that large profits are somehow wicked. In such a context "large" is usually measured in absolute terms, without regard to the size of the assets used to generate the profit, without regard to the risks incurred by the shareholders and without regard to the development time taken to get to the position.

1518 Thus $1 billion profit might be regarded by some critics as excessive, even if it was earned on assets worth $30 billion and thus represented a return on funds of only about 3 per cent. It would be more logical if criticism were directed at those responsible for losses rather than at those producing profits.

1519 A successful enterprise helps the nation economically. It also creates jobs and generates taxation revenue.

Minors

1520 A myth of a different kind is believed by some people— namely that minors cannot own shares. They can, although it is probably undesirable that children not old enough to be able to sign their own names should become registered shareowners (notwithstanding the abolition of the need for share transfer forms bearing signatures).

1521 Companies, for understandable legal reasons, usually do not allow minors to become registered as holders of contributing shares—see para. 414.

1522 The rather punitive tax rate applicable to the investment income of minors, which is referred to in para. 2822, does, however, act as a practical disincentive to some investment transactions by minors.

Dollar Cost Averaging

1523 Another dubious investment strategy involves putting a nominated sum of money into the market, or into a particular stock, at regular intervals for a year or two, regardless of the price level at the time of each payment. This is known as *dollar cost averaging*.

1524 The theory is that as it is impossible to predict the bottom of any market this approach will cause the investor to acquire more shares at times of low prices than at times of high prices. Thus his weighted average cost price will always be below the apparent average price of the shares in the time span concerned.

1525 To illustrate, looking at just two parcels:

Buy 1000 shares @ 600 = $6000

Buy 1500 shares @ 400 = $6000

The average cost of the 2500 shares (total cost $12,000) is now 480, while the average of 600 and 400 is higher at 500.

1526 The trouble is that such an automatic strategy can encourage an investor to acquire a bigger exposure than desirable in a stock which has ceased to be a worthwhile investment.

Arbitrary Targets

1527 Another mechanical strategy involves taking a profit when shares have gone up by a specific proportion—for example, by 25 per cent. However, a share could still be good buying even after reaching such an arbitrary target—in fact, it may go on to prices two or three times as high.

1528 Equally, if circumstances have changed then a share might be good selling even if the price has not reached such a target. If a share is good selling at 125 to an investor who bought at 100 it may also be good selling to an investor who bought at 110-or, for that matter, at 150.

1529 It is always tempting to sell when the market is high. However, investors should bear in mind the risks:

- Even if the index is due for a fall, the market price of an individual stock might not be.

- It is easy to sell too soon.

- Selling can have adverse capital gains tax implications.

- Selling and repurchasing involves two lots of transaction costs.

- Picking the ideal time to repurchase is likely to be difficult.

- Being out of a stock can deprive an investor of the opportunity of benefiting from favourable developments such as takeovers.

Chapter 16—Trading on the Stock Exchange

If you don't know who you are, the stock market is an
expensive place to find out
—George Goodman

The Placement and Execution of Orders

1601 The placing of an order to buy or sell securities with a stock-broker must be carefully distinguished from the seeking of advice from that stockbroker, even if both activities take place (as they frequently do) in the same conversation. See also paras 1410 to 1420.

1602 Advice from a broker may be good, bad or indifferent—whether so regarded at the time or viewed later with the benefit of hindsight. But advice is just that—simply advice, no more, no less—which the client, as the principal in the transaction, is quite free to accept in whole or in part or not at all. However, once he accepts a specific piece of advice and acts on it, then he and he alone becomes responsible for the consequences.

1603 A client is, of course, under no obligation even to seek advice. However, as explained in Chapters 1 and 2, it is important that any client requesting help should make sure that the problem is adequately defined both in regard to the transaction under consideration and in regard to the wider picture—the investor's means, his existing portfolio, his risk aversion, and so on. A broker's advice should extend to discussing the economy at large as well as individual companies and securities, and to advising on portfolio composition and asset allocation.

1604 Orders can be placed:

- in person
- by telephone
- by letter
- by facsimile message
- by e-mail message
- through an Internet site.

Many orders are placed orally—which increases the scope for errors or misunderstanding (but see para. 1654). At this stage not all brokers are willing to accept orders electronically, but this will no doubt change as security is improved.

1605 Notwithstanding the relative informality of such order placements they lead to legally-binding and irreversible contracts. The London Stock Exchange's motto "dictum meum pactum" ("my word is my bond") really applies to the members of all stock exchanges and also to their clients.

1606 Clearly, in everybody's interest, the investor should always make sure that there is no confusion about such key details as:

- the name of the account
- the CHESS reference (HIN or SRN)
- the direction of the transaction (buying or selling)
- the name of the company
- the number of securities
- the class of security, if more than one class exists (for example, fully-paid and contributing shares; "old" and "new" securities; ordinary shares, preference shares, notes and options).

1607 In the case of selling orders, care should also be taken in regard to the precise number of shares held, which may have changed up or down over time as a result of activity such as share splits, consolidations, rights and bonus issues, previous transactions and dividend reinvestment plans.

1608 If the securities have been or are to be registered in the name of any person other than the client then appropriate details should also be given to the broker when the order is placed.

Price Limits

1609 Orders can be given in several ways, the most important being "at best" and subject to a price limit. As shown below, a two-edged sword is involved. Orders can be given on a "good till completed" basis or subject to some time limit, such as "today only" or "while cum dividend".

1610 An order "at best" literally means just that—that the broker should achieve the best available price, regardless of what it may turn out to be in relation to the price prevailing at the time the order was placed. However, in practice brokers will endeavour to confirm orders before executing them if there have been major price changes and/or unexpected announcements affecting the stock.

1611 An order which is subject to a limit means that the broker cannot buy above that price or sell below it, as the case may be. This exposes the client:

- on the one hand to less risk of the deal being done at a price deemed unsatisfactory, but

- on the other hand to more risk that the transaction will not be done at all (or done later, on the basis of revised instructions, at a less satisfactory price than could have been achieved in the first place).

The client has to choose between these two alternatives. There may be an advantage in stipulating limits which are not nice round numbers—for example, to use 801 rather than 800 when buying and 799 rather than 800 when selling.

1612 Some brokers will not accept limits on small orders.

1613 Another form of order is the "stop loss" order, theoretically designed to protect investors who are holding shares against falling markets while allowing them to benefit from rising markets. The idea is that the investor's broker should automatically sell the shares concerned if their price falls to a predetermined level.

1614 However, this price is only the trigger point for the selling order and it may turn out that the actual sale is executed at a much lower figure. Worse still, the trigger price may after the event be seen to have been an isolated low point, with the result that the investor misses out on all the subsequent gains.

1615 Because of these aspects some brokers refuse to accept stop loss orders.

Cancellation of Orders

1616 Provided that it has not already been executed, a client can cancel or amend an order at any time. The onus for initiating such action in the light of changed circumstances is on the client. Amendments should be clearly identified as such in order to avoid duplicated instructions being accidentally recorded.

1617 Orders regarded as "stale"—usually after about a month to six weeks—can also be cancelled by the broker. Some brokers fail to notify clients of such cancellations—a practice which is most unsatisfactory. Orders may also require redefining in the event of a books closing date intervening.

Screen Trading

1618 SEATS, the Stock Exchange Automated Trading System, was mentioned in para. 512. It is a single Australia-wide system now used for all transactions on the ASX. The price differentials which sometimes existed and which disadvantaged investors when each capital city had a separate stock exchange with its own trading floor are no longer possible.

1619 The television-type computer screens which are now used for trading all stocks under SEATS are conceptually similar to the manually-operated boards and their "chalkies" as used on the former trading floors, but with some differences to reflect the size limitations of the screen. Different colours are used for different types of data—blue for buying information (bid prices and quantities and the codes of the brokers involved), yellow for the corresponding selling information (offer prices and quantities and the codes of the brokers involved), green for background information (opening price, highest and lowest prices for the day, latest price), and so on.

1620 The order placed by a client with a stockbroker on the lines described above will be immediately fed into the computer used for screen trading. The current technology enables every stockbroker to have a terminal on his desk. Through this equipment any orders given in person or by telephone or fax can be fed into the central computer as soon as they are received. Where the price limits allow this, an order can be executed immediately and the details can even be confirmed to a client while he is still on the telephone.

1621 The computer matches buying and selling orders automatically, priority being given to the highest bid and lowest offer prices available at any time. As between equal prices, priority is accorded to orders according to the respective times at which they were fed into the computer system.

1622 Of course, as long as the current buying (or "bid") price (meaning the highest price which somebody wishing to buy is willing to pay) remains less than the current selling (or "offer" or "asking") price (meaning the lowest price which somebody wishing to sell is willing to accept) nothing will happen.

1623 However, sooner or later, that buyer, or some other buyer observing the state of the market, will raise the bid price to meet the then current offer price, and a deal will be done at that figure. Alternatively, the seller, or some other seller, will lower the offer price to meet the then current bid price.

Alternatively again, a buyer and a seller will meet somewhere in the middle.

(*Note:* The algorithm used for matching orders placed before the start of normal trading but for execution immediately after that start in circumstances where the highest bid price exceeds the lowest offer price can be illustrated by the following example:

- Suppose that at the head of the queue there is one order to buy 500 shares at "400 or less" and that there are two orders (placed at slightly different times) each to sell 100 shares at "340 or more".

- The first match will involve 100 shares (being the smaller figure of the 500 order to buy and the first 100 order to sell).

- Clearly, the price needs to be in the 340 to 400 range in order to satisfy both parties. The exact price is determined by taking the weighted average:
  $(500 \times 400 + 100 \times 340)/600 = 390$

- The second match will involve 100 shares (being the smaller figure of the 400 remaining order to buy and the second 100 order to sell).

- The exact price for this is now determined by taking a new weighted average:
  $(400 \times 400 + 100 \times 340)/600 = 388$

- This process continues as long as the highest remaining bid price exceeds the lowest remaining offer price.

- After that further matches can take place at equal bid and offer prices.)

1624 SEATS trading takes place on a national basis on each working day from 10.00 a.m. to 4.00 p.m. Eastern time, without a break for lunch. (The local times in States which are not on Eastern time are correspondingly different.)

Contract Notes

1625 Brokers are required to send to their clients a same day written confirmation of all orders executed. This is done in the form of a "contract note", setting out the date of the transaction, the required settlement date (see para. 1680), whether the securities were "bought" or "sold", the names of the broker, the client and the company concerned, the quantity, the class of security, the unit price, the total consideration gross, the brokerage, the stamp duty (see paras 1632 to 1634) and the balance due to or by the broker.

1626 The contract note would also have on it a reference to the fact that the transaction is subject to the rules, customs, etc., of the Australian Stock Exchange (see paras 515 to 516) and that the note is subject to the correction of errors. Securities traded near a books closing date would be identified as being either "cum" or "ex" the entitlement concerned (see paras 461, 713 and 753).

1627 Ownership of the shares takes place at the moment that the orders placed by the buyer and the seller are matched by the exchange's computer (see paras 1618 to 1624). Since September 1990 there has no longer been a physical trading floor on which transactions can be carried out between operators.

1628 The subsequent issue of a contract note only *records* a contract which has already been made. Similarly, payment by the buying client and delivery of scrip by the selling client (where it exists—see paras 1669 to 1681) or its electronic equivalent, while necessary ingredients in order to complete the formalities, do not affect the actual ownership question. As soon as the match has been effected the selling client becomes a creditor for the net proceeds and the buying client assumes the risks and benefits of being a shareholder. Any subsequent price movements, up or down, will affect his pocket.

Notes:

1. Some brokers include with buying contract notes a bank deposit slip making it easy for clients to effect payment though a bank.

2. Correspondingly some brokers include with selling contract notes an invitation to the client concerned to advise his own banking details. This makes it easy

    for clients to receive payment by direct credit to their own bank accounts.

1629 The buying broker will then arrange for details in the share registry of the company concerned to be updated. Shareholders should always advise the company and/or the broker promptly of any subsequent changes of address.

1630 Signed transfer forms are no longer required for shares and fixed interest securities changing hands on the stock exchange.

1631 In a few special cases, such as broadcasting and television companies, certain other formalities need to be complied with by buyers.

Stamp Duty

1632 The stamp duty referred to above is generally levied on both the buyers and the sellers of shares. In each case the rate is 15 cents per $100 consideration (or part thereof). Brokers remit this tax to the relevant State Government in bulk.

1633 Adhesive duty stamps are required only in the case of off-market transactions. The basic rate of duty is:

- 30 cents per $100, all payable by the transferee (listed securities)

- 60 cents per $100, all payable by the transferee (unlisted securities)

1634 The duty stamps of the State in which the company is incorporated must be used for off-market transfers. In some cases a minimum levy applies.

Marketable Parcels

1635 Originally the price fed into the SEATS computer indicated an obligation to deal at that price in a particular quantity (for example, 100 shares) or in some multiple thereof.

1636 This quantity was known as a *marketable parcel*.

1637 A number of shares less than a marketable parcel was said to constitute an *odd lot*.

1638 The precise size of a marketable parcel of shares depended on the market price (a sliding scale being used).

1639 However, such concepts made no sense in a computer age and they have now been abolished. Any desired number of shares from one upwards can now be bought or sold—effectively, a marketable parcel now consists of a single share.

1640 Initial purchases by investors would customarily be some round number. However, share issues are frequently made on bases involving ratios such as one for three or one for seven, meaning that an investor who may have started off with, say, 1000 shares will later on find himself with a number such as 1333 or 1142.

1641 Odd numbers can also arise from dividend reinvestment plans (see Chapter 32) or from capital reconstructions.

1642 There is no particular advantage and some inconvenience in a shareholder deliberately setting out to "round up" or "round down" his holdings each time something on these lines occurs. Small transactions may attract minimum brokerage.

1643 The nuisance value can be increased by the frequent practice of companies to round fractions down. Thus a one for three issue followed by a one for two issue will see a holder of 300 shares with 400 and later with 600 shares. But a holder of 400 shares will have 533 and later 799 shares.

1644 This means that bonus issues—see paras 749 to 764—can actually make shareholders marginally worse off.

Market Bids

1645 As indicated above, prices of shares are always expressed in cents per share. Where the price is in the common 51 cents to 999 dollars range any whole number of cents can be used. At lower levels fractions of a cent can be used. Prices need to be expressed in multiples of the appropriate "minimum bid", according to the following scale:

Price per share (cents)	Minimum bid (cents)
0.1 to 10	0.1
10.5 to 50	0.5
51 to 99899	1
over 99899	100

Deals not Involving Brokers

1646 There is nothing to prevent an investor buying or selling listed securities without using a stockbroker, if he can find another investor with whom to trade and if they can agree on price.

This would save on brokerage, but not, of course, on stamp duty (see paras 1632 to 1634).

1647 Naturally, investors should be wary of dealing with complete strangers—the risks of bounced cheques, stolen documents, forged signatures and so on are obvious enough.

1648 Securities can also be transferred privately without consideration—for example, gifts from one spouse to another in connection with a matrimonial dispute or a rearrangement of assets for tax reasons. Some such transactions may incur stamp duty. (The capital gains tax implications are discussed in paras 2951 to 2952 and the social security aspects are discussed in paras 3135 to 3136 and 3167 to 3169.)

1649 For off—market transactions a "Standard Transfer Form" (white) has to be used to advise the company's registry of the change of ownership. This form requires the signatures of both the transferor and the transferee and appropriate stamp duty (or, if applicable, an endorsement from the stamps office to the effect that the transaction concerned is exempt from duty).

Discount Brokers

1650 While most brokers offer a service which involves both the giving of advice (based not only on research but also on judgement) and the execution of orders, some broking organisations have set themselves up on the basis that they confine themselves to the latter function only, for which they charge correspondingly lower brokerage. They market their services to investors who know what they want. The absence of advice extends to operating aspects as well as to the merits of particular stocks and timing. There is also no scope for reciprocal favours, such as flotations or placements on attractive terms.

1651 Different scales of charges are used by different discount brokers. Orders placed electronically often incur lower brokerage than orders placed by telephone.

1652 There are also associated rules which, while again understandable in the context of keeping the broker's costs down, may not suit the convenience of every client—such as the need to deposit the purchase consideration before placing a buying order and to be a CHESS user sponsored by the broker concerned. However, the introduction of T+5 (see paras 1679 to

1682) has led to some conventional brokers imposing a similar discipline on their own clients.

Other negatives may involve the tying up of cash ahead of a buying order being placed or executed and the absence of anecdotal advice in regard to the feel of the market. Another disadvantage to some investors comes from the lack of access to floats being made on attractive terms and in respect of which good clients of full service brokers may receive priority.

Zero Brokerage

1653 Some companies allow their shareholders to acquire newly-created shares free of brokerage and stamp duty—see para. 777.

Security Aspects

1654 Some brokers record all telephone conservations with their clients on tape, a practice which has much to commend it and which has obvious value in resolving any subsequent disputes between brokers and clients as to the terms of any order. Brokers normally compensate clients for any errors on the part of themselves—and, having regard to the volume of business done, the speed of operations and the frailties of human beings, some mistakes are bound to occur.

1655 The risks of clients in dealing with members of a stock exchange are relatively small. The statutory requirements for brokers to hold dealers' licences under the *Corporations Law* complement self-regulation by the industry itself. All brokers are required to maintain certain minimum levels of net worth appropriate to the size of their operations and to submit peri-odical audited financial statements of their position to the stock exchange. They are also subject to regular and spot inspections.

1656 The Australian Stock Exchange also maintains a National Guarantee Fund which would compensate clients of brokers against losses of money or securities arising from broker fraud or insolvency. (This fund is the successor to the long-standing separate fidelity funds of the State stock exchanges.) Client moneys are placed in a trust account (or, by arrangement, in a cash management trust—see paras 1820 to 1827).

1657 While the assets of the Fund were over $150 million as at 30 June 1997 they are not unlimited and in the event of coverable client losses on a sufficiently large scale the assets could prove inadequate.

1658 Another significant limitation is that the Fund is available only for losses suffered by members of the public in their capacity as clients of a stockbroker, as distinct from in their capacity as clients of any separate entity related to that broker, even if it has a similar name, is managed by the same persons and/or is conducted from the same premises.

Other Considerations

1659 Before purchasing equity securities in companies with more than one class on issue serious consideration should be given to the question of which class is the best buy at the time. Brokers tend to automatically assume that the client wants fully-paid ordinary shares rather than, say, contributing shares or convertible notes. Frequently such securities provide significantly cheaper means of entering the stock, particularly for long-term investors—although the smaller volumes traded may mean that it will take longer to execute the buying order (or any subsequent selling order), with the obvious risks of adverse price movements in the interim.

1660 Orders to buy securities during rights trading (see paras 701 to 734) are best given in the form of "shares or rights, whichever gives the better entry". There are usually price anomalies between them; frequently, the rights plus application money will cost less than the corresponding shares, although in a fluctuating market the reverse can also apply at odd times.

Brokers Dealing as Principals

1661 Normally a client placing an order with a broker would expect that broker to act merely as an agent or intermediary in the transaction. On occasions, however, it can be in the client's interest to deal with the broker as a principal, as when the broker has available some desired shares in a house account or by way of underwriting residuum. Such shares may even be obtainable at a modest discount on the market value at the time. Because of the potential for a conflict of interest in such circumstances the broker is under an obligation to disclose on the contract note that he is dealing as a principal. Unless the client has previously agreed to the transaction being done on this basis he then has the opportunity to reject the deal.

Brokers' Nominee Companies

1662 All stockbrokers maintain nominee companies. In part this relates to the Australian legislative requirement already referred to in paras 453 to 456 to the effect that all shares have to be registered in the name of some specific shareholder, who is known as the "legal owner" of the shares. The real owner of this asset—the person who put up the money, who is entitled to the income, who can direct the vote and who would make any decision to sell—is referred to as the "beneficial owner". (The share register maintained by or on behalf of the company concerned, these days normally in computer form, shows only who the legal owner is.)

1663 Shares owned by clients can be registered in the name of their broker's nominee company for a variety of reasons, including a desire to preserve anonymity or in the case of some overseas investors in order to obtain the use of a local address. Such registrations are also often used for administrative convenience, in order to reduce paper work, to speed up settlements, or to protect the interests of clients in regard to entitlements to dividends or rights. Despite some beliefs to the contrary, there is therefore nothing sinister in the use of such nominee companies by brokers.

Market Price

1664 The concept of *market price* was introduced in para. 517. Actually, there can be up to three different market prices for any share at the one time—the buying price, the selling price and the price of the last sale. If the market price of a share is required as at a particular time such as the close of business on a specified date (a price which is referred to as the *closing price* on that date and which is published in some newspapers under the abbreviated heading "close") then the question arises as to which of these three prices is the most appropriate one.

1665 Sometimes the mean of the buying and selling quotes is used, but a preferable approach by far is to pay the most attention to the last actual trade and to market forces since then. This leads to the definition of market price as "the price of the last sale or a higher buying quote or a lower selling quote".

1666 For some purposes it may be better not to use the price at a particular moment, as that could be a freak result or the result of manipulation. An alternative approach would be to take the weighted average price of all sales during, say, five consecutive trading days (provided that these were all uniformly "cum" or uniformly "ex").

1667 The limitations of a market price should be recognised. The price applicable to 100 shares or so is not necessarily the price appropriate when a large stake is being considered. The vendor of a large parcel may have to accept a discount; alternatively, a large parcel may have appeal to certain buyers who are willing to pay a premium for the privilege of acquiring it in one hit. See also Chapter 11 in regard to the 20 per cent threshold for takeovers.

1668 A statistic sometimes quoted is the market capitalisation of a company—the market price of one share multiplied by the number of shares on issue, as an indication of the total worth of the enterprise. For the reasons given above this is a theoretical measure only; the true total value of the company could be well above or well below this figure according to the circumstances (see also para. 974).

Uncertificated Shareholdings (CHESS)

1669 When companies first started up last century elaborate scrip certificates in copperplate handwriting were the norm. Labour was cheap then and the number of shares changing hands was small. Nobody thought it odd that stock exchange transactions should involve manual processes. The shuffling of pieces of paper between investors, stockbrokers and company share registrars was commonplace.

1670 But now Australians live in an electronic age. Clerical staff is expensive. The volume of stock exchange transactions is enormous (see Appendix 2). Paperwork reduction is a national goal.

1671 Some years ago the need for signatures on share transfers was abolished, originally in respect of buyers only, but later on in respect of sellers as well. In these circumstances it was logical to move towards the complete abolition of scrip certificates.

After all, people depositing money into cheque accounts do not expect to receive a special certificate evidencing their title to the money—and they certainly do not expect to swap certificates every time their account balance changes! Why then should entries in a company share register be treated differently from entries in a bank's ledgers?

1672 More recently CHESS was introduced (the initials standing for *Clearing House Electronic Sub-register System*).

This involves paperless settlements of transactions on the ASX and cost reductions in consequence. The clearing house is a wholly-owned subsidiary of the ASX operating as a self-funding entity. In the case of transactions through stockbrokers investors are protected against any irregularities, through the ASX National Guarantee Fund (see para. 1656). Investors benefit by being relieved of the necessity of keeping track of certificates arising from purchases, new issues, bonus declarations, dividend reinvestment plans and the like. Companies communicate with their uncertificated shareholders in the normal way, except that they no longer issue scrip certificates.

1673 Individual shareholders cannot deal directly with the clearing house. They have to be sponsored by a *participant* to the system, usually a stockbroker. Large institutions, custodian nominees, trustee companies and the like can also be direct participants.

1674 Two distinct versions of CHESS are in concurrent use:

- Under *Broker Sponsorship* a client can arrange with his broker to be sponsored by him. No cost is involved in this, but a formal agreement needs to be executed. The client is allotted a unique *Holder Identification Number* or HIN, which covers the client's holdings in one or more listed companies. This number is effectively a password which needs to be quoted when orders are placed. Clients using more than one broker need to be separately sponsored by each. They would also get a separate HIN from each. If they wish to sell shares covered by one broker's sponsorship through a different broker then they must

first arrange for a transfer of the shares concerned to the latter broker's sponsorship.

- Under *Issuer Sponsorship* a listed company acts
as the sponsor for its own shares, other than
those already covered by a specific broker sponsorship. The shareholder is allotted a unique *Securityholder Reference Number* or SRN, which
covers the shareholder's holdings in that particular company only. Once again this number is effectively a password which needs to be quoted
whenever orders are placed, but this time round
it can be used without any further formality for
orders with any broker selected by the shareholder. No specific agreement is needed for issuer sponsorship, as the contractual aspects
would be covered by the company's rules.

1675 With minor exceptions, it will become compulsory for all
listed Australian companies to convert any remaining scrip
outstanding to issuer sponsorship by the end of 1998. However, for legal reasons companies listed in Australia but incorporated overseas (including New Zealand) will continue to use
scrip certificates.

1676 Periodical transaction statements (resembling bank statements) are issued to shareholders. These are for information
purposes only and have no value beyond that. In particular,
they cannot be used as security for loans—-lenders desiring this
need to have themselves recorded in the CHESS system.

1677 Before issuer sponsorship became common the need for private investors to enter into a sponsorship agreement with a
specific broker before they could participate in CHESS had to
be regarded as a fundamental design fault. Even those clients
who currently used only one broker might not want to lock
themselves into a semi-permanent relationship in this way
merely in order to improve clerical efficiency.

1678 As in the case of the banks' Personal Identification Numbers
(PINs) for obvious reasons both Holder Identification Numbers and Securityholder Reference Numbers should be kept
strictly confidential when not being used as outlined above. A
client should not even quote the HIN being used for transac-

tions with one broker to another broker—this would breach confidentially and not achieve anything beyond highlighting to the broker that competitors were being used.

1679 Shares used as security for loans can, if desired, be covered by the lender's sponsorship or that of a trustee company.

1680 The use of CHESS has no tax implications for investors, except to emphasise the need for them to keep adequate records of transactions. CHESS statements would show only the dates on which transactions were *processed on the share register*, which have no bearing whatsoever on the dates on which the actual transactions might have taken place (or been deemed to have taken place).

1681 Changes of address should be notified to the company's share registrar for issuer-sponsored holdings and to the broker concerned for broker-sponsored holdings. Other communications—for example, in regard to tax file numbers or dividend elections—should always be sent to the company's share registrar.

T+3 and T+5

1682 The rules of the stock exchange have always required speedy deliveries of documents between members. Under the earlier procedures if a selling client did not deliver the appropriate documents on time then the buying broker could "buy in" against him, that is, buy equivalent shares from another seller on a "prompt delivery" basis. The client's own broker would then need to resell the shares to another buyer when the client delivered them in due course, with the difference in the two transactions being for the client's account.

1683 A more modern procedure, usually referred to as "T+5", started on 30 March 1992. This is a rule requiring both broker/broker and broker/client settlements for most stock exchange transactions to take place on the fifth business day after the date of the transaction. In particular:

- Buying clients must pay their broker no later than the morning of the fifth business day.

- Selling clients must deliver scrip to their broker (where still held in certificated form—see above) no later than the morning of the fifth business day.

- Contract notes must show the due date for client settlement (as well as the date of the transaction).

- There are penalties on both brokers and clients who miss the deadlines.

- Settlements under this framework will never again involve claims from "cum entitlement" buyers who are not registered by a company's books closing date for rights or dividends, thus greatly improving the efficiency of the system.

- For "deferred delivery" securities a suitably modified version of "T+5" applies until scrip is available.

1684 This rule also enables the bulk "netting" of transactions between brokers each day, thus reducing the paperwork which previously applied when individual buying and selling orders needed to be matched. In addition, T+5 helps to make the Australian market more attractive to foreign investors, who are used to such a discipline in other countries. The Australian Stock Exchange intends to replace T+5 by T+3 from 1 February 1999.

Short Selling

1685 Normally an investor realises a profit or a loss by buying shares or other securities, holding them for a period and then selling them. However, in conceptual terms the order of the buying and the selling can be reversed. Thus an investor can sell shares which he does not own for, say, $3000, and *subsequently* purchase them for, say, $2000, making $1000 profit in the process. The first leg of such a transaction is called "short selling".

1686 It will be obvious that any person who expects the market to rise can profit from such a belief, if indeed it turns out to be correct, by becoming a buyer of shares. In the same way a person who expects the market to fall can profit from this belief, if it turns out to be correct, by becoming a seller of any shares which he already holds. A system involving short selling in effect extends the opportunity to use this selling strategy to persons who are not already holders of the shares concerned.

1687 The special nomenclature—which, incidentally, also applies in other contexts, such as futures trading—should be noted. A "long" position is said to arise when a person holds a positive number of, say, shares, an asset; correspondingly, a "short" position is said to arise when a person holds a negative number of shares, a liability—effectively when he "owes" shares to somebody else.

1688 Such short selling does not, of course, affect the issuing company. For example, if it has issued one million shares it will still have only one million shares on issue even if collectively investors at some point of time are long in 1,100,000 and short in 100,000. (Naturally, only the owners of one million shares can show up on the company's share register at any point of time.)

1689 Some persons regard it as immoral for persons to sell assets which they do not own, but provided that no deception is involved the practice seems unexceptionable and comparable to the spending of money which a person does not own but has obtained legitimately by raising a loan. It is no more unethical to sell/buy (in that order) than to buy/sell.

1690 Short selling in fact serves a useful economic function by ironing out price fluctuations—for example, if the price of a share rises too much, then selling pressure not only from holders but also from non-holders will help to force its price down.

1691 In the absence of rules to control short selling in an organised way there could be practical problems in relation to settlement aspects—how can the purchaser of non-existent shares receive or enforce delivery and how can the vendor effect delivery?

1692 Worse still, problems can arise if the short seller's judgement that the market will fall turns out to be wrong. A buyer who misreads the market can lose all his investment, but no more. However, the potential losses of a short seller are unlimited. If he sells for a particular sum but is forced to buy back for 10 times that figure then his losses can be enormous and he could even be wiped out.

1693 Short selling can also cause losses for innocent parties. If a short seller is unable to deliver because the market has risen too much for his pocket then the purchasers of the shares concerned—whose good judgement to the effect that the price would rise has actually been vindicated—will miss out. At the time of purchase, of course, they would have had no knowledge of whether their particular parcel really existed or not.

1694 Because of these aspects short selling was illegal in Australia for a long time. However, Sections 846 and 847 of the *Corporations Law* now permit short selling to a limited extent—for example, where it is used as part of an arbitrage transaction or, subject to certain safeguards, where arrangements are in place enabling delivery within three business days (for example, by virtue of the vendor having "borrowed" the necessary securities from some other holder, at a mutually-agreed fee).

1695 The Australian Stock Exchange has adopted a set of complementary rules, although these do not apply to brokers and large institutions. For example:

- Short selling is permitted only in the shares of certain specified larger and more active companies and in public securities.

- Clients wishing to short sell must advise the broker of this when placing the order and must first deposit a 20 per cent margin with the broker concerned, to be held in trust. This margin has to be topped up if the market price rises by more than 10 per cent.

- The short sale must be made at a price equal to or higher than the previous sale price. This requirement is known as the "Uptick Rule".

- Short sales must be identified as such on the trading documentation.

- The total short positions for the shares in any one company must not exceed 10 per cent of the total shares on issue.

1696 However, most brokers do not encourage their private clients to engage in short selling transactions, partly because of the administrative difficulties involved in policing the margins on a daily basis and in arranging "loans" of securities for small quantities. In any case, the same economic effect can often be achieved more readily by the use of options or futures—see Chapters 22 and 23.

1697 Brokers themselves frequently short sell—for example, in order to arbitrage between Australian and overseas markets (see also paras 986 to 988).

1698 Capital gains and losses from short selling transactions are dealt with under the ordinary provisions of the income tax law and not under the special provisions relating to conventional capital gains and capital losses which are discussed in Chapter 29.

Chapter 17—Government Securities

*Blessed are the young, for they shall
inherit the national debt*
—Herbert Hoover

Background

1701 The Federal Government borrows money for public purposes, although these days to a lesser extent than formerly. This allows persons wanting risk-free investments (see paras 1718 to 1721) to buy Commonwealth Treasury Bonds. These are fixed interest loan securities, maturing at various specified dates, in the main up to about 10 years out. Interest is payable half-yearly and the bonds are listed on the stock exchange.

1702 In addition, semi-governmental securities exist. These were originally issued by gas, electricity, water and similar authorities set up under State legislation. Their capital repayment and interest payment obligations were normally guaranteed by the State Government concerned. These securities, which are often called "bonds" or "debentures", are similar in character to Commonwealth Bonds, but they are marginally less secure and this is reflected in the rating awarded to them by the professional ratings agencies. Furthermore, they not as marketable and therefore they normally command a slightly higher yield than the corresponding Commonwealth paper.

1703 In recent years some centralised borrowing authorities have been set up by various State Governments and also by the Northern Territory Administration. These centralised borrowing authorities issue semi-governmental paper on the same lines as above on behalf of the various operating authorities as a group. Some Commonwealth instrumentalities can also be semi-governmental borrowers.

1704 From time to time new money is raised directly from the public by prospectus issues. Existing securities can be purchased and sold in the secondary market—on the stock exchange—in the same way as shares. Lower brokerage rates (based on the face value, rather than on the market value) and exemption from stamp duty apply. However, the turnover in small issues is very low and selling such securities on a reasonable basis can be very difficult.

1705 Small investors can purchase Treasury Bonds over the counter at branches of the Reserve Bank of Australia in each capital city. Some semi-governmental instrumentalities have also made arrangements with panels of market makers so that investors can buy and sell small parcels of their securities at a fair price.

1706 Some people like to subscribe to the loans of specific semi-governmental authorities for social, patriotic or sentimental reasons—for example, they like to support the body providing water and sewerage facilities in their locality because they can see what it does and because they value its services. However, hard-nosed investors would be more interested in two other aspects—the yield and (if there is any likelihood that they might want to quit the stock before its maturity) the marketability.

Yields

1707 The redemption yields on existing government securities as a group go up and down with changes in interest rate levels generally—see paras 263 to 268—and their market values will fluctuate accordingly. A tender system is used for the issue of new Treasury Bonds, allowing market forces to govern the terms.

1708 As explained in para. 227, the redemption yield is the return allowing for both the coupon and the difference between the market price and the redemption (maturity) value. (The flat yield—in other words, the coupon divided by the market price—does not give a useful indication of the worth of a fixed interest security.)

1709 The yield on any specific government security can also go up and down according to supply and demand. At times yields on individual securities can be significantly out of line with the rest of the market. These can be good buying for holders to maturity. However, short-term investors will probably encounter a similar yield anomaly at the time of sale, although they may achieve a higher than normal return until then.

1710 The yield on such paper also varies with the unexpired term. Usually the longest terms command the highest yields, a phenomenon referred to as a "normal yield curve". Occasionally the reverse applies, a phenomenon referred to as an "inverse yield curve". The price of a particular security is thus likely to change as its maturity date approaches, even in the absence of changes in overall interest rate levels.

1711 The market price on a day-to-day basis reflects not only the yield pattern just discussed but also the amount of interest accrued since the last half-yearly interest date. (Between the books closing date and the actual payment date the accrued interest will be negative.)

1712 Potential subscribers to new issues should compare the yield being offered in the prospectus with the redemption yields available on the secondary market for comparable existing securities having similar maturity dates. Often it will be more attractive to buy on the market, particularly if only a small quantity is involved and the investor is flexible as to the precise issue which he is willing to accept and is prepared to wait for a few days till a matching seller can be found. Occasionally new issues offer slightly higher rates to investors subscribing directly to the borrower than to investors using intermediaries.

Inscribed Stock

1713 Commonwealth Bonds are currently issued only in "inscribed stock" form, meaning that there are no bearer bonds available. The Inscribed Stock Register is maintained by the Reserve Bank of Australia. Transfers are effected by lodging the appropriate transfer form at the registry. Semi-governmental securities involve corresponding procedures, usually with the issuing authority itself maintaining its own register. The half-yearly interest can be paid automatically into a designated bank account.

1714 Older Commonwealth Bonds are available in a choice of bearer bonds or inscribed stock. Transfers from one to the other can be made on request. Bearer bonds are in some ways similar to scrip certificates, but they do not show the name of the owner and they are transferable by delivery. However, they need careful safekeeping, as unlike share scrip they are negotiable instruments and their loss by theft or destruction thus has the same effect as the loss of bank notes. Interest is payable by clipping off dated coupons attached to the bonds and presenting them to a bank. In a similar way some semi-governmental "debentures" with attached coupons exist as an alternative to inscribed stock.

Other Aspects

1715 Although semi-governmental securities are redeemable on the designated maturity date investors on the register at the time are often but not always offered conversion to a new loan being raised. The interest rate on this will be governed by the conditions current at that time and the rate can be vastly different, in either direction, from that previously applying. This can be a trap for investors relying on the interest payments for living purposes, as their income can fall in dollar terms at the same time as the dollar itself is losing value. Conversion is, of course, optional and investors who desire to continue in this sector of the market should make the comparisons referred to in the preceding paragraph *before* taking any action.

1716 All the government securities mentioned above are "trustee securities"—see para. 251.

1717 A special tax rebate of 10 cents in the dollar is available for some older government and semi-governmental securities.

Risk

1718 Government paper can be regarded as risk-free in the sense that the regular payment of interest on the due dates and the repayment of the capital on the stipulated maturity date are assured. However, three separate risks should be mentioned for the record.

1719 Firstly, if the Australian Government were ever overthrown by revolution or invasion, then the securities mentioned above would all become as worthless as Czarist loans. But in those circumstances every other asset in Australia would, of course, suffer a similar fate.

1720 Secondly, the only contractual promises refer to punctual payment on the due dates. There is no guarantee that the market value during the currency of the loan will not fall to less than the issue price or the cost price to any subsequent purchaser. As explained in paras 1707 to 1711, market prices can, in fact, move up and down. Furthermore, there is no guarantee that there will always be a convenient market on which orderly trading will take place or that a particular issue will be liquid on the stock exchange.

1721 Thirdly, the only contractual promises refer to a payment in Australian dollars. There is no guarantee that the purchasing power of those dollars will be maintained—actually, investors can be absolutely certain that it will not, and they will obviously need to take that fact into account when making their investment decisions.

Indexed Bonds

1722 Indexed Commonwealth Treasury Bonds were at one stage issued as a variation on the normal Bonds. Two versions exist, both involving quarterly interest payments.

1723 Under the first version, called "Capital Indexed Bonds", the investors get a low coupon, but the amount of interest paid each three months and the prospective amount of capital at maturity both move up in line with changes in the Consumer Price Index (CPI) each quarter. Interest payments are based on the written-up capital value at the time.

1724 Under the second version, called "Interest Indexed Bonds", the investors also get a low coupon, but the amount of interest paid each three months represents the sum of the quarterly coupon and the CPI movement for one quarter. The capital at maturity remains unaltered at its original face value.

1725 The intention behind both these securities (and some similar paper at State level) is to protect holders against the ravages of inflation. However, as all interest payments and the annual write-up of capital in the case of the first version are taxable this objective is not achieved except where the relevant amounts when combined with income from other sources are below the investor's tax threshold (see the sliding scale in para. 2817 and the comments on combining franked dividends with other income in para. 2842).

1726 In fact, the rule relating to discounted and deferred interested securities which is described in para. 2935 and which applies also to Capital Indexed Bonds can mean that the annual tax liability on these can exceed the cash available each year from the coupon. The Interest Indexed Bonds do not maintain the purchasing power of either the initial interest payment or the original capital cost and thus do not seem to serve any useful purpose.

1727 The overall return available on indexed bonds is likely to be similar to the return on conventional bonds. The terms of issue of new bonds are set by public tender.

Australian Savings Bonds

1728 An Australian Savings Bond (ASB) is a version of the Commonwealth Treasury Bonds specially designed for small savers. New series of ASBs are no longer being created by the Government, but bonds issued in earlier years are traded on the secondary market and subject to availability can be bought through stockbrokers. (Australian Savings Bonds are popularly known as "Aussie Bonds".)

1729 Unlike normal Treasury Bonds, the Australian Savings Bonds contain a provision allowing their holders to redeem them at par plus accrued interest. The rate of interest available on current Treasury Bonds from time to time can exceed the rate payable on some series of Australian Savings Bonds. In such circumstances an investor can lift his income by redeeming an ASB and reinvesting the proceeds elsewhere.

Issues by Instalments

1730 Some semi-governmental issues allow subscribers to apply for debentures on the basis of a 10 per cent deposit, with the balance by some specified later date. Apart from helping with an investor's cash flow and possibly facilitating the rearrangement of other investments such a device can be of assistance when interest rates are expected to fall. They allow subscribers to lock in the prospectus rate on the entire commitment and not on just the deposit.

Chapter 18—Other Fixed Interest Investments

Money speaks sense in a language
all nations understand
—Aphra Behn

Mortgages

1801 A *mortgage* is the transfer of an interest in land for the purpose of securing the repayment of a loan or other debt. If the mortgagor (the borrower) defaults then the mortgagee (the lender) has certain rights, including the right to sell up the property in order to clear the debt. (Any balance, after deducting all costs, is paid to the borrower, the former owner of the land concerned.) A "first mortgage" creates a charge which ranks ahead of other charges known as second, third, etc., mortgages.

1802 Loans secured by a first mortgage on prime freehold property are favoured by many highly conservative long-term fixed interest investors, especially where the subject property is income-producing and in a good location and where it involves a long lease to a good tenant. However, such investments clearly give no protection against inflation.

1803 Ideally such loans should not exceed about 60 per cent of a conservative valuation of the property and the annual interest bill should be less than the annual rental (net of the outgo apart from the interest). Such a maximum valuation ratio can be exceeded if mortgage insurance is effected. The borrower should be of good reputation and financial standing and should have other income out of which payments can be made if rent ceases to come in. All loan expenses are borne by the borrower.

1804 Loans taken out by borrowers who are themselves investors are usually on an "interest only" basis for terms of three to five years, at an interest rate which is either fixed for the term of the loan or is subject to variation in accordance with some agreed formula.

1805 Some mortgage lenders confine themselves to loans secured on residential properties, a blind prejudice which does not make very much commercial sense, although it is presumably based on the belief that payments to keep a roof over one's head will have a priority as far as both tenants and owner-occupiers are concerned—a factor which may not be of much help if unemployment, sickness or death strikes.

While obviously each property must be treated on its own merits, tenants of commercial and industrial premises can often have considerably more substance behind them than most residential tenants; businesses can have substantial cash flows, in comparison with the rent; personal guarantees by several directors can complement covenants given by corporations; the gross yields are often better, thus improving the interest cover; and the chance of capital appreciation may also be higher, thus improving the assets cover.

Furthermore, a landlord can have great practical difficulties in evicting a defaulting residential tenant, a factor which does not help a mortgagee at the best of times and which may become acutely embarrassing to a mortgagee actually in possession.

1806 A more sensible criterion for lenders would be to avoid loans secured on "single purpose" buildings. It is much harder to sell such assets, should this ever become necessary, or even to find tenants for them if they are vacant.

1807 Mortgages are not really suitable investments for investors unless their funds are sufficiently large to allow the acquisition of a mortgage portfolio which can provide adequate spread. While a secondary market in mortgages exists to some extent, a mortgage must still be regarded as a relatively illiquid investment. Furthermore, it is impossible to convert part only of a mortgage into cash, in contrast to the position with parcels of shares or unit trust units, which can be broken up and sold off in stages. Again, mortgages cannot readily be disposed of if the investor's view of interest rates, inflation or other economic conditions changes.

1808 Mortgages require more administrative effort than many other forms of fixed interest investment—the policing of the periodical repayments, the policing of insurance cover, the instituting of legal action on default, and so on.

1809 Most of the above-mentioned disadvantages—although not, of course, the loss of purchasing power due to inflation—can be overcome by investing in mortgages indirectly through mortgage trusts—see below. However, these normally involve relatively heavy charges, particularly in the case of relatively short-term holdings, and also some risks in regard to the security of the capital if the trusts are not managed properly or if charges ranking ahead of the unitholders' interests are permitted.

Mortgage Trusts

1810 Some fixed interest trusts invest mainly in mortgages, which tend to produce higher returns than government paper, even after allowing for the considerably greater administrative costs. Good quality first mortgages can under normal conditions be regarded as relatively safe investments, as in the event of default the property which has been charged can be realised and the debt recovered. In fact, in such circumstances penalty interest clauses can add to the profitability of the deal.

However, in times of recession even first class borrowers can fall into arrears in large numbers through no fault of their own, at the very time when properties become virtually unsaleable. Mortgage trusts are thus not risk free in relation to the asset backing of their units. Separate from this is, of course, any liquidity risk.

1811 Some mortgage trusts endeavour to discourage short-term investors by imposing relatively heavy exit fees on unitholders who quit during the first few years.

Loans to the Tax Office

1812 As discussed in para. 2824, salary and wage earners must have tax instalments taken out of their pay packets under the "pay as you earn" (PAYE) system. The law stipulates minimum amounts for this purpose. Some people regard this mechanism as an attractive way of saving in a semi-compulsory fashion for holidays and the like. It is, of course, perfectly legal for the tax deductions to exceed the statutory minima and for the excess to be received back once a year as a refund when the assessment is issued.

1813 However, as an investment such a scheme has no merit whatsoever, as the Australian Tax Office does not pay any interest at all on such savings. It is far better for equivalent deposits to be made into normal interest-bearing savings accounts, either by the employee himself manually or, where the employer is willing to make the necessary arrangements, by automatic transfer.

Bank Bills

1814 As explained in para. 277, bills of exchange can be subdivided into "bank bills" (bills issued or endorsed—effectively guaranteed-by a trading bank) and "non-bank bills". The former are safer and extremely liquid, but the latter command higher yields. Bills do not pay interest as such, but are issued at a discount on their redemption value. For example, a 90-day bill with a face value of $100,000 yielding 15 per cent would cost $96,433.29 (as 15 per cent of this sum, multiplied by 90/365, equals $3566.71, the difference between this sum and the face value). This gives the appearance of "interest in advance", but for many taxpayers (both debtors and creditors) the difference between cost and eventual proceeds is treated as being made on the day of termination. See also para. 1913.

1815 The professional market deals in bank bills in lines of $5 million and upwards. The yields ruling on this market, which vary in accordance with supply and demand, are published in the newspapers each day for 90-day and 180-day bills. Along with the yields on longer dated Commonwealth bonds these yields give a picture of how interest rates are moving generally.

1816 Smaller bills (for example, $100,000 face value) are also available, but at yields to investors slightly below those ruling in the professional market. (Yields to borrowers are similarly slightly above those ruling in the professional market.) It is also possible to obtain interests in bills for smaller amounts, even down to about $5000.

1817 Normal terms go up to about 180 days. Subject to availability and to the yields ruling from time to time bank bills can be a viable and very safe alternative to call or short-term deposits in banks, building societies, cash management trusts and the like. The maturity date can sometimes be chosen to fit in exactly with the investor's specific requirements, for example, in connection with settlements for property purchases.

If a rollover for a further term is desired this can readily be arranged, but at the then current interest rate—except where arrangements have been made for the rollovers to be made on a "fixed basis" instead of a "variable basis". (The initial interest rates for the two bases will be different.)

1818 Bills can be bought or sold through both banks and stockbrokers. Settlement is usually on a "same day" basis. The price obtainable on any resale before maturity would naturally be a function of the interest rate prevailing at that time for new bills having the same unexpired term. This interest rate is likely to be different from the interest rate which applied for the original purchase for several different reasons:

- Because interest rate levels generally may have changed.

- Because shorter bills normally command lower yields than longer bills (but see para. 1517).

- Because there may be a margin between the bases used by the selling organisation when selling and repurchasing the bills.

Thus bills not held till their maturity dates can result in realised capital gains or capital losses, an aspect which should be taken into account when comparisons with interest rates on straight deposits are made.

1819 The purchaser of a bank bill can get immediate delivery of it if he effects settlement by means of a bank cheque. Alternatively, he can get ownership immediately but take delivery a few days later, after a personal cheque has been cleared. However, as bills are negotiable instruments most individual purchasers do not want physical delivery and are content to leave the bills with the bank or broker supplying them, pending either their resale at a later date when the cash is required or their redemption or rollover at maturity.

Cash Management Trusts

1820 A cash management trust (CMT) is a fixed interest unit trust designed specifically for short-term investors. For this reason no front-end or rear-end fees are imposed, the manager's expenses and profits being covered by a periodical charge based on the total value of the fund. Units are normally issued at $1 and redeemed at $1, with interest accruing on a daily basis at a variable rate related to the fund's actual earning rate each day.

1821 New investors must apply on a form attached to a current prospectus, but existing unitholders can make further deposits without such a formality. Deposits can usually be made in person, by mail or through a bank (including by electronic transfer from other accounts). Some trusts do not allow cash deposits, a feature which enables them and their customers to avoid the red tape required under the legislation governing the reporting of certain cash and other transactions and which also applies when new bank accounts are being opened.

1822 Withdrawals can generally be made on not more than 24 hours' notice (subject only to the clearance of any cheques previously deposited). By prior arrangement withdrawals can even be made by telephone, with the proceeds being credited to a designated bank account. Periodical debits can also be arranged.

1823 A cash management trust normally confines itself to investments which are not only extremely safe (such as government and bank paper) but also very short-term (so as to minimise the risk of capital loss due to interest rate fluctuations in the market place).

1824 Some cash management trusts involve a guarantee from a related company in respect of the face value of the units and all previously declared interest. However, unless the shareholders' funds of that company are large in relation to the trust fund then that guarantee may not be particularly meaningful.

1825 Cash management trusts enable small investors to obtain indirect access to the professional short-term money market and to get the same returns from this market as are available to the large players (apart from the above-mentioned periodical charges flowing to the manager who packages this facility).

1826 While the legal format is very different, involving no debtor/creditor relationship, from an investor's perspective using a cash management trust is in some ways similar to using a bank. However, interest rates are much higher than those available from banks, particularly on call deposits, and there are usually no charges for running an account (apart from taxes imposed by governments).

On the other hand, there are no overdraft facilities and there is no "lender of last resort" mechanism such as that once provided by the Reserve Bank of Australia to licensed banks. Each trust also has its own rules regarding the minimum amount required to open an account, the minimum size of subsequent transactions permitted and the minimum credit balance which must be maintained. (However, there are ways around some of these—for example, a rule requiring a minimum of $5000 to open a new account would not prevent $4000 from being withdrawn shortly thereafter—naturally subject to the clearance of any cheques involved.)

Cheque Writing Facilities

1827 A particularly valuable feature introduced by some cash management trusts is the ability for unitholders to write cheques drawn on their own accounts, either in favour of themselves or in favour of third parties (although not usually for cash). This feature presents some important advantages:

- It greatly facilitates access by the investor to the money.

- It often eliminates transaction charges imposed by banks.

- It increases returns (because interest continues to accrue until the cheque is actually presented).

- It avoids the double imposition of government charges which results if money is first transferred from a cash management trust to a bank to enable cheques to be drawn on that bank.

The relatively high cost involved in moving money around is further discussed in para. 3011.

Common Funds

1828 Trustee companies, as a by-product of investing surplus cash on behalf of deceased estates and other trust funds under their administration, have set up *common funds*. These are made up of a large number of small cash balances, pooled for investment purposes in order to get a higher return at a lower cost, with the net return being distributed pro rata.

1829 These days common funds are also open to the general public and operate in a similar fashion to cash management trusts (see above), even to the extent of issuing prospectuses. However, their legal form is different. In terms of security they are comparable to cash management trusts having similar asset portfolios.

Chapter 19—Interest

Money is the wise man's religion
—Euripides Concepts

Interest

1901 "Interest" is the analogue of "rent". Just as one can arrange to get the use of premises owned by someone else for a certain time by periodically paying an agreed amount of rent, so one can arrange to get the use of money owned by someone else for a certain time by periodically paying an agreed amount of interest. Rent can be expressed in dollars per annum per square metre occupied. Interest can be expressed in dollars per annum per $100 borrowed. A few examples are set out below to illustrate some aspects of the subject.

1902 One often talks of "the time value of money". To illustrate, at 15 per cent per annum, a person borrowing $100 for one year would need to pay back not $100 but rather $115. Put another way, a dollar in the future is not as good as a dollar today-$115 in one year's time is worth only $100 now. In the technical language often used in this context, the "present value" of $115 due in twelve months is $100 and, by proportion, the "present value" of $100 due in twelve months is about $86.96. All investment calculations are based around this fundamental concept.

Interest Rate Confusions

1903 However, quoted interest rates are not always what they seem. $100 lent or invested at an "effective rate" of 15 per cent per annum amounts to $115 in one year's time. The 15 per cent just referred to was payable once a year in arrear. What if the transaction instead of this had involved one-twelfth of the 15 per cent each month (1.25 per cent), technically known as a "nominal rate convertible at monthly intervals"? Because of compounding during the year (interest on interest), $100 would grow, not to $115, but rather to about $116.08. In other words, if compounding takes place 12 times a year then the "effective rate" corresponding to a nominal 15 per cent is 16.08 per cent. In fact, the following are all equivalent:

- 15.00 per cent convertible monthly

- 15.19 per cent convertible quarterly

- 15.48 per cent convertible half-yearly

- 16.08 per cent convertible yearly.

All interest rates are not the same and shrewd investors will always ascertain the true interest return which they are receiving or paying. In particular, they will be careful always to compare like with like.

1904 Consumers find all this very confusing. For example, to be invited to pay a yearly subscription of $200 by two half-yearly instalments of $117 sounds not too bad. Actually, the effective rate of interest inherent in that transaction is 98.7 per cent per annum! Many people would regard this as a surprising or even unbelievable result. However, the arithmetic can readily be verified as follows:

- The choice is to pay $200 now or to pay only $117 now and another $117 in six months' time—a total of $234, or 17 per cent more than the single payment.

- In other words, the consumer can "borrow" $83 ($200 less $117) immediately, by agreeing to pay $117 (including an interest component) half a year later.

- The interest is thus $34 ($117 less $83).

- This works out at 40.96 per cent per half-year (34 divided by 83 is 0.4096; 117 divided by 83 is 1.4096).

- To get an effective rate per year it is necessary to assume reinvestment on the same terms for a further half-year.

- 1.4096 squared is 1.9871, giving the seemingly unbelievable but nevertheless correct rate of 98.7 per cent, as quoted above.

Even an offer from an insurance company to allow a $100 yearly premium due to it to be paid by monthly instalments of $9 (a total of $108) instead does not really constitute the "low interest rate of 8 per cent" mentioned in its literature. The last of the 12 monthly instalments is to be paid in 11 months' time, while the first is due immediately. On average, therefore, the 12 instalments are to be paid in 5.5 months' time and the 8 per cent "flat rate" of interest is thus actually equivalent to about 17.45 per cent simple interest (8 multiplied by 12/5.5).

1905 Again, each $10,000 borrowed on a 30-year housing loan at 15 per cent per annum repayable by level instalments of principal and interest would involve a total interest bill of some $35,518 on the basis of monthly instalments in arrear of $126.44. Increasing these instalments slightly to $131.68 (up 4.0 per cent) has the effect of shortening the loan to 20 years and slashing the total interest bill by a quite dramatic-sounding 39.2 per cent to $21,603. (The effect of paying half of a nominally monthly instalment every fortnight-a course of action favoured by some borrowers—is similar but even more dramatic, because this is the equivalent of an increase in annual payments by about 8.3 per cent.)

1906 The interaction of interest and inflation can also produce some surprising results. For example, if $1000 is invested at the end of each year for 25 years in a fund earning 15 per cent per annum after tax, then the $25,000 laid out will have grown to $212,793. However, if inflation at the rate of 9 per cent per annum occurs during this period, then the purchasing power of that accumulation, measured in terms of the dollars current at the commencement of the arrangement, would be only $24,678.

1907 There is also some misunderstanding as to the difference between simple interest and compound interest. $1000 at 15 per cent per annum compound grows to $4046 in 10 years. The simple interest equivalent appears much more impressive at 30.46 per cent per annum—but such a figure would be totally misleading.

1908 Again, interest can be paid on savings deposits either on daily balances or on minimum calendar monthly balances. These two alternatives may sound much the same, particularly when small print is used in advertisements, but the difference can be quite significant for people running active accounts. At 15 per cent, a person with $200 in his account who deposits a further $1000 on 2 April and withdraws it again on 29 April of the same year would get either $13.56 or only $2.47, depending on the system employed.

1909 A further example may assist. If $1000 is invested in a call deposit paying 15 per cent per annum credited yearly then a depositor leaving it there for 12 months will finish up with

$1150 ($1000 original capital, plus $150 in interest). But if the money is withdrawn after six months then the institution concerned will in practice pay interest on a pro rata basis, say $75. If the $1075 is immediately reinvested on the same terms for a further 6 months then it will grow not to $1150 but rather to $1155.63 ($1075 plus 7.5 per cent).

Basis Points

1910 Small differences in interest rates are sometimes measured in "points" or "basis points", each point being 0.01 per cent. Thus a move from 13.29 per cent to 13.41 per cent would be described as a 12 point increase.

Bank Bills

1911 The concept of discount on bank bills is explained in para. 1814. It should be noted that the interest rate quoted for all bills of exchange is a nominal rate convertible at intervals equal to the term of the bill and that for the reasons explained in para. 1903 the effective rate is always higher. Thus, for example, if the nominal interest rate on a bank bill is 10 per cent per annum, then the effective rate to an investor/purchaser is as follows:

- 10.38 per cent on a 90-day bill

- 10.25 per cent on a 180-day bill.

1912 Persons using bank bills as a borrowing mechanism need to bring the bank's "acceptance fee" into their calculations. This fee, which is the charge levied by a bank for guaranteeing the redemption proceeds on the maturity date, is normally expressed as a rate per cent per annum on the face value of the bill. It is levied at the start of the term (on a pro rata basis, in days). The bank's profit comes out of this fee, not out of the basic interest rate.

1913 To illustrate: Consider a 90-day bank bill for $100,000 at 7 per cent per annum, plus an acceptance fee at 3 per cent per annum. The figures are as follows:

Discounted value of Bill	$98,303.25
Less Acceptance Fee	$739.72
Net Proceeds	$97,563.53

The effective rate to the purchaser of the bill would be 7.19 per cent (based on $98,303.25 becoming $100,000.00 in 90 days), while the effective rate to the user of the funds would be 10.52 per cent (based on $97,563.53 becoming $100,000.00 in 90 days).

Junk Bonds

1914 Some corporate fixed interest securities are colloquially (and pejoratively) described as "junk bonds". They are characterised by high apparent interest rates and a greater than average risk of default (poor interest cover and low asset backing—see paras 936 to 944).

1915 The theory expressed by some investors is that, while a few individual bonds might go bad, a portfolio of such junk bonds will do better than an equivalent portfolio of high grade bonds. However, in an economic downturn a very large proportion of such a portfolio can go bad simultaneously.

1916 Companies which have to pay high interest rates in order to attract funds become subject to the vicious circle discussed in para. 3924).

Doubling of Money

1917 A simple but useful rule of thumb is that "the period in which money doubles is 70 divided by the rate of interest". This approximation allows:

- the relevant period to be calculated for a known rate of interest

- the relevant rate of interest to be calculated for a known period.

Thus, for example, at 5 per cent per annum $100 grows to $200 in about 14 years. Conversely, if the period is 7 years, then the required rate for doubling is 10 per cent per annum.

1918 A similar rule can also cover a threefold increase: "the period in which money trebles is 115 divided by the rate of interest".

1919 These rules give acceptable approximations at normal interest rate levels, but, of course, they cannot be used where precision is required.

Compound Interest and Shares

1920 Compound interest principles can also be used to assess returns on ordinary shares. For example, consider a hypothetical portfolio growing at a steady 20 per cent annually over 10 years, including the reinvestment of all dividends, but experiencing a single disaster (such as a market crash) at some time within those 10 years—a disaster which wipes out 50 per cent of the total value in one hit. What does that do to the overall return?

1921 Many people would expect that the return would have become negative in the circumstances just described, but in fact it is still strongly positive—the return is almost the same as from a steady 12 per cent annual growth rate over the entire 10 year period, with no disaster.

Chapter 20—Unlisted Shares

We are ready for an unforeseen event that may or may not occur
—Former US Vice-President Dan Quayle

Local Shares

2001 While all investment in ordinary shares involves some risk, the risk is greater in the case of shares in companies which are not listed on the stock exchange (apart from private companies controlled by the investor himself).

2002 In particular:

- The quality of the information about the company's affairs may not be as good.

- The absence of public scrutiny increases the chance of misfeasance.

- The articles of association may contain all sorts of restrictive provisions.

- The absence of a market may make it virtually impossible to quit the investment quickly.

- The only price available may be totally inadequate and quite unfair.

- The company can be run in the interests of the controlling shareholder(s) and in a fashion quite oppressive to a minority shareholder.

2003 Even if the running of the company is satisfactory at the time the investment is made, the possibility of a change of control at some time in the future needs to be taken into consideration.

2004 Investment in the unlisted shares of listed companies is somewhat safer, especially if listing is likely to take place at a later date. However, the absence of a recognised market is always a disadvantage. Any special conditions attaching to the shares need to be scrutinised carefully. The size and due dates of any uncalled liability should be particularly noted.

Overseas Shares

2005 Shares in foreign companies which are traded on recognised overseas stock exchanges but which are not listed in Australia are in a different category again. They do not pose most of the risks analysed above, but they do expose local investors to a currency risk. This is not necessarily bad—if the Australian dollar falls, then investors benefit from the holding of overseas assets, and in any case many Australian companies with overseas operations or borrowings or which are dependent on imports or exports priced in overseas currencies already expose their shareholders to a similar though less visible exchange risk.

2006 Investors in foreign companies improve their spread and become less reliant on the economy of only one country. On the other hand, overseas investments are sometimes more difficult to monitor—although with the establishment of the Internet the reverse can also apply. Their accounts, compiled in accordance with unfamiliar conventions, may be harder to interpret.

2007 The taxation aspects of overseas investments are discussed in paras 2877 and 2879. Other aspects are discussed in paras 3942 to 3947.

2008 Many foreign companies have dividend reinvestment plans and these can be very useful as a means of avoiding the relatively high transaction costs involved in converting small dividend distributions into Australian currency.

Suspension and Delisting

2009 As mentioned in para. 1223, the *delisting* of a company previously traded on the stock exchange can occur for a variety of reasons, including requests to this effect from the company concerned or its failure to pay listing fees. Delisting, which is permanent, can also occur at the specific request of the stock exchange authorities or the Australian Securities Commission in order to "punish" a company for some serious offence.

2010 Companies are naturally always delisted after a successful takeover bid. Companies can also be delisted after a period of notice if the number of their shareholders declines to less than the threshold required for the maintenance of listing.

2011 Some or all of the securities in a listed company can also be *suspended from trading*. Such suspensions are not meant to be permanent and do not in any way relieve the company concerned from complying with all the listing rules.

2012 In particular, the temporary suspension of trading in a company's equity securities often occurs pending the disclosure of facts thought to be necessary in order to keep the market fully informed.

2013 Again, suspension of all of a company's securities normally follows important technical breaches, such as the non-lodging of accounts by the due date.

2014 Trading in shares normally ceases when a company goes into liquidation or receivership, although shareholders might prefer to have a market available to them even for virtually worthless shares in order to enable them to more readily crystallise a capital loss for income tax purposes. See also paras 2967 to 2968.

Companies not on the Current List

2015 Persons holding scrip in companies which are not on the list can ascertain the current status of the shares from a stockbroker or the stock exchange. It does not automatically follow that the shares are worthless, as the explanation may be that the company has merely changed its name or that it was involved in a scheme of arrangement and the investor now owns securities in some other entity which may well be listed.

2016 Even if the company concerned has been put into receivership or liquidation some proceeds may already be available and/or may result from future distributions by the receiver or the liquidator.

Investor Attitudes

2017 Entrepreneurs starting off an unlisted company often desire access to cash but are reluctant to give up equity.

2018 Some investors choose to put their money into unlisted companies because they are attracted to high expected or promised returns. Others do so because they are willing to support an enterprise being set up by a friend or possibly by a voluntary organisation whose philosophy they support.

2019 This exposes them to a number of risks—for example:

- They may lose some or all of their capital.

- The periodical returns may be small or non-existent.

- They may be unable to cash in their stake at all or only at an unrealistic price.

- Minority holders individually or even collectively may have no influence on the control of
the company.

2020 Depending on the circumstances unlisted companies can raise
cash without the need for a prospectus. This certainly saves
expense but also deprives arms' length investors of some
protection.

Exempt Markets

2021 Some large companies are not eligible for listing on the stock
exchange because of some technical deficiency—for example,
some unacceptable restrictions in their articles of association.

2022 In such cases they might be traded on an "exempt market"
created on a one-off basis by a stockbroker or the company
itself. Sometimes this might be a stepping stone to conventional listing later on.

Chapter 21—Gold and Currencies

*You can fool too many of the people too
much of the time*
—James Thurber

Gold Bullion

2101 To some extent gold can be regarded as an ordinary commodity, similar to, say, copper or lead, with production flowing—through several stages—to end users. Gold has some industrial uses and it is, of course, freely sold to consumers in the form of jewellery. Large quantities of gold are also bought and sold by central banks in connection with trade deficits.

2102 However, interest in gold also comes from individual hoarders who attach a special significance to it as a "store of value". This creates an artificial demand for gold which has no logical basis and which is founded on nothing more substantial than blind faith in the precious metal on the part of numerous gold buffs throughout the world.

2103 While one can understand that political refugees fleeing across national borders would find the conversion of wealth into something small and readily portable as of great advantage, the reasoning of persons in highly civilised countries who wish to control a pile of gold bars as an "investment" permanently kept in some bank vault is less obvious. Massive community resources are devoted to digging gold out of one hole in the ground in order to just put it down another hole in the ground somewhere else.

2104 The supply of gold can be affected by new discoveries, by industrial disputes, by sales from official stockpiles and so on. As indicated above, the demand for gold is really quite unpredictable, although it may well be influenced by war and peace rumours, by inflationary expectations, by happenings on the world stock exchanges, by interest rate movements and so on. However, neither short-term nor long-term gold price movements seem to follow any obvious pattern.

2105 Some governments, including Australia, have in recent years capitalised on collector/hoarder demand by minting special gold coins which, while they technically constitute legal tender, are never intended to be in actual circulation. These are normally issued at a considerable premium to the value of their gold content—a premium which will not necessarily be maintainable in the secondary market. Popular gold coins of this type include:

- the Australian Nugget
- the South African Krugerrand
- the Canadian Maple Leaf
- the American Eagle.

Of course, older coins such as the sovereign, which unlike the above was a genuine coin intended for mass circulation, are also of relevance.

2106 Gold bullion has in the long-term proved a remarkably inefficient "store of value" during times of great inflation, particularly when the absence of any periodical income from it is taken into account. In January 1934 the gold price was officially pegged at $US35 per ounce; 64 years later, the then free market gold price was around $US285 per ounce. This represents an annual compound rate of growth of only a derisory 3.3 per cent per annum.

2107 Investment in gold can take many different forms, including the following:

- Gold bars ("bullion").
- Gold coins.
- Gold jewellery.
- Shares in gold exploration companies.
- Shares in gold producing companies.
- Options on such shares.
- Futures contracts based on gold.
- Gold accounts.
- Gold trusts of various types.

2108 Holding physical gold (bars, coins and jewellery) involves both direct costs (for insurance and storage, etc.) and indirect costs (loss of interest). Trading margins—the difference between buying and selling prices per unit of gold—can also be relatively high, especially for small quantities. In the case of coins and jewellery, the value moves up and down in accordance with fashion changes as well as in line with movements in the underlying gold price. Selling gold bars can incur assay charges, although these can be avoided if arrangements not involving the actual delivery of the gold on purchase are adopted. For example, some banks offer so-called "gold accounts". These are in effect zero interest bank accounts, without cheque facilities, with balances expressed in ounces of gold, but settled in terms of Australian dollars. Deposits are converted at the bank's selling rate on the day of the transaction, while withdrawals are converted at the bank's buying rate.

Other Gold Investments

2109 Investment in the shares of gold mining companies produces much bigger leverage than investment in gold itself. Leverage is at its greatest in marginal producers. For example:

	$A per ounce	
	(1)	(2)
Price of gold	600	660
Cost of production	550	550
Profit	50	110

In this illustration a 10 per cent increase in the price of gold translated itself into a 120 per cent increase in profit.

2110 Futures contracts based on gold are discussed in Chapter 23.

2111 Some unit trusts have been formed specifically to concentrate on gold and gold-related investments such as shares in gold mining companies and gold futures. These trusts have the right to invest for the long or the short-term and to trade actively.

Other Valuable Commodities

2112 Gold is not the only commodity with mystique. Some investors and speculators prefer other precious metals, such as silver or platinum. Others again favour diamonds.

2113 Some investors like to arbitrage between gold and silver or between gold and platinum, following theories to the effect that the price per ounce for the various metals should bear certain relationships to each other.

Foreign Currency

2114 Travellers often hold small amounts of foreign currency in the form of bank notes or travellers' cheques. Neither earns any interest and, in fact, the latter can involve charges.

2115 The more serious investor who wants a foreign currency exposure has a wider choice which includes:

- Foreign currency bank accounts with banks in Australia.

- Foreign currency bank accounts with banks overseas.

- Direct investment overseas.

- Direct investment in Australian companies with overseas interests.

- Units in international trusts.

- Currency futures (see Chapter 23).

2116 Bank accounts with deposits denominated in the major overseas currencies can be arranged with local banks, either at call or for specified terms. If the accounts are interest-bearing then the rate of interest would be at the level prevailing in the home country of the currency concerned. In practice, the chance of making gains from movements in exchange rates needs to weighed against the costs flowing from the interest rate differential.

2117 In line with the explanation given in paras 2005 to 2006, both direct and indirect investment in overseas shares, fixed interest securities, property, etc., exposes investors to the dual risk of fluctuations in market values in the currency concerned and in the exchange rate between that currency and the Australian dollar.

2118 Overseas investment exposures generally are discussed in paras 3942 to 3947.

Tax Aspects

2119 Income from gold mining in Australia was for many years completely exempt from tax. However, from 1 January 1991 the normal income tax rules have applied.

2120 Interest on loans used to purchase gold is not tax deductible, because it is not regarded as an expense incurred in earning assessable income. Gold bars do not, for example, ever pay periodical dividends. However, undeducted interest becomes part of the cost base for capital gains tax purposes (see Chapter 29).

2121 Income tax on overseas investments is discussed in paras 2877 and 2879.

Chapter 22—Options

*Keeping a little ahead of conditions is one
of the secrets of business*
—Charles M Schwab

Company Options

2201 As explained in para. 451, companies from time to time issue options over their own shares, either free in conjunction with a share issue or for a consideration with or without a simultaneous share issue. Such options are in some ways similar to rights, but they usually cover a much longer option period, up to five years (the maximum allowed under the companies legislation), and title to them is evidenced by scrip certificates or through CHESS. They are quoted on the ordinary shares list of the stock exchange and can be traded in the usual way.

2202 Combined issues of shares and associated options (in some specified ratio) can be made by new companies seeking listing for the first time under a prospectus as well as by existing companies to their shareholders by way of proportionate rights entitlements. Except in the case of stapled securities (see para. 489) the shares and options after allotment can be traded separately, but rights to both would be quoted together. Issues of options by themselves are sometimes also made as rights issues. Some companies also issue unlisted options to employees under various incentive schemes authorised under their articles.

2203 Options entitle the optionholder, on one or more specified option dates, to acquire ordinary shares in the company's capital at a stipulated price (the *exercise price*). If the options are not exercised by the last of these days then they become worthless. Naturally enough they will also be delisted. The capital gains tax implications of this are dealt with in paras 2907 and 2931. Options are useful because they give their investor/holders rights but not obligations.

2204 Shortly before each exercise date the company concerned will normally circularise its optionholders to remind them of this date and, particularly before the last available exercise date, to invite them to exercise the option. Such invitations should always be treated on their merits. In particular, if the market price of the shares happens to be less than the exercise price of the options then exercise would be most foolish, as any investor desiring to acquire shares would be better off buying existing shares on the market.

2205 As explained in para. 480, options are useful securities for investors because of the *leverage* effect. The market value of listed options is a function of two quite separate aspects:

- firstly, the *intrinsic value*, namely, the difference between the market value of the underlying shares and the lower exercise price of the option, and

- secondly, the *time value* of the option—the longer the option has to run, the more attractive it is.

This is because, compared with owning the shares, the investor during the currency of the options:

- does not need to tie up so much of his money

- may be able to earn relatively high interest rather than relatively low dividends even allowing for imputation credits

- has the opportunity to make much greater percentage gains if the shares go up

- would suffer a much lower dollar loss if the shares were to become worthless.

See also paras 2261 to 2263.

2206 As options are really deferred equities they should be protected against dilution by future rights and bonus issues. The terms of issue of options do not always provide for this, an aspect which needs to be allowed for by investors when pricing options or making decisions as to their purchase or sale. Some options involve conditions which provide that they can be exercised shortly before the books closing date for a cash issue. This feature is not necessarily attractive, as investors can be faced with a choice between:

- giving up the time value of their options and the leverage which the holding of options confers (if they exercise), and

- having the intrinsic value of their options eroded or even eliminated by the watering (if they continue to hold).

Most options involve conditions which provide for bonus issues made during their currency to be allotted later, if and when the options are exercised.

Exchange Traded Options: Calls and Puts

2207 Quite separate from the company options just discussed are the *exchange traded options* (or ETOs) listed on the ASX Derivatives Options Market, which is part of the Australian Stock Exchange. These are *synthetic* instruments (*derivatives*) created by third parties (investors) without reference to the company which issued the underlying share (the shares to which the option relates).

2208 A full discussion of how to deal in options is outside the scope of this book and the comments below are intended only as a brief introduction to the subject. Appropriate specialist literature should be obtained by those interested in exploring the concept further.

2209 A *call option* is a contract which entitles (but does not require) its holder to buy a fixed number of shares (usually 1000) in the underlying company at a stated price on or before a specified expiry date.

2210 A *put option* is a contract which entitles (but does not require) its holder to sell a fixed number of shares (usually 1000) in the underlying company at a stated price on or before a specified expiry date.

2211 These options involve a *writer* who provides them to the original purchaser (or *taker*) for a consideration (price) arrived at by market forces and called the *premium*. Such synthetic options have been created for about 60 listed companies, the shares of which are very actively traded on the stock exchange. They involve two standardised contract terms, namely a fixed *exercise price* (also called the *striking price*) and a fixed *expiry date* (also called the *expiration date* or the *maturity date*). They also involve a *standard quantity* (such as the 1000 shares of the underlying company referred to above).

2212 For each such company a number of different option series are created, each involving various round number exercise prices (say, 250, 300, 350 and 400) and each expiring on one or more convenient expiry dates over the next few months. Some are more liquid than others.

2213 Options may be exercised by their holders at *any time* up to their expiry date, but subject to supply and demand they can also be traded in the options market. The holder of the option can thus sell it at any time as an alternative to exercising it and then selling the shares received (in the case of a call option) or as an alternative to buying the shares and then exercising the option (in the case of a put option).

2214 Similarly, a writer wishing to quit his position before an option is exercised against him can achieve this objective by buying an option of the right type in the series involved on the secondary market. As all options in a given series are identi-cal—in the same way that all shares of a particular class are identical—it is not necessary for the writer to buy back the specific option which he had created in the first instance.

Advantages for Optionholders

2215 Holders of call options achieve the advantages set out in para. 2205. Buying call options is thus an alternative to buying ordinary shares—whether in respect to the shares of a particu-lar company or in respect to a portfolio situation. Such a strategy can be used to limit downside risk, but, naturally, there is a cost involved.

2216 Put options can be used for *hedging* an existing long position in shares. Buying put options is thus an alternative to selling ordinary shares. This can be particularly attractive in capital gains tax situations —an investor who thinks the market is overpriced can protect himself against falls by taking put options, thus not incurring the tax which might apply if he had sold his actual holding of shares (see Chapter 29):

- If, on the one hand, he is wrong and the market is steady or rises then the tax problem disappears (and if he has offsetting capital gains then he will even be able to claim a capital loss for tax purposes in respect of the option premium out-laid).

- If, on the other hand, he is right and he decides to quit the shares after they have fallen then he will have at least postponed the payment of tax, thus benefiting in terms of interest and indexation.

- If he is right and he decides to hold the shares after they have fallen then he will have avoided the payment of capital gains tax in respect of his holdings, although he will, of course, have to pay tax in respect of the profit made out of the option deal.

2217 Put options can also be used *speculatively* by investors who expect a share price to fall. For example, if the market price of a share is 500 then the premium for a put option exercisable at 550 might be 80 (an intrinsic value of 50 plus a time value of 30). If the market price falls to 450, then even without a time value (as just before expiry) the intrinsic value will be 100, giving a 25 per cent profit. The use of a put in this way is similar in effect to short selling if one is right, but without the risk of limitless losses if one is wrong.

Advantages for Writers

2218 The writer of an option gets the benefit of the premium which he receives at the time of creating the option and which he retains regardless of whether or not the option is subsequently exercised. Writing options can thus boost the revenue returns from portfolio investment, but at the cost of making some losses and foregoing some gains.

2219 The writers of call options make profits out of falling or stagnant markets. The writers of put options make profits out of rising or stagnant markets.

Options on Futures Contracts

2220 Options are also available in respect of the following futures contracts:

- The All Ordinaries Share Price Index (SPI).

- 90-day bank accepted bills.

- 3-year Commonwealth Treasury Bonds.

- 10-year Commonwealth Treasury Bonds.

- Greasy wool.

- Wheat.

    These are discussed in Chapter 23.

Other Aspects

2221 Both writers and takers of options incur brokerage and stamp duty (based on the premium). If options are actually exercised (as distinct from being "closed out" by a transaction in the reverse direction from the original deal) then further brokerage and stamp duty in respect of the share transfer will also apply (based on the exercise price, regardless of the then market value).

2222. The options market is a public market and the prices of transactions and buying and selling quotes are freely available.

2223 Exchange traded options do not involve scrip. Title is evidenced by the equivalent of contract notes. Contracts are registered with a clearing house.

2224 Exercise prices are not adjusted when shares go ex dividend. However, appropriate adjustments are made for capital moves such as rights and bonus issues and share splits or consolidations.

2225 Writers of call options who do not own the underlying shares (or some security convertible into such shares) run the risk of making sizable losses if the shares have to be purchased in the market in order to meet an exercise notice after they have risen significantly (or alternatively if the writers wish to close out their positions in similar circumstances). Such writers are said to be selling "cash covered" options, in contradistinction from writers who are long in the shares concerned and whose options are said to be "scrip covered".

2226 Investors can also adopt a "buy and write" strategy. This consists of buying on the market shares in the companies involving traded options and simultaneously writing call options on those shares.

2227 A call option is said to be "in the money" if the market price of the share exceeds the exercise price of the option. A put option is said to be "in the money" if the market price of the share is less than the exercise price of the option. In the reverse situations the options are said to be "out of the money".

2228 The ability to trade in either shares or options of certain companies can create opportunities to make profits from arbitrage operations whenever the two sets of prices get out of line, and especially if this happens close to the expiry date of the options (see paras 986 to 988).

2229 Dealing in options can often also provide an opportunity to buy the underlying shares at a relative bargain price, although this will mean accepting a minor risk that the strategy will fail. For example, if a share is trading at 550, then the probability is high that any put option with a striking price of 600 which is still held at its expiry date will actually be exercised. If such an option can be written at a premium of, say, 80, then the writer will effectively acquire the share for a net consideration of 520 (600 less 80), or 30 cents cheaper than if he had bought the share at 550 on the market. Similarly, writing call options which are likely to be exercised can be a way of selling shares on attractive terms. However, the fact that the standard size of an option contract is 1000 shares and not just the equivalent of a marketable parcel needs to be taken into account for all such deals.

2230 The simultaneous writing or taking of a call option and a put option in the same stock at the same exercise price and subject to the same expiry date is called a *straddle*.

2231 Finally, optionholders need to watch very carefully the exact expiry dates of their contracts, so that any desired action can be taken before it is too late.

Warrants

2232 The Australian Stock Exchange also lists on its main board a small number of financial instruments called *warrants*. These derivatives are effectively long dated call or put options created by a bank or some other *warrant issuer* over the shares of a listed company or some such.

2233 Each series of warrants has a clearly defined exercise price and expiry date (making all warrants in that series completely interchangeable, as in the case of the other options discussed in this chapter).

2234 Warrants over shares would normally be *deliverable*, meaning that settlement involves the transfer of the underlying security.

Warrants over currencies, commodities or indices need to be *cash settled*.

2235 Warrants can be:

- either "European Style", exercisable only *on* the expiry date

- or "American Style", exercisable *at any time before* the expiry date.

Endowment Warrants

2236 An *endowment warrant* is another form of derivative. Technically, an endowment warrant is a warrant but one without a specific exercise price or expiry date.

2237 The word "endowment" in this context has no legal significance, but was coined by certain promoters for marketing reasons and to distinguish the product from the more conventional warrants described above.

2238 An endowment warrant resembles other warrants in that:

- it is issued by a third party (an entrepreneur here referred to as the *issuer*) and not by the company which issued the underlying shares to which the endowment warrant relates

- it involves a standardised contract

- it is therefore readily tradeable

- it involves the right but not the obligation for its holder to acquire the underlying shares.

2239 However, in economic terms an endowment warrant is really a geared share instrument.

2240 Typically, an endowment warrant:

- relates to a blue chip stock

- has an initial term to maturity of around 10 years

- involves the investor in an initial outlay of about 30 to 75 per cent of the market value of the underlying shares

- involves the investor in a de facto loan called an *Outstanding Amount*

- does not require the investor to make any periodical cash payments

- is so structured that the normal expectation
would be that this loan will have been fully repaid before the maturity date.

2241 The minimum size for an investment in endowment warrants
is much smaller than the minimum size for transactions involving some other forms of loan funds.

2242 In practice, the sum of the initial price of an endowment
warrant and the initial loan exceeds the market value of the
underlying shares by a margin which covers:

- costs including commission

- the premium for the risk being assumed by the issuer

- the issuer's profit margin for putting the deal together.

2243 From its nature, the deal does not represent "value for money"
in a conceptual sense—but this observation applies equally to
many other leveraged products.

2244 For initial purchases the once-only issue price is set by the
issuer on a "free of brokerage" basis. Endowment warrants can
be bought either from the issuer or through a stockbroker or
financial planner (at the same issue price in all cases).

2245 After listing on the stock exchange the market price results
from the interaction of buyers and sellers in the usual way.

2246 The price of an endowment warrant is sometimes referred to
as a *premium* or as a *deposit*.

2247 The endowment warrant works as follows:

- dividends on the underlying shares are credited
to the Outstanding Amount

- interest on the Outstanding Amount is debited to
the Outstanding Amount

- the interest rate is a variable rate and can go up
or down in line with market movements

- because dividends are being received in respect
of the total asset while interest is being paid only
on the portion represented by the loan in normal

circumstances the Outstanding Amount should decline over time

- this process will be speeded up if the company increases its dividend rate each year or so

- this process will also be speeded up as the size of the Outstanding Amount and thus the interest burden falls

- any other cash received—for example, from the sale of rights or from reductions in share capital by the listed company concerned—are also credited to the Outstanding Amount

- company reconstructions such as share splits, consolidations and bonus issues result in an appropriate adjustment to the number of shares represented by each endowment warrant.

2248 When the Outstanding Amount becomes zero or negative the endowment warrant becomes exercisable and on exercise the underlying parcel of shares (or a cash equivalent) together with cash representing any negative Outstanding Amount is handed over to the investor.

2249 If the Outstanding Amount has not become zero or negative by the termination date (the maturity date, the end of the initial term of around 10 years) then the endowment warrant also becomes exercisable.

2250 The exercise price in those circumstances would normally be one cent plus the then Outstanding Amount. On exercise the underlying parcel of shares is handed over to the investor free of any encumbrance. Alternatively, the investor can *cash out* the endowment warrant for a sum equal to the market price of the shares less the Outstanding Amount.

2251 However, because this is a warrant such an exercise of the endowment warrant is not compulsory. If the market price of the underlying shares were to be less than the then Outstanding Amount then naturally the investor would be better off by allowing the warrant to lapse. The loss inherent in this would be borne by the issuer—who, after all, has received the above-mentioned premium for being willing to assume this risk.

2252 The one cent part of the exercise price is actually built into the issue price. However, if the endowment warrant is allowed to lapse then it is forfeited to the issuer.

2253 The dividends for the periodical crediting to the Outstanding Amount as described above may or may not include the attached franking credits, depending on the precise terms of issue. If they do not, then this feature could represent a significant additional cost to the investor as compared with a direct investment in the underlying shares (with or without the use of other loan funds).

2254 Holders of endowment warrants:

- have no cash coming in or going out before the exercise date
- do not pay tax on the dividends
- do not ever get the benefit of any franking credits
- do not get a tax deduction for the interest
- do not get voting rights in respect of the underlying shares.

2255 As there is no taxable income coming in there is less paperwork and no liability for provisional tax.

Instalment Warrants

2256 An *instalment warrant* is yet another form of derivative, this time one designed to resemble a contributing share. Typically, the underlying shares are blue chip stocks.

2257 A purchaser of such a warrant from the issuer pays an initial amount which comprises fees and some tax-deductible interest in advance, as well as a capital amount (part of the share price, roughly half). The precise initial amount would depend on the circumstances at the time. The purchaser would then expect to pay a further *fixed* amount on the defined expiry date of the warrant, about 18 months after its creation; this would comprise tax-deductible interest in arrear as well as a further capital amount (the balance of the share price).

2258 This approach allows the investor to have an exposure to a particular stock of around twice that obtainable through a direct purchase, until the final instalment is paid. As the quid pro quo for the interest being charged on the loan element the investor receives the *full* dividend on the share, plus the benefit of any associated franking credit.

2259 As with all leveraged investments this magnifies both gains and losses. Investors also need to compare the interest rate payable under the arrangement with the cost of borrowing in other ways.

2260 Once created by the issuer, instalment warrants, being standardised contracts, can be bought and sold on the stock exchange in the usual way.

Negative Intrinsic Values

2261 A call option can still have some value even if it is out of the money and thus involves a negative intrinsic value (see para. 2205). For example, a share can have a market price of 88 while its options, with an exercise price of 100, trade at, say, 17.

2262 The scenario in this example would require the shares to go up in value by more than 41 per cent by the expiry date of the options in order for the options to be the better buy (ignoring dividend and interest considerations for the moment):

Shares	88 plus	41 per cent =	124
Options	17 plus	41 per cent =	24
Difference	71 plus	41 per cent =	100

2263 In practice, investors have to place a figure on the time value aspects as well. In particular, they should take into account the difference between:

- the interest, on a daily basis, which can be earned on the exercise price until it has to be paid over, less tax at the investor's marginal rate, and

- the dividends, having regard to the exact number of half-yearly or other instalments involved, which can be received on the shares over the same period, less tax at the marginal rate, plus the related imputation credits (if applicable).

2264 Stamp duty aspects are discussed in paras 1632 to 1634.

Chapter 23—Futures

Beware of barbers, beauticians, waiters
or anyone bringing gifts
of "inside" information or tips
—Bernard Baruch

Background

2301 This chapter does no more than provide a very brief introduction into futures as an investment. The subject is viewed particularly from the narrow perspective of share investors on the stock exchange.

2302 Buyers and sellers on a *physical* market normally exchange commodities for cash, with an immediate transfer of ownership taking place. By way of contrast, trading on a *futures* market involves, not physical commodities, but rather *standardised contracts* for the delivery of a given quantity of a commodity (of a defined quality) at some specified future date, at a price agreed on at the time of the deal. This price can be either higher or lower than the *spot price* (the price for immediate delivery). The buyers contract to take delivery and to make payment at the settlement date and the sellers contract to effect delivery at that time.

2303 Originally futures contracts related to rural products, such as wool, live cattle, boneless beef, and so on, or to minerals, especially gold. Producers and consumers of such commodities often desire to guarantee for themselves a price negotiated long before the intended date of delivery, often before the commodity even comes into existence.

2304 This can be achieved *directly* by entering into "forward contracts"—bilateral contracts between a specific producer and a specific consumer for the delivery of the commodity concerned at some future date, thus facilitating forward planning and reducing uncertainty for both parties.

2305 However, a similar economic effect can also be achieved *indirectly* by means of the "futures contracts" described in this chapter, where the use of standardised terms facilitates the matching of demand from buyers and supply from sellers, without the two parties even knowing each other. In conjunction with cash sales, futures contracts can also be used to iron out fluctuations in price.

2306 A futures exchange, in addition to facilitating the trade in contracts involving real commodities such as those discussed above, also enables dealings in certain artificial "commodities"—financial instruments where physical delivery would not be practicable and where appropriate cash settlements therefore have to be used instead.

The Sydney Futures Exchange

2307 In Australia the futures market is organised by a body called Sydney Futures Exchange Limited (SFE), which trades though a number of *futures brokers*—floor members, associate members and clearing members. Some but not all of these are associated with stockbroking organisations.

2308 The exchange operates between 8.30 a.m and 12.30 p.m. and between 2.00 p.m. and 4.30 p.m. on weekdays. Information about transaction prices each day on the SFE is freely available.

2309 Contracts involving interest rates at various durations—90-day bank accepted bills, 3—year Commonwealth Treasury Bonds and 10-year Commonwealth Treasury Bonds—are currently quoted.

2310 An important contract based on a basket of ordinary shares is discussed in paras 2329 to 2340. Other contracts dealing with specific shares are covered in paras 2341 to 2343.

2311 Other current contracts are based on wool, wheat and electricity. Two of the three wool contracts and the electricity contract involve cash settlements. The other wool contract and the wheat contract are based on physical delivery.

2312 Contracts based on gold and US Treasury Bonds and a "Euro-dollar Interest Rate" contract are no longer available, but Australian investors can readily trade such futures on an overseas exchanges. New types of contract are introduced from time to time.

2313 Futures contracts which enable a number of major currencies to be hedged can also be dealt in on some overseas markets but unfortunately not directly in Australia.

2314 An SFE deliverable "Australian Dollars" futures contract, in units of $A100,000 but with the price quoted in United States dollars, was formerly available, but this has now been discontinued because of lack of customer demand.

Complaints

2315 The SFE is able to investigate investor complaints relating to futures transactions.

2316 Claims for compensation for losses incurred by a client as the result of alleged improper action by an SFE member or other disputes can also be resolved more formally. Subject to agreement by the client this is usually done by arbitration, which is normally faster and less expensive than court proceedings (as well as offering privacy).

Closing Out

2317 Most futures contracts are not actually held until the nominated delivery date, the obligations in practice being "liquidated" (extinguished) by the making of transactions instead. This is known as "closing out an open position". As indicated above, the process is made possible by the use of standardised terms for the contracts, which makes all like contracts for each commodity interchangeable with each other.

The Clearing House

2318 A separate computerised clearing house based in London was formerly used as another part of the market mechanism. However, the current clearing house is a wholly-owned subsidiary of the SFE called Sydney Futures Exchange Clearing House Pty Limited (SFECH).

2319 The main purpose of the clearing house is to guarantee the performance of the contracts. Investors also obtain a measure of protection through statutory licensing requirements and through a fidelity fund maintained by the SFE.

Hedging versus Speculating

2320 When producers and consumers use futures in the way described above they are said to be engaged in *hedging*. Ideally, the commodity in respect of which protection is being sought should be the same as the commodity involved in the futures contract, but if this is not practicable then the risk can still be substantially hedged by using a contract for a commodity which is likely to have similar price movements. For example, a 10-year Treasury Bond contract can be used to immunise the effect of interest rate movements on other long-term paper.

2321 Hedging involves taking an opposite position in the futures market to the one held in the physical market, so that any loss in the physical market will be offset by a corresponding profit in the futures market, thus providing a form of price insurance.

2322 However, while the hedger has the advantage of being able to budget in the knowledge that a specific price has been locked in regardless of any future fluctuations, it has to be realised that any profit in the physical market—which would otherwise have been a windfall gain—will now be offset by a corresponding loss in the futures market.

2323 Futures contracts can also be used for *speculating*. Persons who have no involvement in the physical commodity as either buyers or sellers can trade in futures as a convenient way of benefiting from expected price movements.

2324 By laying out only a relatively small deposit (see paras 2344 to 2352) and transaction charges a speculator can trade a contract many times the value of the deposit and make gains as large in dollar terms as if the speculator had held a "long" or "short" physical position equivalent to the assets represented by the face value of the contract.

2325 This "leverage" aspect can be very attractive, although, as always, leverage is a two-edged sword (see para. 2346). *Wise investors will speculate only if they can afford the losses which may result.* (See especially para. 2349.) The SFE estimates that about 75 per cent of all speculators in futures lose money.

2326 Futures trading is a *"zero sum game"*. For every buyer of a contract there has to be a corresponding seller and vice versa. For every "long" position (a contract promising to take) there must be an equal "short" position (a contract promising to deliver). For every dollar of profit made by one player there must be a dollar of loss made by somebody else.

2327 The participation of speculators in the game thus assists both producers and consumers to find matching parties and helps to broaden the market.

2328 Australian futures brokers can also arrange futures transactions in overseas markets for their clients.

The All Ordinaries Share Price Index Futures Contract

2329 Stock exchange indices are discussed in paras 979 to 985. A futures contract of particular interest to investors on the stock exchange is the one based on the Australian Stock Exchange's All Ordinaries Share Price Index (SPI). This contract naturally involves mandatory cash settlements.

When first introduced it was based on a dollar value of 100 times the Index, but in a successful move to make it more popular this was varied. It is now based on a dollar value of 25 times the Index. A choice of six different delivery dates is available—the end of the current and each of the next five calendar quarters. However, most of the trading activity is always in the contract involving the current quarter and to a lesser extent (and mainly towards the end of the quarter) the one following.

2330 When the Index is at any given level the contract involves a price somewhere in that vicinity, the precise discount or premium to the Index at any particular moment being governed by market forces. In part this will reflect market sentiment—if the Index is expected to be higher by the delivery date then this will naturally be reflected in a premium to the spot price, and vice versa.

2331 Separate from that, the contract price should in theory be at a premium in order to reflect the income advantage which ownership of the contract confers against ownership of a physical portfolio. (The owner of a contract avoids the need to outlay most of the money for the equivalent of the portfolio which the investor controls by virtue of that ownership, thus interest or other investment income can be earned up to the delivery date, instead of dividends at a lower rate. The longer the time to the delivery date the greater the theoretical premium should be on this account.)

2332 If the Index is, say, 2605, then the holder of a share portfolio worth, say, $250,000 who wishes to hedge an exposure can thus sell four contracts, for, say, 2585 (the equivalent of $258,500 for the four). If the value of this portfolio falls by, say, 10 per cent then the investor will have lost $25,000. The contract will have moved down also, although not, of course, by precisely the same percentage. It might have moved down by, say, 9 per cent, to 2352 (the equivalent of $235,200). Buying a contract, in reversal of the original selling transaction, would thus crystallise a profit of $23,300, substantially offsetting the loss on the portfolio itself.

2333 In practice a number of other factors also need to be taken into account—including the incidence of transaction costs; the fact that profits from futures trading are taxable; the probability that pressure from other investors holding similar expectations to the investor's own will usually push the price up or down against the investor; and the likely volatility of the portfolio being hedged (in other words, will its value move more or less than the average represented by the Index?). (Volatility is often expressed by a "Beta Factor". A Beta Factor of 1 represents the same volatility as the market as a whole.)

2334 To give another illustration, an investor wishing to be "long" in the market can buy a SPI contract as an alternative to buying shares in the physical market. That way the investor can achieve exposure to the market while avoiding the need to put up most of the money. Of course, to the extent that the investor can thus earn interest on that money (or save on paying interest on borrowed funds) the investor would need to allow for a likely loss on the contract, as explained above. If the market moves up in line with expectations, then the investor will make a profit; but, of course, if the market moves down then correspondingly the investor will make a loss.

2335 Persons who are already holding a spread of ordinary shares should be careful about buying SPI contracts—as distinct from selling them—as this would serve to *increase* their exposure and thus their risk.

2336 Selling an SPI contract is the equivalent of short selling a basket of shares—see paras 1685 to 1698. Viewed in isolation or through the eyes of a pure speculator, if the market moves down in line with expectations, then the investor will make a profit; but equally if the market moves up then the investor will make a loss. The result for a hedger, long in shares, is naturally different—a loss on the contract will roughly be balanced by a profit on shares of equivalent value and vice versa.

2337 Large investors with portfolios which replicate the Index could in theory arbitrage between their physical portfolios and the SPI contracts—see paras 986 to 989—although the thin Australian markets would make such an exercise on a large scale difficult.

2338 Some large investors use computers to place orders automatically in order to avail themselves of arbitrage opportunities between the share market and futures contracts based on shares. This practice has been blamed for exaggerating market falls and even for precipitating the October 1987 stock market crash.

2339 However, arbitrage activity actually serves to smoothen out market anomalies, by adding buying pressure to the lower of two markets and equivalent selling pressure to the higher of these. The net selling pressure in the two markets combined due to arbitrageurs is by definition nil. Price falls can occur only when there is *net positive selling pressure* from investors.

2340 A small number of leading stocks have a relatively high weighting in the Index. Furthermore, market values on the stock exchange are determined by the relatively small proportion of the total shares on issue which changes hands at any particular time. The existence of the SPI Futures Contract thus increases the risk that—notwithstanding surveillance in both markets—manipulation could on occasions take place, especially near the end of a calendar quarter. For example, an institution with a significant long position in the futures contract is clearly in a position to arrange for its normal purchases of physical stocks to take place at a time of its own choosing.

Share Futures

2341 Other futures contracts of particular interest to investors on the stock exchange are those based on the shares in individual companies.

2342 Contracts over a small number of leading industrial and resource stocks have been created. No doubt others will be created from time to time in line with investor interest.

2343 These contracts normally involve physical delivery (through CHESS). An exception to this exists: Telstra contracts are cash settled, in order to avoid possible complications relating to foreign ownership in excess of the statutory limits.

Mechanics

2344 An investor who wishes to deal in futures needs to make appropriate arrangements with a futures broker. The investor also has to complete a *Client Agreement Form*, which outlines the terms and conditions of the client/broker relationship. This also includes a *Risk Disclosure Document* which spells out the risks involved in leveraged investments. Before placing any order the investor will also have to set up a credit balance in an account with the futures broker. Some of this money will cover the *initial margin* which has to be lodged with the clearing house at the time of the opening leg of each transaction and which cannot be withdrawn while the contract remains open.

2345 The amount of this margin is set by the clearing house and varies with the commodity concerned and the degree of volatility in the market at the time the order is placed. The balance of the money will be available to meet future margin calls. Interest is paid on the credit balances.

2346 The margins and credit balances are small in relation to the effective exposure obtained by the investor and therefore futures contracts constitute highly leveraged investments. For example, a 10 per cent payment means that a 5 per cent movement up or down in the price of the underlying security would result in a 50 per cent movement up or down on the investor's own funds.

2347 As soon as any market movement reduces the investor's stake in the contract the futures broker must make a *margin call* on the investor so as to pass further cover on to the clearing house. If this is not available from any credit balance in the investor's account or from funds otherwise forthcoming within 24 hours then the futures broker has the right to unilaterally close out the investor's open position.

2348 If, on the other hand, a market movement increases the investor's stake, then the clearing house will make an appropriate release of funds, which is then credited to the client's account with the futures broker concerned.

2349 It will be realised that—notwithstanding the system of deposits and margins described above—if the price of a commodity moves sufficiently then the investor's stake in a contract can be wiped out very quickly, even in a matter of minutes. The investor is, of course, left with the obligation to meet any eventual deficiency.

2350 Commission rates are negotiable between members and their clients. Commission is based on a "round turn" (opening and closing). It is levied at the closing out stage and covers also the applicable SFE and clearing house charges.

2351 The interest rate, if any, payable on any credit balance in a client's account with a member is also negotiable. Investors may therefore wish to shop around for the most attractive overall deals. For good clients the interest rate is likely to be the current short-term rate, less a small margin.

2352 For futures contracts on overseas exchanges with prices set in United States dollars or other non-Australian currencies the deposits and margin calls will be expressed in the currency concerned. This exposes the investor to an exchange risk which needs to be taken into account.

Options on Futures Contracts

2353 In addition to allowing trading in the various futures contracts described above, the Sydney Futures Exchange also allows put and call options (see Chapter 22) to be traded in respect of some of the contracts (but not in respect of those based on shares in individual companies).

2354 These options provide great leverage for their holders— greater than the underlying contracts themselves—although as one would expect this privilege is not inexpensive.

Screen Trading

2355 The SFE has its own version of SEATS, an automated screen trading system known as SYCOM (Sydney Computerised Market).

2356 This operates from 4.40 p.m. to 6.00 a.m. Sydney time on week days, thereby opening the Australian market to other dealing centres in the world at times fitting in with their own time zones.

Futures Funds

2357 An alternative method of investing in futures is to acquire an interest in a "futures fund"—a unit trust which is dedicated to trading in futures contracts and options. Some such funds offer limited guarantees, although these are not as good as they might seem on a quick reading—see paras 2416 to 2419 for a fuller discussion of this aspect.

Legislation

2358 Chapter 8 of the *Corporations Law* regulates the futures industry in Australia. These provisions, which replaced the separate *Futures Industry Act 1986*, are sometimes referred to unofficially as the *Futures Law*.

Forecasts

2359 Despite some myths to the contrary, the prices at which futures contracts change hands give no useful information in regard to likely future price movements in the corresponding physical markets. Each market is governed by its own separate supply and demand relationship. Hedgers in particular are buyers or sellers of futures by virtue of their particular circumstances; they seek to eliminate a risk rather than to back a prediction.

General Comments

2360 It goes without saying that investors should always know what they are doing. When they decide to trade in futures this piece of advice becomes even more important than in the case of share investments, as the risks are much greater. Self-education before an investor starts is virtually essential—for example, by attending an SFE course.

2361 Investors should read carefully any proposed agreement between themselves and a futures broker. They should, of course, never sign such an agreement without fully understanding its terms.

Chapter 24—Other Types of Investment

*Spend at least as much time researching a stock as
you would choosing a refrigerator*
—Peter Lynch

Preliminary Comments

2401 Investments other than those described elsewhere in this book exist in many different shapes and forms and it is clearly not practicable to deal with all of them here. However, this chapter discusses some representative types of investment, both as a matter of interest in itself and in order to illustrate some general principles which will have wider application.

Collectibles

2402 Investment is in the eye of the beholder. For example, some people get great pleasure out of collecting coins, postage stamps, jewellery, antiques, works of art, vintage cars, bottles of wine and the like. They may choose to regard their collections as also serving as investments. Persons with the necessary knowledge and experience can undoubtedly make a profit out of buying and selling such collectible items. Whether such profit is as great as it might have been from alternative investment opportunities—particularly when allowance is made for the risks involved and the time spent—is, of course, quite another matter.

2403 An item might have gone up 20-fold in value in 30 years. This sounds pretty good, but it represents only 10.5 per cent per annum compound, not much more than the rate of inflation.

2404 Holding such assets is not free of cost. Whether it is recognised or not, tying up capital always involves an "opportunity cost" equal to the return which would have been obtainable from other investment situations.

2405 Dealing in collectible items can also involve all sorts of hidden costs—breakages, insurance, valuation fees, reference works, high auction commissions, interest and so on.

2406 Persons without the necessary knowledge run the risk that they will make poor bargains on both the buying and the selling legs of their transactions. They can easily be tricked into paying more than an article is worth—particularly in areas where value depends very much on condition. They can be cheated by forgers. They may find that there is no proper market when they want to sell. If they think that they know more than they really do, then they will almost certainly not even buy in that corner of their speciality where the chance of capital appreciation is greatest.

Syndicated Investments

2407 In a different category are various schemes involving some promoter soliciting funds from a series of individual investors with a view to putting those funds, net of the promoter's fees, into some jointly-owned enterprise managed by the promoter or by an associated company. Such investments are often long-term, speculative and highly illiquid. Typically they involve pine tree or jojoba plantations, oyster or emu farms, films or the like. They may present some tax advantages, but the existence of these rarely turns an otherwise unsound proposition into a bonanza.

2408 Sometimes a guarantee of some sort is featured in the publicity material for such schemes—see the warnings given in para. 1512 and the more detailed comments in paras 2416 to 2419.

Property Syndicates

2409 Property syndicates are partnerships of up to 20 people formed in order to acquire real property. They are in some ways similar to unit trusts, but unlike such trusts and unlike companies they are not governed by the companies legislation. This leaves investors relatively unprotected. Except in the case of limited partnerships in the States where this approach is allowed, investments using a partnership format can also expose their members to unlimited liability.

2410 Potential investors in such projects should scrutinise them carefully, paying particular attention to aspects such as the following:

- How realistic is the proposed purchase price of the property?

- Is the vendor of the property at arm's length from the promoter?

- If the intention is to resell the property at some future time, how realistic is the forecast of the sale price?

- What are the terms of the leases?

- How likely is it that the proposed lessees will meet all their obligations?

- Is the proposed rent at a fair market level?

- How realistic are any projections of rent levels following reviews?
- How reliable and experienced is the management company for the project?
- What fees apply during the currency of the project?
- Will the title be held by an independent trustee?
- Is any proposed loan to finance the project firmly tied up, is its duration adequate and is the interest rate appropriate?
- Are any guarantees enforceable?
- Allowing for the risks involved, how does the proposed return compare with that available from more conventional types of investment?

Other relevant questions are:

- How easily can the investor dispose of his interest?
- How long will this take?
- Will he get fair value?
- What fees apply both at entry and at exit?
- What fees apply during the currency of his holding?

Often these projects are put together by professionals such as accountants, who have a vested interest in the ongoing fee income which will be generated.

Mutual Funds

2411 A "mutual fund" operates in a similar fashion to an open end (unlisted) unit trust, but using a different legal format and being subject to different tax rules.

2412 A mutual fund is an unlimited company and the investors are its shareholders. There is no outside trustee, the company's board in effect acting as both manager and trustee. An unlimited company, unlike a limited company or a no liability company (see Chapter 4), is allowed to reduce its capital without much formality, thus allowing shares to be cashed very readily.

However, shareholders are placed in some danger by virtue of the unlimited liability aspect, which means that each shareholder can be sued to the limits of his personal wealth for all unsatisfied liabilities incurred by the mutual fund. For this reason the mutual fund format has fallen out of favour in Australia. (Ordinary companies will be allowed to reduce capital under proposed changes to the legislation.)

Investment Companies

2413 Investment companies involving money subscribed by members of the general public are usually listed on the stock exchange. They are like all other listed companies except that their assets, instead of being plant, stock, land, debtors, etc., consist primarily of ordinary shares in non-investment companies listed on the stock exchange. Investment companies thus resemble closed end (listed) unit trusts in terms of activity, but not in legal form or taxation status.

2414 Investment companies on the lines of open end (unlisted) unit trusts but without the unlimited liability of mutual funds are also possible. These involve redeemable preference shares issued at a substantial premium.

Investment Clubs

2415 Investment clubs are partnerships of up to 20 people who band together in order to invest in a jointly-owned portfolio of shares. Usually each member of the club contributes a small amount of additional investment capital each month. The main purpose of such clubs is self-education, as all decisions as to which shares to buy, hold or sell are made by general meetings of all members. Of course, as a training exercise clubs could also set up hypothetical portfolios and learn the craft without putting up real money.

Special Guarantees

2416 Prospectuses and publicity material for futures funds and other highly speculative ventures sometimes feature a guarantee of some sort in order to make the scheme concerned sound more attractive to conservative investors.

2417 Special attention is drawn to one aspect of this theme—a guarantee from, say, a bank or some other highly reputable institution to the effect that the investor will get all of his money back at the end of a certain period, say seven years. This is made possible by placing about half of the investor's stake in safe fixed interest paper (possibly a zero coupon stock) and using only the balance for the speculative purposes featured by the promoter. At about 10 per cent per annum compound interest, money doubles in seven years, so nothing particularly outstanding is involved in any such arrangements. It is important to note that such guarantees usually operate only at the end of the stipulated term. They thus do little to protect investors wishing to quit before then.

2418 A guarantee on these lines is sound enough—but hardly free of cost. Getting one's own money back without interest and without adjustment for inflation is no great bargain. In any case, any investor so minded can replicate such an arrangement himself. If he is prepared to forego all annual return for some years then he can ensure the preservation of his capital in dollar terms by putting half of his funds into some safe interest-bearing security and exposing only the other half to any investment risk.

2419 While such arrangements may have a certain amount of marketing appeal, there is a distinct lack of logic behind them. Why should an investor who is looking for the excitement and potential gains of some speculative venture and who desires to back the entrepreneurial judgement of the promoter concerned be *forced* to put about half of his stake into decidedly dull fixed interest securities? Having to pay relatively high initial and ongoing fees for the privilege of investing in such paper only makes the whole proposition even less attractive. Promoters wishing to offer such a guarantee to their more timid customers would attract more business from others if the guarantee instead of being compulsory were merely an optional extra.

Property

2420 Investment in property is a specialised form of investment which is for the most part outside the scope of this book. However, many of the comments on the economy in general are, of course, relevant to investors in property, as the share and property markets influence each other.

2421 The subject is dealt with in great detail in a companion volume by the author entitled *Understanding Investment Property*. This discusses investment in residential, commercial and industrial properties.

2422 Investors who favour property will find it useful to own some shares as well, even if only for the ability (which is lacking in the case of real estate) to raise small amounts of money relatively quickly.

Managed Investments

2423 Managed investments (pooled investment vehicles) are very popular these days (see also para. 119). Such indirect investments are explained at length in another companion volume by the author entitled *Understanding Managed Investments*. The products considered there are also complementary to direct share investment. They include unit trusts of all types, conventional and modern life insurance and friendly society policies, capital secure and unit-linked investment bonds, annuities, superannuation and Approved Deposit Funds.

Chapter 25—The Financial Press

Freedom of the press is limited to
those who own one
—A J Liebling

Background

2501 The financial press in Australia is an important source of information for most investors. As indicated in Chapter 10, stories published in the press can affect markets—even when such reports are based on idle speculation, hearsay, rumours, propaganda originated by vested interests or the like.

2502 Daily newspapers in their general pages publish much material of relevance to investors. However, most stories relating to listed companies will appear in a special part of the paper known as the financial pages or the business section. Further special sections may be devoted to the specific needs of various groups of readers. These can range from small savers interested mainly in unit trusts on the one hand to large property investors monitoring developments affecting commercial and industrial real estate on the other.

2503 One specialist newspaper, the *Australian Financial Review*, also appears daily (six days a week), and has the advantage of being able to devote considerably more space to specific investment topics than the other dailies. It also focuses on political stories with an economic flavour.

2504 A number of business journals published weekly or less frequently complement the above-mentioned publications. These journals are more concerned with interpreting and backgrounding news for their readers rather than just recording news as it happens.

Text

2505 The text on the financial pages will include both facts and opinions. Facts will be derived from official announcements by companies, governments, organisations and so on, as well as from the paper's own researches.

2506 Sections 879 to 887 of the *Corporations Law* require financial journalists to maintain a register in which their interests in securities are recorded.

2507 Investors who might wish to rely on newspaper reports will need to bear their limitations in mind:

- The speed of production can lead to typographical and other errors.

- The technical nature of some stories can lead to mistakes by reporters.

- Space limitations can lead to important parts of announcements being omitted or summarised inadequately. Sometimes, as when key dates are left out, this may be obvious, but usually the story will give the impression of being complete even when it is not.

- Remarks can sometimes be taken out of context.

- From their very nature headlines can be misleading.

- Cartoons accompanying stories or captions under photographs can also give misleading impressions.

- Statements by a company, quoted remarks from other parties and comments by the reporter writing the story are not always clearly distinguished from each other.

- Large listed companies are likely to get much more attention than small ones.

- Bad news is more likely to be featured than good news.

2508 Inexperienced reporters can easily misunderstand even some rather fundamental aspects—for example, that the true value of the share consideration in a takeover offer is based on the market value of the shares concerned rather than on their par value. Such reporters can also allow themselves to be trapped into accepting a company's "profit is up" message, even though its *earning rate on funds employed* may be down. They may talk of the "benefit" from rights or bonus issues when their real effect is neutral.

2509 On a different aspect, the law of defamation can prevent newspapers from warning their readers of dishonest corporate behaviour and practices even when they are well aware of them. This law even inhibits investigative reporters doing research, as they know that they will be unable to publish their discoveries and to alert investors accordingly.

Share Tables

2510 In addition to publishing text with facts and opinion, the financial pages also contain tables of current market prices for many listed ordinary shares (and certain other equity issues), together with some related information, such as volumes traded, dividend yields, price earnings ratios, and so on. Unfortunately, typographical and other errors in such tables are by no means unknown and investors should always keep that possibility in mind. Such errors can creep into one particular paper at its production stage, but they can also occur within the stock exchange's own computer system, in which case they will naturally affect all papers taking data from this common source.

2511 Errors seem to be particularly prevalent in the columns showing the high and low prices of a share for the year to date. Apart from containing purely typographical errors such columns often do not treat like with like, ignoring the effect on share prices of cash or bonus issues or spin-offs. For example, a *cum bonus* high price can be set out in conjunction with an *ex bonus* low price, even if the bonus issue had involved, say, a three for one ratio. The use of the calendar year to date, rather than, say, the last 52 weeks, also seems another piece of nonsense.

2512 Some newspapers show in such tables for each company the price of the *last sale*, while others show a *closing price*. The latter is the more sensible concept. It involves the price obtained in the last sale, except where there is either a higher buying price or a lower selling price—in which case the latter buying or selling price is shown.

2513 For understandable space reasons abbreviations are frequently used in such tables, both in respect of company names (which can confuse readers when two companies with similar names are both listed) and in respect of the type of security. A list of the more common abbreviations used in newspapers is set out in Appendix 5.

2514 While the tables list ordinary shares in some detail, the corresponding information for fixed interest securities is rarely published in the general press.

Daily Commentaries

2515 Most newspapers choose to accompany their share tables by some editorial comments, drawing attention to transactions of special interest. They also attempt to explain why the market moved up or down in the way that it did. Such explanations are often quite spurious and even internally inconsistent.

2516 Others are astonishingly naive, as when a reporter, obviously completely unaware of the lead times involved in property deals, wrote: "The government's banning of negative gearing announced yesterday was believed to have caused many property investors to divert funds into the industrial sector of the stock market." Another reporter apparently believed that all bank shares—regardless of factors such as entirely different earnings per share figures—should always be priced equally. Discussing an incident affecting one particular bank she wrote that this was "unlikely to help the ANZ's share price, which has been floundering at about $4.80 a share, well below Westpac's $6.50 and the National's $6.20." What would that reporter have made of a share split?

2517 Price movements are usually discussed in terms of cents per share rather than in percentage terms, which would be far more meaningful. This practice can be quite misleading, as when it is implied that a 20 cent jump, say, from 800 to 820 (which is 2.5 per cent) is more important than a 10 cent jump, say, from 50 to 60 (which is 20 per cent). Tables of "Rises and Falls" for the day are also generally presented in this misleading fashion, a fact which is quite surprising in this computer age.

Radio and Television

2518 A number of radio and television programs, often with "business" in their title, are devoted to investment matters. In addition, some public radio stations broadcast the midday share prices of selected companies each weekday lunchtime.

Defamation

2519 As indicated in para. 1237, the libel laws in the various Australian States are a factor inhibiting the reporting of some matters of considerable relevance to investors. Sometimes journalists and others are aware of malpractices affecting listed companies or pooled investment vehicles—matters which should really be brought to public attention—but those in the know maintain a wall of silence in order to avoid being served with a libel writ.

2520 On occasions this silence is the by-product of what is known as a "stop writ"—the formal commencement of legal proceedings for defamation, not primarily for the purpose of actually winning damages but rather to stop further discussion of the subject by making the matter sub judice and making the publication of further comment a contempt of court.

2521 On other occasions an "apology" will actually be published, withdrawing certain critical comments which had attracted the wroth of the party instituting or threatening to institute libel proceedings. Such messages need to be read between the lines, as they are usually the result of an out-of-court deal and do not necessarily indicate either that the statements complained of were indeed false or that their author has really changed his mind about the malpractice to which he drew attention in the first place.

Internet Pages

2522 Newspaper organisations often maintain pages on the World Wide Web which feature selected articles from their print editions—see Chapter 42.

Chapter 26—Sources of Information

*If Moses were alive today, would God fax
him the 10 commandments?*
—Monica Waldman

Preliminary Comments

2601 Investors will in practice gather their information from a great many different sources—sources of varying standards of accuracy and reliability. This chapter can be regarded as a sort of annotated checklist for this smorgasbord.

2602 One source of information for investors—the financial press—has already been discussed (see Chapter 25). Some miscellaneous additional sources are set out in the List of Further Reading (Appendix 10).

Material from Listed Companies

2603 Listed companies publish much information of relevance to existing and potential shareholders, including:

(a) Material mailed to all shareholders, except where requested otherwise:

• The Annual Report (see Chapter 8).

(b) Material lodged at the stock exchange, which is usually also sent to the media and which may or may not be mailed to all shareholders:

• The Preliminary Final Statement (a brief statement setting out the key figures to be featured in the company's Annual Report, but issued several weeks before this becomes available).

• The Half-yearly Report (a brief statement setting out the key figures covering the company's operations during the first six months of the financial year). A few companies also issue Quarterly Reports.

(c) Material issued at the company's discretion:

• The Chairman's Address (see also paras 856 to 858).

• Miscellaneous circulars to shareholders.

(d) Material issued when appropriate:

• Prospectuses (see Chapter 43).

• Takeover documents (see Chapter 11).

• Rules for dividend reinvestment and dividend election plans (see Chapter 32).

2604 Investors wishing to have back copies of such material or copies of a company's memorandum and articles of association (see paras 411 to 412) can usually obtain them on request to the company concerned.

Material from the Stock Exchange

2605 Stock exchange publications include:

- Statistical and research material relating to listed companies.

- Lists of current new issues, dividends, takeovers, name changes, new listings, calls, etc.

- Daily quote sheets.

- Data relating to the stock exchange indices (see paras 979 to 985).

- Details of delisted companies.

- Investment record sheets.

- Blank charting paper.

- Prices of shares as at 30 June and 31 December each year (these are also available on computer disks).

Commercial Bookshops

2606 The major capital city exchanges formerly maintained modern specialist bookshops, but in a backward move to the cause of investor education these were closed on 30 June 1998. However, many other bookshops sell numerous books dealing with various aspects of investment. Everything from the sharemarket to general finance is covered, including specialist works dealing with taxation, options, futures, commodity trading, company information, accounting, security analysis, the economy, charting, property, company law, superannuation, speculation and even investor psychology. Both beginners and advanced players will find material which will help them to advance their knowledge.

Material from Stockbrokers

2607 Brokers' circulars are discussed in para. 1411.

2608 The opinions expressed in such circulars—while no doubt made in good faith—are, of course, not infallible, as the following case study demonstrates. A leading stockbroking firm once sent a circular to its clients with the following analysis:

"On balance, it seems that, while minor fluctuations in the market could occur over the next month or two, extreme movements in the overall level of prices are unlikely."

On the very next trading day, the market fell many hundreds of millions of dollars.

Government Publications

2609   Numerous publications by the Commonwealth and State Governments and their agencies can have relevance to investment—for example, the Australian Bureau of Statistics publishes a mass of statistical data, while the Taxation Commissioner issues Determinations dealing with aspects of income tax and the Reserve Bank of Australia produces material on money markets and the like.

2610   The Commonwealth and the States maintain in the various capital cities bookshops which sell Acts of Parliament and many other official publications.

Investment Newsletters

2611   A number of commercial organisations publish on a subscription basis periodical investment newsletters intended for specific target audiences. Some of these are virtual tipping sheets, giving rise to the same sort of questions as tipping material in the racing world, namely, why would those with winning information want to share it with many other people instead of just exploiting it themselves.

2612   Section 849 of the *Corporations Law* requires licensed persons who send out circulars containing investment recommendations to include in those circulars details of their interest in any of the investments concerned. This provision was intended to alert readers to any possible bias arising out of security dealings by the publishers of the circulars. In practice the information forthcoming by virtue of this requirement is quite unhelpful—for example, a stockbroker's circular discussing 30 or 40 different stocks will typically contain a declaration to the effect that the broking organisation and its associates "may have a relevant interest in ... all the securities mentioned in this publication".

Libraries

2613 Each capital city stock exchange used to maintain a library which contained, amongst other things, files on each listed company which included copies of all publicly—available reports by the company to the stock exchange. These files were inspectable by investors, usually on payment of a fee. The imposition of such a levy was rather surprising in this day and age, and may well have been counterproductive in the long run if it discouraged greater stock exchange activity. This fee constituted a "tax on knowledge", which seemed particularly inappropriate in the case of material filed with the stock exchange by listed companies for the express purpose of ensuring that users of its market facilities were fully informed.

While the provision of library access undoubtedly involved some costs in respect of staff and accommodation it must be remembered that investors already pay for these indirectly through brokerage whenever they deal and through the listing fees paid by the companies in which they hold securities. Photocopies of any material in the files could also be obtained on payment of a commercially-set fee.

The libraries also contained copies of the Company Review Service reports on listed and delisted companies. (This publication was formerly known as the Sydney Stock Exchange Statistical Service.) Again, an inspection fee per volume was charged.

2614 These libraries were all closed on 30 June 1998, but very up-to-date information is now available electronically—see Chapter 42.

2615 Of course, many stockbrokers also maintain libraries to which clients may be able to get free access on application. These libraries often contain research material produced by the broking organisation itself, as well as non-official information such as newspaper clippings.

2616 Serious investors will, of course, also endeavour to build up their own personal libraries, containing material of particular relevance to them. See Appendix 10.

Recorded Information Services

2617 Recorded information in regard to each day's share prices can be obtained by ringing appropriate telephone numbers in each capital city. The prices, which are updated several times a day, cover the more important stocks traded on that day in alphabetical order. Figures for some stock exchange indices are also included. Similar information is also obtainable:

- on television sets through Teletext
- through World Wide Web sites on the Internet (see Chapter 42 and Appendix 9).

Research Organisations

2618 Detailed research material can also be purchased from several commercial research organisations. However, this is intended mainly for stockbroker and institutional use and the services are priced accordingly.

Information for Property Investors

2619 The comments above refer mainly to the requirements of stock exchange investors. Property investors will need to focus on some information of a different type, for example, in regard to zoning regulations and planning schemes.

2620 Statistical information relating to population movements in different areas and reports dealing with roads and public transport expansion proposals are further examples of information which might be of importance to potential investors in the property market.

Short Courses

2621 Single lectures and short educational courses specially designed for small to medium investors and covering the topics presented in this book are run from time to time. Such courses, which do not involve examinations or lead to formal qualifications, are organised in all States by the various adult education bodies and in relation to their own areas of interest by bodies such as the Australian Stock Exchange, the Sydney Futures Exchange and the real estate institutes.

Tax Deductions

2622 Reference material purchased in connection with investment activities would normally be deductible under Section 51 of the *Income Tax Assessment Act 1936* as an expense incurred in the earning of assessable income.

The Internet

2623 A great deal of information of relevance to investors is available on the Internet, quite apart from the share price and listed company information referred to above. See Chapter 42 and Appendix 9.

Chapter 27—Using Borrowed Funds

*A bank is a place where they lend you an umbrella in
fair weather and ask for it back again
when it begins to rain*
—Robert Frost

Preliminary Comments

2701 A conservative investment portfolio might well be structured to consist of 20 per cent "cash" and 80 per cent "other assets". In this context "cash" does not mean bank notes, but rather "near cash", such as deposits in banks or building societies, deposits with companies, units in cash management trusts, short-term bills or other income-producing assets which can be turned into actual cash (and thus reinvested) very readily. The "cash" might be held in case some particularly attractive investment opportunity turns up, but it might also be kept through inertia or just for general precautionary reasons.

2702 Presumably most investors with such a portfolio mix expect the above-mentioned 80 per cent component to do better than the 20 per cent component—otherwise they would have opted for 100 per cent "cash". If that is so, then the investor would be better off, but for the liquidity aspects, in investing more than 80 per cent in "non cash" and making other arrangements, in the form of undrawn credit lines, for unexpected events.

2703 As shown below, this process can be taken one step further. The investor can invest beyond 100 per cent of his own resources if he chooses to borrow. This will be rewarding whenever the return on the funds employed exceeds the cost of borrowing (allowing for all charges and for tax on both legs of the transaction). The problem is that such a strategy is a two-edged sword. Overall returns are enhanced if all goes well but losses can ensue if anything goes wrong—see, for example, Tables 1 to 3 in para. 2718.

2704 Borrowing in this way is therefore not really a desirable course of action for beginners, quite apart from the difficulties potential borrowers may encounter in dealing with likely lenders, unless they have appropriate chargeable assets and/or an assured cash flow. Investors using other people's money in this way always need to consider what would happen if they cannot meet their interest or capital payment commitments on time or, worse still, at all. As with most other investment decisions, the anticipated extra returns from leverage need to be weighed against all the additional risks.

2705 Situations involving "double gearing" can be particularly dangerous—for example, where a person borrows in order to buy some units in a property trust which is itself a heavy borrower for the trust's own portfolio.

2706 Loans for the acquisition of income-producing freehold property are often thought to be safer than loans raised in order to buy shares, because in normal times the property market tends to be less volatile. Furthermore such loans can often be had for longer terms and at a lower interest cost.

2707 Notwithstanding this, borrowers should always have a long-term strategy for such transactions in mind before entering into them. This would not necessarily involve plans to sell the property—for example, the intention may be to repay the loan from lump sum superannuation, or from the sale of a business, at retirement. The rent with its periodical upward adjustments can then from that point onwards be regarded as an indexed pension to the investor and his spouse for life, with the added benefit that a valuable and unencumbered property can be left as a legacy in his will.

Cash for Stock Exchange Transactions

2708 Investors on the stock exchange will be faced from time to time with the chance to buy further shares, such opportunities arising from rights issues or share purchase plans (see Chapter 7), new flotations (see Chapter 6) or just market happenings which come to their notice. Their demand for funds for these and other investment purposes, including the payment of calls (see para. 414), may easily outstrip their net savings ability, especially in the short-term. Investors are then faced with the choice of abandoning the opportunity, disposing of some existing holdings, borrowing external funds or some combination of these.

2709 Selling shares in a hurry is often inadvisable and temporary accommodation in the form of an overdraft from a trading bank may well be the most appropriate solution. An overdraft is an arrangement permitting customers of a bank to draw cheques for amounts in excess of the credit balances in their accounts, paying interest on the debit balances from time to time, together with certain other fees for the privilege.

Usually such loans are secured by the lodgement of suitable securities—in the case of portfolio investors this could include scrip certificates for good quality listed shares, say, to the value of twice the agreed overdraft limit or its equivalent under CHESS. (This ratio is meant to cover fluctuations in market values and also the dilution which occurs when companies make new cash or bonus issues.)

2710 Loans can, of course, also be secured by other means, for example, on the surrender value of a life insurance policy or by a mortgage on real estate. If the borrower's own residence is to be used as security in this way, as well it might be, then extra care should be taken in documenting the arrangements so as to ensure the tax deductibility of the interest as an expense being incurred in the production of assessable income.

2711 Potential borrowers should always shop around for the best terms, taking into account the interest rate, the front-end charges (which can be relatively heavy) and the conditions generally. Costs on loans from finance companies, on "personal loans" from banks and on "margin loans" arranged through stockbrokers tend to be higher and thus less attractive than those on overdraft facilities, but such loans would have the advantage of being available for defined longer terms instead being granted just "at the pleasure of the bank".

The likely penalties on early discharge should also be taken into consideration. (As their name implies, margin loans secured by shares require the borrower to "top up" the security—for example, to deposit more scrip—if the value of the deposited shares drops by more than an agreed amount.)

2712 However, the interest rate on both overdrafts and other loans is not normally on a fixed basis for the full term of the loan and the possibility of an increase in the rate during its currency needs to be allowed for when a decision to borrow is being made. Of course, this can work both ways—the interest rate on a "variable interest" loan can also fall if interest rates generally drop, to the advantage of the borrower.

Assessment of Leverage Proposals

2713 Sometimes advisers recommend a particular investment on the basis that the investor should increase his exposure to it by "leverage"—by using funds borrowed from other people as well as his own money. The idea is that this will increase the investor's ultimate capital appreciation. It is usually suggested that not borrowing when one should is as unwise as borrowing when one should not. While such "gearing up" will be of advantage to the investor if all goes well it does nonetheless subject him to additional risks to which he may not be being alerted properly.

2714 Naturally the use of such a device also results in a considerably bigger commission payment to any intermediary involved in the transaction, a factor which may have influenced the suggestion in the first place. Furthermore, if the proposed loan is coming from a body related to the adviser then the opportunity for a conflict of interest is opened up.

2715 It is best to approach such a recommendation by analysing the two key elements separately:

- Would the proposed investment be considered attractive in its own right if unleveraged?

- Bearing the risks in mind, is it in the investor's best interests to gear up his whole portfolio? If the answer to the first question is "no" then increasing the exposure would hardly make sense.

2716 It is important, as always, to compare like with like. To contrast the ungeared return from one particular investment with the geared-up return from an alternative proposition would be rather misleading. Any single investment showing an overall "after tax" return—income plus growth—which is greater than the net cost of the corresponding borrowing can obviously be made to look even better by topping up the investor's own equity with borrowed funds.

Portfolio Composition

2717 Another way of looking at this subject is to consider the composition of the investor's entire portfolio, treating any borrowed money as a "negative" fixed interest investment and relating it to the portfolio as a whole rather than to the specific investment being used as the actual security for the loan. For example, three alternative strategies could be as shown in Table 1 below.

2718 If the equity investments go up in value by, say, 20 per cent, then the relative effect is as shown in Table 2. So far, so good; but if, on the other hand, the equity investments go down in value by, say, 20 per cent, then the relative effect is reversed, as shown in Table 3:

	A Balanced Portfolio	A Pure Equity Portfolio	A Leveraged Equity Portfolio
	% of Cost	% of Cost	% of Cost
TABLE 1: THE ORIGINAL INVESTMENT			
Equity Investments	50	100	200
Fixed Interest Investments	50	nil	-100
Total, being the Investor's own Equity	100	100	100
TABLE 2: A 20 PER CENT INCREASE IN EQUITY VALUES			
Equity Investments	60	120	240
Fixed Interest Investments	50	nil	-100
Total, being the Investor's own Equity	110	120	140
TABLE 3: A 20 PER CENT DECREASE IN EQUITY VALUES			
Equity Investments	40	80	160
Fixed Interest Investments	50	nil	-100
Total, being the Investor's own Equity	90	80	60

2719 Of course, apart from considerations related to short-term liquidity fluctuations, there is even less logic in simultaneously :

(a)   investing in fixed interest securities as one component of a broadly-based investment portfolio; and

(b)   borrowing at a higher interest rate than in (a) in order to gear up another part of the same portfolio.

2720 It should also be borne in mind that using borrowed funds which are repayable on a specific date can pose an additional danger, namely, that it may prove difficult at the relevant time for the investor either to repay the loan or to renew it on reasonable terms. "Borrowing short and investing long" is one of the classic investment mistakes.

Taxation Aspects

2721 On the other hand, as explained in Chapters 28 and 29, there are considerable tax attractions in using borrowed funds in order to "gear up" a growth investment:

- As the loan is for the purpose of earning assessable income the interest payments are fully tax deductible.

- Any reduction in investment income also reduces the burden of provisional tax.

- Because "negative gearing" (see para. 2884) is allowed, any excess interest over the immediate income from the investment can be offset against taxable income from other sources.

- Although capital gains are taxed, this tax is imposed only if and when the investment is sold and so the levy can be postponed indefinitely.

- The cost price of the investment is indexed in order to allow for inflation, thus significantly reducing any ultimate capital gains tax burden.

- For assets acquired with the help of borrowed funds, it is the gross cost of the asset, not the much lower net cost after deducting the loan, which counts for this purpose.

2722 The interest cost should be looked at realistically—for example, 16 per cent may sound very expensive, but if the "after tax" cost is 8 per cent and inflation is running at about this level then one is really borrowing for nothing.

Mortgages on Investment Property

2723 Investors can use mortgages either as lenders or as borrowers. Mortgages and their use as an investment vehicle are explained in paras 1801 to 1809. Property investment itself is dealt with in the companion volume by the author, *Understanding Investment Property*, and in the remainder of this chapter the use of mortgages by property investors in their capacity as borrowers is considered.

2724 Basically, property investors find it useful to borrow because this enhances their expected returns both before and after tax and because this allows them to benefit rather than to suffer from inflation. Borrowing involves some risks, but it can also enable larger properties—and to that extent frequently better quality buildings with better quality tenants—to be acquired than if only the investor's own funds are committed.

Borrowing also allows small savers to commence the establishment of a property portfolio at an earlier point of time. Borrowing in order to acquire income-producing assets is, of course, quite different in character from borrowing for consumption purposes.

2725 Sources of loan funds include banks, finance companies, building societies, insurance companies, trustee companies, friendly societies and solicitors. As always it pays to shop around, as different lenders have vastly different ideas as to the types of borrower and the types of property which they will entertain and as to the interest rates, front—end charges, repayment mechanisms, maximum terms, rollover privileges and other conditions which are to apply. The amount of information from borrowers which lenders require and the speed with which they make decisions also vary.

It is, of course, possible to buy one type of asset—for example, shares—with a loan secured on an entirely different type of asset—for example, real estate; this may well result in a lower interest burden.

2726 First mortgage loans are typically granted without mortgage insurance to the extent of 60 per cent of a conservative independent valuation of an income-producing property. Beyond that mortgage insurance, paid for by the borrower in the form of a single premium, is often required if the loan is to proceed. Mortgage insurance protects *the lender* against losses arising from defaults by the borrower. It is quite separate from the fire insurance on any buildings involved, which would also be mandatory in all cases. Borrowers should be of good character.

Apart from the asset cover just referred to, many lenders require a reasonably long lease to an acceptable tenant to be in existence and insist on some interest cover, such as that the annual rent from the subject property net of any outgoings borne by the owner should exceed the annual interest commitment. The loan would be secured by the deposit of the certificate of title with the lender and the formal registration of the mortgage, as well as by the personal covenant of the borrower.

2727   An investor with $100,000 cash can in theory control $2 million worth of property within about 9 years without putting in any more of his own money and without borrowing more than the standard 60 per cent. It works this way:

- He buys a property costing $250,000, using his own initial $100,000 and a further $150,000 borrowed on the security of the property (using the above-mentioned 60 per cent ratio).

- Three years later, at an average growth rate of 11.87 per cent per annum, the property will be worth $350,000 gross. The loan is still $150,000, so that the investor's equity has doubled to $200,000. (If the growth rate is less than 11.87 per cent then this will take a little longer, but the principle is not affected—for instance, at 8.78 per cent per annum the process will take four years.)

- This $200,000 equity will then support a $500,000 property portfolio ($350,000 in the form of the existing property and $150,000 in the form of an additional purchase). This involves a total borrowing of $300,000 ($150,000 from the original transaction and a further $150,000 which is used to purchase this new property).

This process can be repeated indefinitely:

Time	Equity	Property Controlled
years	$	$
0	100,000	250,000
3	200,000	500,000
6	400,000	1,000,000
9	800,000	2,000,000

and so on.

2728 In practice, the position may not be quite as good as this oversimplified description might suggest:

- Purchase and mortgage expenses would need to be taken into account.

- A valuation for mortgage purposes would probably be less than the cost price.

- The growth rate is not likely to be uniform—in the short-term it can even be negative.

- A property of the right type at the required price may not become available at the desired time.

- The original mortgagee may not be willing to advance further funds.

- Some of the dollar growth will be due to inflation and will thus not represent a real increase in wealth.

Nevertheless, the ability to gear up a relatively small sum greatly increases the attraction of property as an investment category.

This principle can naturally be applied to a share portfolio as well as to property investments.

Tax Deductions

2729 As indicated in para. 2721 interest on investment loans is deductible in the usual way under Section 51 of the *Income Tax Assessment Act 1936* as an expense incurred in the earning of assessable income.

2730 Other borrowing expenses are deductible under Section 67. Expenses which are incurred at the time the loan is granted need to be spread over the intended term of the loan or five years, whichever is the shorter. Typically, such expenses would include some or all of the following:

- Establishment fees.

- Procuration fees.

- Mortgage insurance.

- Stamp duty.

- Registration fees.

- Legal charges.

- Search fees.

- Valuation fees.

- Survey fees.

- Bank charges.

- Acceptance fees on bank bills.

- Fees for obtaining a guarantee.

2731 Expenses incurred in discharging a loan can be claimed in the financial year concerned.

2732 Pre-paid interest, where the period covered is up to 13 months, can be claimed in the financial year in which it is paid (under Sections 82KZL to 82KZO).

A Mortgage on the Borrower's Home

2733 As mentioned in para. 2710, it is possible to use the borrower's own residence as the security for an investment loan. This can be attractive in tax terms. However, the likely effect on the lifestyle of the borrower's family if its home should one day be seized by a mortgagee following a default also needs to be taken into consideration. The possibility of such a default through circumstances beyond the borrower's control should not be ignored lightly.

Early Repayment of Home Loans

2734 The question of whether a person with a current home loan who comes into some money should use it to repay some or all of the loan or should instead keep the existing loan arrangements intact and make a separate new investment is discussed in paras 3907 to 3923.

Chapter 28—Income Tax

Business is other people's money
—Mme de Girardin

Preliminary Comments

2801 Tax has been relegated to near the end of this book, not because it is unimportant, but because it seemed preferable to present the non-tax aspects of investments first and then to discuss the effect of tax on investments as a separate topic in its own right.

2802 The main piece of legislation dealing with income tax, the *Income Tax Assessment Act 1936* of the Commonwealth, is a statute about 5000 pages long. In addition there are various other Acts of relevance and numerous Regulations, court decisions, and so on. There are also a large number of non-statutory Rulings and Determinations by the Taxation Commissioner, the official charged with administering the legislation. The Australian Taxation Office (ATO) has also published a series of free booklets, available on application, which endeavour to explain some aspects of the taxation system in lay terms. Much of the material is also on the Internet.

2803 This chapter is accordingly little more than an introduction to a complex subject, providing a brief and deliberately over-simplified description of the more important aspects of tax law which are likely to affect ordinary investors. It also presents some comments on major anomalies. Reading the overview which follows is not intended to be a substitute for the obtaining of competent professional advice.

It should also be borne in mind that the law in this area is constantly changing and that tax rates vary from time to time. All references to sections in this chapter and in Chapter 29 are to the *Income Tax Assessment Act 1936*.

2804 Tax is so significant these days that it is impossible to invest sensibly without taking the tax consequences of one's actions (or sometimes lack of action) into account. For this it is necessary to understand the broad basis of the system. However, as explained in Chapter 1, the aim should always be to *maximise one's net income* rather than just to minimise one's tax.

2805 This chapter deals with:

- Some general principles of the income tax law affecting individuals, companies and partnerships (paras 2806 to 2832).

- The special provisions relating to certain types of transaction (dividend imputation, pooled investment vehicles, overseas income, superannuation, annuities, negative gearing, depreciation, and so on) (paras 2833 to 2886).

- Miscellaneous matters (some fallacies, preference shares, the timing of transactions, tax effect planning, and so on) (paras 2887 to 2899).

Capital gains tax (CGT) is presented separately in Chapter 29. Taxes other than income tax are discussed in Chapter 30. Social security legislation is dealt with in Chapter 31.

Definitions and Concepts

The Tax Year

2806 Income tax is levied separately in respect of the transactions occurring during each "financial year". For most taxpayers this means the period running from 1 July to the following 30 June, both days inclusive. Some company and other taxpayers work on a "substituted year". Appropriate returns have to be filed with the Commissioner, normally by 31 October each year.

Income

2807 Tax is imposed on each taxpayer's "taxable income", which is the "assessable income" less the "allowable deductions". These terms are all defined in the Act.

2808 The term "assessable income", loosely speaking, means "profit" and covers both personal exertion income and the returns on investments. Typically it includes salary, wages, commission, bonuses, professional fees, profits from business operations, pensions, dividends, interest, rent and the like. Some further categories of income are discussed below.

2809 Income does not have to be received in cash in order to attract tax. For example, interest merely credited to a savings account is assessable.

Outgo

2810 "Allowable deductions" fall into two main classes—those incurred in earning assessable income, which are deductible under Section 51, and the so-called "concessional deductions", such as donations to charities and contributions to superannuation funds.

2811 Investment expenditure items are tax deductible—for example:

- fees for professional advice
- the cost of financial journals
- computer software
- financial institutions duty (FID) and debits tax
- bank charges
- postage and telephones.

Also deductible are interest on money borrowed for the purpose of buying shares or making other income-producing investments and all other expenses of such borrowing—see paras 2729 to 2732. Rates, land tax, insurance, repairs, etc., on investment property are similarly deductible. The expenditure and the corresponding income do not have to occur in the same financial year. Money spent in having a tax return prepared is also deductible under a specific provision of the Act. However, penalties under a law, including parking fines incurred in the course of business activities, are not deductible.

2812 More significantly, capital items are not deductible. Thus the cost of investments themselves cannot be claimed as a deduction. Stamp duty and brokerage on stock exchange transactions and fees on pooled investment products are also regarded as part of the capital cost and are thus not deductible at the time of purchase; however, they do affect the capital gains tax calculations—see para. 2942.

2813 Expenditure of a domestic nature is also non-deductible. This term includes rent and interest on a house purchase mortgage where such items are in respect of a person's own home, as this latter is not a loan incurred for the purpose of earning assessable income. (Rent paid for one's business premises or interest on loans made to finance investment property would, of course, be deductible.)

2814 The purpose of any loan and not the nature of the security governs the eligibility of interest and other borrowing costs as a tax deduction. Thus interest on a business loan secured by a mortgage on the borrower's private residence would be deductible.

2815 If the allowable deductions exceed the assessable income of any year then no tax is payable in respect of that year and a "tax loss" is said to be incurred. Such tax losses can be carried forward and used as offsets to assessable income in subsequent years. (See also para. 2896.)

(*Note:* Losses incurred in 1988-89 and earlier years could be carried forward for only seven years.)

Inflation

2816 A major defect of the present Australian tax system is that, except in relation to capital gains, no recognition of inflation is made. Thus, for example, recipients of interest pay tax on the full nominal amount without any offset for the loss of purchasing power on their capital investment. Similarly, depreciation on fixed assets is for tax purposes based on historical cost, rather than, as in logic and equity it should be, on the replacement value. (See also para. 334.)

Individuals

2817 Individuals do not pay a flat rate of tax on their entire taxable incomes. Instead they are taxed on a sliding scale (see Appendix 6). For purely political purposes part of the tax is labelled a "Medicare levy".

2818 A taxpayer on, say, $10,000 income would pay tax at the rate of 20 cents in the dollar on $4600 (being the excess over the $5400 taxfree threshold), that is $920.00. The taxpayer's average rate of tax before applying any rebates would thus be only 9.2 cents in the dollar. However, the *marginal* rate—the rate applicable to each *additional* dollar of income at the top—is the important rate for investment decision making. Of course, it applies to all forms of incremental income, as workers on overtime know only too well.

2819 There is a perception in some quarters that people who move into higher tax brackets can actually become worse off. However, the scale in use means that any given slice of income is taxed at the same rate regardless of the size of the total income, so that even in the worst case taxpayers retain 51.5 cents in each dollar of additional income. See, however, Chapter 31 in relation to the social security income test and paras 2823 to 2828 in regard to provisional tax.

2820 The sliding scale in use also has economic consequences. In conjunction with inflation it allows governments to lift the proportion of gross incomes absorbed in tax in successive years without incurring the political odium which would follow overt increases in the actual tax rates in force. This is known as "bracket creep".

2821 In some cases concessional rebates are available in respect of items such as certain dependants, residence in remote areas, home loan interest payments and large medical expenses. These rebates, which are unrelated to investment strategy, have the effect of reducing or even eliminating the tax which would otherwise be due by virtue of the scale shown above. Interest on Commonwealth loans issued before 1 November 1968 and on certain semi-governmental securities is subject to a special 10 cents in the dollar rebate, but such securities are not often encountered.

Minors

2822 Special rules apply to the investment income of persons who are under the age of 18 years as at the end of the financial year, including investment income channelled through trusts. Where such income exceeds $416 in any financial year a marginal tax rate as high as 66 cents in the dollar can apply.

Provisional Tax

2823 Conceptually all income tax is levied annually in arrear. In any case the exact amount of tax cannot be ascertained until the year's transactions are complete and a return is lodged and assessed.

2824 However, the government prefers to collect its revenue at roughly the same time as the corresponding income is earned by the taxpayers. In the case of salary and wage earners this is achieved through a "pay as you earn" (PAYE) system, also known as "group tax", administered through employers. It is compulsory for all employers to deduct certain instalments of tax when making up pay packets, to remit these instalments to the Australian Tax Office each month and to provide each employee with a "group certificate" at the end of each financial year (and on termination of employment) showing the total gross income and the total tax instalments deducted. In due course, when the employee's return is assessed, allowance is made for the tax already prepaid. Any excess is refunded (however, without any interest) and any shortfall has to be paid to the ATO by a date shown on the assessment notice.

2825 For income which is not subject to the group tax provisions the government's objective is achieved through the "provisional tax" system. This is not an additional impost, as sometimes thought, but only a prepayment of ordinary income tax. It is designed to bring recipients of investment and other non-employment income roughly into line with PAYE taxpayers and to make them pay their tax at approximately the time at which the income is earned rather than about a year later.

2826 Provisional tax is calculated using the tax scale and the other tax rules for the current year applied to a notional income figure for the current year. This notional figure is in the first instance taken as equal to the previous year's non-PAYE income, adjusted upwards by a statutory "Uplift Factor" (5 per cent for 1998-99). This device is designed to allow for inflation and the use of a 5 per cent rate gives some indication of the government's true view as to the underlying rate of future inflation. (This factor is also applied to the imputation credits described in para. 2834.)

Taxpayers have a right to ask for a variation of this notional figure if they believe that their actual income will differ from it, but there are penalties for abuses of this facility (see para. 3509 for a problem in regard to estimating dividends). Capital gains and capital losses (see Chapter 29) are disregarded for provisional tax purposes.

2827 If the notional figure is less than $1000 then provisional tax does not apply. In other cases provisional tax is payable either once a year (around April) or—in the case of provisional tax of more than $8000—by quarterly instalments. When the return for the actual income of the year is processed credit is automatically given for the provisional tax for that year which has already been paid.

2828 It will be noticed that persons becoming subject to provisional tax for the first time are required to pay two lots of tax in the one year—normal tax in respect of the previous year's actual income and provisional tax in respect of the current year's notional income. In subsequent years this doubling up phenomenon applies only in respect of the "growth in income" element.

Partnerships

2829 Partnerships are required to lodge special tax returns, but they do not themselves pay any tax. Instead each partner is required to include the appropriate share of the total partnership income in the personal tax return filed by the partner. (The appropriate share can be negative, if the partnership made a loss.)

Companies

2830 Unlike partnerships, companies are separate legal entities. They pay tax on similar lines to individuals, but at a flat rate (36 cents in the dollar for 1998-99 incomes). Companies are also subject to a special form of provisional tax .

2831 A company which receives a dividend from another company is normally entitled to a rebate under Section 46 of the Act. This ensures that the same profit passing through two or more companies is taxed only once, namely, in the hands of the entity which first earned it.

2832 A further aspect of company tax is discussed in connection with dividend imputation in paras 2833 to 2843.

Dividend Imputation:
Franked and Unfranked Dividends

2833 Before 1 July 1987 corporate profits were subject to two lots of tax. Firstly, companies paid company tax on their earnings. Only the "after tax" earnings were then available for dividend declarations. Secondly, individual shareholders paid personal income tax on any dividends received by them, despite the fact that the companies paying them had already paid tax on the underlying profits. This unfair approach has now been replaced.

2834 Under the current system, which is called "dividend imputation" (or just "imputation"), companies still pay tax on their earnings and then declare dividends, if they wish, out of their "after tax" incomes. However, these transactions no longer involve double taxation. Such dividends are known as "franked" dividends. The company tax which was paid by the company on the portion of the gross profit relating to the dividend is called the "imputation credit" or sometimes the "franking rebate". With a company tax rate of 36 per cent, each $100 gross profit becomes $36 tax and $64 net profit. Each dollar of net profit thus has associated with it 36/64 dollars of imputation credits.

2835 Individuals receiving franked dividends are then treated, for tax purposes, as:

- having received as assessable income both the dividend and the associated imputation credit; and

- having already pre-paid as tax a sum equal to the imputation credit.

The imputation credits at the 36 per cent rate are known as "Class C" credits—see para. 3532.

2836 Individuals on marginal tax rates which are less than the company rate of tax thus become entitled to a "refund" (actually a "rebate") of the amount overpaid. (It should be noted that a rebate is effectively a deduction from tax, as distinct from a deduction from income.) However, this "refund" is not available in cash—it can be used only as an offset to other income tax (including capital gains tax) obligations in the *same* financial year (but, rather illogically, not against the Medicare levy). Unused rebates cannot be carried forward or offset retrospectively against the tax payments of earlier years. They are, to that extent, wasted—a quite unfair anomaly in the system.

2837 Companies receiving franked dividends from other companies also become entitled to the associated imputation credits, enabling them in turn to pay franked dividends to their own shareholders in respect of such receipts.

2838 Actually, companies now earn two types of profit-that out of which they can pay "franked" dividends, because they (or some other company) has already paid Australian taxation, and that out of which they can pay only "unfranked" dividends. The latter can arise because of tax concessions, past losses or the like, or because the profits originated overseas or before the imputation system started. Unfranked dividends do not involve associated imputation credits and are thus fully taxable. Some dividend payments will be partly franked and partly unfranked. (It is also possible in some circumstances for companies to pay exempt dividends.)

2839 The effect of imputation can be illustrated as follows, for a person in the $5,400 to $20,700 a year income range (ignoring the Medicare levy):

- **Company:** $

	$
Gross Profit (say)	1200.00
Less Company Tax at 36%	432.00
Net Profit	768.00
Franked Dividend (say)	640.00
Retained Profit	128.00

- **Individual on a 20% Marginal Tax Rate:** $

	$
Franked Dividend (as above)	640.00
Imputation Credit	360.00
Total (the "grossed-up" Dividend)	1000.00
Personal Tax at 20% (on this "grossed-up" Dividend)	200.00
Less Imputation Credit (as above)	360.00
Tax "Refund"	160.00

The $360 imputation credit (franking rebate) is 36/64 of $640. The $160 tax "refund" is the excess tax ($360 less $200).

2840 The butts on dividend cheques received from companies must always show separately:

- the unfranked dividend
- the franked dividend
- the associated imputation credit.

All three categories represent assessable income, but they need to be set out in separate boxes on tax returns.

2841 One effect of the imputation system is that the Medicare levy on franked dividends is higher than the nominal 1.5 per cent rate, as it is imposed on the associated imputation credit as well as on the actual dividend.

Tax Strategy

2842 Investors can within certain limits arrange to get their income in a mix of franked dividends and other income in such a way as to legally pay no tax at all, apart from the Medicare levy. For example, an individual with $5,000 worth of franked dividends can also earn $12,400 by way of, say, interest and/or pension without becoming liable for any tax:

	$
Franked Dividends	5,000
Interest or Pension	12,400
Actual Income	17,400
Imputation Credits (36/64 of 5000)	2,812
Total Assessable Income	20,212
Tax on this (apart from the Medicare Levy)	2,812
Less Imputation Credits (as above)	2,812
Net Tax Payable	Nil

Imputation makes good quality shares very attractive for many income-conscious investors, although they should bear in mind:

- That tax should never be the only investment consideration.

- That dividends can vary from year to year, while a fixed interest return, in the absence of a default, is constant for the duration of the agreed term.

- That market values of shares are likely to be more volatile than the market values of fixed interest investments.

- That the cost of shares on the market would in practice already to some extent reflect the tax advantages.

- That prudent investors would wish to spread
  their risks by investing in different categories of
  assets.

2843 For all practical purposes a franked dividend of $64 is as
valuable to a taxpaying shareholder as an unfranked dividend
of $100 (for example, at a marginal tax rate of 21.5 per cent,
each is worth $78.50 net). This aspect, which is discussed in
much greater detail in Chapter 35, should also be borne in mind
when comparing dividend yields from companies which are
paying fully franked dividends with dividend yields from other
companies which are paying unfranked or partly franked
dividends.

It should, furthermore, be noted that the proportion of the total
dividend which any particular company can pay out as a
franked dividend may vary from year to year. When comparing
returns in the form of franked dividends with returns in the
form of unfranked dividends or other returns such as interest
or rent, the "grossed-up" dividend figures should be used (that
is, the face value of the franked dividend multiplied by 100/64
or 1.5625).

Bonus Share Issues

2844 As explained in Chapter 7 bonus shares issued on a pro rata
basis to all ordinary shareholders are really nothing more than
share splits in a slightly different legal form. An allotment of
bonus shares while increasing the number of pieces of paper
in circulation leaves its recipients owning exactly the same
proportion of the company as before. The imposition of a tax
on bonus shares thus has no logical rationale whatsoever.

2845 The law reflects this in relation to bonus issues made out of a
so-called "genuine" share premium reserve, apparently because such issues are regarded by the authorities as giving back
to the body of shareholders some of the funds which they
themselves had contributed on earlier occasions. Although
exempt bonus shares do not result in any tax, taxpayers are still
required to mention them by way of note in their tax papers.

2846 However, some bonus issues are made out of other sources,
such as an assets revaluation reserve. Taxation law since 1 July
1987 has treated such bonus shares as "dividends" and they
are now taxed accordingly—a quite absurd position. No sen-

sible company would therefore make a bonus issue other than out of a share premium reserve.

Other Share Issues

2847 Voluntary dividend reinvestment and dividend election plans and their tax implications are described in Chapter 32. Employee share schemes are discussed in Chapter 36.

Bank Bills

2848 The use of the term "discount" in connection with the issue of bank bills gives the appearance of "interest in advance", but for most taxpayers (both debtors and creditors) the difference between the original cost of a bill and the eventual proceeds is treated as being a payment in the nature of interest made on the day of termination.

Thus, for example, a 90-day bill issued at $97 in May and maturing at $100 in August would give rise to $3 assessable income or to a $3 tax deduction, as the case may be, in the financial year containing the August maturity date. It would have no effect in the financial year containing the May issue date; neither would the interest component be apportioned between the two years. Before a sale or maturity this component is regarded as merely an expectation.

2849 Any acceptance fee paid by the user of the funds to a bank for its signature on the bill is deductible under Section 51. However, any establishment fee charged for its services generally is a borrowing expense definitely and not contingently incurred. It is thus deductible on a pro rata basis in each of the financial years concerned.

Tax File Number

2850 An investor who receives unfranked dividends or interest payments from listed companies or savings institutions will have tax deducted from such payments at the top marginal tax rate of 48.5 per cent, except where he has "voluntarily" supplied his tax file number (TFN)—or an exemption claim, if applicable—to the paying entity.

Most organisations send out specially coded forms to facilitate the accurate processing of this information, but standard forms provided by the Australian Taxation Office or even plain paper could also be used. It should be noted that the onus is on the investor to take the necessary action, not on the paying entity or on any broker involved.

2851 Franked dividends, on the other hand, will be paid without such deductions, notwithstanding the fact that the tax liability in respect of such payments can exceed the imputation credit.

2852 Payments in respect of which the above-mentioned deductions have been made still need to be included in the recipient's tax return, but in due course full credit will be allowed for the tax deducted. Thus any excess tax deducted at source in respect of persons on marginal rates which are lower than 48.5 per cent is not permanently denied to them. However, apart from the liquidity disadvantage the deduction and refund process will naturally involve them in a small loss of interest in the meantime.

2853 The tax file number is not required for insurance or friendly society bonds, as the organisations issuing these do not make periodical dividend or interest payments to their bondholders.

Tax Agents

2854 Tax returns can be lodged by taxpayers either personally or through a registered tax agent. The latter approach will naturally enough involve the payment of an appropriate fee, although this fee will itself tax be deductible under Section 69 of the Act and the agent may be able to find ways of reducing tax through the use of provisions of which the taxpayer may be unaware. The fee is likely to be lower if the records handed to the tax agent for his task are in good shape.

2855 The employment of a tax agent can also result in an extension of time for the lodging of returns, leading to a later issue of assessments. For taxpayers with large tax liabilities this can mean an interest advantage greater than the cost of using the agent.

Appeals

2856 Taxpayers dissatisfied with income tax assessments can lodge, within 60 days, objections against them. Beyond that, there is a right to appeal to the Administrative Appeals Tribunal (AAT) or to the courts. Such appeals are not cheap: apart from legal costs, use of the AAT involves a prescribed fee of several hundred dollars for each separate matter. (In earlier times the fee was a nominal $2.) However:

- This fee is itself a tax deduction under Section 69(1) of the Act.

- If the taxpayer is at least partially successful then the fee is refundable.

Further Information

2857 Attention is drawn to two other self—contained books by the present author which deal with the subject matter of this chapter and of Chapter 29 in much greater detail:

- *Taxation and the Small Investor*, which covers income tax, particularly in relation to fixed interest securities, shares, property, unit trusts, insurance policies, friendly society bonds, superannuation, annuities, negative gearing, capital gains, and so on. It has 26 chapters and six appendices.

- *Understanding Dividend Imputation*, which is the first definitive work on this important topic. It covers the new imputation system from a number of different angles in 12 chapters and seven appendices and explains how investors can benefit from franking credits.

Unit Trusts

2858 Unlike companies, listed and unlisted unit trusts do not pay tax themselves, provided only that they distribute all their taxable income. Instead, the investors in the trusts, the unitholders, have to include their share of the trust income in their own tax returns. (Trustees are liable for tax on income to which no beneficiary is presently entitled. Trading trusts are taxed in the same way as companies, but the only trusts likely to be encountered by most portfolio investors are trusts which invest solely in shares, property, fixed interest paper, etc., and therefore do not fall into this category.)

2859 Trust income always retains its character when distributed to unitholders. Thus distributions can include components regarded as "interest" or as "franked dividends" (with associated imputation credits) or as "realised capital gains" or as "overseas income" and so on. The trust manager will supply appro-priate details with each distribution cheque. Unlike investment income generally, income from trusts is regarded as having been earned in the financial year to which it relates, which is not necessarily the year of receipt; this can be a nuisance administratively.

2860 Some portions of a trust distribution may be described as "tax-free income" or as "tax exempt income" on such docu-ments or in prospectuses. This exempt status can come about because the trust has made a distribution out of capital instead of out of profits— unlike companies, trusts are legally permit-ted to make such distributions, although this is an unethical practice, often designed to deliberately mislead investors. In that case, as no element of profit is involved, it would be absurd to tax a unitholder for taking out some of his own money.

Exempt distributions can also come about, particularly in the case of property trusts, because certain tax deductions are available to the trustee (for example, in respect of deprecia-tion) and because "income" as defined in the trust deed is larger than "taxable income" as defined in the taxation legis-lation. (Trust "income" may, for example, include the proceeds from the sale of rights.)

It should also be noted that depreciation allowances can be higher in the early years of a new project than later on; investors should bear in mind that the proportion of a distribu-tion treated as exempt may thus decline in the future. Such so-called "exempt" payments can lead to an additional capital gains tax liability at a later stage—see in particular paras 2942 to 2945.

2861 The price of units in unlisted trusts is normally related to the asset backing. If, as is usually the case, asset values are published on a gross basis, without adjustment for any capital gains tax element due on disposal of the asset, then unitholders on the register at the time of such a disposal could find themselves landed with a capital gains tax liability of which they had had no prior warning, which was not allowed for in the unit price which they would have paid and which may relate to a gain which had not even arisen in the time during which they held the units.

2862 It is also possible for unit trust structures to involve their unitholders in double capital gains tax. If, for example, an unlisted property trust sells a particular property at a significant capital profit which it retains, then the trustee would pay tax on the indexed capital gain, calculated by the usual formula. This tax would be a charge on the trust fund, but the "after tax" proceeds would remain in the fund and would be reflected in the asset backing and thus in the unit price. Any unitholders selling their units at the unit price prevailing after the property sale would also be regarded as having realised their own separate capital gains. Thus in effect the original gain would have, quite unfairly, been taxed twice.

Life Insurance and Friendly Society Policies

Life Insurance

2863 Life offices are companies but pay tax at a 39 per cent rate in respect of their non-superannuation business. They pay tax on investment income, but unlike most other categories of taxpayer they are not allowed to claim the bulk of their expenses as tax deductions. They are also taxed on net realised capital gains, but without the benefit of indexation.

2864 Life offices allow for their tax obligations when setting premium rates, when declaring bonuses on conventional policies and when fixing unit prices for investment—linked business. This means that policy benefits paid to policyholders are, generally speaking, free from all forms of income tax at that stage. This also means freedom from provisional tax. Although sometimes misleadingly described as "tax exempt", life insurance policies—including the popular "investment bonds"—are really "tax paid" products.

2865 Premiums paid on non-superannuation life insurance policies no longer qualify for any tax relief.

Friendly Societies

2866 The above comments on life offices apply equally in regard to friendly societies, except that these are subject to a special tax rate, namely, 33 per cent, rather than the 39 per cent life office tax rate.

Interest on Policy Loans

2867 If a life policy is used as the security for a loan (whether from the life office concerned or from a bank or other third party), then the interest is eligible as a tax deduction in those cases where the loan monies are used to acquire assets which are used to produce assessable income. However, interest on a loan taken out in order to pay premiums on a life policy, whether secured on that policy or not, would not normally be deductible. Neither, in line with the principles enunciated earlier, is interest on a loan used purely for domestic purposes.

The 10-year Rule

2868 As explained above, as a general principle the benefits paid under life insurance or friendly society policies do not attract income tax or capital gains tax in the policyholders' hands, as the institution has already been levied on their behalf in regard to such items. However, one important exception to this principle was introduced in 1983—the so-called "10-year Rule", now set out in Section 26AH of the Act. This was devised in order to tax "bonuses" on "short-term policies", in the belief that persons in high tax brackets were exploiting the lower tax rates applying to life offices and friendly societies.

2869 A non-superannuation policy discontinued otherwise than by death, disability or "serious financial hardship" (in the view of the Taxation Commissioner) within 10 years of its commencement is caught by this provision, which applies to policies taken out after 7 December 1983. (A similar 4-year rule applies to policies effected between 29 August 1982 and 7 December 1983.) The rule thus catches short-term policies at maturity and all policies regardless of their original term if voluntarily discontinued (that is, surrendered) within 10 years.

2870 The excess of benefits received over premiums paid (whether called "bonuses" or not) is treated as part of the policyholder's assessable income and is taxed at the policyholder's marginal rate. However, a special rebate of 39 cents in the dollar in the case of life offices or 33 cents in the dollars in the case of friendly societies (even where the marginal tax rate is lower) is allowed against this, thus freeing the transaction from tax for some policyholders.

This rebate is meant to allow for the tax already paid by the institution concerned. It should be noted that this provision involves double taxation—for example, a life policyholder with a 48.5 per cent marginal tax rate would pay tax at 9.5 per cent on his share of the life office's income—this latter being income net of the tax already paid by the life office itself.

2871 The use of the word "bonus" in this context is rather confusing—the word "gain" would have been more readily understood. It should, however, be noted that life policies are not subject to capital gains tax as such in the hands of policyholders at any duration. A "gain" can also arise from the addition of "interest" under investment account policies or from changes in unit values under investment-linked policies.

2872 A phasing-in mechanism applies in the last two years—in the ninth year only two-thirds of the "gain" is taxed. In the tenth year only one-third is taxed. (For 4-year rule cases: the third and fourth years respectively.)

2873 While insurance bonds and other products are often marketed under slogans implying that the policies are "free of tax after 10 years" the reality is that they are free only of *double* tax after that period.

2874 If a policy is only partially surrendered then the tax treatment is the same as it would have been if two quite separate policies had been used for the portion being quit and the portion being continued. In other words, everything happens—reasonably enough—on a proportionate basis. Thus, if one-third of the total available surrender value is being taken in cash, then one-third of the amount which would have been taxable if the whole policy had been surrendered becomes taxable. It is, of course, quite immaterial whether the cash value is regarded by either the office or the policyholder as all "original capital" or all "gain" or anything in between.

2875 It should be noted that the 10-year period dates from the commencement of the contract and not from the payment of any particular premium. However, the premiums paid in any one policy year must not exceed the premiums actually paid in the previous policy year by more than 25 per cent. In the case of investment bonds this means that a single premium of, say, $10,000 can be followed by a further payment of $12,500 at any time during the period commencing exactly 12 months later and ending a further 12 months less one day after that. If such a payment is actually made, then an additional $15,625 could be paid in during the next policy year, and so on.

Furthermore, a payment made at, say, the start of the tenth year is effectively a one-year contract in the same "tax paid" form as the original 10-year contract was. This can be a considerable attraction.

2876 However, if policies are altered from one type to another (other than by being made paid-up)—even within the same life insurance company or friendly society—then the 10-year "clock" starts all over again. This would catch capital secure contracts being altered to investment-linked or vice versa.

Overseas Income

2877 Australia has double taxation agreements with many other countries. Usually this results in income earned by the residents of one country from sources in a different country being taxed only once, but at the higher of the two possible rates. However, the imputation system applies only to company tax paid to the Australian government, so double tax still applies to corporate profits earned overseas by Australian companies.

2878 Dividend and interest payments made by Australian companies to overseas investors are subject to a special deduction known as "Withholding Tax". This eliminates the need for the non-resident investors concerned to lodge Australian tax returns. The rate of withholding tax depends on the particular agreement but is mainly 15 per cent on dividends and 10 per cent on interest.

2879 Similar arrangements work in reverse. Australian taxpayers include overseas income (often called "foreign income") in a special section of their local tax returns and receive appropriate credits for tax paid or payable to overseas governments, all amounts being converted to Australian currency. However, foreign losses cannot be offset against domestic income, although they can be carried forward. Since 1 July 1990 Australia has had an "accruals tax" system and certain "attributed income" connected with overseas investments also constitutes assessable income for Australian income tax purposes. This provision is unlikely to affect normal portfolio investors.

2880 Overseas shareholders in Australian companies receive franked dividends free of withholding tax, but apart from that do not benefit from the imputation system. Because of this it was formerly advantageous for overseas investors to sell Australian shares to local investors on a "cum dividend" basis and to repurchase them on an "ex dividend" basis if this could be done at prices which allowed both parties to share in some way the benefit from the imputation credit. Such a process, sometimes referred to as "dividend washing", is no longer feasible following amendments to the legislation.

Superannuation Funds and Approved Deposit Funds

2881 The taxation ramifications of superannuation funds and Approved Deposit Funds are discussed in a companion volume by the author, *Understanding Managed Investments*.

Immediate Annuities

2882 An annuity is a pension purchased from a life office. The instalments of an annuity come within the prima facie definition of "assessable income", but are subject to special treatment designed to ensure that an annuitant effectively has to pay tax only on the notional "interest component" of each instalment. These instalments in part represent interest and in part constitute a return of the purchaser's own capital; the latter element is, quite reasonably, given tax exemption—although in the convoluted language of the Act the whole annuity payments are first regarded as income and the notional capital repayment is then called a "deduction" under Section 27H of the Act (formerly Section 26AA).

2883 It works this way. If a person pays $1000 in order to buy an annuity of $100 per annum payable for 15 years—a total of $1500—then the $500 "gain" is regarded as subject to tax but the "return" of the taxpayer's own $1000 is not. A deduction of $66.67 per annum ($1000 divided by 15) would therefore be allowed. In the case of life annuities the term of the annuity for this purpose is taken as a suitable "average" value, namely, the expectation of life on a prescribed mortality table.

The amount of usable capital for this exercise is the total purchase price less any portions which have been subject to the former concessional deduction or rebate provisions; or which have been rolled over as an alternative to attracting the tax on lump sum superannuation benefits; or which have been provided by an employer or other third party. In the formal language of the Act this amount of usable capital—as calculated by the statutory formula—is referred to as the "undeducted purchase price".

Immediate annuities are subject to "pay as you earn" (PAYE) tax deductions and group certificates—except, of course, where the income is below the tax threshold. Annuities are thus not subject to the provisional tax system. This applies even to "annuities" which closely resemble debentures in that they involve a return of the full purchase price.

Negative Gearing

2884 If an investment property, say, is purchased with the assistance of borrowed funds then it is possible for the rental income (especially after the deduction of other expenses) to be less than the interest commitment in the course of a year, as in the following typical example:

Property	$100,000	Rent	$8,000
Mortgage	$60,000	Interest	$9,000
Equity	+ $40,000	Net Income -	$1,000

In such cases the property is said to be "negatively geared". For tax purposes this negative net income can be offset against any positive income from other sources. Negative gearing can also apply in the case of share investments. Group taxpayers who are subject to negative gearing can apply for a variation of their "pay as you earn" (PAYE) deductions under Section 221D of the Act.

Depreciation

2885 For tax purposes the value of all plant and equipment used to produce assessable income may be written down to zero over its working lifetime, using one of two methods set out in the legislation. The amount of depreciation each year is a tax deduction. Property investors are affected by these provisions, because certain components of buildings, such as lifts, air-conditioning units, carpets and many other items come within the definition of "plant".

Some items, such as amenities for employees, are even subject to depreciation claims at specially generous rates (although, of course, for correspondingly shorter periods). Depreciation for tax purposes is always based on the unindexed historical cost of the asset concerned, rather than on its replacement value.

2886 The remainder of the cost of a building (but, naturally enough, not of the land) can also be subject to depreciation claims, provided that construction commenced on or after a certain date:

Period Commencing	Depreciation Rate %
Residential income-producing buildings:	
18 July 1985	4.0
16 September 1987	2.5
Non-residential income-producing buildings:	
20 July 1982	2.5
22 August 1984	4.0
16 September 1987	2.5

Some Fallacies

2887 A few listed companies attract criticism from uninformed commentators because they are paying tax at rates which appear to be abnormally low. There is usually a very good explanation for such a phenomenon. For example, a company making a $1 million loss one year and a $1 million profit in the next year would pay no tax at all in that second year. Over the two years combined it would have made nil profit and paid nil tax, a perfectly logical and equitable outcome. To look at the figures of the second year in isolation would be quite misleading.

2888 Again, a company may receive its entire income in the form of dividends from other companies. Such dividends are effectively tax-free in its hands by virtue of the Section 46 rebate referred to in para. 2831. However, there is no element of tax avoidance in this, as the underlying profits out of which the dividends are declared will already have borne full tax in the hands of the companies which first earned these profits.

2889 It is also thought by some people that highly leveraged companies, including successful bidders in takeover situations, somehow avoid tax because interest on loans is a charge before the taxable profit is arrived at and because a tax deduction thus becomes available to the payer. However, such interest is also assessable to the recipient and thus the net interest within the system arising from such a transaction is probably nil. In any case, under the imputation system the effect on tax collections is identical whether the payments to the suppliers of the funds happen to be classified as dividends or as interest.

Preference Shares

2890 From a legal and taxation point of view dividends on preference shares can be either franked or unfranked. However, unless the terms of a preference share issue specifically provided for the dividends to be franked and the company took this feature into account when setting the coupon it would be unfair to the ordinary shareholders for any preference dividends to be franked. Such a course of action would deprive the ordinary shareholders of a portion of their limited available imputation credits.

The Timing of Transactions

2891 The fact that each financial year (see also para. 2806) is effectively a watertight compartment can at times be used to advantage. For example, arrangements can be made to make payments in respect of deductible items in June rather than in the following July. Investment in short-term fixed interest paper can similarly have regard to the due date of the interest, so that if desired a security with a July maturity date rather than one with a June maturity date can be chosen.
This may result:

- In the payment of income tax a year later than would otherwise have been the case.

- In the payment of provisional tax a year later than would otherwise have been the case.

- In the payment of less actual tax if the tax scale is lowered.

- In the payment of less actual tax if the taxpayer's marginal tax rate falls because of a change in his personal circumstances.

Of course, if the tax rate is expected to go up, then the above approach can be reversed.

Names to be used for Registering Assets

2892 One effect of the personal income tax sliding scale shown in para. 2817 is that a given income spread over more than one taxpayer incurs less tax than the same income earned by only one person. This fact is not of much assistance in the case of personal exertion income being earned by a specific person, but in the case of married couples it is very relevant to decisions as to into whose name income-producing assets should be registered.

The optimum position is reached when the income of the husband equals the income of the wife. If, for example, a husband is the sole breadwinner, then investments are (from a tax point of view) best made in the wife's name as long as the total return from such investments (including imputation credits) is less than the husband's existing income.

On the other hand, putting shares paying franked dividends in the name of a spouse whose income is such that the imputation credits cannot be used is not advantageous and even less so if it also prejudices a spouse rebate.

2893 Furthermore, in such circumstances assets should not normally be put into joint names, as in the absence of a formal partnership arrangement specifying a different distribution formula, this would lead to half the investment income being attributed to each party.

2894 Existing assets which are found to be in a different name from that desired in the light of the above comments can, of course, be transferred to a new owner by way of gift or sale, but this may incur stamp duty and/or it may trigger off immediate capital gains tax. It may also result in the permanent loss of pre-1985 status or in a lowering of the benefits which could flow from the indexation provisions in the future (see Chapter 29).

2895 While registering assets in a particular name can be attractive in terms of income tax reductions it can also have unforeseen consequences in the event of a matrimonial dispute. Furthermore, the long-term consequences may be different from the short-term consequences—for example, a particular investment can produce a return which is initially negative but which becomes strongly positive over time; or the personal exertion income of one spouse may change significantly (up or down) later on. Again, a capital loss in one name may not be offsetable against a capital gain in another. See also para. 2822 in regard to assets registered in the names of children.

Corporate Tax Losses

2896 As mentioned in para. 1137, the existence of tax losses in the books of an offeree company can be one of the attractions in a takeover. However, certain restrictions apply, apart from the seven year limitation referred to in the *Note* to para. 2815. In particular, either a "continuity of shareholding" test or a "same business" test must be satisfied—thus ruling out most take-overs. Furthermore, the value of tax losses will depend on the rate of tax applying in the years in which the losses are used up.

Tax Effect Planning

2897 Taxation is black letter law. To suggest that there is an obliga-tion on taxpayers to observe the "spirit of the law" is arrant nonsense. Nevertheless, if a sufficient number of taxpayers engage in conduct which deprives the authorities of revenue to which they think they are entitled then the letter of the law will be changed.

2898 For this and other reasons there can be no guarantee that either the present tax rules or the current tax scale will continue to apply indefinitely and this aspect must be taken into consid-eration when engaging in any long-term planning. Many rec-ommendations of recent enquiries into the Australian taxation and financial systems have not yet been implemented (for example, Asprey, Mathews, Campbell, etc., as well as the 1985 "Tax Summit").

2899 While changes in the law are unlikely to be retrospective in the sense of creating a liability for past transactions the future performance of arrangements entered into in the expectation that a particular tax regime will prevail indefinitely can, of course, be significantly affected—in either direction—by statutory amendments made down the track.

Chapter 29—Capital Gains Tax

*Money can't buy friends, but you can get
a better class of enemy*
—Spike Milligan

Background

2901 Australia has had a formal capital gains tax (CGT) since 1985. It now covers the disposal of most assets, but there are some important exceptions—see paras 2958 to 2970. Strictly speaking, the CGT is not really a separate tax at all. It is part of the wider income tax system, although a number of special rules discussed below apply to it.

Notes:

1. Before the CGT legislation came in capital gains on investments were often taxed on a "hit or miss" basis, some being treated as totally exempt because the investor concerned was not regarded as a trader and others being taxed in full at the investor's marginal tax rate. Neither outcome was necessarily equitable and the inconsistencies and lack of certainty were in themselves highly undesirable.

2. Many people regard a capital gains tax as unfair. However, in the context of a system which imposes tax on incomes at large it seems perfectly appropriate to also tax capital gains. Why should an increase of wealth by one dollar be treated differently if it is derived from wages rather than from acquiring and disposing of assets? The effect on the recipient of the dollar is much the same in both instances.

3. Of course, investors need not concern themselves with the rationale for or morality of capital gains tax-they just have to accept it as a fact of life in Australia today. The only aspect they might wish to consider is the possibility of amendments to the legislation—for example, on a change of government.

4. Actually, two features of the current capital gains tax regime make it fairer than the income tax on revenue transactions:

    •   The first is the recognition of inflation (as shown in para. 2903, only real rather than nominal capital gains are taxed—although rather illogically this recognition does not extend to capital losses).

- The second is the concept of averaging, thus minimising the effects of irregular receipts of money pushing people into higher tax brackets than warranted by their overall position (see paras 2817 and 2904).

5. The "grandfathering" of assets held at the commencement of the legislation was a relatively generous concession by the authorities, although its value is somewhat reduced by the absence of rollover provisions (other than to the limited extent described in paras 2924 and 2925).

6. The permanent exemption of these "pre-1985" assets was very clever politically. It made the new tax much more acceptable to the electorate. In the early years the revenue from the CGT provisions was negligible, but it now raises several billion dollars a year (directly and indirectly) and thus helps to keep other tax imposts down.

Capital Gains

General Principles

2902 The distinction between a capital gain and a revenue gain can best be illustrated by an example. If a shopkeeper buys an article wholesale for $6 and sells it retail for $10 then the $4 profit which he has made on the deal is regarded as part of his regular income and as a "revenue gain". It is taxed accordingly. Most investors are not in the business of share trading and any similar profit which they make by buying shares at one price and selling them at a higher price is regarded as a "capital gain" for income tax purposes. Capital gains are taxed under special provisions of the legislation instead of as normal income of a revenue type.

Generally speaking, any assets acquired before the introduction of capital gains tax on the evening of 19 September 1985 (Budget night) remain outside the scope of the CGT legislation imposts (now set out in Part IIIA of the *Income Tax Assessment Act 1936*, Sections 160AX to 160ZZU). This is because the government of the day very properly did not want to impose any legislation which had a retrospective effect. By virtue of this provision investors who hold pre-1985 shares, for example, now own a valuable and irreplaceable asset. Unrealised capital gains remain exempt, but correspondingly unrealised capital losses remain unclaimable.

(*Note:* For convenience assets acquired or deemed to have been acquired before 20 September 1985 are here described as "pre-1985" assets. Other assets acquired after that cut-off date—here described as "post-1985" assets—give rise to a capital gains tax liability, but only if and when they are sold or otherwise disposed of.)

Indexation

2903 For post-1985 assets held for 12 months or less this liability is based on the excess of the sale price (net of selling expenses) over the original purchase price (including all acquisition costs). The purchase price adjusted for associated capital costs is referred to in the legislation by the technical term "cost base". For assets held for longer periods than 12 months this cost base is indexed for inflation, thus producing a lower tax liability. The Australian Statistician's Consumer Price Index (CPI) figures for the relevant calendar quarters of acquisition and disposal are used for this purpose.

The cost base can consist of more than one component, as for example when contributing shares are purchased subject to calls paid later on or when capital improvements are made to a property. Each component is indexed separately; indexation applies even to components involving 12 months or less, provided that the original asset was held for more than 12 months.

However, expenses of a revenue nature, such as rates, taxes, repairs, insurance premiums, interest, etc., are disregarded. For assets purchased with the aid of borrowed funds the indexation factors are applied to the gross value of the assets, and not to the net value allowing for the loan—a considerable advantage for investors.

Averaging

2904 The rate of tax applied to capital gains can be less than the rate for revenue gains of equal size, because special averaging provisions apply. In effect, income tax is first calculated on 20 per cent of the total capital gain in the usual way. The average rate of tax applying to this 20 per cent (treated as the top slice of income) is then applied to the other 80 per cent. For some taxpayers this approach will give them the benefit of the lower rates applying to some slices of income (see para. 2817). In an extreme case, a taxpayer with no other income could realise $27,000 worth of capital gains (after indexation) without actually paying any tax other than the Medicare levy, as 20 per cent of this is $5400 (the tax threshold figure).

Bonus Shares

2905 For capital gains tax purposes, bonus shares are deemed to have been acquired at the same time as the original shares to which they relate. Thus bonus shares arising on pre-1985 holdings fall outside the capital gains tax net. Bonus shares on post-1985 holdings are quite logically treated as having been received at a nil cost and on any subsequent disposal both the old shares and the bonus shares are deemed to have been acquired at an average price per share arrived at by dividing the total cost of the old shares by the new total number of shares. See also paras 2845 to 2846.

(*Note:* Sometimes the bonus shares are a different class than the original shares. In such cases the deemed cost prices of the shares in the two classes would need to be apportioned in proportion to the initial market values on an ex bonus basis.)

Rights Issues

2906 On the other hand, shares arising out of rights issues are treated as having been acquired at the time of issue and the cost price of the old shares is not adjusted. If the original shares have pre-1985 status then any rights can be sold without incurring capital gains tax and any new shares are, consistently with this principle, treated as having been acquired for a consideration equal to the sum of the actual application money and the market value of the rights.

However, if the original shares have post-1985 status then any rights which are sold incur CGT in respect of the sale price (the cost having been nil) and any new shares are, consistently with this principle, treated as having been acquired for a consideration equal to the application money only. It should be noted that the mere *exercise* of rights, as distinct from a sale of rights on the market, does not constitute a "disposal" for CGT purposes. The same principle applies to the exercise of options and the conversion of convertible notes or convertible preference shares.

(*Note:* For rights purchased on the market the cost base in the event of their resale as rights is naturally the actual price paid. If the shares arising out of the exercise of these rights are sold then the cost base is the sum of the purchase price paid on the market for the rights and the application price of the shares paid to the company. Both elements are subject to indexation from the respective dates of payment.)

2907 Many investors seem to think that proportional rights issues made at a deep discount to the market price of the existing shares confer an advantage on them. As explained in Chapter 7, shareholders—apart from tax considerations—are really equally well off, per dollar invested, irrespective of whether companies issue a large number of shares at a low price or a smaller number of shares at a higher price. However, from a CGT point of view, it is the latter approach which is considerably more attractive than the former.

As explained above, the CGT legislation does not allow any adjustments to be made to the cost price of shares going ex rights. For example, if a company with shares selling at, say, 500, makes a one for one issue at 300, then the theoretical ex rights price would be 400. In other words, a purchaser of one share before the issue at 500 who takes up one share at 300, a total cost of 800, would then hold two shares worth 400 each, at an unchanged total value of 800. For CGT purposes, however, an investor who sells at that stage would be regarded as having made a "gain" of 100 on the "new" shares and a "loss" of 100 on the old shares.

In the fullness of time this will be to the investor's disadvantage, as the CGT legislation is not symmetrical—as explained below, loss situations, unlike situations in which gains are recorded, do not get the benefit of indexed cost prices, therefore the claimable losses are always less than conceptually they should be. The position is even worse if the old shares have pre-1985 status, as losses from such shares are not deductible at all.

2908 Despite the above-mentioned impression to the contrary, the most sensible rights issues in the future will thus be those made at modest discounts to the prevailing market price. The only difficulty is that companies pitching an issue price at such a level (as well as their underwriters, if any) run the risk that the issue could fail if there were to be even a minute downturn in the market during the period between the setting of the issue price and the closing date of such an issue. Thus in practice discounts involving some safety margin are likely to be the norm.

Options and Convertible Securities

2909 All shares arising from the exercise of pre-1985 options or the conversion of pre-1985 convertible securities are deemed to have pre-1985 status (see also para. 2906).

Composite Assets

2910 For capital gains tax purposes a single asset is sometimes deemed to be two separate assets, one with pre-1985 status and the other with post-1985 status. For example, an investment property could comprise land purchased before 20 September 1985 and a building erected after that date.

Capital Losses

2911 The capital gains tax legislation just described for capital gains situations also applies to capital loss situations, but with some important differences. In particular, the purchase price (cost base) of assets sold at a loss (or even at a gain which is not big enough to be subject to CGT after allowing for inflation) is not indexed (see para. 2939).

2912 Furthermore, capital losses can be offset against capital gains, but not against normal income. Unused capital losses can, however, always be carried forward indefinitely (not just for seven years, as used to be the case in regard to revenue losses).

Partial Sales

2913 An investor selling some but not all of his shares in a particular company will have to nominate which portion of his holdings is being disposed of, in all cases where the original parcel was acquired in stages. He does not have to treat either his oldest or his most recent purchases as the shares being sold unless that happens to suit his purpose. Thus he can choose to nominate those shares which produce the lowest realised capital gains if he wishes to minimise the tax burden at that time. Alternatively, he can choose to nominate those shares which produce the highest realised gains if he wishes to use up some tax losses or if he expects to be on a higher marginal tax rate in the year in which he quits the remainder of the parcel.

2914 Again, an investor is entitled to choose between selling pre-1985 and post-1985 shares. Selling the former may have the short-term advantage of allowing tax-free capital gains to be realised at that time. But such a strategy will also have the long-term disadvantage of destroying for ever the unique and irreplaceable pre-1985 status of such investments.

Transaction Dates

2915 It will be obvious from the above description of the system that the precise dates of transactions can be important for capital gains tax purposes. The date of a purchase or sale on the stock exchange will be set out on the relevant contract note. The date of acquisition of new shares in a rights issue is less clear cut—it could be the date of mailing the application form and cheque to the company; the date of receipt of this material by the company; the official closing date of the issue; or even the date of the formal allotment of the new shares by the board of directors of the company.

An even greater list of possible dates applies in relation to shares issued in takeover situations (for example, there is the date on which an offer is declared unconditional). In the absence of a court case to determine this matter shareholders can presumably use their discretion. In most cases the precise choice will make little difference.

2916 In any event, the date on a scrip certificate (or CHESS statement) is not helpful, as this is governed by the administrative routine of the share registrar and can be completely unrelated to any transaction date, as when "balance" certificates are issued after partial sales, or when new certificates are issued after changes of name or register or as replacements for lost or defaced documents or following conversion of uncertificated holdings.

2917 As mentioned in para. 2903, the indexation adjustment for capital gains tax purposes depends on the calendar quarter of the transaction. There is therefore an advantage in buying just before the end of a quarter rather than just afterwards. Similarly, there is an advantage in selling just after the end of a quarter rather than just before. Because of the 12-month rule there is an even bigger advantage in selling at a profit just after the end of the first year rather than just before. As explained in para. 2889, there can also be other advantages flowing from selling in July rather than the previous June. However, altering the timing of a purchase or sale for tax reasons can expose the investor to market fluctuations, a risk which he may wish to avoid.

Takeovers

2918 Takeovers are described in Chapter 11. For capital gains tax purposes the acceptance of a takeover bid is regarded as a "disposal" of shares and the consideration received, if wholly in cash, is treated in the same way as the proceeds from a normal sale. If the consideration consists wholly or partly of shares or other securities then these are brought into account at their market value at the time. This latter amount also becomes the cost of acquisition of the new securities, a figure which will become relevant if and when they are ever disposed of in the future.

2919 Although a long-term investor might logically regard the receipt of a bidding company's shares in exchange for shares in the target company as a continuation of the original investment rather than as a disposal and a fresh acquisition the law does not give any rollover relief in such situations. This applies regardless of whether the investor voluntarily accepted the offer or had the shares compulsorily acquired at the end of the bid. If the consideration consists entirely of shares then it is even possible for tax on a large realised capital gain to become payable without the investor having received any cash flow out of which to meet this obligation.

2920 The 12-month clock for indexing purposes (see para. 2903) starts all over again in such share swaps. Thus if the shares in the original company had been held for, say, 11 months before the takeover and the shares in the new company are then held for a further 11 months before being sold, then despite the total investment having lasted well over 12 months no indexation would apply.

2921 Again, if the shares received in a takeover are subsequently disposed of at a lower figure than the deemed acquisition cost referred to in para. 2918, then the consequential loss cannot be offset against any capital gain levied in respect of the disposal of the original shares where that occurred in any previous financial year.

2922 Worse still is the position of investors in the target company whose shares enjoyed pre-1985 status. While in accordance with the savings provisions applying to such assets these investors do not incur capital gains tax at the time of the takeover, they do lose for ever this valuable privilege, as the new shares issued in the takeover naturally have post-1985 status.

2923 Shareholders desiring to avoid the above-mentioned disadvantages face an insoluble dilemma. They can, of course, always reject the bid, especially if its terms do not adequately compensate them for the tax aspects. However, this strategy will not avoid the problems if compulsory acquisition takes place in due course and in any case it poses the risk that the investor will become "locked in" as a minority holder in a company which is then controlled by the bidder and the shares of which may become delisted.

Rollovers

2924 Certain involuntary asset disposals are accorded rollover relief, so that the ownership of the replacement asset is in effect regarded, at the option of the taxpayer, as a continuation of the ownership of the original asset. This preserves any pre-1985 status existing and postpones any liability for capital gains tax in respect of post-1985 assets to the time of disposal of the replacement asset.

2925 These provisions cover some situations of direct relevance to investors, including:

- the compulsory acquisition of an investment property by a government body

- the replacement of a destroyed asset by an insurer

- the transfer of assets between spouses on the breakdown of a marriage.

As mentioned in para. 2923, they do not cover the compulsory acquisitions in takeovers.

Death of the Investor

2926 The death of a person is not regarded as the disposal of that person's assets for capital gains tax purposes, but special provisions apply from that time on. The incidence of capital gains tax is deferred until the assets are disposed of by the executor or administrator or—possibly many years later-by the beneficiaries. Transfers of assets by an executor or administrator to beneficiaries are also not regarded as disposals for capital gains tax purposes.

2927 In the case of pre-1985 assets these are treated as having become post-1985 assets acquired as at the date of death by the legal representative (if he disposes of them), or by the beneficiaries, at the market value prevailing at that date. No tax is payable at the time of death, but the pre-1985 status is lost from that time on. A careful record of the market value of all relevant assets should be made at the time, particularly for assets other than listed shares where special steps to obtain a valuation may need to be taken.

2928 In the case of post-1985 assets these are treated as post-1985 assets acquired as at the date of death by the legal representative (if he disposes of them), or by the beneficiaries, at the original cost price indexed to the date of death. In other words, they are regarded for CGT purposes as a continuation of the deceased investor's holdings, with no tax payable at the time of death. Appropriate records should be passed on to and retained by the beneficiaries concerned.

Liquidation of the Company

2929 If a company is wound up then any monies received by shareholders from the liquidator, to the extent that these are not deemed profit distributions taxed as such, are treated for capital gains tax purposes in the same way as if the shares had been disposed of by sale.

2930 Shareholders who are asked to vote on a resolution to place a company in voluntary liquidation would need to take the loss of any pre-1985 status into account—both in regard to assets owned by the company and in regard to the shares in the company owned by the investors. This aspect may make it more attractive to keep the vehicle in existence and to merely change its line of business.

Expiry of Options

2931 If post-1985 options or warrants are allowed to expire, as distinct from being exercised (see para. 2907), they are regarded as having been disposed of for a nil consideration, thus triggering off a capital loss in respect to their unindexed cost.

Failed Loan Securities

2932 On occasions companies which have raised loan funds from investors go into receivership or liquidation. In such circumstances the lenders, as well as missing out on interest payments and encountering considerable delays and uncertainty, may eventually finish up with less than 100 cents in the dollar of capital. In the case of post-1985 investments this would lead to a claimable loss in terms of the capital gains tax legislation, but only when the amount of the loss has been crystallised— either by the receipt of a "final distribution" from the receiver or liquidator or by the sale of the loan security (that is, the equity in the outstanding loan balance) to a third party. See also para. 2968.

Superannuation Funds

2933 The capital gains tax liability of superannuation funds is set out in a companion volume by the present author, *Understanding Managed Investments*.

Brokerage and Stamp Duty

2934 Brokerage and stamp duty on investment purchases are regarded as part of the capital cost and are therefore not deductible as expenses incurred in the earning of assessable income. However, for post-1985 assets such items enter the capital gains tax calculations by lowering the capital gain which would otherwise have applied.

Brokerage and stamp duty on a purchase, written up by the usual indexation factor, can thus effectively become deductible at the time of realisation (although this may involve a different tax rate from that which would have prevailed if such items had been regarded as revenue items at the time, and there is furthermore no allowance for interest). Brokerage and stamp duty on investment sales enter the CGT calculation in a similar way, except that naturally indexation is not applicable for these.

Discounted and Deferred Interest Securities

2935 Certain fixed interest securities do not involve the annual payment of interest in the usual way, the return to the investor being achieved wholly or mainly at maturity by virtue of the redemption price significantly exceeding the issue price. The former are often referred to as "zero coupon" bonds (or colloquially as "DINGO stocks", after a bond-stripping exercise labelled "discounted investment in negotiable government obligations").

Such securities are an exception to the normal rule that unrealised capital appreciation is not taxed, because the legislation (Division 16E, Sections 159GP to 159GZ) requires that in place of capital gains tax at maturity an equivalent amount of interest is treated for tax purposes as income progressively each year. This also means that such paper does not get the benefit of indexation.

Traditional Securities

2936 Certain other fixed interest securities acquired after 10 May 1989 come within the definition of "traditional securities". These are governed by Sections 160ZB(6), 26BB and 70B of the Act, which collectively take them out of the capital gains tax net. As a result:

- Realised capital gains are taxed as ordinary income—a disadvantage, because indexation does not apply.

- Realised capital losses are allowed as an ordinary tax deduction—an advantage, because such losses can be offset against ordinary income instead of only against realised capital gains.

These provisions have no relevance to equity investments, such as shares. To summarise:

	Capital Gains	**Capital Losses**
Shares, etc.	Indexed gains taxed on realisation	Unindexed losses allowed on realisation, but only against realised capital gains
"Traditional Securities"	Unindexed gains taxed on realisation	Unindexed losses allowed on realisation against ordinary income
Discounted Securities	Unrealised gains taxed year by year, with a balancing item (gain or loss) on disposal	

Notes:

1. The distinct lack of symmetry in the above provisions should be noted—for example, gains are treated differently from losses; amounts taxed as income in the hands of lenders are not necessarily deductible to the borrowers.

2. The term "traditional securities" includes convertible notes.

3. The term "traditional securities" is rather misleading. It includes, for example, deposits with failed building societies—thus providing some unfortunate depositors with a partial refund of their losses and providing a tax benefit which was probably not intended when the legislation was enacted.

Provisional Tax

2937 Both capital gains and capital losses are disregarded when provisional tax is calculated.

Switches

2938 The existence of capital gains tax can make shares which are already held poor selling even if they are felt to be overpriced on the market and they have reached a level at which further acquisitions would be regarded as poor buying. Consider the following numerical example, which excludes brokerage and stamp duty:

Cost price of a particular share	100
Indexed cost price	130
Market price now	300
Hypothetical "true value"	250
Capital gains tax liability, say 48.50% of (300-130)	82
Market price net of this CGT liability = 300-85	218

Thus, while to sell a share worth 250 (in relation to alternative investments) for 300 would make sense, to sell it for an effective 218 would not.

A Numerical Example

2939 The following numerical example sets out three alternative scenarios. The relevant facts are as follows:

> An asset was purchased for $1000 in November 1985.
> This asset was sold in January 1988.
> The Consumer Price Index for the December 1985 Quarter was 147.1.
> The Consumer Price Index for the March 1988 Quarter was 176.0.

> The indexed cost price at the date of sale was thus
> 1000 x 176.0 / 147.1 = $1196.

Scenario	(a)	(b)	(c)
Sale Price	900	1100	1300
Actual Cost	1000	1000	1000
Indexed Cost	1196	1196	1196
Actual Profit/Loss	100 Loss	100 Profit	300 Profit
Indexed Profit/Loss	296 Loss	96 Loss	104 Profit
Taxable Profit/Loss	100 Loss	nil	104 Profit

Record Keeping

2940 In order to be able to comply with the capital gains tax legislation shareholders will have to keep very detailed records of their holdings. In respect of *each separate parcel* of the shares of each company in which they invest they will need to keep track of the key details, such as:

- the exact number of shares
- their total cost

- the date of acquisition
- the total sale proceeds
- the date of disposal
- the actual or deemed CGT-status.

Notes:

1. Forms which can be filled in to facilitate the task of keeping track of such data are contained in another work by the author, *The Australian Wills & Record Keeping Book.*

2. The obligation is to keep the appropriate records relating to an asset for five years after disposing of the asset.

3. It should not be assumed that an investor's stockbroker will have the necessary records. For one thing, many transactions, such as new issues and dividend reinvestment plan shares taken up, do not involve brokers. For another, the broker may dispose of old records after a period, or he may cease his operations down the track.

4. See also Appendix 8.

2941 It is important to realise that shares received at the one time can involve a mixture of pre-1985 and post-1985 shares, as when bonus shares are issued (see para. 2905) or when an investor participates in both dividend reinvestment and dividend election plans (see paras 2847 to 2857).

Partial Capital Returns

2942 Investors holding shares or units in a unit trust sometimes receive payments (under various names) which are effectively partial returns of capital (as distinct from revenue items, such as dividends or normal trust distributions).

In the case of shares, such payments may occur because the company concerned has legally reduced its capital or because it has made a *cash* payment out of a share premium account.

In the case of unit trusts such payments include some but not all of the "exempt income" amounts described in para. 2860. In particular, the benefit from the building depreciation allowance described in para. 2886 is ignored for CGT purposes.

Sections 160ZL and 160ZM of the Act deal with such partial capital returns.

2943 Where these payments are less than the indexed cost price of a post-1985 asset then no capital gains tax is payable at the time of the payment. Instead, the indexed cost price is written down by the amount of the payment, so that that payment (with appropriate future indexation, in the case of gains) is taken into account if and when the asset is disposed of.

2944 Where these payments are more than the indexed cost price of a post-1985 asset then capital gains tax is immediately payable on the excess and the cost price for future CGT purposes is written down to zero.

2945 The legislation as originally enacted introduced an undesirable side effect. The 12-month clock for indexing purposes (see para. 2903) started again each time such a partial capital return was made and furthermore if the payment was made within 12 months of the acquisition of the asset then the benefit of indexation for that initial period was also lost.

Thus unit trusts which made exempt distributions could involve their investors in more tax than if the trusts had just retained the relevant amounts and allowed them to be reflected in a higher asset backing and unit price. This anomaly has been rectified in respect of distributions made after 15 August 1989, provided only that the units are held for at least 12 months.

Economic Effects of the CGT Legislation

2946 The existence of a tax liability on realised capital gains without any corresponding levy on unrealised gains provides a strong incentive for investors who do not require immediate cash to hang on to existing investments which show real profits rather than to switch into alternative situations. This incentive is, of course, even greater in respect to pre-1985 assets. A considerable number of investors are thus "locked in" to their portfolios—a fact which discourages the efficient use of assets and harms economic growth.

2947 Notwithstanding such theoretical considerations, the pool of pre-1985 assets seems to be falling quite rapidly, as investors sell for liquidity reasons or in takeover situations, and as individuals die. Commonwealth tax revenue must benefit accordingly.

2948 It is sometimes alleged that the capital gains tax is a disincentive to investment. Such claims have little logic:

- Capital gains less tax are still more attractive than no capital gains at all.

- Tax on capital gains, by virtue of being subject to an indexation component, is still more attractive than tax on income, which is not subject to an indexation component.

Effect on Turnover

2949 One consequence of the CGT legislation has been the reduction in turnover on the stock exchange because of the "lock in" aspect described above. This actually affects both pre-1985 and post-1985 shares, although in different ways:

- Investors are reluctant to sell pre-1985 shares, because no replacement investment would enjoy this valuable status.

- Investors are reluctant to sell post-1985 shares where disposal would result in a capital gain, because this would trigger off an immediate tax liability, whereas continuing to hold would not. As explained in para. 2938, continuing to hold is usually also more attractive than switching into another investment.

- Investors are also reluctant to sell post-1985 shares where disposal would result in a capital loss, because they might not be able to utilise that loss. Furthermore, continuing to hold would not create any extra CGT liability on an eventual disposal, except to the extent that future growth took the price to more than the (indexed) original cost price. By way of contrast, buying an alternative investment would create a CGT liability on disposal in respect of the entire (indexed) future growth.

To illustrate, consider a shareholder with shares which cost 200 but which are now worth only 100. Any future capital appreciation between this 100 and the original 200 plus indexation will be tax-free. But all capital appreciation on this

100, if it is used to acquire a replacement asset, would be fully taxable (apart from indexation on the 100, which would be much less than the indexation component on the 200 which covers both a larger base figure and an earlier starting date).

Dividend Reinvestment and Dividend Election Plans

2950 The tax consequences of shares issued under dividend reinvestment and dividend election plans (however called) are explained in Chapter 32. In brief, shares issued in lieu of cash are regarded as having been purchased for the relevant cash amount and bonus shares are treated in the same way as the other bonus shares discussed above (see para. 2905).

Gifts

2951 If an asset is disposed of by way of gift then for capital gains tax purposes it is treated as though there had been a sale at the market value. This applies in respect to both parties, so that the recipient of the gift is on any subsequent disposal treated as though he had made an arm's length purchase on the day of the gift.

2952 It follows from the above that if an asset with pre-1985 status is given away then it automatically loses that status.

Transfers between Spouses

2953 Sometimes it is desired to transfer income-producing assets from the spouse who is subject to the higher marginal tax rate to the spouse who is subject to the lower marginal tax rate.

2954 While such transactions may reduce the burden of income tax in the future, they also constitute the disposal of assets for capital gains tax purposes and may therefore trigger off an immediate capital gains tax liability and/or create a potential CGT disadvantage down the track.

Spin-off Companies

2955 As explained in para. 741, sometimes a listed company floats off a subsidiary company by offering shares and/or options in it to its own shareholders, usually as a preliminary to having that subsidiary listed separately on the stock exchange: a "spin-off".

2956 Such issues where made after 19 September 1985 and before 16 August 1989 have post-1985 status.

2957 However, issues made on and after 16 August 1989 are treated in the same way as if the company had made a rights issue to its own shareholders (see para. 2906).

Personal Use Assets

2958 The legislation distinguishes between "listed" personal use assets (basically, jewellery and collectible items costing at least $100) and "non-listed" personal use assets. It accords special capital gains tax treatment to both categories, as follows:

	Listed Assets	Non-listed Assets
Gains from sales up to $5000	Taxable	Exempt
Gains from sales above $5000	Taxable	Taxable
Losses	Deductible, but only against gains from the sale of other Listed Assets in the same or a later financial year	Not deductible

Each personal use asset is treated individually, except where it is part of a set.

Share Traders

2959 Persons who trade in shares are taxed using the same rules as persons who *trade* in, say, vegetables. Profits and losses are then treated under the ordinary income tax rules and not under the special provisions relating to capital gains. This has some advantages and some disadvantages.

2960 One advantage is that trading losses are offsetable against all income, whereas capital losses are offsetable *only* against capital gains.

2961 Furthermore, traders have an option to value trading stock at market value for tax purposes at the end of each financial year, and can thus claim *unrealised* as well as realised losses as tax deductions.

2962 The disadvantage is that indexation does not apply. For genuine long-term holders indexation can be very valuable, as it exempts part-perhaps all—of the capital appreciation for an asset being disposed of. Investors presumably acquire assets in the expectation of making gains rather than losses, and should thus not lightly declare themselves as share traders.

2963 Investors are entitled to have a "long-term" portfolio for some of their holdings and a "trading" portfolio for the rest of their holdings. However, under Section 52 of the Act (which governs only pre-1985 assets) the taxpayer was required to advise the Commissioner of the profit-making nature of the arrangements no later than the date on which the first return was lodged after the relevant asset was acquired.

Overseas Assets

2964 Capital gains and capital losses in respect of overseas assets can be aggregated with capital gains and capital losses in respect of local assets. Both the cost and the proceeds have to be converted to Australian currency at the exchange rate applicable at the time of the relevant transaction. Capital gains are not aggregated with overseas income of a revenue nature, although credit for any tax payments to foreign governments with which Australia has double tax agreements would be brought into account in the usual way (see paras 2877 and 2879).

Short Selling

2965 As explained in para. 1685, short selling shares involves selling shares which the vendor does not own, with a view to buying them later as the second leg of a transaction and hopefully at a lower price.

2966 Capital gains and losses from short selling transactions are dealt with under the ordinary provisions of the income tax law and not under the special provisions relating to conventional capital gains and losses. The first leg of the transaction does not constitute the "disposal" of an asset, and acquisitions do not trigger off CGT.

Worthless Shares

2967 Shares in companies which have gone into receivership or liquidation are often worthless in any practical sense, but because they have been suspended from trading on the stock exchange (or because the company concerned has been de-listed) the formal and irreversible "disposal" of the shares, which is necessary in order to allow a capital loss to be recognised for CGT purposes, is difficult. Investors are thus adversely affected not only by the commercial loss on their investment but also by an anomaly in the tax system.

2968 Parliament has started to address this problem, but workable legislation and/or administrative rulings from the Australian Taxation Office to assist investors in regard to this important matter are still awaited. The following are relevant:

- Section 160WA allows a liquidator to make a written declaration that no distributions are likely and this gives the shareholders concerned a right to claim an immediate loss, as though they had disposed of their shares for a nil consideration. (Any subsequent distributions would naturally then be taxed in full when received.)

- However, there is no machinery in place to force liquidators to make such a declaration or even to advise shareholders individually or collectively that one has been made.

- Nor is there any corresponding provision governing receivers of defunct companies not in liquidation.

- Of course, shareholders can always crystallise a loss by actually selling the shares concerned to some third party for a nominal consideration.

Tax Returns

2969 For a number of reasons the "Capital Gains Tax Worksheet" included in official Australian Taxation Office publications is not very suitable for active share investors or even inactive long-term members of dividend reinvestment and dividend election plans. An alternative approach is presented in Appendix 8.

Exempt Transactions

2970 Disposal of the following does not give rise to any capital gains tax:

- The sole or principal residence (but not a second house, such as a holiday house, or an investment property).
- Motor vehicles.
- Life insurance policies (including investment bonds).
- Friendly society policies (including investment bonds).
- Superannuation.

Furniture and ordinary household effects are also generally exempt, but works of art, collectible items, etc., are not. Certain receipts of money are also regarded as not appropriate for taxation—for example:

- Winnings from lotteries and other forms of gambling.
- Damages and compensation awards.

Strategies

2971 Investors have some control over when they incur capital gains tax. They may, for example, be able to realise gains in financial years when their normal income is relatively low. However, sometimes this choice is not available to them either literally or as a market reality, as when disposals are forced on them by takeovers or schemes of arrangement.

2972 In such cases one way to minimise the cash required to pay tax on the capital gains could be to sell off some other holdings where the disposal would result in an offsetting capital loss. If the investor still wants an interest in the shares concerned then they can be repurchased either immediately or when the price looks more attractive (or, if appropriate, other comparable shares could be bought instead).

2973 Such a strategy can have some long-term negatives—for example, it might result in the loss of any existing indexation component and future indexation will take place only in respect of the lower repurchase price. However, it may be useful in terms of solving a liquidity problem in the case of disposals involving share exchanges rather than cash.

Reconstructions

2974 Shareholders affected by reconstructions such as share splits or consolidations (see para. 772) can protect themselves by lodging a Section 160ZZP election with the Australian Taxation Office with their first tax return after the change.

2975 This ensures that the replacement shares are treated as a continuation of the original holding—as indeed they are—and that no disposal of the former shares has taken place.

2976 Of course, in some cases shareholders might prefer to have the transaction treated as a disposal and a fresh acquisition, in which case they would just refrain from lodging the election.

Section 51AAA

2977 Interest on loans used to purchase assets such as gold bars or derivatives which do not pay periodical income is not tax deductible, because it is not regarded as being an expense incurred in the earning of assessable income. Section 51AAA of the *Income Tax Assessment Act 1936* specifically stipulates that the expectation of making a taxable gain is not sufficient.

2978 However, any interest previously undeducted does become part of the cost base of the relevant asset for capital gains tax purposes.

Endowment Warrants

2979 As with all options and warrants, capital gains tax is not payable at the exercise stage of an endowment warrant (see paras 2236 to 2255). If it is sold then a capital gain or loss crystallises. Naturally also if an endowment warrant lapses as worthless then this constitutes a disposal and a capital loss is realised.

2980 If a share which arose from the exercise of an endowment warrant is sold then a capital gain or loss arises at that time, with the cost base then comprising quite logically both the original cost of the endowment warrant and the exercise price (both amounts being subject to indexation from the respective dates of payment, in the case of capital gains).

Company Assets

2981 If more than 50 per cent of a company's shares change hands then its pre-85 assets become post-85 assets as at the date this threshold is exceeded. (The detailed rules for this are quite complex.)

Special Rulings

2982 From time to time unusual market happenings lead to one-off rulings from the Australian Taxation Office.

2983 For example, shares issued by AMP Limited to its former policyholder at demutualisation free of charge in exchange for their previous voting rights are deemed for CGT purposes to have been acquired at 1043 each. (Shares purchased on the market or in other ways are, of course, not affected by this special ruling.)

Superannuation Surcharge

2984 In contrast to the approach used for provisional tax (see para. 2937) this income for purposes of the superannuation surcharge legislation includes net capital gains. Thus, for example, a on-off capital gain which happens to take an investor's total income above the threshold can have the effect of increasing the tax levied on the superannuation contribution.

Installment Receipts

2985 The payment of the final instalment under instalment receipts (see paras 493 to 494) and the transfer of the title to the underlying shares from the trustee company to the investor do not constitute a disposal for CGT purposes. As in the case of contributing shares which become fully-paid the capital gain on a subsequent disposal of the shares has regard to all the amounts previously paid (indexed in the usual way from the respective dates of payment.)

Chapter 30—Other Taxes

To be clever enough to get all that money, one must
be stupid enough to want it
—G K Chesterton

Preliminary Comments

3001 To round off the subject dealt with in the preceding two chapters, this brief summary mentions the main taxes other than income tax which are relevant to investors. It should be regarded as a broad outline only and fuller details of the position in the State concerned should be sought out in appropriate cases. The warnings set out in para. 2803 apply here.

Stamp Duties

3002 Stamp duties are levied by State Governments on a wide range of transactions and at rates which often differ from State to State. However, in the case of transfers of shares the duty is almost uniform throughout Australia (see paras 1632 to 1634). The same rate as for shares also applies to transfers of rights and options and of units in unit trusts.

3003 For sales on the stock exchange the rate is generally 15 cents per $100 consideration (or part thereof), payable by each of the buyer and the seller. The amount of this duty is shown on contract notes and the actual duty is remitted in bulk by the brokers to the authorities.

3004 For private sales the rate is generally 30 cents per $100 consideration (or part thereof), levied on the buyer only. This duty is payable by adhesive or impressed duty stamps on the transfer form.

3005 Transactions such as the issue of new shares by a company or the creation or redemption of units in a unit trust are not regarded as transfers for duty purposes.

3006 Transfers of company debentures and notes and of government and semi-governmental securities are also exempt.

3007 The stamp duty on the transfer of real property is much higher than the corresponding duty on the transfer of shares, a fact which along with the incidence of other transaction costs and the imposition of capital gains tax may "lock in" some investors to their existing holdings and thus slow down overall economic activity.

Transfer duty is levied on a sliding scale, with the peak marginal rate in Victoria being as high as 6 per cent for properties within the popular $100,000 to $760,000 range. Possibly a lower rate structure might actually result in more transfers and thus greater revenue for the government, although it is impossible to prove or disprove this proposition. Certainly, even with the present incidence of duty property turnover figures are quite high. It is also possible that this level of duty actually encourages the redevelopment of properties, as "value added" by an owner is naturally free of any transfer duty.

3008 It follows that, in pure duty terms, it is cheaper to buy a plot of land plus a contract to erect a building than to buy the land with the building already in place. It is similarly cheaper, from a stamp duty point of view, to buy property in the form of units in a property trust than to buy equivalent property directly. Buying a series of smaller properties involves less duty than paying the same number of dollars for a single larger property.

3009 Stamp duty is also payable on property leases, licences and guarantees. This duty is normally borne by the tenant and not by the landlord.

3010 Stamp duty is payable on most new life policies, including investment bonds. However, this duty is normally absorbed by the life company, although, of course, it is indirectly paid for by the customer in the form of higher premiums.

3011 All investment transactions involve the payment of money and thus incur Financial Institutions Duty (FID) and Debits Tax at the State level. While in the aggregate these taxes raise a great deal of money the rates of tax are in general too small to be material to investment decision making. However, FID at 0.06 per cent *per transaction* is the equivalent of interest at 21.9 per cent for one day. This can mean that the duty on a deposit in, say, a cash management trust is of the same order of magnitude (7.3 per cent per annum) as the interest payable for three days, thus making frequent switches between trusts in order to finesse the yields available relatively unattractive. The existence of both FID and the debits tax also makes transfers of money between different bank accounts quite expensive.

Death Duties

3012 State and Federal death duties (under various names such as "probate duty", "succession duty" and "estate duty") have mainly been abolished. However, one aspect of capital gains tax (see Chapter 29) should be mentioned in this context. This tax is triggered off when post-1985 assets previously owned by a deceased person are actually sold, irrespective of whether this sale is instituted by the executors or administrators of the deceased estate shortly after the death or by the beneficiaries to whom the particular assets were transferred when these beneficiaries dispose of the assets many years later. Because of the former feature some critics of the legislation regard CGT as a quasi-death duty.

Property Taxes

3013 Although Australia has no wealth tax as such, certain annual levies are imposed on one particular asset, namely, real property. These levies directly affect owner-occupiers as well as investor-owners. As shown below, indirectly they also affect tenants.

3014 At State level there is *land tax*, imposed on the site value (also called the "unimproved value") of property—in other words, on the value of the land only, disregarding any "improvements" or buildings. This approach is designed to encourage owners to fully develop their land, as the tax burden is the same in dollar terms for an empty plot of land as for a plot with a large and costly building on it. In "percentage of total value" terms the burden is, of course, much less for the latter.

3015 Land tax is imposed on a sliding scale, the rate having regard not to the value of the particular piece of land but rather to the aggregate value of all pieces of land held in the State concerned by the same owner. It follows that, in pure land tax terms, an investor would be better off holding property in more than one State—although any tax advantages would need to be weighed against possible disadvantages, such as costlier administration or lower growth rates.

3016 At a local government level there are *rates*, payable to municipal councils and also separately to water and sewerage authorities (under various names). Some rates are imposed on site values, as in the case of land tax, but not using a sliding scale. However, others are imposed on the net annual value of the property, which is a notional rent covering both the land and the buildings on it. A few councils even levy "shandy" rates—a compromise between these two approaches.

3017 In the case of residential investment property land tax and rates are usually borne by the landlord and passed on to the tenant implicitly through the level of rent. This "gross rent" method can also be employed for commercial and industrial property, although under modern leases in most areas it is more common to use a "net rent" method. Under this approach the tenant explicitly meets all outgoings.

A third method is also in use, under which the annual outgoings in force as at the commencement of the lease are built into the rent, with the tenant then being responsible for any increase in these outgoings over a stipulated base figure.

It should be noted that these three methods are only alternative ways of expressing the same commercial reality. The overall accommodation costs of tenants and the net investment returns to owners are both governed by market forces, not by labels in contracts.

3018 Because land tax is imposed on a sliding scale basis the actual amount levied on a particular property really depends on the land value of the owner's total property portfolio rather than on the value of the actual site occupied by the tenant concerned. For this reason the amount of land tax to be met by the tenant is often expressed as being the amount which would be due on a "single holding" basis, thus putting the tenant in exactly the same position as if the landlord owned no other property. The landlord is then out of pocket to the extent of the difference between the sum of the separate "single holding" figures applicable to his various tenants and the actual aggregate holdings figure which applies to him.

3019 The valuations placed on properties for land tax and rating purposes are usually well below the true market levels, thus reducing the likelihood that these valuations can be upset on appeal. For administrative reasons they are also invariably out of date, as in order to ensure equity among all taxpayers or ratepayers a common date embracing all properties in the area concerned needs to be used.

3020 The legal liability for both land tax and rates is imposed on the owners registered as such on a particular date each year. Appropriate pro rata adjustments between buyers and sellers during the period covered by the levies are made on a change of ownership (except where these are the responsibility of an ongoing tenant).

Chapter 31—Social Security Aspects

So, this doesn't mean anything, but at least it's not obvious nonsense
—Hugh Young

Preliminary Comments

3101 Investors are affected by more than just the income tax provisions discussed in Chapter 28. In some cases they may also need to be aware of the means test under the legislation governing social security and veterans' affairs benefits.

3102 As is the case with taxes, the legislation governing social security and veterans' affairs benefits is subject to frequent change. Furthermore, the rates of benefits and some of the various thresholds are subject to half-yearly adjustment to allow for inflation.

3103 A detailed discussion of this complex piece of legislation and all its ramifications, and of the various extra-statutory provisions which somewhat surprisingly are applied in practice, is outside the scope of this book. The comments which follow relate specifically to the age pension under the *Social Security Act 1991,* and should therefore be regarded as illustrative of the broad principles rather than as an exposition of the fine print.

3104 Subject to certain tests described below, eligibility for age pensions arises at age 65 for males and at a slightly lower age for females, irrespective of whether or not actual retirement has taken place. The commencement age for females is 61 as from 1 July 1997 but this age will be increased by six months every second 1 July until it reaches 65.

3105 The summary in this chapter is intended as only a brief outline of the subject, with particular reference to the rules governing investments and their effect on age pensions. Brochures describing the various social security pensions and benefits in lay language in greater detail are available from Centrelink offices. (Centrelink is the new Commonwealth Government agency set up in 1997 in order to provide social security payments and services.)

Background

3106 Although many people believe that the taxes paid by them during their working life time have in part been by way of prepayment for an age pension for themselves and their spouses and that therefore such a pension is their moral due, the reality is that such benefits to the retired generation on a national level can come only from the efforts of the working generation at that time.

3107 Consumption by the elderly of food, clothing, entertainment and the like really requires the contemporaneous production of these items by other people—in the form of production in excess of their own consumption—and no rearrangement of bookkeeping for the national accounts can alter this fundamental fact.

3108 For this reason social security benefits in Australia have traditionally always been means tested, so as to keep the cost to the current taxpayers down, while rationing the limited resources for the benefit of those persons regarded as most in need of them. The present means test involves both an income test and a separate assets test, pensions being paid under whichever of the two formulae produces the lower rate of benefits.

3109 The assets test is unlikely to have much effect on genuine investors in ungeared situations, as in most cases their investment returns will be such that the income test by itself will govern the rate of pension.

3110 The main effect of the means test is on persons who for lifestyle reasons insist on being "assets rich and income poor" (for example, art collectors or farmers) or who deliberately arrange their affairs in a quite uncommercial fashion (such as leaving a large sum of money in a zero interest bank account, where the loss of interest is likely to far exceed any possible gains to be made from exploiting the social welfare system).

3111 However, in a geared situation the net return on the net asset can also be very small or negative, causing the assets test to come into play. Broadly speaking but subject to the more detailed comments below, in the case of an asset which is subject to a debt regard is had to the *net* value of the asset—its gross market value less all outstanding debts.

3112 These debts may include items other than a formal loan on mortgage—for example, a bank overdraft secured by the lodgement of title deeds, accumulated interest, arrears of rates and so on. An unsecured loan raised specifically to purchase a particular asset also ranks.

3113 Similarly, with one significant exception regard is had to the *net* income—the actual gross return less the corresponding outgoings. Thus in the case of, say, property investments the *gross rent less expenses and interest* is used. The exception refers to shares and other financial investments, which are subject to the special rules relating to *extended deeming*, an important concept which is explained in paras 3142 to 3149.

3114 However, unlike the income tax position, a negative investment return from a geared investment is taken as zero. Negative amounts cannot be offset against positive income from other sources or carried forward.

Means Tests

3115 Means tests have many drawbacks. For instance, they discourage thrift before retirement and they make it unattractive for people to remain in the workforce after reaching an arbitrary "statutory age of senility".

3116 Such tests are expensive to administer and, by discriminating in favour of those who fail to provide for their own old age, they also unfairly penalise those who act more responsibly.

3117 Nevertheless, the present means test is a fact of life which needs to be taken into account by investors. Despite the occasional rhetoric of some politicians removal of the means test is most unlikely in the foreseeable future.

Rate of Pension

3118 Whereas the income tax legislation regards each individual person as a separate unit for tax purposes, the social security legislation, in the case of married persons or persons who are living in a de facto relationship, treats the couple as the primary unit for benefit purposes.

3119 This affects the rate of pension, which for a couple is at about one and two-thirds times the single rate, rather than twice (as, for example, in the case of two elderly siblings living together).

3120 This principle also governs the various thresholds, which have regard to the combined incomes or assets of both parties (even where only one person is receiving the pension).

Income Test

3121 As one would expect, "income" for the purpose of the income test under the social security and veterans' affairs legislation is widely defined. It includes:

- all personal exertion income, such as salary and wages and business and professional income

- pensions from past employers

- in the case of property, rent

- in the case of "financial investments", the *deemed* investment income under the extended deeming rules discussed in paras 3142 to 3149

- in the case of other assets, the *actual* investment income in the form of interest and dividends.

3122 Distributions from family trusts are also treated is income. This covers both income distributions and—not at all logically—capital distributions. Capital distributions to persons regarded as disabled for social security purposes and used to make home improvements were previously exempt, but this is no longer the case.

3123 Regard is had to the total of the relevant amounts received in the preceding 12 months. The following all rank:

- amounts paid in cash

- amounts credited to a beneficiary loan account

- amounts reinvested

- amounts expended in paying bills on behalf of the beneficiary.

3124 However, income does not include, in the case of pensioners, one-off or periodical payments from immediate relatives which are not made through a family trust.

3125 It should be noted that the full definition of "income" for income test purposes is rather different from the corresponding income tax usage of that term.

3126 Understandably enough, the age pension itself is treated as income for tax purposes only.

3127 In the case of private company shares, which unlike listed or widely available but unlisted public company shares are not treated as financial investments, the dividend imputation system introduces yet another important distinction.

3128 Franked dividends themselves are naturally regarded as "income" under both systems. However, the attaching imputation credits—which are, of course, never received by shareholders in cash—are regarded as income under the tax system but are not counted as income under the income test.

3129 In the case of business operations, the net income after allowing for certain outgoings rather than the gross profit is taken into account for the income test. The relevant outgoings consist of deductions under Section 51 of the *Income Tax Assessment Act 1936*, as well as depreciation and employee superannuation contributions, but not certain concessional items or the borrowing expenses which are deductible under Section 67.

3130 Similarly, in the case of property investments, the net rent after allowing for all expenses borne by the landlord rather than the gross rent is taken into account for the income test. The expenses for this purpose include interest on a loan used to acquire the property and normal depreciation but not borrowing expenses or the special building allowance available under Division 10D.

3131 The expenses other than interest are based on taxation return data where this is available or, failing that availability, they are taken as a minimum of one-third of the gross rent in order to allow for rates, land tax, insurance premiums, body corporate charges, repairs and the like. However, a higher figure can be used where it can be supported by appropriate evidence. If the net rent on this basis for any one property is negative then it is taken as zero.

3132 The income test allows pensioners to earn up to a certain level of "other income" each week and still receive the full pension. For each dollar of gross income beyond this rather small limit the pension drops by 50 cents per single pensioner or by 25 cents per pensioner in the case of couples, until it eventually becomes nil.

3133 As the remaining 50 cents is for most incomes also subject to income tax the total marginal rate of abatement can be higher than the 48.5 per cent marginal tax rate being imposed on millionaires—for example:

Extra gross income	$100
Reduction in pension	$50
Extra income before tax	$50
Tax at, say, 20 per cent	$10

Extra income after tax	$40

equivalent to a 60 per cent marginal rate of abatement.

3134 It should be noted that, even in the absence of a specific social security income test, the sliding scale used for income tax would to some extent act as a de facto income test.

Gifts Received

3135 Gifts received from the immediate family are never treated as income under the income test.

3136 Gifts received from other than the immediate family are not treated as income where they are one-off lump sums. However, they are regarded as income where they are received on a regular basis.

Borrowings

3137 In the case of shares or other financial investments (see paras 3146 to 3147) the deemed income based on the *gross* value of the asset is used *regardless of any offsetting interest obligations.*

3138 Furthermore, interest on a loan secured on a property but actually used to buy shares is not deductible from anything.

3139 It follows that persons proposing to buy both property and shares should ensure that as far as practicable any loan funds raised are used to buy the property rather than the shares.

3140 Rather strangely, the legislation provides that private borrowings (including those from both family trusts and individual family members) should be considered as "income", although conceptually these are clearly capital sums, similar in character to withdrawals of deposits previously made. However, this provision is rarely enforced in practice.

3141 The legislation also makes an exception for the first $40,000 of loan funds under home equity conversion loans.

Extended Deeming

3142 In order to counter a perceived abuse of the system, a concept known as "extended deeming" now applies in the case of certain assets called "financial investments". For these, the actual investment return is disregarded for the purpose of the income test and a notional or *deemed* rate of return applied to the value of the asset is used instead.

3143 It is important to note that for this purpose the *gross* value of the asset is used, rather than the more logical *net* value after allowing for any loan (which, in contrast, is the approach used for purposes of the assets test). Quite unfairly no allowance at all is made for the interest payable on loans used to acquire financial investments.

3144 This deeming concept is meant to take into consideration both regular income and capital growth.

3145 The deeming rate is adjusted up or down from time to time in order to reflect current interest rates. As from 20 September 1997 the rate was 3 per cent for amounts up to $30,400 (single) or $50,600 (couples, combined value). Beyond this threshold the rate was 5 per cent.

3146 Financial investments include cash, bank and similar deposits, loans, listed and unlisted public company shares, units in unit trusts other than unitised family trusts, life insurance and friendly society bonds and the like.

3147 Financial investments do not include a home or its contents, other real estate, cars, boats, collectibles, shares in private companies, conventional life insurance policies and the like.

3148 The extended deeming provisions do not lead to the notional amounts of income also becoming subject to income tax.

3149 Despite some concerns expressed by pensioner groups when deeming first came in, pensioners who convert low interest or zero interest deposits into deposits earning the deeming rate will always be better off. The additional interest payments received, even allowing for any tax on that extra income, more than offset any reductions in the pension.

Assets Test

3150 The term "assets" for purposes of the assets test under the social security and veterans' affairs legislation includes all types of investment—shares, Commonwealth bonds, bank bills, debentures, unsecured notes, deposits, options, warrants, futures, property, units in share and property trusts, and so on, as well as life insurance policies (at their surrender value).

3151 Quite consistently, it also includes all loans to family trusts and to relatives (whether bearing interest or not), as well as units in unitised family trusts.

3152 Assets are taken into account at their market value at the time of application for a pension or at the time of a review, not at their original cost price. In the same way, the replacement value of the assets, which value may well have been used— quite advisedly—for insurance purposes, is quite irrelevant to the assets test.

3153 The value of a pensioner's home is excluded from the test, but a higher threshold applies in the case of persons not living in their own homes.

3154 The assets test allows pensioners to own a certain level of assets and still receive the full pension. For each $1000 of assets beyond that the pension drops by $3 per fortnight (per single pensioner or per couple, as the case may be) until it eventually becomes nil. (This reduction in pension is the equivalent of a return on the assets of 7.8 per cent per annum before tax. This rate does not move in line with changes in the deeming rate.)

3155 There is, of course, nothing under the income tax law which corresponds to the social security assets test.

3156 As indicated above, the general principle is that for any assets which are subject to outstanding loans the net value after deducting such loans is used.

3157 In the case of income producing property, each asset is taken separately. It is possible for an outstanding loan to exceed the current value of the gross asset. In such cases the net asset is taken as having a zero value.

3158 In the case of a loan secured by a portfolio of shares, the same principle would apply but the entire share portfolio would be treated as a single asset.

3159 In the special case of a loan secured by a home, the loan would be completely disregarded even if it had been raised for investment purposes.

Capital Gains and Losses

3160 Capital gains are disregarded for purposes of the income test. This applies to both realised and unrealised gains.

3161 This is perfectly logical in the case of financial investments, as the deeming rate is meant to be the proxy for both capital growth and periodical income.

3162 Such a rule is quite generous in the case of other assets, as it allows pensioners to arrange their portfolios so that they hold mainly investments with low immediate returns and high growth prospects, rather than the other way round.

3163 Naturally, capital losses are also disregarded and cannot be offset against income.

3164 For persons who have been declared share traders—see paras 2959 to 2963—realised capital gains and realised capital losses from share trading are now covered by the extended deeming rules and they are no longer treated under the rules applying to traders in other commodities.

Deprivation

3165 People who "deprive" themselves of assets or income in order to get around the means test are affected by special provisions in the legislation designed to counter this. Such persons are deemed to be still owning the relevant assets in full, and also to be earning certain income, for a further five years after disposal.

3166 Deprived assets are included in the "financial investments" category described above, regardless of their previous status. This results in the actual former income on these assets being disregarded and notional income calculated in accordance with the extended deeming rules being used instead.

3167 The above deprivation principle covers gifts to family trusts and to relatives. It also embraces deprivations within the five-year period leading up to qualification for the pension. However, gifts made more than five years previously do not count for means test purposes.

3168 Furthermore, disposals aggregating up to $10,000 a year (single persons or married couples) are permitted and only the excess is relevant for deprivation purposes.

3169 Sales of assets for a consideration less than the true market value are regarded as involving gifts to the extent of the shortfall.

3170 These provisions naturally enough do not extend to normal sales of assets where the proceeds are:

- spent on consumption items
- used to pay interest

- used to repay loans

- invested in other ways.

3171 In the last-mentioned case, of course, the replacement assets and the income produced from them would be included in the means test in the usual way. Certain other transactions are also regarded as quite acceptable—for example, the reduction in assets caused by the purchase of an annuity.

Home Improvements

3172 A legal way of overcoming the means test is, of course, provided by the above-mentioned treatment of the pensioner's own home. Investing in an expensive residence or upgrading an existing building can take money out of reach of the test. It can also create a hedge against inflation and assist in regard to capital gains tax-but naturally it does not provide an income stream.

Changed Circumstances

3173 If a person's circumstances change then the pension entitlement may change also and the person concerned is allowed or required to lodge an "application for review" form giving up-to-date particulars or alternatively to advise the relevant details to Centrelink by telephone or letter.

3174 This would, for example, be appropriate in the following cases:

(a)   Where the income test applies:

- ceasing to derive personal exertion income on giving up work

- suffering a permanent cut in investment income if a company folds up

- suffering a temporary cut in investment income if a private company fails to pay its normal dividend

- suffering a cut in investment income if a savings institution becomes subject to a moratorium

- experiencing a significant variation in the amount of distribution from a family trust

- incurring a larger or smaller interest bill on borrowings.

(b) Where the assets test applies:

- incurring a reduction in the capital value of shares if a company goes into receivership or liquidation

- incurring massive unrealised capital losses if the market overall slumps.

Planning Aspects

3175 Persons who are planning their affairs should not look at social security and taxation provisions in isolation. Regard should always be had to the combined effect of both.

3176 Several differences between the legislation relating to income tax and that relating to social security benefits have already been mentioned (combined incomes used in the case of couples, definition of "income", assets test, notional income for certain categories of investments).

3177 One further difference needs discussion. Income tax law has regard to the total income received in a *financial year* running from 1 July to 30 June following. The social security system in contrast looks at the current "per fortnight" income basis prevailing at the time a claim for benefits is assessed or reviewed.

3178 For salary and wage payments received weekly, fortnightly or monthly this causes no conceptual problems, although if the amounts vary from period to period then they need averaging.

3179 However, some other categories of income may be being received in irregular licks at greater intervals or may be being calculated notionally under the extended deeming rules.

3180 Deductions such as loan interest may also be payable quarterly —or, if bank bills are used, at irregular intervals depending on the frequency of rollovers.

3181 For such payments the income or outgo per fortnight for purposes of the income test is taken as one twenty-sixth of the annual amount at the time at which the claim is processed, having regard to the actual or notional figures for the most recent full year for which information is available.

3182 Clearly, the means test is not going to be of concern to persons who are either well below the lower thresholds (and thus not adversely affected) or well above the upper thresholds (and thus in a position where attempting to avoid the provisions is not practicable or worthwhile).

3183 It is only persons in between these two categories who should ever consider rearranging their affairs in order to improve their position. Even then, the aim should always be to maximise the overall net returns allowing for the payments to and from the government, not either to minimise tax or to maximise social security entitlements as ends in themselves.

3184 But such planning should never overlook the other relevant aspects, such as ensuring a cash flow in line with requirements and peace of mind from holding worry-free investments. (Any desired level of cash flow can, of course, be achieved by a suitable mix of capital withdrawals and income receipts.)

3185 When married persons are planning on the above lines, consideration should also be given to the situation likely to arise if one spouse predeceases the other.

3186 Quite apart from the loss of any non-investment income peculiar to the person concerned which may follow such a death, there can be significant consequences flowing from the "combined income" and "combined assets" thresholds of the means test. Income which previously satisfied the limit for two people may not satisfy the limit for one and thus an age pension previously payable at the full rate for a couple falls, not to the full rate for a single person, but rather to that rate reduced in respect of the then excess "other income".

The Pensioner Rebate

3187 Pensions are treated as part of assessable income for income tax purposes. (In the case of pensioner couples, each spouse is regarded as having received half of the joint benefit.)

3188 However, a special *pensioner rebate* is available. This ensures that persons who derive no other assessable income apart from the age pension will not pay any tax despite its amount exceeding the normal tax-free threshold.

Group Certificates

3189 The Department of Social Security after the end of each financial year issues statements of pension earnings to pensioners to assist them in the preparation of their tax returns. If "pay as you earn" (PAYE) tax has been deducted at any pensioner's request then a group certificate will be issued instead.

Investment Advice

3190 Centrelink provides a free service for existing social security and veterans' affairs pensioners and also for persons currently planning their retirement.

3191 Called "Financial Information Service" (FIS), this offers advice on a range of matters including the effect of various types of investment income on pension entitlements and taxation. However, it does not recommend particular investments or individual investment advisers.

Conclusion

3192 To sum up, the means test can affect investments in up to three different ways:

- income each year

- asset value

- capital gains on disposal

with some special rules applying to certain types of investment.

3193 Unspent income, even where it has had an effect under the income test, becomes an asset under the assets test in the usual way.

3194 Even relatively small savers can be affected by these tests —for example, at the deeming rates mentioned in para. 3145 any financial assets in excess of $64,160 are automatically regarded as producing more than the permitted $100 per fortnight ($2600 per annum) for single persons (as at June 1998).

Chapter 32—Dividend Reinvestment and Dividend Election Plans

But it is pretty to see what money will do
—Samuel Pepys

Background

3201 Many companies offer their shareholders an alternative to receiving dividends in cash, allowing the shareholders at their option to take up newly-created shares instead (or to take a mixture of cash and shares).

Advantages

3202 Such shares are generally offered at a discount of 5 to 10 per cent of the market price at the time, although some issues are made at no discount. No brokerage or stamp duty is incurred. Such issues tend to be attractive to both parties.

3203 The company gets money for expansion at a modest administrative cost and at the same time the company cements shareholder relations.

3204 Such semi-automatic capital raisings also reduce the need for conventional rights issue and thus avoid the pressure on market prices which such issues normally create.

3205 The shareholders have the opportunity to increase their investment in the company at a bargain price and without incurring expenses or hassle.

3206 The facility can also suit:

- Investors wishing periodically to make modest increases to their total portfolios in an economical way.

- Investors who prefer to build up existing holdings rather than increase the total number of companies in which they hold shares.

- Investors seeking to avoid handling small dividend payments.

- Investors not wishing to incur the normal bank charges and associated taxes for small receipts and disbursements.

- Persons setting up trust funds designed to accumulate income for some years—for example, until a child or grandchild reaches a certain age.

3207 Dividend reinvestment plans also flourish in some other countries. Australian investors with overseas shares can avoid the relatively high bank charges involved in converting dividend cheques in currencies other than Australian dollars by joining such plans.

Types of Plan

3208 There are two main versions of such plans:

- A "Dividend Reinvestment Plan" (DRP) involves the company declaring dividends in the normal way and then applying these dividends to the cost of the newly-issued shares.

- A "Dividend Election Plan" (DEP) involves the company issuing bonus shares out of a capital source (usually the share premium account) in lieu of declaring the normal dividends.

3209 There are some significant tax differences between these two versions—see below. For this reason many companies offer both types of plan to their shareholders and allow them to choose participation in either or both.

Nomenclature

3210 The nomenclature for dividend election plans which involve distributions out of capital sources is unfortunately far from uniform. Names such as "Bonus Share Plan" (BSP), "Bonus Option Plan" (BOP), "Dividend Option Plan" (DOP), "Dividend Bonus Plan" (DBP), "Stock Election Plan" (SEP) and "Share Investment Plan" (SIP) are all in use.

3211 On the other hand, the nomenclature for the true dividend reinvestment plans is fairly standard, although some variations such as "Dividend Investment Plan" (DIP) and "Dividend and Interest Reinvestment Plan" (DIRP) do exist.

Plans are Voluntary

3212 It should be emphasised that any such participation in a dividend plan is quite voluntary. Enrolment normally requires the signature of the shareholder on an appropriate application form.

3213 However, investors should not hesitate to join these plans:

- if they continue to like the idea of investing in the company concerned

- if participation suits their cash flow requirements and other circumstances, and

- if they do not object to the record keeping
  needed for capital gains tax purposes (see paras
  2940 to 2941).

3214 Shareholders can elect to participate in such plans for some or all of their holdings and can reverse or modify their elections (in respect of future distributions) at any time. However, it should be noted that an election once made normally remains in force until the shareholder takes a specific initiative to vary it. Shareholders need to watch the deadlines for joining or withdrawing from a plan. No action is required from shareholders receiving dividends in cash who wish to continue to receive their dividends thus.

Disadvantages

3215 One minor disadvantage of participation in dividend reinvestment used to be the creation of odd lots, but this concept has now been abolished.

3216 An ongoing negative is the need to keep detailed track of the issue dates and issue prices of dividend reinvestment plan shares to enable compliance with the capital gains tax legislation (see para. 2940).

3217 On a separate aspect, it is, of course, also possible that the market value of the new shares will fall below their issue price, notwithstanding the buffer often provided by any discount granted at the time of issue. But the risk of that happening is no different in character from that applying to the original holding.

3218 A further disadvantage can be the need for shareholders to write to the company if they ever change their minds and wish to withdraw from a plan.

Tax Consequences

3219 Another disadvantage in some cases and for some investors is that a non-cash dividend can result in a tax obligation without providing the necessary liquidity to meet it—especially in the case of unfranked dividends.

3220 It should be noted that all shares issued under dividend reinvestment plans are regarded as new shares purchased with the dividend proceeds. The dividends, despite not being received in cash, are thus taxed either as franked or as unfranked dividends in the usual way. Where franked they have the normal imputation credits associated with them.

3221 Appropriate franking details must be set out on the plan statements issued by the company concerned. On any subsequent disposal the plan shares would for capital gains tax purposes be treated as having been purchased at the time of the dividend distribution for a consideration equal to the dividend which was not taken in cash.

3222 By way of contrast, the bonus shares issued out of a share premium account (or share premium reserve) under a dividend election plan (however called) are treated in the same way as other bonus shares issued in this way (see paras 2844 to 2846) and in particular:

- They constitute exempt income at the time of receipt.

- If they relate to pre-1985 shares, then the bonus shares also acquire pre-1985 capital gains tax status.

- If they relate to post-1985 shares, then the bonus shares also acquire post-1985 capital gains tax status and the cost base applying to the original parcel is then regarded as the cost base of both the original and the bonus shares.

3223 The 5 to 10 per cent discount at which dividend reinvestment plan shares are usually issued does not constitute assessable income at the time of issue. However, it does result in a lower acquisition cost for the new shares and this will result in a correspondingly higher taxable capital gain on any subsequent disposal.

Social Security

3224 The dividend used to acquire new shares under a dividend reinvestment plan or a dividend election plan has no effect under the social security income test, as income is assessed under the extended deeming rules (see Chapter 31). However, the value of the additional shares would need to be counted in the usual way for asset test purposes.

Mechanical Aspects

3225 Companies with such plans normally send detailed statements to all participants in respect of each distribution and arrange for the listing of the new shares.

3226 Different companies adopt different rules in regard to aspects such as the treatment of the small cash balances left over after each transaction. Some companies carry them forward, others eliminate them by rounding up the number of shares allotted.

3227 Some companies allow their convertible noteholders to participate (by using the interest to acquire new ordinary shares, not new notes). This is a desirable extension of the plan concept. In some cases dividends on convertible or participating preference shares can be used to acquire more preference shares of the same class.

3228 Another important question is, "Will the plan still operate if the formula issue price drops to a figure below par"? As explained in para. 1246, the *Corporations Law* does not allow companies to issue shares at a discount on their face value and this feature is usually allowed for in the plan rules. However, for plan shares to be issued at above their then market value is not doing their recipients any favour and until foreshadowed changes in the law come into effect it would be much better to provide for the automatic suspension of the plan in such circumstances.

3229 The precise mechanism for setting the issue price (before applying the discount factor) also varies from company to company. Clearly, in conceptual terms an *ex dividend* price is needed (or an *ex dividend, ex rights, ex bonus* price if the same books closing date applies to rights and/or bonus entitlements also and the new shares do not rank for these issues).

3230 Common approaches are to use the weighted average market price either for the five days immediately following the books closing date for the dividend or the five days immediately preceding this date (when the shares are, of course, already being quoted on an ex dividend basis).

3231 From a practical point of view a market price set much closer to the actual dividend payment date would more nearly correspond to the scenario applying in the case of non-automatic reinvestments and would reduce the scope for significant variations in the market price of the shares between the two dates (in either direction). Falls in the market value in respect of new shares which were issued at a price not involving a discount do little for a company's goodwill.

Optional Share Purchase Plans

3232 Some companies—regrettably, not very many in Australia, although the pattern is different in some overseas countries—supplement their dividend reinvestment plans with optional share purchase (or "top up") plans, allowing the acquisition of further shares up to some limit free of brokerage and stamp duty. These plans are discussed in paras 776 to 777.

The Legislative Changes of Recent Years

3233 In combination the introduction of capital gains tax and the dividend imputation system significantly altered the rules of the game. Previously it made sense for companies to pay out as small a proportion of their profits as seemed prudent in terms of shareholder relations—this minimised the double taxation of income and in effect converted the retained profits into tax-free capital gains as the market value of shares rose to reflect this element.

3234 For post-1985 investors the position is now reversed—the distributed franked dividends confer tax advantages, while retained profits (whether revenue gains or capital gains) will in due course increase the capital gains tax burden of the shareholders.

3235 A major complicating factor is that some present shareholders owned their shares before the new capital gains tax rules came into force in 1985 and for them the arithmetic is completely different because of savings provisions in the law.

3236 Overseas investors are in a different category again, as they may not be able to utilise Australian imputation credits in the same way as local shareholders.

The Response of Companies

3237 One of the more pleasing developments of recent times has been the great flexibility shown by listed companies in adapting to the problem just described. Some companies refined their dividend reinvestment plans, even to the extent of offering Australian shareholders up to seven different choices, arising from different combinations of cash and/or new shares purchased with the dividends and/or exempt bonus shares. The latter in effect increased the pool of pre-1985 shares in circulation.

3238 Correspondingly, one of the less pleasing developments has been the action by the authorities in treating such arrangements as tax avoidance schemes and altering the rules to stop some of them being worthwhile with effect from 1 July 1990.

3239 The range of choices was no doubt confusing for elderly investors and it must have greatly complicated each recipients' record keeping. However, the companies' approach was very fair in that it, quite legally, minimised each investor's individual tax burden.

3240 Other variations to this theme had also been devised, including "compulsory" non-cash distributions, designed to use up franking credits without reducing the company's cash flow. This aspect is further discussed in paras 3250 to 3253.

3241 Some Australian companies had furthermore introduced special plans which enabled overseas investors to elect to exchange Australian dividend entitlements for dividends from associated companies offshore in a way which gave those shareholders benefits from the imputation rules in overseas countries, while at the same time enabling the company itself to preserve Australian franking credits to the maximum advantage of local shareholders.

3242 Other companies had given their investors a choice between lower dividends on a franked basis and higher dividends on an unfranked basis. Again, this provided an incentive to preserve the available franking credits for those shareholders who could derive the most benefit from them. Some overseas companies operating in Australia arranged for Australian shareholders to get franked dividends made possible by those companies' Australian tax payments. Most of these variations have, for all practical purposes, disappeared as from 1 July 1990.

Abandonment of Dividend Election Plans

3243 In the light of these tax changes some listed companies have rather foolishly withdrawn their dividend election plans (however called). Participation in such a plan is of considerable advantage to holders of pre-1985 shares, as the new shares issued under such a plan, unlike the new shares issued under a dividend reinvestment plan, remain outside the capital gains tax net for ever.

3244 Allowing participation in a dividend election plan is of no disadvantage whatsoever to other shareholders or to the company. It is true that the advantage prevailing until the law was changed—namely, the absence of debits to the Franking Account when bonus shares are issued in lieu of dividends—no longer applies, but this translates into a neutral situation, not a disadvantage. Debits to the Franking Account are now *the same* for all dividends irrespective of whether these are

- paid in cash

- used to acquire new shares under a conventional dividend reinvestment plan, or

- used to acquire new bonus shares under a dividend election plan.

3245 While as a matter of bookkeeping the issue of such bonus shares results in a debit to the share premium account there is a corresponding credit to the capital account, so that a company's total shareholders' funds are not affected by such entries.

3246 It is true that this can limit the ability of a company to make conventional bonus issues to all its shareholders in the future, but as these confer no real benefit on anybody this does not really matter. If a company ever feels that the market price of its shares is too high then it can split its shares instead.

What Should Shareholders Choose?

3247 For holders of pre-1985 shares an allotment of bonus shares is usually more attractive than participation in a dividend reinvestment plan, especially where dividends are not fully franked.

3248 For holders of post-1985 shares a sensible choice is less clear-cut. For these investors the bonus shares result in a worse capital gains tax liability on any subsequent disposal, as the cost of the new shares is effectively taken as nil instead of as a sum equal to the amount of the dividend (thus increasing the amount of the capital gain in due course). However, working in the opposite direction there is an immediate income tax saving in respect of any amount which would otherwise have been an unfranked dividend.

3249　Franked dividends for holders of both pre-1985 and post-1985 shares can result in either a small tax liability or a small tax rebate, depending on the investor's marginal tax rate relative to the rate of company tax.

"Compulsory" Non-cash Distributions

3250　The tax effect of "compulsory" non-cash franked dividend reinvestment distributions on shareholders depends on their particular capital gains tax status, as well as on the aspect mentioned in the previous paragraph.

3251　Holders of pre-1985 shares would be better off with a system involving higher retained profits, as this would almost certainly boost the market price of their existing shares without any capital gains tax detriment.

3252　However, holders of post-1985 shares, on balance, become better off by virtue of such distributions, because the cost price of their holdings becomes increased by the amount of the dividend, thus ultimately reducing their CGT burden, particularly when allowance is made for indexation (but, of course, only if and when they actually sell and only then if they realise a sufficiently large profit).

3253　The non-tax effect of such "compulsory" distributions is neutral, as the equity of each shareholder remains the same. To that extent they have a similar effect to a share split.

Underwriting

3254　Some companies with a need for more capital would prefer it if all their shareholders participated in their dividend reinvestment plans. As this is not really practicable they accordingly make arrangements with an underwriter for the placement of any shares which would have been available to those of their shareholders as elected not to participate in the plan.

3255　This device retains the voluntary nature of the plan for individual investors while simultaneously preserving the company's cash flow. Its availability is a useful encouragement to a high pay-out ratio (see para. 928).

Suspension of Plans

3256 Some companies choose to temporarily suspend the operation of their dividend reinvestment plans (as they are entitled to under their rules) during times when they have no need for any additional capital.

3257 Of course, even companies with a great need for extra capital should still suspend their plans in some circumstances—as explained in para. 3228.

Comparison with Rights Issues

3258 Investors are sometimes faced with the possibility of taking up shares in a dividend reinvestment plan at a modest discount on the market price at the time, while simultaneously being presented with the opportunity to subscribe for new shares in a rights issue being made at a much lower price.

3259 In such cases the "best value for money" will normally be the plan shares, notwithstanding their seemingly higher issue price.

3260 This comes about because the rights themselves will usually have a market value (see para. 714), so that effectively the price of the new shares will be the sum of the application money being paid to the company and the value of the rights foregone by virtue of their being exercised instead of being sold on the stock exchange. This sum will in practice be close to (and in theory identical with) the *full* "ex rights, ex dividend" market price of the old shares and thus higher than that price less the usual plan discount.

Miscellaneous

3261 Companies with dividend reinvestment and/or dividend election plans should always take steps to assist their shareholders, on taking up rights or exercising options, to enrol their new shares in the plans (where their earlier enrolment application was confined to shares in existence at the time and to plan shares arising out of such holdings).

3262 Having regard to the data needed for capital gains tax calculations, it would also be helpful if each company which currently has, or which has ever had, a dividend reinvestment plan included with its plan statements and/or published in its annual reports, a list of the dates of issue of all plan shares since commencement of the plan, together with their respective issue prices and the indexation factors for the quarters concerned. Such conveniently-located information would make the task of preparing tax returns when plan shares are sold much easier.

3263 Shareholders enrolled in dividend reinvestment plans seeking to sell their entire holdings need to take care when placing selling orders on an ex dividend basis, as otherwise their orders might overlook the small number of additional shares to which they are becoming entitled.

3264 An investor who is enrolled in a dividend reinvestment plan for some but not all of his shares and who sells some but not all of his total holdings will have the extent of his future participation in the plan governed by automatic provisions in the plan rules. If these do not suit his purpose then he needs to send a variation form to the company setting out his revised wishes.

3265 It should be noted that the customary five-day window for setting issue prices for plan shares can encourage price manipulation. For example, institutions enrolled in such plans and thus with a vested interest in a low price can easily sell or simply refrain from placing purchase orders during the relevant period, thus allowing the market price for the existing shares to become lower than it otherwise would have been.

3266 Investors should regard the existence of a plan as a fringe benefit when acquiring shares, rather than as a prime motive for choosing a particular company.

3267 Some companies with dividend reinvestment plans also engage in buy-backs (see Chapter 40). To some extent this is contradictory, but the plan may exist more as a deliberate shareholder benefit than as a device to raise fresh capital.

3268 In fact, some companies set out to buy back roughly the same number of shares as are being allotted through the plan each six months, so as not to water their total issued capital and lower their earnings per share.

Chapter 33—Continuous Disclosure

Traditionally, most of Australia's imports
come from overseas
—Former Australian Minister, Kep Enderby

Background

3301 For people who have always put their savings into a bank, building society or credit union the thought of using the stock exchange and actually buying ordinary shares for the first time can be quite dramatic. However, the float of Commonwealth Bank of Australia shares in 1991 brought many new investors onto the scene and further privatisation issues since then and the demutualisation of several life offices has extended this pattern.

3302 At the same time some of Australia's major corporate collapses have become household words—everybody has heard of Alan Bond and Christopher Skase, of John Spalvins and Bob Ansett. Investors in companies headed by such figures have collectively lost many billions of dollars.

3303 It is therefore understandable that investors are now insisting that something should be done to stop recurrences of such disasters. As discussed below, the Australian Stock Exchange has recently revised its listing rules, but it can be stated at the outset that this by itself will not and cannot solve all the problems.

3304 For one thing, some of the more spectacular disasters hitting investors' pockets in recent years have not even involved listed companies—for example, Pyramid (a building society), OST (a friendly society), Occidental and Regal (two life offices) and Estate Mortgage (an unlisted unit trust).

3305 For another, the task of prosecuting corporate criminals quite properly belongs to public bodies such as the Australian Securities Commission, the Director of Public Prosecutions and the police—not to a private organisation such as the Australian Stock Exchange.

3306 Apart from that, not all investor losses are the result of criminal or even unethical behaviour by company directors. Many are the result of management decisions made in good faith, of economic conditions unexpectedly changed or of measures imposed for policy reasons by governments.

3307 Investing in companies from its very nature involves investors undertaking certain commercial risks in return for the opportunity to join in an enterprise which they hope will make profits in due course.

3308 The function of the stock exchange is to provide and run a market place for investors in ordinary shares and in certain other securities. The aim of the listing rules is to provide a mechanism for fair dealings, not to duplicate the *Corporations Law* or accounting standards. In part, this involves ensuring that investors are fully informed at all times. Many of the more important changes to the listing rules in recent times have been directed toward that key objective.

The Continuous Disclosure Rule

3309 To illustrate, after much research and public discussion the Australian Stock Exchange has brought in a revised listing rule, effective from 1 January 1992, which requires all companies traded on the exchange to report relevant data on a basis which is usually referred to as "continuous disclosure".

3310 The new wording of Listing Rule 3A(1) is based in part on the prospectus provisions in Section 1022 of the *Corporations Law*, which came into force exactly one year earlier and which, of course, apply only to new capital raisings on a one-off basis.

3311 Listed companies now have to "immediately notify the exchange" of (and thus effectively publish to the world) any information in their possession *at any time* which is likely to materially affect the price of their securities or which is necessary in order to avoid the establishment or continuation of a false market in those securities.

3312 Any information which investors or their professional advisers "would reasonably require" must be disclosed. This very wide general wording would appear to cover just about everything.

3313 But in order to make doubly sure that not even inexperienced company directors or managements can possibly misunderstand their obligations, the rule also refers specifically to the making of an informed assessment of a company's assets, liabilities, profits and losses, as well as of its current financial position and future prospects.

3314 The effect of this significant provision on investors requires some comment. Obviously, better information will allow individuals and institutions to make sounder investment decisions. However, it should be borne in mind that fuller and earlier disclosure will not in itself affect the underlying profitability or performance of a company or a group.

3315 It is, of course, true that if an adverse change in fortune is revealed in, say, May, rather than in the following August, then this no doubt will help those investors who might have bought shares at high prices during these three months whilst ignorant of the true position.

3316 But the benefit to them will be exactly balanced by the detriment to those shareholders who thus lost the opportunity to sell at those prices. The total position of all market participants in this *zero sum game* will naturally remain unchanged.

3317 This is not to say that this revision to the listing rules is not worthwhile:

- The need for prompter disclosure can act as a brake on reckless corporate activities or expansion and may also act as a spur to greater efficiency.

- The earlier cessation of trading by a failing enterprise which the more timely revelation of its near insolvency induces could prevent it from accumulating yet further losses. To that extent the revised rule may well help to contain the size of a disaster, thus benefiting lenders, customers and employees, as well as investors.

- Even short of actual failure, early disclosure of problems, by causing a fall in the market value of a company's ordinary shares, will in practice stop it from raising—and thus putting at undue risk—further equity capital, whether in the form of placements or proportionate rights issues or through dividend reinvestment plans.

3318 Unrealistically high market values have on occasions in the past prejudiced lenders to associates of a company who have pledged its shares by way of security under loan agreements requiring "topping up" if the margin in asset values drops too much.

3319 The new rule may also be useful in other ways. The earlier flow of information to the market will no doubt assist security analysts to make better forecasts and it will probably also result in less violent price fluctuations.

3320 It may in addition help market participants to reassess other listed stocks. It will certainly reduce the scope for insider trading. And, importantly, it will do no harm to Australia's credibility overseas.

3321 However, as indicated above, more frequent reporting cannot directly affect a company's actual profits or losses. If, for example, a company through poor management misreads its market or underestimates the skills of its competitors or gets its timing wrong—or if the government of the day increases taxes or passes undesired legislation —then even a previously highly profitable company can start to incur losses.

3322 Some events—such as the 1987 stockmarket crash, the 1990-91 Gulf war or the 1997 Asian melt—down cannot easily be foreseen. The severity or duration of recessions or changes to interest rate levels or exchange rates can also impact on companies.

3323 Companies can also lose money very quickly through dishonesty—as when their directors divert public company income or assets into private company pockets.

3324 Sometimes a company falls into the trap of thinking that distant fields look greener and attempts to diversify into an unrelated industry (for example, a property developer acquiring television interests). Or it may seek to expand into geographical areas in which it has no experience. Many Australian companies have had their fingers burnt in the tough world of North America.

3325 Another classic way of losing money is to pay too much for assets. If a company compounds the problem by using borrowed funds in order to buy such assets then the risk of being wiped out increases quite dramatically. For example, if assets costing $100 million are purchased with the help of $60 million in loan funds—a seemingly quite conservative ratio—then the halving of the gross asset value would turn a $40 million net asset into a $10 million net liability.

3326 It must also be obvious that corporate assets which do not earn their keep will not make shareholders wealthy.

3327 One final point should be made in regard to all this. In times of high inflation all balance sheets prepared on traditional lines have very serious limitations. Current Cost Accounting is not a popular concept at the moment and it is not normally used in Australia. To some extent this is because the taxation legislation for the most part ignores inflation—but managements also are reluctant to face up to the unpleasant fact that profits in dollar terms may be disguising losses in real terms. The rule requiring continuous disclosure in no way addresses this vital issue.

Other Developments

3328 The setting up of a single national exchange in 1987 to replace the six separate capital city stock exchanges which dated back from the last century has helped to increase the overall protection for shareholders—for example, in regard to market surveillance.

3329 The listing rules have also been tightened so as to require fuller half-yearly and preliminary final reports and better details regarding "conflict of interest" items such as management fees and loans to directors.

3330 Better disclosure of significant changes to accounting policies is also now being required.

3331 Furthermore, in certain circumstances—see also Chapter 34—the listing rules require advance approval of a transaction by a company's shareholders, with the notice of meeting being accompanied by copies of reports, valuations and other material from independent qualified persons, to enable shareholders to judge whether the proposed transaction is really in their best interest.

3332 Still further strengthening of the listing rules to reflect the best international practice can be expected over the next few years.

Electronic Company Announcements

3333 To complement the above-mentioned approach the stock exchange has introduced an "Electronic Company Announcements System" (ECAS). Under this system listed companies are in effect expected to send their official announcements to the exchange in electronic form, speeding up the process greatly and eliminating the possibility of error in transcribing hard copy into the stock exchange computer database, as was the position under the old system.

3334 Naturally, a number of precautions are being built into the ECAS software and procedures in order to provide safeguards against fraudulent or hoax messages.

Chapter 34—Experts' Reports

He knows so little and knows it so fluently
—Ellen Glasgow

Background

3401 Investors on the stock exchange entrust the running of the companies in which they hold shares to their respective boards of directors. The law imposes some general obligations on the directors of all companies, but apart from that does not normally interfere.

3402 Thus, for example, Section 232 of the *Corporations Law*, which is mentioned in para. 1225, reads in part as follows:

"An officer" (a term which here includes directors as well as executives)" shall at all times act honestly in the exercise of his or her powers and the discharge of the duties of his or her office ... An officer ... shall at all times exercise a reasonable degree of care and diligence in the exercise of his or her powers and the discharge of his or her duties".

3403 In theory, investors on the stock exchange could hardly want any greater protection of shareholders' rights and interests than these plain and seemingly unambiguous words provide.

Conflicts of Interest

3404 In this approach the drafters of the legislation appear to have made several different assumptions, such as:

- that the directors will themselves normally be shareholders

- that therefore their interests will be broadly the same as those of other shareholders

- that, as shareholders at an annual meeting have chosen certain persons to be their directors, such persons must have the full trust and confidence of the shareholders

- that, if the shareholders are not satisfied with the performance of their directors, then they will replace them at a shareholders' meeting

- that, if shareholders want to impose any specific conditions on their directors, then they can do so through the company's articles of association.

3405 As these implicit assumptions have some obvious limitations the law goes on to deal with some special situations of potential conflict of interest. For example, Section 648(1) of the

Corporations Law deals with a takeover bid by one company for another where these have one or more common directors or where the bidding company is deemed by virtue of a 30 per cent shareholding to already be in effective control of the target company.

3406 Again, Section 703 deals with the mopping-up on equitable terms of options and convertible notes after a bidder has acquired a company's ordinary shares.

3407 The approach which legislators have adopted in such circumstances is to require that investors be given appropriate information to allow them to make informed judgements. In particular, the law prescribes that each shareholder be sent a copy of a report by an independent expert.

Independence

3408 In this connection "independent" means not having an association with any of the companies or other parties involved and "expert" means holding qualifications and a reputation giving authority to any statements made by that person when acting in a professional capacity. Reports are often prepared by bodies such as:

- merchant banks
- major accountancy firms
- corporate advisory services of stockbrokers.

3409 In the case of mining or property companies, specialist groups practising in those areas of expertise would normally be used. For purely legal issues, firms of solicitors would naturally be engaged.

3410 If a target company obtains two or more reports a copy of each has to be provided. This requirement is designed to ensure that boards do not "shop around" until they get a report which suits their particular purposes.

3411 The former National Companies and Securities Commission issued a number of releases setting out its views on aspects of the relevant legislation. For example, in Release 102 the Commission set out its philosophy in the following terms:

"The Commission expects market participants and company managements to seek maximum rather than minimum probity in takeovers. The Commission would be concerned if mere technical compliance with the legislation, whether concerning expert reports or any other matter, were to impair the market system or result in diminishing public expectations of corporate accountability."

3412 The legislation requires the expert to say whether the particular offer being reported on is "fair and reasonable" and to set out the reasons for his opinion. While lay readers of such reports might have thought that "fair and reasonable" was a compound term, in fact these two elements need to be examined separately.

3413 Fairness refers to the relationship between the takeover consideration and the value, on various alternative bases, of the underlying assets. Reasonableness refers to other factors of relevance to investors, such as the existence of controlling interests and the liquidity or otherwise of holdings on the stock exchange.

Help for Investors

3414 Independent reports are meant to help investors both directly and indirectly.

3415 On the direct side, shareholders will obviously wish to look closely both at the recommendations and at the reasoning leading to those conclusions, even if the shareholders lack the time and patience to read every word of a lengthy report. They should also focus on aspects of particular relevance to them—for example, tax considerations (not all investors may be affected in the same way) and short-term versus long-term considerations.

3416 Each shareholder must make up his own mind—both the advice of disinterested experts and the views of interested parties such as bidders and incumbent directors should be studied. However, ultimately investors themselves must make the actual decisions.

3417 On the indirect side, shareholders benefit from the creation of a better-informed market (reducing the chance that they will be ripped off) and from the fact that any views formed by security analysts engaged by their own stockbrokers and personal advisers will be more soundly based.

3418 The need for independent reports is probably also a useful spur to keeping boards and managements honest—although it has to be remembered that if there is outright fraud then no system of experts or auditors can provide a foolproof remedy in all cases.

3419   In recent times small shareholders have criticised some independent reports for their length, complexity and cost, while institutional investors and regulatory authorities have been more concerned at a perceived lack of quality. A few reports have been subject to judicial review and have been criticised by the courts in regard to questions of true independence and unprofessional procedures. The experience gained from some of these cases has led to the promulgation of tighter guidelines.

3420   Investors are sometimes suspicious of the bona fides of a report because it has been paid for by an interested party. However, an expert subject to a professional code of conduct would normally give objective advice regardless of who was meeting the costs. Notwithstanding that general proposition, it would not be appropriate for the size of the fee to be dependent on the outcome of the matter; the use of a *success fee* is incompatible with the concept of independence.

3421   Of course, not all expert reports provided to shareholders are meant to be *independent* reports. This aspect will be made plain by the document itself—for example, by the use of words such as:

"This report has been prepared by us in our capacity as corporate advisers to ABC Limited. It has not been prepared pursuant to the requirements of Section 000 of the *Corporations Law*."

The size of any success fee payable to the expert should be disclosed. The facts and arguments in such reports should still be given appropriate weight by readers.

Other Aspects

3422   Apart from their use in takeover situations, a need for independent expert reports can also arise under other statutory provisions and under certain stock exchange listing rules—for example:

- Implicitly, under Section 206E(2) of the *Corporations Law*, in relation to buy-backs by companies of their own shares (see Chapter 40).

- Implicitly, under Section 412, in respect of schemes of arrangement involving connected parties.

- Explicitly, under Listing Rule 3J(3), when assets are acquired from or disposed of to associated parties.

- Implicitly, under Listing Rule 3S, when a company proposes to change the nature of its activities in a significant way.

- In the case of mining exploration companies seeking listing, under Listing Rule 1A(3)(f).

- In the case of listed stockbroking companies making non-proportional share issues, under Listing Rule 3E(24).

3423 Experts' reports can also be included in prospectuses, in accordance with the general requirements for the disclosure of all information which investors might reasonably require.

3424 Such reports are sometimes also commissioned on a voluntary basis—for example, where directors (or trustees, in the case of unit trusts) wish to follow the spirit of the law in circumstances which are not directly covered.

Chapter 35—The Mathematics of Dividend Imputation

'Tis money that begets money
—Thomas Fuller

Background

3501 The dividend imputation system is explained in paras 2833 to 2843. It has great relevance to investors, particularly retired persons and other income-conscious savers, but it is unfortunately not widely understood by many of the people who could benefit from it.

3502 For example, a typical fixed interest investor with other income may not realise that an 8 per cent dividend yield from a share paying fully franked dividends is 25 per cent more valuable to him on an "after tax" basis than a higher-sounding 10 per cent interest rate.

3503 On the other hand, some brokers and investment advisers are recommending ordinary shares in companies which are paying wholly or mainly franked dividends on the basis that these are virtually tax-free to investors or that they can even lead to negative amounts of tax.

3504 Statements on these lines, while technically correct, are actually slightly misleading, because they ignore the fact that in practice the prices of shares which are listed on the stock exchange already to some extent reflect the country's existing tax regime.

3505 This is not to say that such shares might not be well worth buying in their own right, in terms of their expected returns and/or growth prospects. However, investors should not delude themselves that they are always getting something for nothing by virtue of the imputation system.

Dividend Yields and Imputation

3506 Dividend yields in general are explained in paras 930 to 935.

3507 As mentioned in para. 2843, for all practical purposes a franked dividend of $64 is as valuable to a taxpaying shareholder as an unfranked dividend of $100. This aspect needs to be borne in mind when comparing dividend yields from companies which are paying fully franked dividends with dividend yields from companies which are paying only unfranked dividends—see para. 3511.

3508 It should, furthermore, be noted that the proportion of the total dividend which any particular company can pay out as a franked dividend may vary from year to year.

3509 In practice this phenomenon can pose some difficult problems for taxpayers who wish to lodge provisional tax variation applications (see para. 2826), as investors naturally have no control over the profits of companies in which they hold shares or over their dividend payout and franking ratios (see paras 2823 to 2828).

3510 Before imputation was introduced the customary way of quoting dividend yields was to divide the full year dividend in cents per share by the market price in cents per share. The result, expressed as a percentage, was then perfectly comparable with the yields from other forms of investment.

3511 This is no longer true in all cases. To make yields from shares paying fully franked dividends comparable on an "after tax" basis with returns from:

- shares paying unfranked dividends

- deposits or securities paying interest

- property investments paying rent

it is necessary to multiply the yield as calculated in the previous paragraph by 100/64, to reflect the current 36 per cent company tax rate. The term "grossing-up" is often used in this context, when the face value of a franked dividend is multiplied by 100/64 (in other words, by 1.5625).

3512 In the case of partly franked dividends the grossing-up process should naturally be applied only to the franked portion of the dividend.

Earnings Yields and Imputation

3513 Earnings yields in general are explained in paras 920 to 925.

3514 The "earnings yield" of a share indicates what the return (the dividend yield) from an investment in ordinary shares would be if all earnings (net of preference dividends) were paid out as ordinary dividends. It is calculated by dividing the earnings in cents per share in a full year by the market price in cents per share, again expressed as a percentage.

3515 It should be noted that the earnings yield multiplied by the price earnings ratio always equals 100.

3516 The earnings yield is an important measure of the performance of the company to an investor. Earnings yields can be compared with interest rate levels generally. The earnings yield of a particular share—subject, however, to the comments below—is a much more useful yardstick than the dividend yield discussed in paras 3506 to 3512 which—because it is a function of the dividend payout ratio—ignores the fact that ordinary shareholders benefit from a company's earnings irrespective of whether these are distributed or not.

3517 Before imputation was introduced earnings per share figures and earnings yields on shares (and price earnings ratios) were, very logically, based on a company's earnings net of company tax. Earnings yields calculated in this way represented the return to the investor before deducting his own personal income tax—as in the case of yields from fixed interest securities or property investments.

3518 Most published earnings yields and price earnings ratios in newspapers and stockbrokers' circulars are still calculated in this traditional way.

3519 However, this approach is no longer logical. For example, if a company which operates solely in Australia retained none of its earnings in the business, then the effect on its shareholders collectively would be that they would receive by way of dividends and associated imputation credits the *whole* of the company's gross profit-in other words, the earnings *before* rather than *after* the deduction of company tax.

3520 On distribution each shareholder's portion of this would effectively be subject to personal tax at his marginal tax rate—see para. 2818. To be strictly comparable with yields from fixed interest securities or property investments all earnings per share figures and the earnings yields derived from them should now be based on company profits *before* tax.

3521 The above theory implies that the shareholder concerned is able to use the imputation credits. Persons in respect of whom this assumption does not hold would rarely be investors in such shares and their activity would be most unlikely to affect the market overall.

3522 In the case of companies which receive franked dividends from other companies such calculations should in fact be based on the sum of the company's profits *before* tax and the imputation credits attached to the dividends which the company received and included in those profits.

3523 In the case of companies with overseas operations the above approach needs some modification. The effective entitlement of the shareholders collectively (see para. 3519) is the gross profit figure reduced by any taxes paid to overseas governments and this latter amount, rather than the total gross profit, needs to be employed in the calculations.

Dividend Cover and Imputation

3524 As indicated in para. 927, the "dividend cover" of a share is a yardstick which gives an indication as to how secure the continued payment of a company's rate of dividend might be.

3525 For the reasons discussed above, the dividend cover for ordinary shares should no longer be calculated in the traditional manner by simply dividing a company's profits after tax (net of preference dividends, if any) by its total ordinary dividend payout for the full year.

3526 The correct method now involves dividing the sum of the company's profits before tax and any imputation credits attached to the dividends which it received (net of its own grossed-up preference dividends, if any) by the sum of its total ordinary dividend payout for the full year and any imputation credits attached to the ordinary dividends which it paid.

3527 In the case of companies with dividend election plans (see Chapter 32) a further adjustment should be made. The cash equivalent of the bonus shares should be treated as part of the dividend payout for purposes of the above calculation, despite this amount not being debited to the profit and loss account. In other words, regard should be had to economic realities rather than to accounting conventions, legal fictions or taxation concepts. Such an approach would also be consistent with the pre-imputation concept of looking at dividend cover as the ratio of earnings per share to dividends per share.

Nomenclature

3528 The nomenclature adopted by companies when referring to imputation credits on cheque butts, dividend reinvestment plan statements and the like is unfortunately anything but uniform.

3529 The following are among the terms in use—some of them ungrammatical, but all really meaning exactly the same thing:

- Franked Credit.

- Franking Credit.
- Imputation Credit.
- Imputation Tax Credit.
- Imputed Credit.
- Tax Credit.

3530 The most common usage by the Australian Taxation Office is "Imputation Credit" when considering assessable income and "Franking Rebate" when working out tax. In most cases these two amounts will be the same, but the aggregate of rebates of all kinds cannot as a matter of law exceed the total pre-rebate amount of tax. On occasions the ATO uses other combinations of words—for example, "Imputation Rebate".

Miscellaneous

3531 If an investor with a 48.5 per cent marginal tax rate buys a fixed interest security yielding, say, 8 per cent, then that is worth 4.12 per cent net to him. If he buys ordinary shares with a franked dividend yield of 6.4 per cent (that is, 10.0 per cent on a "grossed-up" basis), then that is worth 5.15 per cent net to him. Thus the share has to have only about 1 per cent per annum capital growth for it to be a better investment than the fixed interest security.

3532 The current 36 per cent company tax rate has applied since 1 July 1995. Franking credits under this rate are known as "Class C". (Class A" involved a 39 per cent rate. "Class B" involved a 33 per cent rate.)

Chpater 36—Share Issues to Employees

If Harold Wilson ever went to school without any
boots, it was merely because he was too big for them
—Harold Macmillan, discussing
a political opponent

Background

3601 Employees sometimes use the stock exchange in order to buy shares in the company which employs them (or the parent company of their group), possibly in the belief that their greater knowledge of the company or the industry enables them to spot bargains more readily than outsiders.

Employee Share Schemes

3602 Apart from that, some listed companies have formal schemes in place which enable their employees (or those in associated entities) to take up newly-created shares at a discount to the market price (up to some limit, possibly dependant on wages and/or length of service).

3603 Sometimes the shares in such special schemes are contributing shares, paid up to only one cent or some such, possibly on the basis that dividends will be applied towards paying up further amounts. Alternatively, the company may offer interest-free or low interest loans to employees taking up fully-paid scheme shares. Similar schemes involving options also exist. There may be rules limiting the voting power of scheme shares and/or restricting their disposal.

3604 The theory underlying such arrangements is:

- that they give the recipients a positive incentive to increase their company's profitability

- that they help to create a greater awareness of the company's operations

- that they can keep wage costs at lower levels than would otherwise be the case

- that they are good for morale

- that they are another form of superannuation

- that they help to attract and retain key staff.

3605 However, there are some problems with this:

- Share prices can move up for reasons quite unconnected with employee performance—lower interest rates, tax reductions, creative accounting, and so on. This can result in large undeserved windfall gains.

- Share prices can also move down for reasons unconnected with employee performance-mistakes
at board level, interest rate changes, new taxes,
government intervention, and so on. In such an
event all shares offered to employees in earlier
times at higher prices—even if they represented
good value at the time-may result in a negative
reaction. Particular embarrassment can arise if
the outstanding balance of loans used to make
share purchases exceeds the current market
value of the relevant shares.

3606 If things go wrong in a more serious way then some employees
may well lose both their jobs and a major portion of their life
savings —in the form of shares in the employing company—at
the same time and from substantially the same set of circumstances.

3607 In the case of partly-paid shares the possibility can even arise
that a liquidator will seek to enforce calls involving large sums
in respect of shares which at that stage are completely worthless.

3608 Apart from those aspects, serious conflicts can arise. The
interests of outside shareholders and employees do not always
coincide.

3609 The statutory prohibitions on insider trading pose another
disadvantage, severely restricting the ability of employees—
especially senior executives—to sell any shares owned by
them at times of their own choosing, even if those shares are
held by them unconditionally and the motive for disposing of
them is unconnected with the performance of the company.

Superannuation Fund Placements

3610 There are also other variations to the general theme described
above. A relatively common one involves placements at a very
favourable price made to the trustees of a staff superannuation
fund, giving rise to most of the problems referred to above. In
addition, conflicts of interest can occur in the event of a
takeover offer being subsequently received.

Distortions to the Published Accounts

3611 From the perspective of non-employee shareholders, such issues to employees or superannuation funds on special terms can amount to an unwarranted watering of capital. The discount usually constitutes a hidden cost not reflected in the profit and loss account, and one which, unlike other labour costs—such as those for wages, bonuses or conventional superannuation contributions—is not even tax deductible.

Taxation Aspects

3612 If shares under an employee share acquisition scheme are issued at a discount on the market price, then the amount of that discount constitutes assessable income to the employee at the time of issue. Correspondingly, it is not subject to fringe benefits tax (FBT) in the hands of the employer.

3613 For capital gains tax purposes the cost of the shares is then taken, again quite consistently, as the market price at the time of issue and not the lower actual subscription price.

Company Performance

3614 It is sometimes suggested that companies with employee share schemes perform better than companies without them. This may well be so, but which is cause and which is effect?

3615 It is likely that a company which is progressive and well managed will do well *and* will bring in such a scheme. Furthermore, a company which is already performing well can more readily afford to be generous to its employees.

Chapter 37—Investment under a Goods and Services Tax

Judgement is forced upon us by experience
—Samuel Johnson

Background

3701 At the time of writing the parties constituting the Federal Government, the Liberal and National Coalition Parties, have promised to reform the taxation system if they are re-elected. The main change will involve a Goods and Services Tax (GST).

3702 This chapter offers brief comments on some aspects of such a proposal which are of particular interest to investors.

Stock Exchange and other Investment Transactions

3703 The 15 per cent or so levy will not apply to any basic sums being invested or disinvested, or presumably to interest or dividends either paid or received.

3704 However, it will catch all associated expenses whether of a capital or a revenue nature—for example:

- brokerage
- fees to investment advisers
- fees to accountants
- fees to solicitors
- fees to tax agents
- fees to valuers
- bank charges
- loan charges
- subscriptions to financial journals.

3705 There may be one important exception to this—government charges will probably not give rise to a "tax on a tax". If so, then this would exempt some items of relevance to investors—for example:

- stamp duty
- financial institutions duty (FID)
- debits tax.

The Economy

3706 Of greater relevance to investors than the effect on their own transaction costs is the question of how the economy will perform under the GST regime.

3707 If the economy at large booms as a result of the changes, then company profits will rise, boosting returns from shares and from managed investments based on shares. However, the operative word is "if".

3708 Again, interest rates may rise in line with an increased demand for borrowed funds, thus benefiting new fixed interest savers (whether investing directly or through unit trusts or insurance bonds). However, existing investors will naturally see the capital values of long—dated securities and shares fall as interest rates rise.

3709 Because there is to be no phasing—in period for a vast range of new measures involving massive changes, the task of predicting the future becomes much more difficult both for investors and for government planners. The population may well react to the reform package in strange and unexpected ways.

3710 On a separate aspect, there will undoubtedly be some minor chaos during the transition period. In the six months or so leading up to G-day many goods will probably disappear from shelves as hoarding at pre-GST prices takes place. This will neither help consumers nor boost business confidence.

Costs of Collection

3711 There will also be a further factor lifting prices in the future, quite apart from the tax itself. The enormous private sector administrative cost burden of complying with the GST legislation will inevitably have to be passed on to consumers and/or shareholders.

3712 Even allowing for computers, sales tax returns from about 100,000 wholesale outlets under the present regime will be replaced by GST returns from 10 times as many retail outlets. Each ultimate sale will need to be processed three or four times en route. Somebody will have to pay for all this additional paperwork or its electronic equivalent.

Income Tax

3713 Income tax rates may fall if a GST at a high enough rate is introduced. However, it is more likely that a GST will replace only some existing indirect taxes.

3714 It is also noteworthy that the Coalition has shied away from guaranteeing automatic indexation adjustments to the income tax scale in the future.

3715 In the absence of this the customary bracket creep will clearly continue and the credibility of any income tax reductions must be in considerable doubt.

3716 It has to be remembered that it was the Fraser Government which abolished the indexation provisions in the income tax legislation.

3717 It also seems likely that the absurd Medicare levy, which has little connection with actual health costs, is to be continued.

Capital Gains Tax

3718 The Coalition has failed to consider some long overdue reforms to another form of tax which is very relevant to all investors—namely, capital gains tax.

3719 For example:

- Realised capital losses should be subject to indexation in the same way as realised capital gains.

- A loss realised in a financial year later than that involving a previously taxed gain should be capable of being retrospectively offset against that gain.

- Shares becoming worthless should more readily be treatable as disposals.

- Capital losses brought forward and not used up at a person's death should be capable of being transferred to beneficiaries of the estate.

- Interspousal transfers of assets should not be regarded as disposals.

- Some switches of investments should be subject to rollover relief, particularly in connection with takeovers at large and even more so when compulsory acquisition occurs.

Effect on Existing Savers

3720 If Australia moves to a broad-based consumption tax system, even in conjunction with lower income tax, then there could well be some significant disadvantages for those people who are already retired or near retirement at the time of the change.

3721 These persons will have been exposed to the present high income tax regime whilst still earning money, only to be subjected to a high expenditure tax when—in old age—they come to spend the savings which they had built up in earlier years out of the net income remaining after income tax has been levied.

3722 Unlike many other people who will get long-term benefit from the reforms, the generation of retired persons at the start of the new system will inevitably experience the worst of both worlds.

3723 On G—day the purchasing power of their accumulated savings will fall dramatically, as prices rise to reflect the 15 per cent or so GST.

3724 It is true that on average prices will not rise by the full 15 per cent, because of the elimination of the wholesale sales tax, the State payroll tax and some other imposts, and because competition will keep shopkeepers on their mettle. But clearly each dollar of past savings will buy less than it used to.

3725 To some extent this will be a one-off effect, although some "second round" price rises will filter through the system for another year or so. However, savers have always lived with the gradual reduction in the purchasing power of their money due to creeping inflation. Viewed objectively, a single price rise of, say, 8 per cent—while clearly unpleasant—is not going to be all that different from the less dramatic series of price rises totalling 8 per cent over a 12—month period which was often experienced in the past.

3726 The G-day effect on prices needs to be distinguished from the underlying inflation trend, which depends on other factors, such as wage movements, productivity improvements and changes to the exchange rate or monetary policy.

Indexed Bonds

3727 Because a GST will feed into the Consumer Price Index indexed bonds will increase in value.

Conclusion

3728 Finally, a general comment. There is a natural inclination for commentators to compare and contrast the pre-GST and post-GST positions of various individuals and to judge the Coalition package according to the winners and losers on this basis. However, such a yardstick implies that the present distribution of wealth and incomes and the current tax and social security systems which are used in this comparison are ideal.

3729 Such an assumption is, of course, quite unwarranted. No meaningful reform of the system can possibly leave everyone in exactly the same net position as before.

Chapter 38—The Future

*You want to know a sure way to lose money? Buy
what's popular and don't know
what you are investing in.*
—Marty Whitman

Background

3801 The stock exchange, the securities industry and the system under which the share market operates in Australia are all likely to experience some very dramatic changes over the next few years. As indicated in the Preface, to some extent this period of change has already started. However, those who think that the last few years have involved a fair pace of change will find that only the surface has been scratched so far and that the rate of evolution will, if anything, accelerate.

3802 This chapter sets out to describe a possible scenario for the remainder of the second millennium and the start of the third. It does not attempt to forecast movements in share prices or the likely performances of individual companies or industries, but rather some of the more interesting changes which *may* occur in regard to the environment and the institutional arrangements.

Innovative Legislation

3803 Further innovative legislation can be expected—innovative at least in the Australian context, even if some of the ideas are well known overseas.

3804 Further reforms will make the principle of "one share, one vote" which was mentioned in para. 1232 compulsory at all shareholder meetings and will require proportional representation to be used for the election of company directors. (Proportional representation is the method used for electing the Australian Senate.)

3805 This system will automatically ensure that groups of small shareholders with common interests—as well as large investors who build up significant stakes in companies—could obtain, as an entitlement, board seats based on the size of their respective holdings, should they so wish.

3806 Of course, some such persons might not desire involvement as members of the board, either because of potential conflicts of interest or because the "insider trading" legislation would unduly reduce their freedom to buy and sell shares in the company concerned. They might also not want to devote the necessary time to the task or to become exposed to the statutory and common law liabilities faced by directors these days by virtue of holding such an office. However, this should not interfere with the ability of independent minority shareholders to be adequately represented if they so desire.

3807 In order to make this system work properly it will, of course, be necessary to have quotas of reasonable size. This can be achieved by prescribing a minimum number of members for each board and by limiting their terms in office to one year at a time.

3808 Listed companies will also be prevented from watering their capital by offering ordinary shares (or securities convertible into ordinary shares) other than to existing holders strictly on a pro rata basis.

3809 On a separate matter, the institution at public expense of civil actions on behalf of shareholders and/or creditors in a particular company on suitable occasions will be greatly stepped up. After all, at present investors directly and indirectly make considerable contributions to State and Federal Government coffers!

Stock Exchange Practice and Procedures

3810 The trend for brokers and investment advisers to become more highly qualified will continue and this will be of benefit to their clients. Not long ago it was the exception rather than the rule for a stockbroker to have formal professional qualifications, but the new generation is much keener on training.

3811 Clients in the future will also make much greater use of more sophisticated investment means—put and call options, more complicated convertible and hybrid securities, and so forth.

Current Cost Accounting

3812 There will also be major developments in the area of accounting standards. Changes here will be of great importance to all investors. Hopefully accountants and company directors will have regard to the fact that inflation is an ongoing fact of life and that a 1978 dollar has a different value from a 1998 dollar in the same way that a New Zealand dollar is not identical with an Australian dollar.

3813 To pretend that all dollars are equal is as absurd as to pretend that one foot has the same length as one metre—even though this is the view of the taxation authorities (except in relation to capital gains).

3814 In the celebrated words of one State Attorney-General (F.J.Walker of New South Wales, in June 1978):

"There are lies, damned lies and true and fair profit statements".

3815 If a company is not making adequate allowance for the replacement cost of its stock or its plant and equipment then it is overstating its profit and may even be paying dividends out of capital without this being obvious. When this happens universally then the nation's capital base is being eroded.

3816 A business enterprise cannot be regarded as having made a true profit unless the proprietors' net worth at the end of an accounting period exceeds their net worth at the beginning of that period, after allowing for any money put in or taken out.

3817 The tax rules will also change to reflect inflation. After all, the levying of income tax on illusionary profits raises serious issues of inequity between different taxpayers.

Internationalisation

3818 Australian shares will be traded much more freely on overseas stock exchanges. Correspondingly, shares of foreign companies which are traded on recognised offshore stock exchanges will also be dealt in much more readily on Australian markets, with appropriate modifications to local listing rules continuing to be made in order to facilitate this.

3819 Australian companies will also choose to expand overseas to a much greater extent, thus providing their Australian shareholders with a partial currency hedge, giving some protection in the case of a fall in the value of the Australian dollar. Investors in such companies also become less reliant on the economy of only one country.

3820 "Foreign currency shares" will be created by some local companies.

3821 The dividend imputation system will be extended to cover the genuine overseas business of Australian companies, eliminating the double taxation implicit in the present provisions.

The Corporate Sector

3822 There will also be major changes in the corporate sector. Small listed companies will tend to disappear, as the desire to achieve economies of scale and the need for international competitiveness will encourage rationalisation—quite apart from the needs of institutional investors for stocks which can be bought and sold in large quantities quickly.

3823 Many more takeovers will inevitably occur, if only because in many cases it will be much cheaper to take over an existing enterprise than to start a brand new one.

Trade Unions and the Voting Power Attached to Shares

3824 Ordinary shares owned by trade unions and in particular the voting power attached to them can be used in at least five different ways, namely:

- To promote traditional investment objectives, such as maximising the return on funds invested and ensuring the security of capital.

- As part of a profit-sharing mechanism. This object is, of course, also the concept behind the employee share schemes further discussed in Chapter 36. An argument frequently used in this context is that the suppliers of labour should have a similar stake in the company to the suppliers of capital. However, dividends and company earnings can go down as well as up. Dividends can even become zero, while wages cannot move in a like fashion. A shareholder can lose his total investment. It is, of course, true that an employee can lose his job, but in such circumstances he still has an opportunity to put his labour to work elsewhere, whereas capital once lost is gone for ever.

- To improve employee conditions—wages, fringe benefits, the physical conditions of the workplace, provisions relating to redundancy, etc.— or to force formalised discussions between trade unions and the management. Some of these objectives may involve conflicts of interest—for example, higher wages may mean lower profits. Alternatively, increased wages may lead to higher prices for goods and services and in consequence to lost sales. On the other hand, more dialogue may lead to increased productivity and greater profitability and thus to other benefits for both workers and shareholders.

- To preserve or create jobs. Such an objective may lead to gains in the short-term, but at the risk that Australia could ultimately be priced out of world markets. Mindless opposition to mechanisation or computerisation and to other rationalisation moves may do job prospects more harm than good in the long run.

- To take political action in areas unrelated to the above-for example, to use the annual general meeting of a listed company as a forum to make speeches relating to issues such as the environment, pollution, conservation, afforestation, uranium, South Africa, aboriginal land rights, the preservation of historic buildings and so forth, or to argue for greater benefits to consumers, such as lower prices or the wider provision of credit.

3825 None of these approaches is necessarily bad in itself—after all, companies have a duty to the whole community, as well as to their own shareholders, but a question of degree is involved. Share ownership can provide a useful exercise for employees and trade union officials to learn the facts of economic life. Inevitably there will be conflict between investment and non-investment criteria.

3826 In an extreme situation the control of a large pool of investment funds could in theory be used as a means of "punishing" or threatening a company, or even a State, by making positive decisions not to invest, as distinct from merely making speeches at annual general meetings. However, such a strategy would not work in practice, as once large sums of money are involved investment performance will inevitably become more meaningful and relevant than political rhetoric.

3827 The control of specific companies would also become possible if various trade unions were to adopt a cohesive investment policy, but only at the expense of a proper spread, with the result that if anything were to go wrong with the company concerned (whether because of the trade union intervention itself or for quite unconnected reasons) then the employees involved would inevitably lose some of their hard—earned savings.

3828 One further point needs to be considered if trade unions ever become major share investors—should unions seek directions from their own members before exercising the voting power attached to union-held shares, and, if so, should they cast all their votes in accordance with the wishes of the majority or should they cast them in proportion to the differing views of the membership?

3829 Also, should trade unions seek representation on boards of directors by virtue of owning large blocks of shares?

3830 Finally, a look at another scenario. In a labour—intensive industry, the total shareholders' funds of one company can easily be of the same magnitude as the assets of the superannuation fund relating to the employees of the company concerned. It would, therefore, be feasible for the employees to make a successful takeover bid and thus acquire the whole of their own company's capital—in effect turning it into a sort of workers' co-operative and in the process becoming their own bosses, with all the advantages and disadvantages and risks which this might entail.

Employee Shares

3831 Staff share and option purchase schemes are discussed in Chapter 36. Such arrangements will no doubt expand over the next few years. However, this will be a mixed blessing. Obviously employees owning shares in their employing company have a vested interest in increasing its profits, and such ownership of shares can thus act as useful incentive to good performance.

3832 But if anything goes wrong with the company—possibly through external factors beyond the control of the management and the staff—employees can lose both their jobs and their savings at the same time and from the same set of circumstances. Apart from that, falling share prices can easily sour the goodwill which might originally have attached to share issues on favourable terms.

3833 Similar remarks apply also in the case of shares issued by corporate employers to superannuation funds which provide benefits for their own employees.

3834 On the whole, it would be better if incentive and profit-sharing schemes were not to be based on shares (or securities convertible into shares), notwithstanding the good intentions of those who introduce such arrangements.

Prospectuses

3835 Another reform is likely in the prospectus area—in fact, the trend has already started. Two versions of a prospectus will exist—a simplified one for individuals and a much fuller one for institutions and for others who specifically request it.

3836 This will overcome some of the practical problems of the present system described in Chapter 43.

3837 It would also be useful (and would save trees) if prospectuses included four to six application forms each instead of the customary two.

Chapter 39—Miscellaneous

There are three types of statistics: lies,
lies, and damned lies
—Mark Twain

Background

3901 This chapter discusses a number of unconnected topics of relevance to investors but which do not logically fit into the other chapters.

Share Issues: Privatisation Stocks

3902 A number of State and Federal Government instrumentalities have been privatised in recent years. Others may be privatised in the future, possibly including Medibank Private and the Australian National Line.

3903 The two-thirds of Telstra still in the hands of the Commonwealth Government will no doubt also be sold off.

3904 Many respondents to a recent survey indicated interest in subscribing to other privatisation floats, although the validity of such views in the absence of firm data such as an issue price, a dividend yield, a price earnings ratio and a net tangible asset backing per share figure has to be questioned.

3905 Partial floats in particular pose some risk for investors, although if the terms of a particular issue are generous enough then the potential rewards could well justify the taking of the risk. For example:

- The stock remaining in the Government's hands is likely to be sold off at some stage, increasing the amount of stock publicly available and thus likely to push prices down.

- Until that happens, knowledge of the overhang and the expectation of the next move will adversely affect market prices.

- The chance of a takeover offer being made in such circumstances is likely to be much lower than in the case of conventional companies.

- The privately-held shares will effectively have no voting influence as long as the Government concerned retains its large voting block.

- The "culture" of the organisation is more likely to resemble that of the public sector than that of the private sector.

- There may be political pressure on the organisation to offer consumer services on an uncommercial basis.

- The privatised entity may have inherited unfunded superannuation liabilities to its staff.

3906 After listing, privatisation issues with the above disabilities are (deservedly) likely to command lower price earnings ratios than if they were conventional private sector companies.

The Early Repayment of Home Loans

3907 The question often arises as to whether a person with a current mortgage on his own home who comes into some money should:

- use it to repay some or all of the loan, or instead

- keep the existing loan arrangements intact and make a separate new investment.

3908 If the proposed new investment involves fixed interest securities then the question is easily answered by comparing the two interest rates, allowing for tax. Often the rate of interest on the investment will be less than the rate of interest on the loan even before tax, thus clearly making repayment of the loan the more attractive option.

3909 As explained in para. 2813, interest on a home loan is classed as domestic expenditure and is therefore not deductible as an expense for income tax purposes. On the other hand, the interest to be earned on the new investment would be fully taxable in the usual way, at the investor's marginal tax rate. The required comparison is therefore between the *gross* interest rate on the loan and the *net* interest rate on the proposed separate investment.

3910 Thus persons with a housing loan who later acquire funds available for investment purposes will normally find that the best fixed interest "investment" which they can make is to pay off some or all of their own loan. This usually applies even if they are getting the benefit of a concessional interest rate and/or a penalty for early repayment applies.

3911 To illustrate: Except in the case of persons below the tax threshold it is usually better to avoid paying 8 per cent non-deductible interest on a mortgage than to earn, say, even 9 per cent taxable interest on a deposit elsewhere. This applies both in the case of a direct investment by the investor himself (incurring tax at his marginal rate) and to an indirect investment through a superannuation fund or rollover vehicle (incurring tax at 15 per cent). Furthermore, an external investment carries with it a risk of default, whereas an "investment" in one's own home loan does not.

3912 Similarly, it will usually be better to pay off a housing loan in preference to paying off an existing loan which was raised for business or investment purposes.

3913 Again, for a person aged over 55 years and under 65 years who is retiring it will normally be less attractive to roll over an "eligible termination payment" (ETP) than to pay off a mortgage, despite the relatively low 15 per cent tax rate applying to the investment income of rollover vehicles. (For persons aged under 55 years the additional lump sum tax alters this relationship.)

3914 The term "eligible termination payment" is defined in the tax legislation. It includes lump sum superannuation payments and "golden handshakes".

3915 If the proposed new investment involves equities then the same considerations as discussed above for fixed interest securities apply. The new investment will be worthwhile only if its expected "after tax" yield, allowing for the anticipated growth element, is greater than the actual interest rate on the existing home loan.

3916 Of course, there is also a non-financial reason for giving priority to paying off a housing loan as early as possible—the peace of mind that an unencumbered home gives its owner—occupiers and the flexibility that such an asset offers.

3917 For social security recipients in particular it can be better to have a home with a high value and no other investments than to have a home with a low net value (by virtue of an attaching mortgage) and a separate investment, even if the total value of the assets in the two cases is the same. This is because not only is interest on a home mortgage not a deduction from gross income under the income test but also because the assets test treats a home on a concessional basis.

3918 A partial repayment of a housing loan ahead of time without reducing the amount of the periodical "principal and interest" instalment will shorten the remaining term of the loan and can reduce the total interest burden over the life of a loan quite dramatically.

3919 However, it would not make sense to "save up" separately in order to make such a partial repayment, unless the "after tax" rate of return from the chosen savings vehicle exceeded the loan rate of interest. It is usually better to arrange a permanent or temporary stepping up of the pace of periodical loan repayments instead.

3920 The above analysis assumed that the money concerned was available for investment on a permanent or at least on a long-term basis. If the money is available only temporarily then it is not advisable to use it for loan reduction purposes with a view to reborrowing the sum concerned later on. This would incur relatively heavy transaction costs and there is always the danger that the lender might not allow the desired reborrowing.

3921 Persons with house purchase loans from some savings institutions are allowed to maintain "offset" (credit) accounts with those institutions, the interest on which is effectively tax-free. Thus instead of paying, say, $1000 non-deductible interest to a house purchase lender and receiving, say, $100 taxable interest on the credit account, the taxpayer is treated as having paid a non-deductible net $900 interest in respect of the housing loan. This approach is particularly suitable for money known to be available only temporarily.

3922 It should be noted, however, that some institutions take a quite unfair advantage of those of their customers that use this facility because of its tax attractions. These institutions pay a much lower rate of interest on the credit balances than they charge on the debit balances.

3923 There is a third choice, apart from the two mentioned in para. 3907. A home owner who wants to continue to have the benefit of the loan funds currently in place in order acquire new investments can first of all repay the housing loan, having regard to its "non-deductible interest" status. Such a person can *then* raise a fresh loan (on the security of the same home, if desired, and/or on the security of his investment portfolio), this loan being devoted exclusively to investment purposes and thus giving rise to tax deductibility for the interest (see, however, para. 2710 in regard to the documentation aspects and paras 2713 to 2720 in regard to certain risk aspects). However, some lenders charge a higher interest rate on commercial loans, and this aspect and the incidence of further transaction charges need to be taken into consideration.

Risk and Reward

3924 The traditional saying, "The greater the interest rate, the greater the risk", may warrant some illustration. Consider a savings institution which is keen to increase its market share:

- It decides to pay higher rates of interest on its deposits than those available from its competitors.

- This succeeds in attracting new funds.

- It is then faced with the necessity to on-lend these funds at a suitable margin in order to cover its costs.

- It can achieve this only by charging higher rates of interest on its loans than those being charged by its competitors.

- The only borrowers willing to pay such higher rates in practice are those who constitute a greater-than-normal risk of default.

- On a typical portfolio such defaults will then indeed occur.

- Defaults mean not only trading losses instead of trading profits but also a reduction in cash flow.

- The institution therefore needs to step up its deposit-taking even further.

- It thus needs to offer even higher rates of interest to its depositors.

- This sets up a vicious circle of greater defaults, higher interest rates, greater defaults, and so on,

- Eventually the regulators will have to step in and/or the institution will need to close its doors for ever.

3925 Higher-than-normal interest rates should serve as a clear warning to investors. Commercial organisations do not offer above average returns for the fun of it.

3926 The above scenario should also re-emphasise the importance of spread—although, of course, putting all of one's savings into more than one high interest/high risk organisation is not a satisfactory solution either.

Runs on Financial Institutions

3927 The concept of a "run on the bank" (or on some other financial institution) is mentioned in para. 272. The term implies a panic rush by anxious customers to withdraw their money and the formation of queues outside its premises.

3928 Unfortunately, a run can happen to any financial institution. However, runs are more likely in the case of organisations which "borrow short and lend long", as by definition these will never have sufficient cash reserves to meet unexpected demands.

3929 The best strategy for an individual depositor when such a run develops—or probably even when there are just rumours in circulation which could lead to a run—is to withdraw his money as fast as possible.

3930 Panic is sometimes started accidentally—for example, by some ill-chosen words in the media. Rumours may also be propagated for malicious reasons. However, at the time the separation of fact from fiction by investors is not feasible.

3931 Once an organisation closes its doors—or when a moratorium is imposed by the authorities—it will be too late to take any useful action. Even if such a development does not lead to a permanent loss of capital for the depositors it can result in money becoming frozen and not earning any interest for many years.

3932 Depositors in savings institutions are effectively faced with a one-way option once a run is in progress and have little to gain by remaining loyal.

3933 The position with rumours in regard to a company listed on the stock exchange is entirely different—the risk of loss if the facts asserted by the rumours are true could be offset to some extent by the chance of gains if the company concerned prospers and the rumours turn out to have been ill—founded.

3934 Furthermore, a rumour causing excessive sales of a company's shares on the stock exchange does nothing to directly undermine the well—being of the corporate entity, whereas the withdrawal of funds from a deposit—taking institution can ruin it very quickly. (Of course, a fall in a company's share price can affect it adversely in the long-term, by making it harder for the company to raise additional funds.)

3935 It should be realised also that a rumour of financial problems can easily become a self—fulfilling prophecy: for example, a highly liquid institution can quickly become illiquid if enough people act on the rumour concerned.

3936 Even sensible commercial steps to deal with the problem— such as attempts to sell assets and/or to raise loan funds in a hurry and in secrecy—may just fuel additional harmful rumours and speculation.

3937 Furthermore, denials of problems in such circumstances cannot ever be relied upon, as such denials would invariably be made for obvious commercial reasons, whether justified by the facts of the particular situation or not. This warning applies equally to denials by the organisation concerned, to denials by friendly competitors, to denials by industry associations and even to denials by government spokesmen. Of course, such statements may suffice to stop a run.

3938 Naturally, depositors should also act consistently—there is no logic in drawing money out of, say, a building society in the form of a cheque because of concern as to its liquidity or solvency, and then hanging on to that cheque. (Of course, getting cash and putting it under the bed is also not a desirable investment strategy!)

3939 Similarly, there is not much merit in a depositor drawing out only a portion of his total deposits. If the rumours have suddenly made him a belated convert to the concept of spread then he would be better off in withdrawing the lot and entrusting it to two or more other institutions.

3940 Runs can also be infectious. As money is frozen in some organisation, runs are likely to affect its competitors. Partly this is because of psychological factors, but the more significant reason is that as customers lose liquidity because one of their normal cash sources is not available they need to access alternative sources.

3941 Temporary freezes are sometimes imposed by institutions for reasons unconnected with liquidity or solvency—for example, unlisted property trusts may wish to prevent the cashing in of units at prices based on asset backing figures which are suspected as being too high pending a sale or revaluation.

Overseas Investment Exposures

3942 Investments involving exposure to overseas currencies and economies are favoured by some investors in several different contexts:

- Where they believe that the chosen overseas economy will outperform the Australian economy.

- Where they believe that the Australian dollar will fall against the chosen currency.

- Where they desire exposure to an industry not represented locally.

- Where they desire to participate in a country with a higher expected growth rate than Australia's.

- Where they believe that a specific investment will do particularly well.

- Where they desire to participate in a market which is more liquid than their own.

- Where they want a greater spread than is obtainable purely by investing in Australia.

3943 In one sense overseas investment doubles the risk, as market prices expressed in Australian dollars will fluctuate with both the market prices expressed in the overseas currency concerned and in the exchange rate. However, the overall volatility of a portfolio with both local and overseas exposure may be less than that of a purely locally-based portfolio. To a logical equity investor there is nothing inherently different between the risk of share price fluctuations and the risk of "share price cum currency" fluctuations.

3944 Overseas currency exposures can be hedged, but the expense of doing this is likely to offset the benefits for long-term investors. Normally investors who go offshore decide to deliberately stay unhedged because they have formed a view in regard to the weakness of the Australian dollar.

3945 Overseas investment exposures can be obtained in a number of different ways, including the following:

- Through listed Australian companies with large overseas interests.

- Through listed Australian companies involved with the export of mineral or other commodities priced in overseas markets. These involve a "leverage" effect—a small movement in commodity prices can have a much larger proportionate effect on profits.

- Through listed overseas companies. These can be purchased without difficulty through local offices of overseas brokers or through local brokers with overseas connections. See also paras 2005 to 2006.

- Through international trusts and mutual funds (although these may involve relatively high charges).

- Through foreign currency bank accounts—see paras 2114 to 2116.

3946 One Australian company was proposing to issue foreign currency shares, to enable local investors to obtain (or, for that matter, to avoid, if so desired) a specific interest in its overseas operations. However, to date nothing has come of this worthwhile proposal.

3947 The taxation aspects of overseas investments are discussed in paras 2877 and 2879.

Share Registers as Mailing Lists

3948 As indicated in para. 453, share registers are public documents. They may be inspected free of charge by any shareholders of the company concerned by virtue of Section 216F of the *Corporations Law*, thus enabling shareholders to communicate with each other freely and in particular to seek proxies for forthcoming votes. This principle also extends to registers of optionholders and debenture holders.

3949 The registers may also be inspected by other persons, although companies are entitled to charge a fee for this service.

3950 Interested persons can also purchase a copy of a share register or any part thereof. Some companies are willing to provide this information in the form of computer disks.

3951 Such information allows offers for the shares to be made (in compliance with the other provisions of the *Corporations Law*).

3952 Of course, the information in the register relates only to the *nominal* owner of the shares. This person may or may not also be the *beneficial* owner.

3953 Before the law was changed in 1995 some persons and organisations used to acquire share register details in order to use them as mailing lists for purposes unconnected with the company. For example:

- Stockbrokers who wished to send out promotional material, offering their services to the recipients in the hope of attracting them as new clients.

- Publishers of investment journals who wanted to send out invitations in the hope of obtaining new subscribers.

- Promoters of various investment schemes who wished to mail prospectuses to likely targets.

- Other merchants who desired to send out miscellaneous junk mail.

However, Section 216J of the *Corporations Law* now limits such activities.

3954 The registers contain not only names and addresses (and possibly telephone numbers), but also information relating to the size of the holdings, enabling mail to be specifically targeted to investors who meet certain criteria.

3955 Many public companies object to the practices because of the nuisance to them in having to supply the data and also because of the danger that their corporate names might improperly become associated with promotions or advice-giving by third parties.

3956 Some shareholders resent such mailings either because they do not want to get junk mail in general or because they regard the use of their names in this way as an unwarranted invasion of their privacy. Nevertheless, such practices are perfectly legal at present, although they are viewed with some concern by the Privacy Commissioner.

3957 Of greater worry are unsolicited circulars to shareholders by persons with vested interests of their own, making specific recommendations to the effect that the shares in the company concerned should be sold or alternatively that more should be purchased. Such advice may or may not be soundly based, but in any case it would obviously not take the particular circumstances of the recipients into account. Such communications should always be viewed with some suspicion.

Twenty Largest Shareholders Lists

3958 Listed companies are required to lodge with the stock exchange at the time of first listing and annually thereafter a list of their 20 largest shareholders for each class of equity securities and the number of such securities held by each (as well as the total held by the 20 largest shareholders as a percentage of the grand total). Many companies include such data in their published annual reports.

3959 These lists can show the influence of various categories of investor—for example, the founding family, the major institutions, potential takeover bidders, overseas parents, and so on. They supplement the statutory requirements for substantial shareholders (that is, those with beneficial interests of 5 per cent upwards) to disclose themselves.

3960 Interpreting the information is more difficult. Large holdings by the founding family can indicate a mark of confidence in the enterprise and a force for making it perform, but they can also cause problems because the interests of such insiders and other investors may not always coincide and because such shares could one day be dumped on the market. Even if existing shares are not sold, a similar effect may result from the non-taking up of rights issues.

3961 Furthermore, while some members of the founding family may have built the company up originally their successors might be less capable and might be given managerial positions and/or board seats for the wrong reason.

3962 Sometimes different groupings in the founding family adopt different philosophies. Such splits can be a destabilising factor.

3963 The absence of institutions can be a danger sign, but it can also foreshadow greater-than-normal share price growth if the company does well and attracts institutional support later on. Institutions often avoid small companies not because these are inherently bad investments but rather because their shares cannot readily be traded in volume.

3964 Large holdings in few hands can facilitate takeovers because control can change very quickly. Equally they can frustrate takeovers if the large shareholders decide to follow an agenda of their own. Of course, an entity which is already a large holder may one day become a bidder itself.

3965 In practice large shareholders will often be represented on the board of directors—which again can present both advantages and disadvantages.

3966 Finally, the attitude to important topics such as dividend rates, the size and timing of new capital raisings and merger or expansion plans may well differ as between large and small shareholders.

Clerical Errors

3967 Investors need to keep an eye on the accuracy of documents prepared by others in relation to their financial affairs. Clerical and computer errors in documents ranging from bank statements to taxation assessments are all too common these days and it is foolish to assume that mistakes will not occur in official-looking material.

Percentage Movements

3968 Some aspects of percentage movements seem to confuse investors. To illustrate:

- If a share moves up in price from 200 to 300, then this represents a 50 per cent increase.

- But if a share moves down from 300 to 200, then this represents only a 33.33 per cent decrease— not 50 per cent.

3969 Some aspects of percentage movements also seem to confuse listed companies when reporting to the stock exchange. To illustrate:

- If a company has a $2 million loss this year against a $4 million profit last year, then the percentage change is actually "minus 150 per cent".

American Depository Receipts

3970 Shares in some listed Australian companies are traded in the United States, with a special document of title called the "American Depository Receipt" (ADR) being used as the trading unit. An ADR may represent, say, two shares or four shares in an Australian company, with the market value in US dollars then being the equivalent of the market value of two or four Australian shares.

3971 ADRs are created by certain US banks, which hold the underlying scrip and become the registered shareowners as far as the Australian company is concerned. This device facilitates changes of beneficial ownership when trading occurs on the stock exchange in America. Naturally, all dividends belong to the beneficial owners in the usual way.

Savoy Clauses

3972 Some listed companies which are involved in 50/50 joint ventures have contracts involving a "Savoy Clause". Such a provision means that one party to the joint venture can at any time nominate a price to the other party, which must then (at its option):

- *either* buy the first party's interest in the joint venture from the first party at that price

- *or* sell its own interest in the joint venture to the first party at that price.

Charge-Free Bank Accounts

3973 Some banks rebate account maintenance and/or transaction fees for customers who maintain certain minimum credit balances in a zero interest bank account during a calendar quarter or some such. Such arrangements often represent remarkably poor value.

3974 To illustrate, a rebate formula based on 1 per cent per quarter represents only 4 per cent per annum interest in the ideal situation—and even less in practice because of the "minimum balance at all times" and "excess amounts" aspects. It would thus be much more economical to earn, say, 10 per cent per annum elsewhere and to meet the normal bank charges in full.

Greed

3975 Commentators sometimes assert that markets are driven by only two factors, "greed and need"—presumably referring to the desire of investors to get capital growth or income. However, greed can also be a factor affecting corporate performance.

3976 To illustrate, a banking company can decide that it will lift its gross profit margin by increasing the interest rate which it charges certain of its commercial borrowers. If this does not reduce the volume of its lending business then it may congratulate itself on its success in having achieved greater profitability. However, down the track it may encounter huge losses from bad debts.

3977 What will probably have happened is that some of the bank's potential customers, particularly those with the best management skills, the best net worth and the best cash flow, will have been able to negotiate deals on better terms with one or other of the bank's competitors. The remaining customers, who present a much greater credit risk and who thus have a weaker bargaining position, will have accepted the original bank's offer. Thus the proportion of defaulting loans in the bank's portfolio will have been much bigger than if it had been less greedy in the first instance. The extra interest seemingly earned will have been more than offset by the subsequent capital losses.

Further Information

3978 Attention is drawn to three other self-contained books by the present author which may assist investors who have found this volume of interest:

- *The Retirement Handbook*, a book of 19 chapters and seven appendices which looks systematically at all the relevant financial, lifestyle and legal aspects of retirement—including budgeting, investments, income tax, social security, wills, housing, leisure, health and superannuation. Subjects which have special significance in today's conditions are dealt with at length —for example, retirement villages, enduring powers of attorney, rollovers, annuities and second careers.

- *Wills & Record Keeping*, a unique book designed to help families cope with one of the unavoidable difficulties of modern life—the need to keep track of a mass of essential personal and financial information. It contains a set of 35 specially designed forms for recording such data systematically and in an easily retrieved format. The accompanying text introduces the subject of maintaining adequate family and investment records. It explains some of the ramifications in regard to powers of attorney, computer records, income tax and capital gains tax. The points to be considered when drawing up a will are discussed in some detail.

- *Understanding the Australian Economic Debate*, a different type of book which has been described as a lucid and opinionated primer to the key economic issues facing Australia in the 1990s. It discusses privatisation, class actions, interest rates, recent changes to superannuation, and so on. It analyses a number of proposed taxation reform measures which, if enacted, would have significant ramifications for all investors.

Complaints against Stockbrokers

3979 The Australian Stock Exchange maintains its own "Ombudsman" service, although strangely enough not under that name. Any complaints which clients have against stock exchange member organisations and which they have been unable to resolve themselves can be impartially investigated by this service, which can be contacted through the ASX in each capital city.

The Stock Exchange Referral Service

3980 The Australian Stock Exchange runs a general advisory service as well as a referral service which enables new investors without a stockbroker to be introduced to one who can cover their needs.

Dual Listed Companies

3981 The concept of a *dual listed company* (DLC) has existed overseas fo many years. Well-known examples include Unilever and Shell.

3982 One local company of this type exists: Rio Tinto. Shares in Rio Tinto Limited, an Australian company, are linked to shares in Rio Tonto plc, a United Kingdom company. Legally these two corporations are separate, but effectively they are treated as a single entity by virtue of carefully-devised reciprocal arrangements and complementary articles of association. On a "per share" basis the shares in both companies rank equally, except that dividends are paid in the local currency and with the benefit of local franking rules.

Chapter 40—Buy-backs

October. This is one of the peculiarly dangerous months to speculate in stocks in. The others are July, January, September, April, November, May, March, June, December, August, and February.

—Mark Twain

Synopsis

4001 The term *buy-back* refers to the purchase by a company of its own shares.

4002 Buy-backs are usually instituted for one or both of two main reasons—to boost the earnings per share for the remaining shares and to mop up surplus cash by making an "investment" which is regarded as better than the available alternatives.

4003 As discussed in greater detail below, some buy-backs are made on-market and no special action on the part of individual shareholders is called for. They will benefit indirectly in the future from the increased performance of the company in respect of the lower number of shares outstanding and from the higher market prices arising from the extra buying pressure.

4004 Other buy-backs involve offers to shareholders to buy portions of their holdings. These need to be assessed by investors on their merits and having regard to their individual circumstances. They are effectively rights issues in reverse. Acceptance of such offers is entirely voluntary.

4005 Offers which are judged by investors as being too generous may result in acceptances being reduced proportionately.

Historical Background

4006 Until a few years ago Australian companies were not allowed to buy back their own shares. There were a number of reasons for this.

4007 Because creditors ranked ahead of shareholders the authorities were worried that letting a company reduce its shareholders' funds could prejudice the security of that company's creditors. In an extreme case, permitting a company to distribute too much of its assets to shareholders could increase the risk of corporate failure later on.

4008 Another concern was the scope for both insider trading and the manipulation of share prices. For example, allowing a company to prop up its share price artificially by buying on the market could be unfair to other investors who purchased shares in good faith while the market was temporarily inflated and who subsequently suffered losses when prices dropped back to their normal level.

4009 Buy-backs could also unduly advantage unscrupulous directors and associates of a company who were trying to reduce their own holdings for as high a price as possible and who would thus benefit from a rigged market.

4010 There was also the danger of cross—subsidisation. If the price being paid out of corporate funds for the shares being bought back was on the high side then this would be quite unfair to the ongoing shareholders of the company.

4011 Furthermore, if the price per share being bought back exceeded the net tangible asset backing per share—as well it might in many cases—then this would reduce the asset backing of the remaining shares.

4012 Another problem was the danger of "greenmail"—the practice under which the shares of one particular significant shareholder are acquired by a company at a premium to the then market price in response to threats by that investor to initiate a hostile takeover bid or otherwise disrupt the company's affairs.

4013 However, notwithstanding these negatives buy-backs are permitted in the sophisticated markets of the United States and other countries, so Australian companies were at a disadvantage internationally. Furthermore, although companies as such were prohibited from buying back their own shares unit trusts were allowed to buy back their own units.

4014 There were also a number of loopholes. A company could indirectly buy its own shares either by interposing another company which it controlled or by using a jointly-owned company.

Law Reform

4015 In September 1987 the Companies and Securities Law Review Committee issued a detailed report entitled "A Company's Purchase of its own Shares". Partly as a result of this the *Corporations Law* was changed in 1990 to permit self—acquisition schemes in a controlled way. The rules were further simplified in 1995.

4016 Subject to certain legal formalities five types of buy-back became possible:

On-market purchases

A listed company can buy its own shares in the ordinary course of trading on the stock exchange. The actual shares come from investors who choose to place selling orders in the normal way and who would not even be aware at the time that the purchaser of their particular shares was other than a normal investor. (They would hardly complain even if they did know, as the additional buying pressure would do them no harm!)

Buy-back schemes

These involve the company making an identical offer to all its existing shareholders as at some date to buy a defined proportion of each holding. In a sense this is a non-renounceable rights issue in reverse. Apart from the identity of the bidder it is also very similar to a partial takeover bid. Acceptance is not compulsory, so shareholders who wish to hang on to their entire holdings or to sell on the market can still do so.

Employee share purchases

Many employee share ownership plans contain provisions allowing shares held by current or former employees to be sold back to the company in certain circumstances—for example, on resignation, retrenchment, retirement or death.

Odd lot purchase schemes

Before the concept of odd lots was abolished (see para. 1637) these schemes involved the company making an offer to its existing shareholders to sell back shares constituting an "odd lot", that is, shares not making up a defined "marketable parcel" such as 100 shares. These schemes could also be used to mop up the entire holdings of investors holding less than a single marketable parcel, free of brokerage, stamp duty and odd lot charges. Some mining companies in the "penny dreadful" class have many thousands of very small shareholders in this category. These are very expensive to service—the cost of mailing an annual report even once can exceed the entire market value of a holding. The shareholders concerned cannot effectively quit their stakes in the ordinary way because of minimum brokerage charges.

Selective buy-backs

These are buy-backs that do not fall into any of the above categories—for example, purchases of one or more particular members' shares (hence the name "selective"). Such arrangements could be used to buy out a large shareholder as an alternative either to a sale by that investor on the market (which would depress the share price for everybody) or to a proportionate offer to all other shareholders. They could also be used to mop up small holdings—see the previous item.

4017 Generally speaking, a buy-back scheme no longer requires specific authority to be included in a company's articles of association. Greater formalities can apply if a company wishes to buy back more than 10 per cent of its capital in any 12—month period.

4018 It will be appreciated that directors who in their own right are large shareholders and/or optionholders in their companies may have conflicts of interest when putting buy-back proposals forward.

4019 Selective buy-backs present greater opportunities for abuse than the other categories. For this reason they are subject to more stringent rules.

4020 If a company happens to have cash which is surplus to the immediate requirements of its traditional activities then it is preferable by far that the company should return that cash to the shareholders in some form of capital reduction, thus allowing the individual shareholders to then spend that money or reinvest it as they see fit. (While legally the company's board of directors can control the company's cash, morally the board only holds it in trust for the shareholders as beneficial owners.)

4021 A buy-back scheme which allows individual investors to choose whether or not to accept could be a useful alternative to a conventional capital reduction of so many cents per share for everybody.

4022 A further advantage should be mentioned. If the market price happens to be less than the realistic worth of the company then a buy-back arrangement could make sense on investment considerations alone-it could be the means of increasing the earnings per share and net asset backing per share figures.

4023 Furthermore, the buying pressure and the possible removal of stock overhang would also tend to push share prices up to more realistic levels, to the benefit of both quitting and ongoing investors.

4024 Despite the advantages to both shareholders and company managements which the new legislation provided relatively few share buy-backs have actually taken place, although the dollar amounts of those that have taken place have not been insignificant.

Takeover Protection

4025 The use of buy-backs as a defence against an actual or threatened takeover can be rather a mixed blessing for small shareholders.

4026 On the one hand, the ability for a company to push up the market price of its shares could result in a higher offer than might otherwise have been available. On the other hand, this higher price and the reduction in the cash held by the company—which might have been one of the attractions of the company for a bidder—might result in no offer at all.

Overseas Experience

4027 American companies were able to support the market price of their shares through buy-backs at bargain prices in the days immediately following the 19 October 1987 stock market crash. Australian companies could not do this at that time.

4028 By law any shares bought back by a company in Australia have to be cancelled. In overseas countries companies usually have the right to be holders of their own shares (the so-called "treasury stock") and to reissue them later on. However, the Australian requirement for cancellation seems cleaner and results in more understandable balance sheets. And, of course, a company can always issue brand new shares if it finds that such a cash raising suits its purposes.

4029 United States studies show that companies making buy-backs tend to outperform other companies. Although this correlation is of interest it does not, of course, prove that such a capital move was the *cause* rather than the *result* of their success.

Market Slumps

4030 Some companies use times of market weakness to accelerate their share purchases under on—market buy-back programs previously announced. The additional buying pressure at that time naturally helps to support the market price of the shares. Apart from that, purchases of a company's own shares at such a time often constitute an attractive investment in its own right.

4031 Such transactions also increase the liquid resources of the market as a whole. Normal buying and selling transactions do not have this effect, as the cash being paid out by one investor is exactly matched by the cash being taken in by another investor.

Tax Aspects

4032 Buy-backs have no effect on the tax position of companies making them. The tax effect on the shareholders depends on the circumstances.

4033 In an on-market purchase the shareholder is, naturally enough, treated the same as in the case of any other market disposal—a capital gain or a capital loss would be calculated in the usual way.

4034 In an off-market purchase by the company the shareholder is treated for capital gains tax purposes as having sold the shares for that part of the consideration as is debited by the company to its capital or share premium accounts. Any remainder is then treated as a taxable dividend (either franked or unfranked).

Chapter 41—Targeted Shares

I have enough money to last me the rest of my life,
unless I buy something
—Jackie Mason

The Problem

4101 Some large Australian companies which are listed on the stock exchange have a number of separate divisions. Inevitably, some of these are more highly regarded than others.

4102 Investors in such companies have to take the good with the bad and this aspect tends to depress the market price of the shares concerned.

The Solution

4103 One possible solution would be to hive the various divisions off as separate listed companies. The likelihood is that the market would regard the various parts as free—standing entities to be worth more than the whole.

4104 Frequently, boards do not support such an approach, taking the view that their company derives much of its strength from being a single large entity with a portfolio of different activities.

4105 However, this argument overlooks the possibility of an even better third alternative—namely, the creation of "letter stock" or "targeted shares" on the lines used in North America and also nearer home by the locally listed New Zealand company, Fletcher Challenge.

4106 Such a formula would give an Australian diversified company the best of both worlds and would in practice no doubt boost its share price.

4107 As discussed in Chapter 4, many listed companies already have two different classes of shares—ordinary and preference, or fully-paid and contributing. In each case the various categories of shareholder draw their dividends from a single pool of money—the profits of the relevant company as a whole.

4108 However, it is also possible for a company to create two or more distinct series of "targeted" ordinary shares, each of which participates in the profits of only a defined division of the company rather than in those of the entire enterprise.

The Legal Structure

4109 Under such a scenario the company would remain a single legal entity for all external purposes, including taxation and the rights of creditors, but each relevant division can be thought of by investors as a sort of pseudo-company.

4110 Investors could continue to hold both classes of shares if that suited their overall investment purposes, but they would also have the opportunity of selling the shares of one class while keeping those of the other (and of buying more on the market if they so wished).

4111 In the United States companies with targeted shares are relatively common. The following random examples will illustrate the method:

- General Motors Corporation, which invented the concept in 1984 (Class E shares for its Electronic Data Systems operations and Class H shares for its GM Hughes Electronics business, in addition to its original common stock).

- USX Corporation (separate shares for its U.S.Steel, Marathon and Delhi Groups, reflecting the company's steel, oil and natural gas interests).

- Tele-Communications Inc. (Liberty Media Group shares for its entertainment, educational and electronic retailing activities and TCI Group shares for its separate cable, telephony and communications businesses).

4112 No change in the legislation would be required in Australia. However, any company wishing to introduce targeted shares would, of course, need shareholder approval to make appropriate changes to its articles of association.

The Mechanics

4113 The arrangements would work as follows. At the commencement of a targeted share program all existing shareholders would be given shares in each class without further payment and in proportion to their existing holdings. Each division of the company would be allocated its own distinct assets and liabilities.

4114 Such arrangements would benefit both management and shareholders:

- Investors could concentrate on the class shares in the industry they particularly favoured, without having their stake diluted by unrelated activities.

- The publication of separate balance sheet and profit and loss figures for the various divisions would help market understanding.

- The various divisions could reflect their different circumstances by declaring individual dividend rates and by implementing separate capital raising or buy-back programs.

- This factor can be particularly useful if a new venture with a long start-up period is formed as a separate division.

- The market would give the shares in each division their own market values.

- The creation of distinct pseudo-companies with high visibility would be good for staff and management morale and would facilitate the development of better incentive schemes.

- In practice pure "plays" trade at a premium to conglomerates.

- The above factors can be expected to lead to a net increase in the overall buying pressure and thus (other things being equal) to a higher total market value for the company's shares.

4115 The ongoing use of a single corporate structure rather than a break-up would allow the shareholders to retain all the benefits of size—economies of scale, a better credit rating and thus lower borrowing costs, bulk buying power, greater international competitiveness, access to key management expertise, and so on.

4116 The existence of different classes of shares would also create scope for selectively using these as currency in takeover bids.

Control

4117 The company concerned would continue to be controlled by a single board—a cost advantage over having boards of separate companies. The company would also have a single annual meeting, with the various classes of ordinary share having a different voting power on some appropriately defined basis— for example, in proportion to market value.

4118 Furthermore, separate class meetings to deal with matters affecting only the relevant business unit concerned could also be held as required. Such meetings would be compulsory before articles governing class rights could be amended, as such changes would need endorsement from the shareholders affected.

4119 In addition to using externally raised loan funds which are an obligation of the group as a whole, the various divisions could no doubt also lend to and borrow from each other so as to maximise their own profitability from time to time.

4120 Other variations to this theme are, of course, possible. For example, one division instead of being a pure play could if desired have a small equity interest in another division, especially in the early stages when this asset is often referred to as a "retained interest". However, in the long run too much of this would probably defeat the object of the exercise. (Such an interest would also give rise to awkward questions in regard to voting rights at shareholder meetings.)

4121 The overall concept could naturally also be taken one step further if desired—for example, by creating divisions based on geographical regions or particular foreign currency operations instead of on different types of business activity. Any company contemplating the use of targeted shares could tailor the idea to its own requirements.

Taxation Aspects

4122 The initial reconstruction, unlike a divestiture of assets into various new legal entities, would mean that no capital gains tax or stamp duty liabilities would be incurred by either the company or its shareholders (where these opt to continue to hold intact their entire interest). All pre-1985 assets would retain their CGT status.

4123 The use of a single legal entity would enable tax losses in one division to be offset against profits in another.

The Future

4124 The terms of each class of targeted shares would provide the relevant shareholders with dividends and entitlements to retained profits based on the actual performance of a particular division. However, each targeted share would also rank as part of the equity of the whole company. As such it would naturally be subordinate to all the company's external liabilities.

4125 After a while, as trading on the stock exchange took place and as separate divisional data was built up, the registers of the various classes of shares would no doubt reflect the different groups of investors favouring each particular division rather than the company as a whole. Of course, those institutions seeking to build up portfolios replicating the All Ordinaries Index would no doubt wish to hold shares in all divisions in proportion to their size.

4126 However, in the process of realignment the total market capi- talisation of the group would no doubt rise, to the benefit of all concerned.

Chapter 42—Investors and the Internet

Commerce is the greatest of all political interests
—Joseph Chamberlain

Background

4201 The Internet can be used by investors in a number of different ways, some of which are discussed briefly below. The listings are meant to be illustrative of the vast amount of material available rather than exhaustive.

4202 Furthermore, the technology and the practices in this area are changing so rapidly that any detailed comments would probably become out of date very quickly.

4203 A number of sites of interest to investors on the World Wide Web are set out in Appendix 9. In addition there are available a number of specialist books which deal with the subject in greater detail than is practicable here.

Types of Sites

4204 Web sites of especial relevance to stock exchange investors include those put up by organisations such as:

- **Stockbrokers**. These sites may feature general advice in regard to investment; selected research reports; market prices; details of prospectuses available; and so on. Some sites enable orders to be placed online and/or by e-mail. Naturally enough, all broker sites are designed to generate goodwill and indirectly to boost stock exchange turnovers—in much the same way as brokers' circulars seek to do that and with corresponding limitations.

- **Australian Stock Exchange**. This is a very large site. However, it could be made even more useful by including items such as a list of companies which have been delisted over, say, the last 25 years, showing their fate (takeover, liquidation, or whatever) and another list dealing with companies which have changed their names. Each day's closing prices are available after midnight at no charge.

- **Australian Securities and Investments Commission**. This is another large site. It also includes the means of checking the status of investment advisers.

- **Commercial service providers**. See paras 4209 to 4212.

- **Australian Taxation Office**. The latest media releases and information such as tax rulings can be obtained.

- **Australian Bureau of Statistics**.

- **Listed companies.** At the time of writing most listed companies have no Internet presence at all. Others have surprisingly poor sites or sites aimed at potential customers rather than at their own shareholders—although no doubt the latter would also be interested to see how companies go about marketing their wares. See also paras 4226 to 4269.

- **Financial institutions**. These sites tend to market financial products, including managed investments.

- **Newspapers**. Business stories are featured each day. The sites also provide access to archived material and sometimes to the full version of important material published for space reasons only in a summarised form.

- **Radio and television**. Transcripts of some business programs are featured.

- **Australian Shareholders' Association**. This site includes details of the organisation's own meetings and of its position papers on various important issues.

4205 A number of online glossaries of investment terms are also available.

Share Price Information

4206 Share price and related information is available on the Internet from both stockbrokers and other organisations. Most of this is on World Wide Web sites, but some is also available by e-mail.

4207 A wide variety of charging bases apply; a brochure detailing these can be obtained from the Australian Stock Exchange.

4208 Typically, the services covered include:

- real time share prices
- end of day share prices
- historical share prices
- charts
- headlines of company announcements
- full company announcements (see below).

Service Providers

4209 The sites put up by a number of commercial service providers give members of the public access on a fee-for-service basis to official company announcements made to the Australian Stock Exchange and/or the Australian Securities and Investments Commission.

4210 These sites thus provide an electronic version of the hard copy files which used to be available for inspection at ASX information centres in each capital city but with the convenience of access to readers in their own homes or offices or through Internet facilities in public libraries or Internet cafes.

4211 New information is available as soon as it is released by the ASX and can be read online or downloaded at any time convenient to the user, 24 hours a day, seven days a week. Historical information is also available.

4212 Users can, if desired, keep the information on their own systems without its taking up physical storage space. They can easily print it out for their own use and can study it in detail at their leisure.

General Resources

4213 The usual Internet search engines can, of course, also be used to seek out information on many investment—related topics, just by typing in one or two keywords.

4214 Investors can also use the Internet to buy books on investment subjects or to access library catalogues.

4215 Software of interest to investors can also be purchased online. This includes general accounting programs as well as programs specifically aimed at stock exchange investors—for example, to draw charts.

Some Warnings

4216 Frequently the date of creation of a web page is not shown, which substantially detracts from the usefulness of the whole exercise.

4217 There are also sites put up by various enthusiastic amateurs. Often these include useful links to other sites. The experimentation is a healthy phenomenon, but some care is needed in regard to the information presented (in much the same way as care is needed when reading printed material produced by strangers).

4218 In particular, the information could well be:

- inaccurate, even though it has been put up in good faith

- accurate but incomplete

- out of date

- deliberately false by way of hoax

- deliberately false in order to manipulate prices fraudulently.

4219 Sometimes "unofficial" rival sites are set up, especially by people who feel that the corresponding official pages are inadequate —as indeed they may be. There is nothing wrong with this as long as all the pages concerned are clearly labelled as not being official (preferably with a hyperlink to the real site, if there is one) and as long as investors allow for the status of the site when interpreting the data.

4220 Information on screen, particularly if it is neatly set out, somehow looks very creditable. However, all general information suffers from the obvious defect that it can have no regard to the circumstances of any particular reader.

4221 Comments from the supporters of a particular stock, even if propagated with the best of intentions, can easily lead to an unwarranted price escalation, followed in due course by a collapse and many burnt fingers.

4222 In a different category are web sites marketing esoteric investments, such as ostriches or whatever happens to be the flavour of the month at the time. As persons who have poured money into such schemes in response to print advertisements know only too well the failure rate of such arrangements is very high.

A glossy Internet presence is unlikely to reduce the inherent risks.

Legislation

4223 Various sites allow existing State and Federal legislation and new Bills to be read online or downloaded.

4224 Sites put up by government departments often feature Ministerial media releases, official reports and the like, as well as key documents such as the annual Budget papers.

4225 Parliamentary sites give details of Parliamentary inquiries and provide access to Hansard.

Listed Companies

Background

4226 These days all Australian companies have a great need to communicate effectively with their owners, creditors, employees and customers. Many companies listed on the stock exchange produce expensive and otherwise elaborate annual reports. It is thus somewhat surprising that so few have taken the logical next step and established for themselves a presence on the Internet.

4227 It is unfortunately true that not all persons who own shares are computer literate. Nor do all investors have ready access to the Internet. It is also a fact that not all persons who own shares take that ownership seriously and want to absorb company information directly themselves, preferring just to act on the advice of their stockbrokers.

4228 Nevertheless, many less apathetic investors would welcome the opportunity to inform themselves rapidly and inexpensively of developments by companies in which they hold shares. They might also wish to peruse data relating to other companies which they are studying because they have in mind acquiring a parcel.

4229 Space limitations in the financial press mean that announcements to the stock exchange and to the media by listed companies—except possibly in the case of a small number of leaders—often get very little exposure. Conventional company communications to shareholders, unless the development concerned is truly a major one, may not deal with a matter until several months after the event.

4230 In all such cases if companies co-operated then interested investors with Internet access could, virtually at the press of a button, call up the full announcement on their own computers at home or at work (or possibly in a public library or at an Internet cafe), either reading it on screen while online or more probably saving it to a file for more detailed study offline later on. If desired, they could also readily produce a hard copy of the text on their own printers.

4231 The additional cost to a listed company of providing such a service would be negligible, both absolutely and even more so on a "per shareholder" basis. The actual words of the announcement would not only already exist but these days they would also in practice already be available in electronic form. Thus adding them to an existing set of web pages on the Internet would be both cheap and extremely simple in administrative terms. Furthermore, this could happen literally within seconds of the relevant information being made public.

4232 Because no expenses for paper, printing or postage would be involved the size of any material put on a web page would not really matter. Unlike the position at present its distribution would also be friendly to the environment, as it would not use up any forests.

4233 If as a result of such developments a significant number of shareholders elected to opt out of receiving some bulky documents in their conventional form then in due course there could well be a considerable net cost saving to companies overall.

4234 It is, of course, true that some initial effort in designing and setting up a good quality shareholder—based home page would be involved, but such a one-off effort and the associated ongoing running costs would have their payback in enhanced image and greater goodwill.

Links

4235 To illustrate further, such a home page could contain an index of hypertext links to other pages containing information of direct relevance to investors, such as the following:

- A computer version of the company's last annual report in full.

- A summary of this report.

- The chairman's address to the last annual general meeting.

- Details of the questions asked at that meeting and appropriate replies to these. (Admittedly, some of these questions might be trivial—but it is better to have a "warts and all" approach rather than to engage in censorship.)

- The results of any polls taken at a general meeting.

- Recent quarterly or half-yearly reports.

- Announcements relating to declared dividends, giving details of amounts, books closing and payable dates, franking status and so on.

- An indication of the likely size of future dividends.

- Announcements of new rights issues, giving full details of the issue price and the relevant dates (such information is generally reported very inadequately in the daily press).

- The notice convening any forthcoming meeting of the company.

- All other recent announcements to the stock exchange and/or to the shareholders.

- Other media releases likely to be of interest to shareholders.

- Non—private communications between the company and the Australian Stock Exchange (such as those formerly included in the company files made available for inspection by the general public).

4236 Other pertinent reference material could also be included—see paras 4261 to 4267.

4237 Ideally, the index should indicate the size in kilobytes of the relevant file, its date of creation and, where relevant, a two or three line synopsis of its contents. To aid users who have downloaded material onto their own systems and who later on wish to get more files online it would generally be preferable for absolute rather than relative addresses to be used in all hyperlinks.

4238 Such links could also be provided to other unrelated web sites likely to be of interest to shareholders, such as those mentioned earlier in this chapter. Many companies would no doubt also wish to add links to other sites of specific relevance to their own investors.

4239 A favourite device on many parts of the Internet is the "FAQ"—a list of *frequently asked questions* and their answers. In the case of listed companies several different such lists might be appropriate:

- One about the company's activities and performance, as viewed from an investor perspective.

- Another about the company's products and services, as appropriate from a customer perspective.

- A third about administrative matters affecting shareholders—for example, how to get dividends paid into a bank account or the various options for receiving additional shares in lieu of cash dividends.

4240 On wider issues, it should be remembered that such Internet pages would present a particularly good opportunity for the board and management of a company to speak out and explain themselves at length without having their words distorted. The company's strategic thinking and its plans for future growth could readily be presented in a positive way.

4241 If desired, corporate logos and appropriate graphs, tables, cartoons and photographs could, of course, also be provided. However, having regard to the extra time it takes for users to load down such non-textual material, such items—no matter how pretty—should preferably be made available only on separate pages for the benefit of those readers who specifically wish to call them up.

4242 The inclusion of a sound file featuring a welcoming message from the chairman or the managing director can be a nice touch, but it has to be regarded as rather a gimmick. Once again, large files are involved even for very short messages and serious investors might thus appreciate an opportunity, as an alternative, to read a text version instead.

4243 From a shareholder perspective an approach on the above lines would enable each investor to call up information directly targeted to his needs, instead of getting a pile of paper of mainly irrelevant information. Furthermore, researchers would know that whatever current data they looked at would always be completely up to date.

4244 Although participating investors would incur the usual telephone and Internet access charges they would be able to examine both topical and historical material without having to pay inspection fees of the type recently being imposed by the stock exchange libraries in relation to the official ASX files of listed company data. And they would be able to do all this without leaving their own desks and at any hour of the day or night.

4245 Furthermore, any textual material downloaded could readily be searched by users for announcements containing appropriate keywords.

4246 For persons keen to do their own sums any pertinent figures could also be fed directly into a spreadsheet for more detailed analysis.

e-mail

4247 Apart from the World Wide Web another part of the Internet has relevance to listed companies—namely e-mail. This could be used in at least four different ways:

- For questions and comments relating to company performance or prospects and the like— which investors could send to an e-mail address at the company's head office.

- For investor requests for annual reports or other company documents in hard copy form.

- For investor requests to be put on an electronic mailing list to get some or all company announcements automatically as and when they are made. It is clearly not practicable for investors to search on a continuous basis the web pages of every company in which they are interested.

- For mechanical questions relating to their share-holdings or for notifying changes of address, bank details, tax file numbers, annual report mailing requests and the like—which investors could send to an e-mail address at the company's share registry. In appropriate cases investors could very easily send identical electronic messages to more than one company.

4248 The Internet could also be used to feature prospectuses for new issues. In addition, it could be used to provide forms which enabled members of the public to order hard copies of such material electronically.

Other Aspects

4249 Companies need to publicise the availability of their Internet facilities by specific advice to their own shareholders and by mention in the directory pages of their annual reports.

4250 Possibly an official central register of Internet addresses could be maintained and kept up to date by the ASX and in various other places, inspectable both manually and electronically (with hyperlinks).

4251 Companies would be able to measure the number of "hits" made to their shareholder information pages each day. This could itself give them some useful information as to shareholder interest.

4252 Initially, no doubt, usage would be relatively small. However, as knowledge of the facility spread its use would grow rapidly and its existence would in itself become an additional reason for persons to get themselves on as subscribers to the Internet. In 10 years' time web pages will no doubt be regarded as the norm.

4253 In due course it could even become compulsory for listed companies, whenever they file public information electronically with the Australian Stock Exchange and/or the Australian Securities and Investments Commission, to also put a copy onto the Internet, thus facilitating authoritative searches.

4254 In the meantime shareholders who are keen to speed up this process and who would like to get a "code of best practice" established in this area could raise the matter during the question time at a few company annual general meetings (or even by snail mail to their chairmen). Topics such as the lack of an Internet presence or the inadequacies of any existing web pages are worthy of much greater public debate.

4255 Companies should also include an electronic search facility on one of their pages. This would enable readers to enter a keyword in an appropriate field on their own computer screens and instantly gain access to all material produced by the company which dealt with that particular subject.

4256 During proxy battles each side soliciting votes could readily publish its own arguments on the Internet. Copies of relevant media releases and correspondence could easily be included.

4257 Similarly, during hostile takeovers the home pages of both the bidding and the target companies could set out their respective cases.

4258 Because of the international nature of the World Wide Web the ready access to the home pages of Australian companies might encourage further investment in these companies by foreign parties, thus boosting local share values.

4259 Especially for the benefit of investors resident overseas, every company's site should also feature the latest market price and dividend yield, etc., of each class of listed security (updated at frequent intervals and with the corresponding figures as at selected preceding dates). For the benefit of local investors the corresponding grossed-up yield (allowing for the franking credits) should also be shown.

4260 Following recent legislative changes the Internet can also be used to facilitate proxy voting by shareholders. This can be much more convenient than sending in proxies by snail mail or even by fax.

Summary

4261 Data on the following lines would greatly assist investors trying to trace information which, while no doubt publicly available, is otherwise scattered over numerous separate pieces of paper:

- A brief history of the company.

- A description of the business.

- A list of the company's corporate objectives (preferably in meaningful rather than in motherhood terms).

- A summary of the major announcements made during the preceding 12 to 18 months, with appropriate hypertext links which allow the full text to be called up.

- A financial calendar for the next 12 months (the expected dates of reports, meetings, dividends and the like and the closing dates for enrolments to any plans and for eligibility to vote at meetings).

- Profiles of the company's directors and senior executives, especially any who were appointed since the last annual report.

- The amounts (both per share and in the aggregate) and all relevant dates for dividends, calls, share issues and other capital changes over the last five to ten years.

- The franking status of each of the above-mentioned dividends.

- The balance of the company's franking account.

- Details of the terms and conditions relating to all outstanding convertible securities and options, including especially any created since the end of the last reporting period.

- Full details of the dividend entitlement, calls program and voting power of any contributing shares.

- A table showing the number of shares of each class on issue as at a convenient starting date about five years earlier and all changes since.

- The company's ASX Code (to help shareholders to get used to it).

- The state or territory of incorporation (which is relevant for the stamp duty on off-market transfers).

- Where applicable, details of the company's dividend reinvestment and similar plans.

- Statistics as to their utilisation.

- Details of any employee share and option schemes.

- Details of any shareholder discount schemes.

- If material, details of any pending litigation.

- Details of any successful prosecutions against the company or its officers over the last few years.

- A list of significant transactions by insiders over a similar period.

- A 10-year table of key financial data and ratios, and of figures such as the number of shareholders and the number of employees.

- A 10-year table setting out selected market prices (both actual and adjusted) for each class of the company's listed securities—for example, the highest, lowest and closing prices each calendar quarter.

- Addresses, telephone and facsimile numbers and e-mail addresses for the company's main offices and also for those of its share registry.

- Recent speeches by senior company executives.

- Information designed for the company's customers.

- School project material.

- Details of any significant sponsorships.

- A statement such as "This page (http://www.xxx.com.au) was last updated on ...".

4262 A similar list to the above is set out in para. 852—but, of course, information on a web site is available to shareholders instantaneosly and does not involve printing, distribution and storage costs.

Capital Gains Tax Aspects

4263 There are really no limits as to what could usefully be included on a company's home page. To illustrate, one matter which greatly troubles many shareholders is complying with the capital gains tax disclosure rules discussed in Chapter 29. The Internet could provide an effective solution to this problem.

4264 Having regard to the data needed for the capital gains tax calculations it would be very helpful if each company which was listed before 20 September 1985 and which has made any rights issues since that date set out a table itemising all such issues, showing in particular the market value per right as at the time of exercise on each occasion and the indexation factor for the calendar quarter concerned.

4265 This information is required by shareholders who sell shares arising out of rights issues accruing on their pre-20 September 1985 holdings in order to take advantage of the "grandfathering" concession, Section 160ZYO(4) of the *Income Tax Assessment Act 1936*.

4266 In the same way it would be useful if each company which currently has, or which has ever had, a dividend reinvestment or top up plan also set out a list of the dates of issue of all plan shares since the commencement of the plan, together with their respective issue prices and the indexation factors for the calendar quarters concerned.

4267 Such conveniently located information would greatly facilitate their shareholders' task of preparing tax returns for the financial years in which any of the relevant shares are sold.

Assessing Companies

4268 A listed company's web site provides another way for shareholders to judge the company. For example, the absence of a web site probably indicates that a company is not technologically minded. A poorly designed site may be a symptom of poor management. Information which is boring, out of date or hard to follow carries its own message.

4269 Correspondingly, a company successfully using a site to boost its sales is likely to have increasing profitability, even if takes time for them to build up. A site with good product information and comparative data for different models is a positive asset.

A site with useful after-sales information demonstrates that the company is interested in preserving goodwill.

Overseas Sites

4270 Most of the local sites mentioned above have their counterparts overseas. Sometimes such sites are of much better quality than found in Australia and they may also be more easily accessed.

4271 By virtue of free e-mail mailing lists it is to some extent easier to monitor United States stocks from a computer in Australia than it is to monitor local stocks.

4272 On the other hand, it is also possible for overseas senders out of reach of the Australian authorities to send illegal "get rich quick" proposals to unsuspecting and gullible Australian investors.

Chapter 43—How to read a Prospectus

*The big print giveth and the small
print taketh away*
—Tom Waitts

Background

4301 Raising money from the general public in the way described in Chapters 6 and 7 requires the issue of a *prospectus*—a legal document, registered with the authorities, and complying with Section 1022 of the *Corporations Law*.

4302 The essential words of this section are reproduced below. The law requires that prospectuses shall "contain all such information as investors and their professional advisers would reasonably require, and reasonably expect to find in the prospectus, for the purpose of making an informed assessment of:

(a)   the assets and liabilities, financial position, profits and losses, and prospects of the corporation; and

(b)   the rights attaching to the securities".

4303 This is actually a more stringent requirement than applied under earlier legislation which provided a statutory checklist of the information which had to be set out.

4304 In practice a modern prospectus must also set out in considerable detail the precise terms of the issue—its size, the issue price, the opening and closing dates, the asset backing, the proposed annual return to the investors, the dividend policy, the expected franking status of any dividends, the maturity dates (if applicable), and so on.

4305 The prospectus should also set out the existing capital structure and the background of the company and its directors, together with details of any proposed or existing dividend reinvestment, shareholder discount and employee share plans or the like.

4306 Thus, for example, in the case of an established business, certain up-to-date accounting information would need to be provided. Usually a pro forma balance sheet is included, showing both the actual balance sheet and what it would have looked like if the proceeds of the issue (net of expenses) had been received and if any pre-float rearrangements had already been implemented.

4307 Frequently reports by independent experts are included (see Chapter 34).

4308 Sometimes a glossary of technical terms used in the prospectus is presented.

4309 A prospectus does not need to reproduce all the law of the land—for example, it would not need to recite such well-known facts as that transfers of shares involve stamp duty.

4310 In an endeavour to protect potential investors there are severe penalties for false or misleading statements or material omissions.

4311 Nevertheless, prospectuses can be bulky documents and it is always possible for important information to be buried away in small print under innocuous headings such as "additional statutory information" at the back. However, prospectuses issued by responsible organisations would normally go out of their way to highlight any unusual features and do their best to ensure that investors always went in with their eyes wide open.

4312 Prospectuses cannot remain in force for more than 12 months.

The Issue Price

4313 The usual Australian practice has been to set out a firm issue price for securities offered by a prospectus. However, some large recent issues have used a tender process for applications by institutions, but with a provision for smaller investors to pay a price based on that paid by the successful tenderers but subject to a defined maximum figure and/or involving a small discount.

4314 Tender issues involve some additional risks for individual applicants—for example:

- The issue price may turn out to be at the high end of an indicated range rather than near the middle, as might have been expected.

- Alternatively, the price may turn out to be at the low end of the indicated range—while this provides a cheap entry it also demonstrates to the world that the issue was not regarded as attractive.

- The tender price may turn out to be an accurate reflection of the true value of the shares and of their market value on listing, thus removing the scope for stag profits (see para 624).

4315 Another variation to this theme is to have one issue price for applicants taking their chances in a portion of the issue made available to the public at large and a different, higher, issue price for applicants receiving a firm number of shares from their broker. (A firm allocation ensures that clients do not miss out getting stock and do not have any money tied up pending the processing of refund cheques in the event of rationing due to oversubscriptions.)

Reading between the Lines

4316 Apart from considering the specific aspects discussed in Chapter 6 and above, intelligent readers of prospectuses will also need to read between the lines and to take into account numerous miscellaneous aspects such as the following (in no particular order):

- the reputation of the directors
- the size of their holdings in the company
- the reputation of the underwriter (see paras 614 to 616)
- the underwriter's track record in regard to previous floats
- the reputation of any experts whose reports are included in the prospectus
- the attractiveness of the industry
- the company's position in its industry
- the reasons for the issue
- the use to be made of the money being raised
- the quality of the company's assets (both tangible and intangible)
- whether floats of other comparable companies are likely in the foreseeable future
- whether the size of the issue is likely to overload the market
- whether the interests of insiders and outside investors are likely to coincide

- whether the value being attributed to the assets is consistent with the earnings on those assets

- the amount of any goodwill flowing to the vendors

- details of all related party transactions

- whether the company is proposing to change direction

- whether the issue offends current market prejudices in regard to aspects such as diversification, gearing ratios, complex structures, unfamiliar concepts and the like

- temporary features, such as a low or zero tax rate for the time being due to past losses

- franking credits from the pre-listing period

- the effect of any restrictions imposed in regard to who may and who may not apply for the shares.

4317 The above checklist is not meant to imply either that these are the only relevant matters to be considered or that there are "right" and "wrong" answers to any of the questions raised.

4318 For example, an accumulated credit balance in a franking account is a "plus" as representing additional value which is not shown in the balance sheet. However, it is also a non-recurring item and is thus not as attractive as something ongoing.

4319 Again, a high gearing ratio has both advantages (potentially higher returns for shareholders) and disadvantages (greater risk).

4320 Another factor to be considered is the critical mass of the enterprise. Small companies, if successful, have the potential to grow at much faster rates than large ones—but they also have much higher failure rates. Large companies benefit from economies of scale and from lower borrowing costs. The level of reserves available for a "worst case" scenario should be taken into account, especially in the case of new enterprises or new ventures by existing operators.

4321 Some companies use stapled securities (see para. 489) in order to make tax-free distributions to investors in the early years of a project when losses are expected. In effect, they are just giving investors some of their own money back, as distinct from declaring dividends out of profits in the normal way. Subscribers to such issues should be aware of the difference.

4322 Another variation of this theme involves projects with an income guarantee provided by the vendor of assets to the company. While money provided under such a guarantee is technically income (and taxable as such) it really represents a refund of the investors' own capital as its value would have been built into the consideration paid for the assets.

4323 In the case of issues which are not being listed on the stock exchange, another question arises: How easy will it be for investors to get out at reasonable prices when they wish to quit their investment?

4324 Other clues as to the likely success or otherwise of an issue and a possible indication of any scarcity value for the stock are provided by factors such as:

- Was the prospectus sent to the investor as a special favour or alternatively because he took the initiative in requesting it?

- Was the investor offered a firm allocation of stock and, if so, was it particularly large or particularly small?

- Are prospectuses being sent out widely to persons on junk mailing lists?

- Is the availability of prospectuses being advertised in media not conventionally used for such a purpose?

- Do applicants for prospectuses receive unsolicited follow-up telephone calls from personnel in the underwriter's office?

4325 See also paras 3902 to 3906 in regard to privatisation issues.

4326 For legal reasons relating to the personal liability of the directors and experts who sign a prospectus such documents, despite their great size—and possibly even because of it— have become less and less meaningful. Understandably, no promoter will want to say outright that an issue is a dud. The solution usually adopted is to set out a long list of "risk factors". Unfortunately, this approach tends to give equal prominence to minor matters and to more serious aspects. Furthermore, the prospectuses of brilliant issues are likely to carry similar lists.

4327 However, it is possible to identify some warning signs. These are particularly relevant in combination:

- a high number of vendor shares relative to the number of shares being issued for cash to new investors (this indicates a transfer of wealth away from the applicants to the promoters)

- a high number of vendor options (these will be a drag on the share price if the company does well but will leave any pain to be borne only by the new investors in the reverse situation)

- a right to accept oversubscriptions (this will reduce the pent-up demand for the shares if the float is successful but with no countervailing benefit if it flops; it may also reduce the earnings per share)

- a cash payment for goodwill which is large in relation to the cash being raised from the public (this also deprives the company of finance for future growth)

- a low net tangible asset backing per share, compared with the issue price

- a small number of listed shares after the issue is concluded (this will make the market in the shares illiquid and will also mean that the institutions will avoid the company)

- the inclusion of major assets in the balance sheet at a valuation by the directors instead of at a valuation by an independent expert (and/or at a valuation date some time ago)

- the absence of a prominent organisation as underwriter

- a higher than normal underwriting fee—for example, 5 or 6 per cent of the funds being raised—

and/or one involving a large number of "free" options

- easy availability of the prospectus to anybody who asks for it even when there is no existing business relationship

- an absence of media comment, possibly because of a fear that a meaningful analysis might invite defamation proceedings (this silence will probably contribute to a lack of investor interest after the float).

4328 Accounting is an art rather than a science. It is possible to divert profit to some reserve or provision—perhaps even on the basis of just being very conservative—and to release it from this reserve or provision later on.

4329 Consider the following scenario relating to the five years before listing:

Year	-4	-3	-2	-1		Total
Actual Profit $'000	500	500	500	500	500	2500
Transfers to/from Reserves $'000	-195	-120	-24	95	244	0
Published Profit $'000	305	380	476	595	744	2500
Growth Rate %		25	25	25	25	

4330 This gives the quite misleading impression:

- that the profit is growng at 25 per cent per annum

- that the most recent profit, which would strongly influence the issue price, is much higher than it really is.

Managed Fund Prospectuses

4331 As discussed above, a prospectus is a legal document issued by an organisation seeking to raise investment funds from the general public. Prospectuses are used not only for share issues but also for issues involving managed funds—for example, unit trusts (both listed and unlisted).

4332 Such documents are meant to give their lay readers sufficient information about a proposed investment to enable them to make proper decisions as to whether to invest or not.

4333 Prospective investors in a unit trust may wish to start their study by reading the trust's investment objectives. They should satisfy themselves that these are in line with their own requirements, risk profile and priorities. If they are not, then there is clearly no point in proceeding any further.

4334 It is, of course, necessary to distinguish between the intentions of the management as set out in the prospectus on the one hand and the formal investment powers available under the trust deed on the other. The latter would normally be much wider, to cover as many eventualities down the track as possible without the need to amend the deed. This can, of course, mean that a trust can change direction in a manner not to an investor's liking—the possibility of this happening is the price which has to be paid for flexibility.

4335 Some prohibitions in the trust deed can also be relevant-for example, risk—averse investors may welcome undertakings not to deal in derivatives or not to breach certain debt ratios.

4336 The power to borrow also needs consideration. Using borrowed funds is a two-edged sword, enhancing equity returns when things go well but increasing the losses if anything ever goes wrong. However, a limited right to borrow in order to meet redemption requests is probably in investors' best interests even in conservative funds which do not allow borrowing for permanent investment purposes.

4337 Borrowing is not uncommon in property trusts, where its main effect is to reduce the amount of income which is subject to immediate taxation and to replace it by greater capital growth. There is nothing wrong with this in principle as long as the investor is aware of what is going on and allows for it in his overall portfolio composition. It would, for example, clearly be unwise to increase the leverage risk by borrowing on the security of units in trusts which are themselves heavy borrowers.

4338 The manager and the trustee should both be reputable organisations. (Legislation removing the need for trusts to have both a manager and a trustee was passed recently.)

4339 The trust's distribution policy should also be examined to ensure that it is tax effective for the investor concerned. Some trusts make distributions out of capital sources (in effect giving the investor back some of his own money), thus creating an impression of profitability which is not in accordance with the facts.

4340 In the case of established trusts the actual portfolio as at a recent date, as set out in the prospectus, will give an indication of how the manager's philosophy is given effect to in practice. It will also show the degree of spread and how liquid the trust is.

4341 The prospectus will set out whether the trust is to be listed on the stock exchange or not. In the case of unlisted trusts, the investor's ability to cash in units should be examined closely. For instance, can they be redeemed at any time? How much notice must be given? Are there any exit fees? Are the minimum and maximum amounts in line with the investor's requirements?

4342 Other information in the prospectus which should be considered includes the following:

- The level of fees and commission.
- The minimum investment amount permitted at entry.
- The minimum investment amount permitted for additional contributions.
- The minimum amount permitted for partial withdrawals.
- The minimum balance which must be retained after a partial withdrawal.
- The opening and closing dates of the issue (if applicable).
- The likely distribution rate and its tax status.
- The frequency of distributions.
- The policy in regard to distributing capital gains.

- The net tangible asset backing per unit.

- The requirements for amending the trust deed.

- Details of any distribution reinvestment plan.

- Details of any arrangements for making switches between related funds.

- Details of any contracts to buy assets for the trust.

- The rights of unitholders to transfer units privately.

- The rights of unitholders in regard to general meetings.

- Details of any cooling-off period.

4343 Many stockbrokers, understandably conscious of their expense rates and the time which can easily be spent in explaining even simple things to inexperienced investors, discourage some clients from initiating market transactions. Instead, the brokers head the clients into pooled investment vehicles. Unit trusts have many advantages, but they are not the best investment avenue for everybody. Persons who would prefer to invest directly should always insist on their right to do so.

Managed Fund Fees

4344 The fees charged by different unit trust managements vary enormously both in size and in the way in which they are expressed in trust deeds and prospectuses.

4345 Of course, fees by themselves can be misleading—a labourer is worthy of his hire; it may be better to pay a high fee and get a good quality investment rather than to pay a lower fee and suffer from poor performance.

4346 Naturally, it is also possible to get the worst of both worlds—high fees and low (or even negative) returns. A high level of fees does not in itself ever guarantee success.

4347 Fees are normally built into the buying and selling unit prices quoted to the general public and into the amount of each periodical distribution. Fees can be charged:

- At entry ("front-end" fees), usually as a percentage of the assets being acquired.

- Monthly or quarterly, usually as a percentage of the assets represented by the units and/or the income.

- At exit ("rear-end" fees), usually as a percentage of the assets being disposed of.

4348 Prices are normally rounded up to buyers of units and down to sellers of units. The effect of this can be greater than is often realised—for example, to convert a theoretical price of 47.01 cents per unit to 48 cents amounts to a surreptitious 2.1 per cent increase in the price.

4349 In comparing different funds, like should always be compared with like. A fund charging 5 per cent of the assets being acquired as a front-end fee is giving better value than a fund charging 5 per cent of the amount being contributed:

Price	Assets	Effective Charge
105	100	5.000 per cent
100	95	5.263 per cent

4350 Similarly, entry and exit fees and the periodical charges should be looked at in combination. Some funds allow the charges which would otherwise be paid upfront to be paid instead in the form of lower income distributions in, say, the first year. This results in a tax saving for the unitholder.

4351 Many funds use a sliding scale for the front-end fees. While this is, no doubt, justifiable on economic grounds, it must also discourage investors from spreading their money over several different funds.

4352 The fees mentioned above, which flow to the manager and to the trustee, should ideally cover all the marketing and administrative costs. Investors would need to take into account any other disbursements which are to be charged directly to the trust fund, apart from the expenses of acquiring or disposing of trust assets (which are properly treated as part of the capital cost).

4353 It is clearly not appropriate that any expenses relating to future prospectuses or otherwise applying to the marketing of new units should be borne by the existing unitholders.

4354 Some trust managers provide certain services in house—for example, in relation to the management of properties owned by the trust, on the basis of fees equal to those which might be paid to outside experts under some formula. On the surface this might seem reasonable enough, but it actually poses yet another conflict of interest problem—the fund manager should really be expected to shop around for the best deal available from any outside source.

4355 The total fees set out in the prospectus are relevant in relation to the assets and income being acquired per dollar invested.

4356 Quite separate from that is the commission (part of the front-end fee) which flows to the intermediary. This commission entitlement should be looked at in regard to the possible bias which its level may induce in the recommendations being proffered by the intermediary.

4357 Intermediaries who charge a fee for service may choose to pass their commission entitlements back to their clients, either in cash or in the form of additional units. Some intermediaries who operate on the basis of not giving advice are also willing to rebate a proportion of their commission to investors lodging applications through them.

4358 If a trust proposes to invest not in direct investments but rather in units in other unit trusts then investors need to have regard to any double impost of fees which may be involved in such an arrangement.

4359 When comparing the costs of using listed and unlisted trusts regard should always be had to the *sum* of the buying and selling expenses in both cases.

4360 Ideally, the purchase or sale of an asset by a unit trust should not affect its unit price, as the total assets and the number of units on issue should not be affected by a swap of cash for other assets. However, the market value of an asset is unlikely to be the same as the value of that asset in the trust fund, as such a value would need to allow for transaction costs.

4361 Some newly-formed trusts undertake to keep the unit price fixed for an initial period, such as one month. This may mean that they keep their funds in a liquid form during that period, rather than start to build up a portfolio in accordance with the announced long-term intentions. In a rising market this can be unfair to early subscribers. Alternatively, such a provision may result in cross-subsidisation between different investors.

4362 Current unit prices are always obtainable on application from the fund manager concerned. Prices for a large number of funds are also published on a weekly basis in some newspapers.

Some Hidden Traps

4363 Apart from the fee structure, certain other information in a unit trust prospectus will be very relevant to investors.

4364 Past results by the manager and/or by companies associated with the manager, both in the trust itself (if it has been in existence for some time) and in other trusts in the same stable, should be looked at carefully. While a brilliant past performance is, of course, no guarantee that the future will be equally good, a poor track record—for example, a low return on funds invested or a growth rate in unit prices at less than the rate of inflation—is a danger sign.

4365 Figures should always be compared with industry norms. To illustrate, in isolation a 28 per cent increase in a unit price over a 12-month period might sound excellent. However, if the comparable index moved up by some 54 per cent then the result is revealed as almost disastrous—a point which would not be apparent from merely reading the prospectus by itself.

4366 Forecasts of future performance should always be treated with considerable caution. Any indicated growth rate should have been calculated using proper compound interest principles.

4367 While the future rate of return is relevant in the context of getting value for money, the form of that return may also be of consequence to a particular investor. For example, a pensioner in need of periodical income would probably not be well served in a trust dedicated to high growth and low income, although, of course, any desired cash stream can be achieved by selling off some units from time to time. Nevertheless, this would involve additional hassle and probably higher than necessary charges.

4368 Particularly in the case of property trusts, the manager's policy on revaluations should be studied. There is no point in having increasing asset values if the benefit from these does not flow to the right generation of investors.

4369 The wording in prospectuses should always be read cynically. For example, "No exit charges after three years" probably means "Exit charges imposed if investors quit within three years".

4370 Extra care should be taken if the trust has acquired or proposes to acquire assets with one or more of the following characteristics:

- Assets belonging to parties who are not at arms' length from the promoters.

- Property which has been on the market for a long time.

- Very specialised proposals—for example, interests in time sharing schemes.

4371 Some funds have a system of incentive fees. Such an approach has obvious advantages for unitholders, provided that the incentives are not too generous—especially in relation to performance measured in dollar terms to the extent that it is virtually automatic as a result of inflation rather than due to the skill of the manager.

4372 The period over which performance is measured can have some relevance. For example, a fund with a mediocre performance over a whole year may have had three poor quarters and one excellent quarter. To pay an incentive fee based on the performance in the latter without regard to the former may not really be warranted even though the deed may allow this.

4373 The existence of an incentive formula on these lines may even be counterproductive as far as the investors are concerned, as it can encourage a fund manager to seek out the more speculative investment situations in the hope of boosting short-term results.

4374 The following remarks apply only to those unlisted trusts which have units which all rank equally—as distinct from, say, cash management trusts, were income is credited on a daily basis to each unitholder having regard to the balance in his individual account.

4375 The basic concept of a unit price representing the asset backing of the unit plus or minus certain loadings and round—figuring is fundamental. The asset backing at any point of time between successive income distributions would normally include some accrued income.

4376 The unit price immediately after the books close for a distribution has to fall in order to reflect that entitlement. Thus an investor buying newly-created units shortly before the books closing date for a half-yearly distribution will always get a distribution covering the full six months, which on the surface may sound attractive.

4377 However, this feature has been made possible by the pricing mechanism—and an investor has, in effect, paid for his own distribution in the form of a higher unit price. (A buyer of existing Commonwealth bonds shortly before an interest due date would similarly get six months' worth of interest for a holding of much shorter duration. This, too, will have been built into the price.)

4378 Worse still, in the circumstances just described a unitholder will normally pay tax on the full distribution, notwithstanding the underlying fact that most of it is really a return of the investor's own capital. (Collectively, the accrued income adjustments out of capital can enable the trust to declare part of the distribution in tax-free form.)

4379 Whether a particular unit trust issue offered by a prospectus represents good value for money obviously depends in part on the alternatives available. Investors should, of course, always decide first of all the category of investment which they want.

4380 On the assumption that a particular issue would suit the requirements in that regard the next question is, how does it measure up in relation to:

- Other unit trust issues available under current or imminent prospectuses?
- Unit trusts available on the stock exchange?
- Direct investments?

Appendix 1—Share Price and Inflation Indices

The table below has five columns of data:

(1)   Australian Stock Exchange
      All Ordinaries Index for the date shown

(2)   Consumer Price Index for the quarter
      ending on the date shown (eight capital cities)(ABS
      6401.0)

(3)   Australian Stock Exchange
      All Ordinaries Accumulation Index for the date
      shown

(4)   Dow Jones Industrial Average (DJIA) for the date
      shown

(5)   Ratio of the DJIA to the All Ordinaries for the date
      shown

	(1) ALL ORDS	(2) CPI	(3) ALL ORDS ACCUM	(4) DOW JONES	(5) RATIO (4)/(1)
31/12/79	Base 500.0		1000		
1989-90	Base	100.0			
31/12/85	1003.8	72.7	2622	1546.67	1.54
30/06/86	1179.8	75.6	3134	1892.72	1.60
31/12/86	1473.2	79.8	3991	1895.95	1.29
30/06/87	1764.1	82.6	4841	2418.53	1.37
31/12/87	1318.8	85.5	3678	1938.83	1.47
30/06/88	1555.0	88.5	4424	2141.71	1.38
31/12/88	1487.4	92.0	4335	2168.57	1.46
30/06/89	1521.1	95.2	4580	2440.06	1.60
31/12/89	1649.0	99.2	5089	2753.20	1.67
30/06/90	1500.7	102.5	4767	2880.70	1.92
31/12/90	1279.8	106.0	4198	2633.66	2.06
30/06/91	1506.2	106.0	5047	2906.80	1.93
31/12/91	1651.4	107.6	5635	3168.83	1.92

	(1) ALL ORDS	(2) CPI	(3) ALL ORDS ACCUM	(4) DOW JONES	(5) RATIO (4)/(1)
30/06/92	1644.7	107.3	5720	3318.52	2.02
31/12/92	1549.9	107.9	5505	3301.01	2.13
30/06/93	1738.1	109.3	6287	3516.08	2.02
31/12/93	2173.6	110.0	8002	3754.00	1.73
30/06/94	1989.1	111.2	7448	3624.96	1.82
31/12/94	1912.7	112.8	7308	3834.44	2.00
30/06/95	2017.0	116.2	7873	4551.95	2.26
31/12/95	2203.0	118.5	8783	5117.12	2.32
30/06/96	2242.1	119.8	9119	5654.63	2.52
31/12/96	2424.6	120.3	10065	6448.27	2.66
30/06/97	2725.9	120.2	11541	7672.79	2.81
31/12/97	2616.5	120.0	11296	7908.25	3.02
30/06/98	2668.4	121.0	11731	8952.02	3.35

See paras 979 to 985 for an explanation of the stock exchange indices.

Between 31 December 1986 and 30 June 1998 the All Ordinaries and the Dow Jones increased by factors of 1.81 and 4.72 respectively—a strikingly different performance.

This period included the stock market crash of October 1987. Even allowing for this, share investors in Australia who continued to hold would have averaged an annual growth rate of 5.30 per cent on top of dividends. Their United States counterparts would similarly have averaged an annual growth rate of 14.45 per cent on top of dividends (in US dollar terms).

Since it was formed as at 31 December 1979 the All Ordinaries Accumulation Index has increased over eleven—fold. The return to investors over the 18 years has been 14.42 per cent per annum, including both income and capital growth but excluding charges and taxation.

Appendix 2—The Size of the Market: Selected Statistics

ASX Main Board:	30/06/87	30/06/97	Growth Rate
Listed Companies (number)	1320	1198	
Market Capitalisation:			
equities ($ billion)	226.3	734.5	12.5% p.a.
fixed interest ($ billion)	44.1	122.3	10.7% p.a.

Turnover 1996-97:

Transactions (million)	5.4
Shares (billion)	90.0
Value ($ billion)	212.7
Call Options (million)	6.9
Value ($ billion)	3.0
Put Options (million)	3.3
Value ($ billion)	1.0

Warrant Types Available:	30/06/96	30/06/97
Call warrants (number)	26	102
Put warrants (number)	0	20
Endowment warrants (number)	25	40
Instalment warrants (number)	0	22
Capital Plus warrants (number)	0	4
Total (number)	51	188

Liquidity Ratio (the value of turnover divided by the average market capitalisation) for 1996-97: 55 per cent

Number of active ASX Member Organisations as at 30/06/97: 87

Source: derived from Australian Stock Exchange Limited, Annual **Report 1997**

Appendix 3—Australian Shareownership Patterns

Note: In the figures below "direct investment" refers to shares owned personally or through family companies or trusts, as distinct from through managed funds, superannuation or the like.

Adults (18 years and over) who owned shares directly (May 1997):

Number:	2,822,000
Proportion:	20.4 per cent
Males:	23.2 per cent
Females:	17.9 per cent

The proportion of each of the following groups which owned shares directly (May 1997):

	Per cent
Professionals	23.6
Managerial	28.8
Skilled office workers	21.3
Skilled trade workers	14.8
Unskilled workers	11.7
Age 18 to 24	10.1
Age 25 to 34	18.2
Age 35 to 44	23.1
Age 45 to 54	27.0
Age 55 and over	21.4

The total value of the share portfolios of direct shareowners (May 1997):

Value of the Portfolio		Per cent of Shareowners
$1,000 to	$ 4,999	22.8
$5,000 to	$ 9,999	16.7
$10,000 to	$24,999	18.6
$25,000 to	$49,999	10.7
$50,000 to	$99,999	5.1
$100,000 and over		9.9
not known		16.2
Total		100.0
Average	$33,000	

The number of companies represented in the share portfolios of direct shareowners (May 1997):

Number of Companies in the Portfolio	Per cent of Shareowners
1	24.8
2	13.5
3	14.0
4	9.2
6 to 10	18.2
more than 10	10.3
not known	3.0
Total	100.0

Source: derived from Australian Stock Exchange Limited, Australian Shareownership Survey 1997

Appendix 4—Can you Bear to be a Bull?

This is an edited version of a paper by the author on the occasion of the opening of the new Stock Exchange building in Melbourne on 30 March 1992.

Despite its light-hearted heading the paper contains a serious message, particularly for newer investors.

These days many people have large sums of money to invest—for example, lump sum superannuation benefits or the proceeds from selling a house or a business. Such people often realise that they know very little about investment matters and accordingly they seek out professional advice.

They then encounter an unexpected problem. Their adviser uses technical terms which they do not understand. Should they stop him there and then and thus display their ignorance? People hesitate before doing that. They do not want to look silly, particularly if they have made it in life and are expert in their own field.

Nor do they want to add to the complications of the interview itself. They may already have been caught out in not having pat answers to some significant questions being put to them, such as their investment objectives, their attitude to taking risks, or their likely future cash flow pattern.

So they pretend to understand what is being said to them and they make intelligent noises—but a lot of the advice goes over their heads. This can be highly dangerous when large amounts of money are at stake, particularly if that money has to last for the rest of their lives.

Most advisers will be only too pleased to answer even elementary questions—they realise that informed investors are more likely to be long-term clients. Usually they use jargon without realising it, not in order to confuse.

Newspaper headlines and television bulletins have helped to make names such as the "All Ordinaries Index" and concepts such as "negative gearing" widely understood.

However, the communications task is not assisted by practices such as the following:

- The use without explanation of slang terms, such as "bull" (an investor who expects the market to rise), "bear" (one who expects the market to fall) and "stag" (an investor who takes up new shares in a float with a view to selling them for an immediate profit).

- The growing use of deliberately-coined stock exchange acronyms, such as "SEATS", "FAST" and "CHESS".

- The use of several rather different expressions to mean virtually the same thing, such as "imputation credit" and "franking rebate".

- The use of the same technical term in two or more unconnected senses—for example, "call" in relation to contributing shares and call options.

- The use of ordinary words in special senses, such as "rights" or the "writing" of options or the "passing" of a dividend or "Chinese walls".

- The tendency for listed companies to invent their own pet terms for Dividend Election Plans and the like.

- The practice of unit trust managers to employ non-uniform expressions for the entry and exit prices of their units.

- The paradoxical use by life offices of the (normally) fixed interest expression, "bond", to refer to an equity-linked product.

- The occasional use of London terms such as "jobber" or "acceptance house" in inappropriate Australian contexts.

- Differences in United States and local terminology—for example, "stockowner" for "shareholder" or "common stock" for "ordinary shares".

- The gradual change in the meaning of certain terms, such as "warrants" (originally, "bearer shares"; more recently, "company-issued options").
- The use of metaphors such as "white knights" or "junk bonds".

Why does the world of finance have its own peculiar jargon? The answer is simple enough—most experts like to save time by employing shorthand expressions for concepts frequently used by them. However, an everyday phrase to a stockbroker, an accountant or a financial planner is not necessarily a term previously encountered by his clients.

Changes in technology mean that phrases such as "screen trading" and "program trading", which were unknown a few years ago, are now part of the language of finance.

Some expressions are derived from the Corporations Law, some from taxation or social security legislation, some from stock exchange rules and practice. Others come from the usages of accountants, actuaries, auditors, bankers, chartists, commodity dealers, computer experts, economists, futures dealers, geologists, institutions, journalists, lawyers, security analysts or statisticians.

Technical terms abound in all types of financial literature—the market pages of daily newspapers, brokers' circulars, prospectuses, company reports, specialist financial publications, and individually-tailored plans prepared by investment advisers.

But wise investors will ask the right questions and prosper.

Appendix 5—Abbreviations in Newspaper Listings

The listings of share prices and other information which are published in newspapers normally use abbreviations for space reasons. Unfortunately each paper makes up its own version instead of following a uniform approach. Sometimes two or more different symbols for the same type of security are even used within the one list. The more common abbreviations include the following:

b	bonus shares	del	deferred delivery
bon	bonus shares	dl	deferred delivery
c	contributing shares	gr	growth units
call	call paid	i	interest
cb	cum bonus	in	income units
cbr	cum bonus and rights	new	new shares
cd	cum dividend	nts	convertible notes
ce	cum entitlement	o	options
cf	cum offer	opt	options
ci	cum interest	p	priorty
cn	convertible notes	pf	preference shares
cnt	convertible notes	pref	preference shares
contrib	contributing shares	prf	preference shares
conv nts	convertible notes	r	rights
cp	cum priority	rts	rights
cr	cum rights	w	warrants
ctg	contributing shares	xb	ex bonus
cvnts	convertible notes	xbr	ex bonus and rights
dd	deferred delivery	xd	ex dividend
defd	deferred shares	xe	ex entitlement
defd del	deferred delivery	xf	ex offer
		xi	ex interest
		xp	ex priority
		xr	ex rights

Notes:

1. Some of these abbreviations can also occur in combination—for example, "cdl" for "contributing shares, deferred delivery".

2. Figures after the letters usually indicate the year of expiry for options or warrants (for example, "o98" or "w99"), or the paid-up face value of shares.

Appendix 6—Marginal Income Tax Rates

The rates in these tables allow for the Medicare Levy and the Low Income Taxpayers' Rebate.

THE NORMAL SCALE FOR INDIVIDUALS
FOR 1998-99

Income Bracket $	Rate per cent
0-	0.0
6150-	-20.0
13389-	-40.0
14192-	-21.5
20700-	-39.5
24450-	-35.5
38000-	-44.5
50000-	-48.5

THE SPECIAL SCALE FOR MINORS
FOR 1998-99

This scale applies to persons under age 18 at the end of the financial year, in respect to investment and trust income (assuming that that is the only income).

Income Bracket $	Rate Per cent
0-	0.0
644-	66.0
1446-	47.0
13389-	67.0
14192-	48.5
20700-	52.5
24450-	48.5

Appendix 7—Adjustments for Capital Changes

Various ratios relating to company accounts are discussed in Chapter 9, which introduces a number of theoretical concepts of relevance to investors and security analysts.

In para. 964 it is pointed out that the use of "end of year" figures is not appropriate where a company has issued shares or made other capital changes during the course of the year. In particular, suitable adjustments for bonus issues, share splits or consolidations, cash issues, capital returns or shares issued as consideration for assets need to be made.

The following oversimplified examples will illustrate this point:

Example 1

A company which balances on 30 June makes a bonus issue on 31 March, details being as follows:

Number of shares at start of year:	2,000,000
Number of shares at end of year:	3,000,000
Total earnings for the year:	$930,000

Bonus issue: One for two (1,000,000 shares)

While the average number of shares on issue over the whole financial year just counting the pieces of paper seems to be 2,250,000, the shares on issue during the first nine months were not of the same quality as the shares on issue during the last three months (effectively being 50 per cent more valuable).

To be meaningful the earnings must be related to "end of year" shares, both as to number and quality:

Earnings per share = $930,000 / 3,000,000 = 31 cents

Example 2

A company which balances on 30 June makes a pro rata rights issue closing on 31 March, details being as follows:

Number of shares at start of year: 2,000,000
Number of shares at end of year: 3,000,000
Total earnings for the year: $765,000

Rights issue: One for two, at 200, fully-paid (1,000,000 shares, raising $2,000,000).

Closing price cum rights: 400

For every two shares worth 800 (being 2 multiplied by 400) immediately before the issue there were then three shares worth 1000 (being this 800 plus the additional 200) immediately after the issue.

The new cash was received three quarters of the way through the year.

Thus the adjusted number of "end of year" shares over the whole financial year is:

(3/4 x 800/1000 + 1/4) x 3,000,000 = 2,550,000
Adjusted earnings per share = $765,000 / 2,550,000 = 30 cents

Example 3

A company which balances on 30 June makes a pro rata rights issue closing on 31 March, details being as follows:

Number of shares at start of year: 2,000,000
Number of shares at end of year: 3,000,000
Total earnings for the year: $714,500

Rights issue: One for two, at 200, being 100 on application and 100 a year later (1,000,000 shares, raising $1,000,000 during the financial year, with a further $1,000,000 yet to come).

Closing price cum rights: 400

For the purpose of the exercise it is desirable to produce a single "earnings per share" figure which relates to fully-paid shares. The contributing shares are therefore treated as being fully-paid, and the company is treated as though it had had the use of an amount equal to the calls yet to be paid. This accords with the economic reality of the situation.

For every two shares worth 800 (being 2 multiplied by 400) immediately before the issue there were then three shares worth 1000 (being this 800 plus the additional 200) immediately after the issue.

The new cash was received (or deemed to have been received) three quarters of the way through the year.

Thus the adjusted number of "end of year" shares over the whole financial year is:

$$(3/4 \times 800/1000 + 1/4) \times 3,000,000 = 2,550,000$$

	$
Actual Earnings	714,500
add notional earnings on the amount not yet received, say $1,000,000 at 10 per cent net for three months	25,000
	739,500

Adjusted earnings per share = $739,500 / 2,550,000 = 29 cents

Appendix 8—A Ledger and Worksheet for Capital Gains Tax

The sample "Capital Gains Tax Worksheet" which is included with the Australian Taxation Office's various booklets on the subject is not really suitable for active share investors.

A typical investor may well in the one financial year have disposed of a number of separate share parcels acquired at different times in each of a number of different listed companies.

Participants in dividend reinvestment and top up plans and investors who take up rights will find that they have acquired many distinct parcels over the years, even where they have not in addition actively purchased any further shares on the stock exchange.

The instruction to "use a separate worksheet for each asset or parcel of shares or units" is not very helpful in such circumstances. It could lead to quite a large pile of paper.

The ATO worksheet also deals with confusing aspects such as "deductions" and "reduced amounts" which normally have no application to investors in ordinary shares.

With the advent of self—assessment and its penalties for error, it seems highly desirable that an investor should use a worksheet which allows the data on it to be reconciled against his own accounting ledgers and which in addition enables the arithmetic to be carried out in readily understandable steps.

Apart from that, many sophisticated investors like to keep track of their realised capital gains and losses even when these relate to pre-1985 assets and thus have no particular tax implications.

It should be noted that use of the above-mentioned sample ATO worksheet is not in any way compulsory. Ordinary paper using any logical setting out which is found convenient can be used instead.

For example, a single sheet on the following lines and covering *all* share disposals during the financial year might be found useful:

No	Company	Type of Security	Pre or Post	AQUISITION			DISPOSAL			Indexed Cost	GAINS		LOSSES	
				Date	Cost	CPI	Date	Proceeds	CPI		Taxable	Exempt	Taxable	Exempt
(1)	(2)	(3)	(4)	(5)	(6)	(7)	(8)	(9)	(10)	(11)	(12)	(13)	(14)	(15)

Such a sheet can be produced either manually or by computer.

(1)   "No." refers to the number of shares, etc., in each separate parcel disposed of (or, where these parcels do not precisely match the parcels originally acquired, in a portion of the parcel disposed of so that this matching is achieved).

(3)   "Type of Security" refers to Ordinary Shares, Preference Shares, Options, Convertible Notes, etc.

(4)   "Pre or Post" refers to the actual or deemed CGT status of the security ("pre-20 September 1985" or "post-19 September 1985"). Although capital gains tax commenced on 20 September 1985 any bonus shares issued after that date are regarded as pre-20 September 1985 shares if they accrued on pre-20 September 1985 shares; this rule extends to bonus shares under dividend election plans.

(5)   "Date" refers to the actual date of acquisition, except in the case of bonus shares. Bonus shares are always deemed to have been acquired at the same time as the original shares to which they relate.

(6)   "Cost" usually refers to the actual cost, including brokerage and stamp duty. However, if bonus shares have been issued then a deemed cost is applied to both the original shares and the bonus shares: the *total* cost of the original shares is applied pro rata to the original shares and the bonus shares. In the case of shares arising out of the exercise of rights accruing on pre-20 September 1985 holdings a special deemed cost is to be used: the sum of the actual application money and the market value of the rights at the time of their exercise.

(7)   "CPI" refers to the Consumer Price Index figure for the calendar quarter in (5).

(9)   "Proceeds" refers to the money received on sale or redemption, net of brokerage and stamp duty.

(10)   "CPI" refers to the Consumer Price Index figure for the calendar quarter in (8).

(11)   The "Indexed Cost" = (6)x(10)/(7). However, indexation is not available if the asset has been held for less than 12 months and for these (11) = (6).

(12) "Taxable Gains" refers to gains beyond indexation on post-19 September 1985 assets.

(13) "Exempt Gains" refers to:

  (a)   gains within indexation on post-19 September 1985 assets and

  (b)   all gains on pre-20 September 1985 assets.

(14) "Taxable Losses" refers to all losses on post-19 September 1985 assets. These can be offset against "Taxable Gains" of the current financial year; any balance can be carried forward for offset against "Taxable Gains" of a future financial year.

(15) "Exempt Losses" refers to all losses on pre-20 September 1985 assets.

Transactions details are best entered at the time the transactions are made; however, the CPI figures need only be inserted when they are actually needed. For shares acquired in dividend reinvestment plans the cost is the actual amount of the relevant dividend; the discount in the issue price of the plan shares does not need any further treatment.

The calculations for columns (12) to (15) proceed as follows:

For pre-20 September 1985 assets, calculate (9)-(6).

If

  (9)-(6)   is positive, it is the Exempt Gain, to be shown in (13).

  (9)-(6)   is negative, it gives the Exempt Loss, to be shown in (15).

For post-19 September 1985 assets, calculate (9)-(11).

If

  (9)-(11)   is positive, it is the Taxable Gain, to be shown in (12);

  (11)-(6)   is the Exempt Gain, to be shown in (13).

  (9)-(11)   is negative, then calculate (9)-(6).

  (9)-(6)   is positive, it is the Exempt Gain, to be shown in (13).

  (9)-(6)   is negative, it gives the Taxable Loss, to be shown in (14).

Calls, etc.

If the acquisition cost was paid in stages, as, for example:

- when shares were subject to calls
- when rights were purchased on the market
- when options were exercised

then separate entries are required in columns (1) to (7) and (11) for each payment. The calculations shown above to the extent that they involve columns (6) and (11) should be performed on the totals in those columns of the individual items for all the relevant stages relating to each separate parcel disposed of-for example, the original purchase price and each call.

Partial Sales

An investor who sold some *but not all* of the shares in a particular company will need to nominate which portion of the total holding was disposed of. This will be relevant in all cases where that holding was acquired at various times.

Investors do not have to treat either their oldest or their most recent purchases as the shares being sold unless that happens to suit their purpose.

Thus they can choose to nominate those shares which produce the lowest realised capital gains if they wish to minimise the tax burden at that time. Alternatively, they can choose to nominate those shares which produce the highest realised gains if they wish to use up some tax losses or if they expect to be on a higher marginal tax rate in the year in which the remainder of the parcel is quit.

In the same way an investor is entitled to choose between selling pre-20 September 1985 and post-19 September 1985 shares. Selling the former may have the short-term advantage of allowing tax-free capital gains to be realised at that time. But such a strategy would also have the long-term disadvantage of destroying for ever the unique and irreplaceable pre-20 September 1985 status of such investments.

For a whole variety of reasons share certificates (even where they exist) are at best only a poor guide as to the date on which any particular shares were actually acquired. Furthermore, the one scrip certificate can encompass some bonus shares deemed to have pre-1985 status as well as other bonus shares deemed to have post-1985 status.

In any case, certificates do not exist under the CHESS system. Thus the maintenance of good records by shareholders becomes essential for tax purposes and in order to allow investors to demonstrate to the authorities precisely what transactions have been undertaken and which nominations they may have made.

Property Trusts

The periodical distributions paid to unitholders in property trusts often contain components which are exempt from ordinary income tax but which affect the capital gains tax on a subsequent disposal. These components fall into two distinct categories, commonly called *tax free* and *tax deferred*.

The *tax free* amounts arise from the building allowance available to investors in certain properties. These amounts are ignored in capital gain situations but need to be brought into account in capital loss situations (thus producing a worse result for the investor).

The *tax deferred* amounts arise from conventional depreciation. These amounts need to be brought into account in both capital gain and capital loss situations.

The procedure for the amounts brought into account is the same as for calls (see above), except that in the case of trust distributions received the "cost" is, of course, a negative figure.

Appendix—9 Examples of useful Internet Links

1. General Sites

Australian Stock Exchange
http://www.asx.com.au/

Sydney Futures Exchange
http://www.asf.com.au/

Australian Securities Commission and Investments Commission
http://www.asic.gov.au/

Australian Shareholders' Association
http://www.asa.asn.au/

Financial Planning Association of Australia
http://www.fpa.asn.au/

Australian Financial Review
http://www.afr.com.au/

Australian Bureau of Statistics
http://www.abs.gov.au/

Australian Taxation Office
http://www.ato.gov.au/

Centrelink (for social security information)
http://www.centrelink.gov.au/

Australian Prudential Regulation Authority
http://www.apra.gov.au/

Australian Broadcasting Corporation
http://www.abc.net.au

Legislation and Litigation
http://www.austlii.edu.au/

A useful meta search engine, Metacrawler
http://www.metacrawler.com

Another useful meta search engine, Inference Find
http://www.infind.com

Dictionary and other tools
http://www.iTools.com/research-it/research-it.html

New York Stock Exchange
http://www.nyse.com

Securities and Exchange Commission (United States)
http://www.sec.gov

Banned and Disqualified Investment Advisers
http://www.search.asic.gov.au/ban.html

2. Glossaries

Australian Stock Exchange
http://www.asx.com.au/I1000.htm

County NatWest
http://www.county.com.au/dict.htm

WebLink Investor Centre
http://203.24.211.10/webinvestor/doc/ASX/glossary.html

New York Stock Exchange
http://www.nyse.com/public/glossary/glss10.htm

Washington Post
http://www.washingtonpost.com/wp-srv/business/longterm/glossary
/glossary.htm

Market Guide
http://www.marketguide.com/MGI/HELP/glossary.html

Ten Finance and Investing Related Glossaries
http://www.e-analytics.com/glossdir.htm

3. Share Prices

Trading Room—a Fairfax site which allows investors to get personalised share price and other information:

- instant prices can be obtained for a fee
- the previous day's closing prices can be obtained free of charge
- the value of a nominated portfolio can be monitored
- a watchlist of selected stocks can be set up

http://www.tradingroom.com.au/

Infobeat—a useful site for getting US company share prices and announcements by e-mail

http://www.infobeat.com/

Appendix 10—List of Further Reading

Many interesting books on different aspects of investment exist these days, covering everything from the sharemarket to general finance.

Specialist works dealing with taxation, options, futures, commodity trading, company information, accounting, security analysis, charting, property and company law are readily available. There are also books describing corporate fraud, other historical aspects and even investor psychology.

Both beginners and advanced players will be able to find material which will help them to advance their knowledge. Serious investors will probably wish to build up a personal library of their own.

The list of further reading below may assist in this task. It is meant to be illustrative rather than exhaustive.

Armstrong, Merril:	*Charting Made Easy* (Information Australia, 1990, 117 pp)
Band, Richard E:	*Contrarian Investing for the '90s* (Information Australia, 1989, 260 pp)
Baxt, R:	*An Introduction to Company Law* (Law Book Company, 1985, 3rd ed., xx+271 pp)
Bruck, Connie:	The Predators' Ball (Simon and Schuster, 1988, 385 pp)
Bruns, Gordon R:	*The Stock Exchange* (Bruns, 4th ed., 1962, x+152 pp)
Carew, Edna:	*The Language of Money* (Allen & Unwin, 1988, x+267 pp)
Donnelly, Austin:	*More Wealth with less Risk* (Information Australia, 1990, 410 pp)
FitzHerbert, Richard:	*Blueprint for Investment* (Wrightbooks, 1998, 2nd ed., xii+210 pp)

Galbraith, John Kenneth:	*The Great Crash 1929* (Penguin, 1961, 221 pp)
Graham, B, Dodd, DL and Cottle, S:	*Security Analysis: Principles and Technique* (McGraw Hill, 4th ed., 1962, x+778 pp)
Hewat, Tim:	*The Intelligent Investor's Guide to Share Buying* (Wrightbooks, 3rd ed., 1994, 135 pp)
Koch, David:	*Your Money & Your Life* (Information Australia, 1993, 466 pp)
Lipton, Phillip and Herzberg, Abraham:	*Understanding Company Law* (LBC Information Services, 7th ed., 1998, lx+850 pp)
McIlroy, John:	*Superannuation Simplified* (Wrightbooks, 1989, 163 pp)
Renton, NE:	*Company Directors: Masters or Servants?* (Wrightbooks, 1994, xviii+206 pp)
Renton, NE:	*Family Trusts* (Wrightbooks, 1997, xiv+226 pp)
Renton, NE:	*Guide for Meetings and Organisations: Volume 2: Meetings* (Law Book Company, 6th ed., 1994, xxviii+269 pp)
Renton, NE:	*Negative Gearing* (Wrightbooks, 1998, xix+186 pp)
Roth, Martin:	*The Internet for Investors* (Wrightbooks, 1996, x+164 pp)
Rubner, Alex:	*The Ensnared Shareholder* (Penguin, 1965, 237 pp)
Stammer, Don:	*Unlimited Success in Personal Investments* (Wrightbooks, 1989, 97 pp)
Sykes, Trevor:	*Two Centuries of Panic: a History of Corporate Collapses in Australia* (Allen and Unwin, 1988, xi+593 pp)
Tate, Christopher:	*Understanding Options Trading in Australia* (Information Australia, 1990, 96 pp)
Wasiliev, John:	*The Intelligent Investor's A-Z* (Wrightbooks, 1989, 120 pp, being a glossary of financial terms)
Wheeler, David and Wilkinson, Rick:	*Shareholders' Rights* (Information Australia, 1990, xvii+76 pp)
	Australian Investment Handbook (Stock Exchange Research Pty. Ltd., published every six months, covers 50 major Australian companies)
	Australian Shareownership Survey 1997 (Australian Stock Exchange Limited, 1997, 28 pp)
	Australian Stock Exchange: Annual Reports

Dictionary of Stock Exchange Terms (Information Australia, 1990, vi+167 pp)

Managing your Share Portfolio (Australian Stock Exchange Limited, 1996, 24 pp)

Personal Investment(John Fairfax Ltd., published monthly)

Shares (John Fairfax Ltd., published monthly, includes statistics of all listed companies)

Your Guide to Investment (Australian Stock Exchange Limited, undated but c.1992, 52 pp)

Note: Other books on this subject will be found in libraries, often under the Dewey decimal number 332.6.

Appendix 11—Industrial Groupings

The 24 classifications below are used for the purpose of the ASX Share Price Indices. It is, however, likely that Banks and Insurance will be combined, to reflect the convergence of these two industries.

Investors aiming at spread and desiring to diversify their portfolios might find this a useful categorisation of industries.

- Alcohol and Tobacco
- Banks
- Building Materials
- Chemicals
- Developers and Contractors
- Diversified Industrials
- Diversified Resources
- Energy
- Engineering
- Food and Household Goods
- Gold
- Health Care and Biotechnology
- Infrastructure and Utilities
- Insurance
- Investment and Financial Services
- Media
- Miscellaneous Industrials
- Other Metals
- Paper and Packaging

- Property Trusts
- Retail
- Telecommunications
- Tourism and Leisure
- Transport

Index

All references are to paragraphs

Dispute resolution, 2316, 3979
Diversification (companies), 255, 1057-1062, 1129
Diversification (investors), 256-262, 1335
Dividend cheques, 459, 828
Dividend cover, 927-928, 935, 943, 3524-3527
Dividend election plans, 770-778, 779, 853, Chapter 32
Dividend imputation, 436, 928, 2833-2846, 2890, Chapter 35
Dividend payable date, 461
Dividend reinvestment plans, 779, 853, 2008, Chapter 32
Dividend yield, 930-931, 934, 1033-1034, 1038, 3506-3512
Dividends, 211, 458-461, 474, 926-935, 1032-1038, 1324
Dollar cost averaging, 1523-1526
Double tax, 2877-2880
Doubling of money, 1917
Dow Jones, 981, Appendix 1
Dual listed company, 3981-3982
Earnings yield, 920-921, 1038, 3513-3523
Earnings before interest and tax, 818, 917, 940-942, 952
Earnings, 915-925, 1022-1031
EBIT, 818, 917, 940-942, 952
ECAS, 3333-3334
Economic entity, 821
Economic factors, 1004
Election of directors, 1230-1232, 1325-1326, 1339-1343
Electronic company announcements, 3333-3334
Electronic payment of dividends, 459
e-mail, 4247-4248
Employee ratios, 957-958
Employee reports, 832-833
Employee shares, Chapter 36, 3831-3834
Endowment warrants, 2236-2255, 2979
Equation of issues, 734
Equity accounting, 823
Equity securities, 246, 424-430
Equity, 2727
Errors, 1606-1607, 1626, 1654, 3967
Estate duty, 3012
Ethics, 526
European style, 2235
Ex bonus, 753
Ex dividend, 461, 1070, 2880
Ex interest, 461
Ex rights, 713, 723, 1046

Independent reports, Chapter 34
Index funds, 619, 647-654, 4125
Indexed securities, 1722-1727, 3727
Indices (stock exchange), 979-985, 2329-2340, 2617, Appendix 1
Industrial groupings, Appendix 11
Inflation, Chapter 3, 1009-1011, 1722-1727, 2816, Appendix 1
Information, Chapter 26
Initial Public Offering, 607
Inscribed stock, 1713-1714
Insider trading, 1085-1088, 1195
Instalment receipts, 493-494, 2985
Instalment warrants, 2256-2260
Instalments, 414, 1730
Insurance bonds, 3146
Intangible assets, 810, 972-978
Interest, 211, 263-268, 458-461, 474, Chapter 19, 2120, 2811-2815
Interest cover, 940-942, 959-961
Interest in advance, 2732
Interest indexed bonds, 1724-1727
Interest rate expressions, 1901-1910
Interest rate levels, 263, 324, 1005-108
Interim dividend, 458, 1036
Internet, 2522, Chapter 42, Appendix 9
Intrinsic value (options), 2205-2206, 2217, 2261-2263
Inverse yield curve, 266
Investment, 207-211
Investment advisers, 113-119, Chapter 14
Investment and gambling, 279-286
Investment bonds, 3146
Investment clubs, 2415
Investment companies, 2413-2414
Investment in relation to the investor, 231-243
Investment myths, 742, 1074, 1327, Chapter 15, 2359, 2887-2889
Investment newsletters, 2611-2612
Investment objectives, 223-224, 1404
Investment reserve, 466
Investment return, 212-222
Investment risk, 225-226, 237, 1069, 1718-1721, 3924-3926
Investment spread, 256-262, 1335
Investment types, 244-250
Investor attitudes, 108-112
Irredeemable securities, 247
Issue price, 618-623, 1047

Marginal tax rates, 2817-2818, 2822, 2836, 2839, 2843,
2850-2853, Appendix 6
Market, 475, 501-503, 512
Market bids, 1645
Market capitalisation, 962
Market price, 517, 1621-1623, 1622, 1664-1668, 2512
Market rigging, 1078-1080
Market value of assets, 812-813
Market value of property, 3019
Market value of stock, 813
Marketable parcels, 1635-1644
Means test, Chapter 31
Media, 1236, 1321, 1334, Chapter 25, Appendix 5
Meetings, 858, 1218-1221, 1236, Chapter 13
Memorandum of Association, 410-411, 1215-1216
Millennium bug, 136-137
Minimum bids, 1645
Minimum brokerage, 532, 766, 1234
Minimum shareholdings, 1239-1240
Mining companies, 415-416
Minority interests, 470
Minors, 414, 1520-1522, 2822, 3206, Appendix 6
Misleading figures, 969-971
Mistakes, 1606-1607, 1626, 1654, 3967
Monetary assets, 326
Mortgage debentures, 447
Mortgage insurance, 1803
Mortgage offset accounts, 3921-3922
Mortgage trusts, 1810-1811
Mortgages, 272, 473, 1801-1809, 2723-2728
Mutual funds, 2411-2412
Myths, 742, 1074, 1327, Chapter 15, 2359, 2887-2889
Names for registration, 2892-2895, 2951-2954
National Guarantee Fund, 1656, 1673
Near cash, 276
Negative gearing, 2721, 2884
Negative intrinsic value, 2261-2263
Net assets, 907, 937-939
Net tangible assets, 812, 909-914, 959-961, 1039-1043
New issues, Chapter 6, Chapter 7
New products, 124-128
New shares, 535, 1068
Newness, 1071-1072

Index

Senior securities, 442, 472-474

Service providers, 4209-4212

Settlements, 1682-1684

SFE, 2307-2314

Share capital, 462, 809

Share capital account, 496, 750

Share exchanges, 772-775, 1107, 1183

Share futures, 2341-2343

Share issues, Chapter 7, 1233-1235

Share premium account, 463, 467, 496, 750, 772-775

Share prices, Chapter 10, 4206-4208

Share purchase plans, 776-777

Share registers, 453-456, 1662, 3948-3957

Share splits, 754, 772-775

Share traders, 2901, 2959-2963, 3164

Shareholder discounts, 1257-1262

Shareholders' equity, 806, 907

Shareholders' funds, 463, 806, 809, 907

Shareholders' rights, Chapter 12

Shareownership patterns, 1335, Appendix 3

Shares, 424-441

Shares (existing), 625-627

Shares of no par value, 781-782, 1241-1256

Shark repellents, 1166

Short selling, 989, 1685-1698, 2336, 2965-2966

Silver, 2112-2113

Single purpose buildings, 1806

Size of company, 1061, 1075

Small holdings, 483-485

Small investors, 296, 828-831

Small orders, 532, 766, 1234, 1612

Social security, Chapter 31

Special dividend, 1036

Speculation, 279-286, 2217, 2320-2328

SPI contract, 2329-2340

Spin-off companies, 741-742, 2955-2957

Splits, 754, 772-775

Splitting of orders, 528

Spot price, 2302, 2330

Spouses, 2953-2954

Spread, 256-262, 1335

Stags, 624

Stakeholders, 410